123491

M. R. EVANS

DATE

The Works of John Newton

M. R. EVANS

The Works of
JOHN NEWTON

*

VOLUME 2

The Banner of Truth Trust

THE BANNER OF TRUTH TRUST
3 Murrayfield Road, Edinburgh EH12 6EL
PO Box 621, Carlisle, Pennsylvania 17013, U.S.

*

First published by
HAMILTON, ADAMS & CO, LONDON, 1820

Reprinted by
THE BANNER OF TRUTH TRUST
1985

*

ISBN 0 85151 460 X for complete set
Volume 2 0 85151 462 6

*

Printed and bound in Great Britain at
The Camelot Press Ltd, Southampton

THE

WORKS

OF THE

REV. JOHN NEWTON,

LATE RECTOR OF THE UNITED PARISHES OF ST. MARY WOOLNOTH,

AND

ST. MARY WOOLCHURCH HAW, LONDON:

WITH

MEMOIRS OF THE AUTHOR,

AND GENERAL REMARKS ON HIS LIFE, CONNECTIONS,

AND CHARACTER;

BY THE

REV. RICHARD CECIL, M.A.

THIRD EDITION.

IN SIX VOLUMES.

VOL. II.

LONDON:

PRINTED FOR HAMILTON, ADAMS, AND CO.,

33, PATERNOSTER ROW.

M.DCCC.XXIV.

CONTENTS.

CARDIPHONIA (CONTINUED.)

SIX DISCOURSES (OR SERMONS), AS INTENDED FOR THE PULPIT.

SERMON I.
On the Deceitfulness of the Heart.

Jer. xvii. 9, 10.—*The heart is deceitful above all things, and desperately wicked ; who can know it ?   I the Lord search the heart, I try the reins, even to give every man according to kis ways, and according to the fruit of his doings* 259

SERMON II.
On the Saviour and his Salvation.

1 Tim. i. 15.—*This is a faithful saying, and worthy of all acceptation, that Christ Jesus came into the world to save sinners ; of whom I am chief* 276

SERMON III.
On the Christian Name.

Acts. xi. 26.—*And the disciples were called Christians first at Antioch* 290

CARDIPHONIA

CONTINUED.

SEVEN LETTERS

TO

MRS. ****.

LETTER I.

My dear Madam,   November, 1775.

Too much of that impatience which you speak
of, towards those who differ from us in some religious sentiments, is observable on all sides. I do
not consider it as the fault of a few individuals,
or of this or that party, so much as the effect of
that inherent imperfection which is common to
our whole race. Anger and scorn are equally
unbecoming in those who profess to be followers
of the meek and lowly Jesus, and who acknowledge
themselves to be both sinful and fallible; but too
often something of this leaven will be found
cleaving to the best characters, and mixed with
honest endeavours to serve the best cause. But
thus it was from the beginning; and we have
reason to confess that we are no better than the
Apostles were, who, though they meant well, manifested once and again a wrong spirit in their
zeal; Luke ix. 54. Observation and experience
contribute, by the grace of God, gradually to
soften and sweeten our spirits; but then there
will always be ground for mutual forbearance and
mutual forgiveness on this head. However, so
far as I may judge of myself, I think this hastiness
is not my most easy besetting sin. I am not
indeed an advocate for that indifference and luke-
warmness to the truths of God, which seem to
constitute the candour many plead for in the
present day. But while I desire to hold fast the

sound doctrines of the Gospel towards the persons of my fellow-creatures, I wish to exercise all moderation and benevolence : Protestants or Papists, Socinians or Deists, Jews, Samaritans, or Mohammedans, all are my neighbours ; they have all a claim upon me for the common offices of humanity. As to religion, they cannot all be right ; nor may I compliment them by allowing the differences between us are but trivial, when I believe and know they are important ; but I am not to expect them to see with my eyes. I am deeply convinced of the truth of John Baptist's aphorism, John iii. 27, " A man can receive nothing, except it be given him from Heaven." I well know, that the little measure of knowledge I have obtained in the things of God has not been owing to my own wisdom and docility, but to his goodness. Nor did I get it all at once : he has been pleased to exercise much patience and long-suffering towards me, for about twenty-seven years past, since he first gave me a desire of learning from himself. He has graciously accommodated himself to my weakness, borne with my mistakes, and helped me through innumerable prejudices, which, but for his mercy, would have been insuperable hindrances : I have therefore no right to be angry, impatient, or censorious, especially as I have still much to learn, and am so poorly influenced by what I seem to know. I am weary of controversies and disputes, and desire to choose for myself, and to point out to others, Mary's part, to sit at Jesus' feet, and to hear his words. And, blessed be his name ! so far as I have learned from him, I am favoured with a comfortable certainty ; I know whom I have believed, and am no longer tossed about by the various winds and tides of opinions, by which I see many are dashed one against the other. But I

cannot, I must not, I dare not, contend ; only, as
a witness for God, I am ready to bear my simple
testimony to what I have known of his truth,
whenever I am properly called to it.

I agree with you, that some accounted evangelical teachers have too much confined themselves
to a few leading and favourite topics.   I think this
a fault ; and believe, when it is constantly so, the
auditories are deprived of much edification and
pleasure, which they might receive from a more
judicious and comprehensive plan.   The whole
Scripture, as it consists of histories, prophecies,
doctrines, precepts, promises, exhortations, admonitions, encouragements, and reproofs, is the
proper subject of the Gospel ministry ; and every
part should in its place and course be attended
to ; yet so as that, in every compartment we exhibit, Jesus should be the capital figure ; in whom
the prophecies are fulfilled, the promises established ; to whom, in a way of type and emblem, the
most important parts of Scripture history have an
express reference ; and from whom alone we can
receive that life, strength, and encouragement,
which are necessary to make obedience either
pleasing or practicable.   And where there is *true
spiritual faith* in the heart, and in exercise, I believe a person will not so much need a detail of
what he is to practise, as to be often greatly at a
loss without it.   Our Saviour's commandments
are plain and clear in themselves ; and that love
which springs from faith is the best casuist and
commentator to apply and enforce them.

You are pleased to say, " Forgive me if I transgress ; I know the place whereon I stand is
holy ground." Permit me to assure you, my dear
madam, that were I, which I am not, a person of
some importance, you would run no hazard of

offending me by controverting any of my sentiments: I hold none (knowingly) which I am not
willing to submit to examination; nor am I afraid
of offending you by speaking freely, when you
point out my way. I should wrong you, if I
thought to please you by palliating or disguising
the sentiments of my heart; and if I attempted
to do so, you would see through the design, and
despise it. There may perhaps be an improper
manner of chiming upon the name of Jesus, and
I am not for vindicating any impropriety; yet,
could I feel what I ought to mean when I pronounce that name, I should not fear mentioning it
too often. I am afraid of no excess in thinking
highly of it, because I read it is the will of God,
that all men should honour the Son as they honour
the Father. Laboured explications of the Trinity
I always avoid. I am afraid of darkening counsel
by words without knowledge. Scripture, and
even reason assures me, there is but one God,
whose name *alone* is Jehovah. Scripture likewise
assures me, that Christ is God, that Jesus is
Jehovah. I cannot say that reason assents with
equal readiness to this proposition as to the former.
But admitting what the Scripture teaches concerning the evil of sin, the depravity of human
nature, the method of salvation, and the offices of
the Saviour; admitting that God has purposed to
glorify, not his mercy only, but his justice, in the
work of redemption; that the blood shed upon the
cross is a proper, adequate satisfaction for sin;
and that the Redeemer is at present the shepherd
of those who believe in him, and will hereafter be
the·judge of the world; that, in order to give the
effectual help which we need, it is necessary that
he be always *intimately with those* who depend
upon him in every age, in every place; must

know the thoughts and intents of every heart; must have his eye always upon them, his ear always open to them, his arm ever stretched out for their relief; that they can receive nothing but what he bestows, can do nothing but as he enables them, nor stand a moment but as he upholds them; admitting these and the like premises, with which the word of God abounds, reason must allow, whatever difficulties may attend the thought, that only he who is God over all, blessed for ever, is able or worthy to execute this complicated plan, every part of which requires the exertion of infinite wisdom and almighty power; nor am I able to form any clear, satisfactory, comfortable thoughts of God, suited to awaken my love or engage my trust, but as he has been pleased to reveal himself in the person of Jesus Christ. I believe with the Apostle, that God was once manifested in the flesh upon earth; and that he is now manifested in the flesh in heaven; and that the worship, not only of redeemed sinners, but of the holy angels, is addressed to the Lamb that was slain, and who, in that nature in which he suffered, now exercises universal dominion, and has the government of heaven, earth, and hell, upon his shoulders. This truth is the foundation upon which my hope is built, the fountain from whence I derive all my strength and consolation, and my only encouragement for venturing to the Throne of Grace, for grace to help in time of need.

> Till God in human flesh I see,
>   My thoughts no comfort find;
> The holy, just, and sacred Three
>   Are terrors to my mind.
>
> But if Immanuel's face appear,
>   My hope, my joy begins;
> His name forbids my slavish fear,
>   His grace removes our sins.

I am, however, free to confess to you, that, through the pride and unbelief remaining in my heart, and the power of Satan's temptations, there are seasons when I find no small perplexity and evil reasonings upon this high point: but it is so absolutely essential to my peace, that I cannot part with it; for I cannot give it up, without giving up all hope of salvation on the one hand, and giving up the Bible, as an unmeaning, contradictory fable, on the other: and, through mercy, for the most part, when I am in my right mind, I am as fully persuaded of this truth as I am of my own existence; but from the exercises I have had about it, I have learned to subscribe to the Apostle's declaration, that " no man can say that Jesus Christ is Lord, but by the Holy Ghost." I am well satisfied it will not be a burden to me at the hour of death, nor be laid to my charge at the day of judgment, that I have thought too highly of Jesus, expected too much from him myself, or laboured too much in commending and setting him forth to others, as the Alpha and Omega, the true God and eternal life. On the contrary, alas! alas! my guilt and grief are, that my thoughts of him are so faint, so infrequent, and my commendations of him so lamentably cold and disproportionate to what they ought to be.

I know not whose letters are rapturous, but I wish mine were more so: not that I am a friend to ungrounded sallies of imagination, flights of animal passions, or heat without light. But it would be amazing to me, were I not aware of human depravity (of which I consider this as one of the most striking proofs), that they who have any good hope of an interest in the Gospel salvation, do not find their hearts (as Dr. Watts expresses it) all on fire; and that their very looks

do not express a transport of admiration, gratitude, and love, when they consider from what
misery they are redeemed, to what happiness they
are called, and what a price was paid for their
souls. I wish to be more like the Apostle Paul
in this respect, who, though he often forms and
compounds new words, seems at a loss for any
that could suitably describe the emotions of his
heart. But I am persuaded you would not object
to the just fervours of Scriptural devotion. But
this holy flame can seldom be found unsullied in
the present life. The temper, constitution, and
infirmities of individuals will mix more or less
with what they say or do. Allowances must be
made for such things in the present state of infirmity; for who can hope to be perfectly free
from them ? If the heart is right with God, and
sincerely affected with the wonders of redeeming
love, our gracious High Priest, who knows our
weakness, pities and pardons what is amiss, accepts our poor efforts, and gradually teaches us to
discern and avoid what is blameable. The work
of grace, in its first stages, I sometimes compare
to the lighting of a fire, where for a while there is
abundance of smoke, but it burns clearer and clearer.
There is often, both in letters and books, what might
be very well omitted; but if a love to God and souls
be the leading principle, I pass as gentle censure
upon the rest as I can, and apply to some eccentric
expressions, what Mr. Prior somewhere says of
our civil dissensions in this land of liberty,

> A bad effect, but from a noble cause.

I am, &c.

LETTER II.

My dear Madam,   February 16, 1776.

It gave me great comfort to find, that what I

wrote concerning the divine character of Jesus, as
God manifest in the flesh, met with your approbation. This doctrine is, in my view, the great
foundation-stone upon which all true religion is
built: but, alas! in the present day, it is the
stumbling stone and rock of offence, upon which
too many, fondly presuming upon their own wisdom, fall and are broken. I am so far from won-
dering that any should doubt of it, that I am
firmly persuaded none can truly believe it, however plainly set forth in Scripture, unless it be
revealed to them from Heaven; or, in the Apostle's
words, that " no one can call Jesus Christ Lord,
but by the Holy Ghost." I believe there are
many who think they believe it, because they
have taken it for granted, and never attentively
considered the difficulties with which it is attended
in the eye of fallen reason. Judging by natural
light, it seems impossible to believe that the title
of the true God and eternal life should properly
belong to that despised Man who hung dead upon
the cross, exposed to the insults of his cruel
enemies. I know nothing that can obviate the
objections the reasoning mind is ready to form
against it, but a real conviction of the sinfulness
of sin, and the state of a sinner as exposed to the
curse of the Holy Law, and destitute of every
plea and hope in himself. Then the necessity of
a Redeemer, and the necessity of this Redeemer's
being Almighty, is seen and felt, with an evidence
which bears down all opposition; for neither the
efficacy of his atonement and intercession, nor
his sufficiency to guide, save, protect, and feed
those who trust in him, can be conceived of without it. When the eyes of the understanding are
opened, the soul made acquainted with and attentive to its own state and wants, he that runs
may read this truth, not in a few detached texts

of a dubious import, and liable to be twisted and
tortured by the arts of criticism, but as interwoven in the very frame and texture of the Bible,
and written, as with a sun-beam, throughout the
principal parts both of the Old and New Testament. If Christ be the shepherd and the husband
of his people under the Gospel, and if his coming
into the world did not abridge those who feared
God of the privileges they were entitled to before
his appearance, it follows, by undeniable consequence, " that he is God over all blessed for
ever." For David tell us, that his shepherd was
Jehovah; and the husband of the Old Testament
church was the Maker and God of the whole
earth, the Holy One of Israel, whose name is the
Lord of Hosts; Psal. xxiii. 1; Is. liv. 8. with
xlvii. 4. I agree with you, Madam, that among
the many attempts which have been made to
prove and illustrate the Scripture-doctrine, that
the Father, the Word, and the Holy Spirit, are
one God, there have been many injudicious, un-
warrantable things advanced, which have perplexed instead of instructing, and of which the
enemies of the truth have known how to make
their advantage. However, there have been tracts
upon these sublime subjects which have been
written with judgment and an unction, and I
believe attended with a blessing. I seem to
prefer Mr. Jones's book on the Trinity to any I
have seen, because he does little more than state
some of the Scripture evidence for it, and draws
his inferences briefly and plainly; though even
he has admitted a few texts, which may perhaps
be thought not quite full to the point; and he has
certainly omitted several of the most express and
strongest testimonies. The best and happiest
proof of all, that this doctrine is true in itself and
true to us, is the experience of its effects. They

who know His name will put their trust in Him :
they who are rightly impressed with His astonishing condescension and love, in emptying himself,
and submitting to the death of the cross for our
sakes, will find themselves under a sweet constraint
to love him again, and will feel a little of that
emotion of heart which the Apostle expresses in
that lively passage, Gal. vi. 14. The knowledge
of Christ crucified (like Ithuriel's spear) removes
the false appearances by which we have been too
long cheated, and shews us the men and the
things, the spirit, customs, and maxims of the
world, in their just light. Were I perfectly master
of myself and my subject, I would never adduce
any text in proof of a doctrine or assertion from
the pulpit, which was not direct and conclusive ;
because if a text is pressed into an argument to
which it has no proper relation, it rather encum-
bers than supports it, and raises a suspicion that
the cause is weak, and better testimonies in its
favour cannot be obtained. Some misapplications
of this kind have been so long in use, that they
pass pretty current, though, if brought to the
assay, they would be found not quite sterling :
but I endeavour to avoid them to the best of my
judgment. Thus, for instance, I have often heard,
Rom. xiv. 23 ; " whatsoever is not of faith is sin,"
quoted to prove, that without a principle of saving
faith we can perform nothing acceptable to God ;
whereas it seems clear from the context, that
faith is there used in another sense, and signifies
a firm persuasion of mind respecting the lawfulness of the action. However, I doubt not but
the proposition in itself is strictly true in the other
sense, if considered detached from the connection in which it stands ; but I should rather choose
to prove it from other passages, where it is directly
affirmed, as Heb. xi. 6 ; Matth. xii. 33. In such

cases, I think hearers should be careful not to be prejudiced against a doctrine, merely because it is not well supported; for perhaps it is capable of solid proof, though the preacher was not so happy as to hit upon that which was most suitable; and extempore preachers may sometimes hope for a little allowance upon this head, from the more candid part of their auditory, and not be made offenders for an inadvertence which they cannot perhaps always avoid in the hurry of speaking. With respect to the application of some passages in the Old Testament to our Lord and Saviour, I hold it safest to keep close to the specimens the Apostles have given us, and I would venture with caution if I go beyond their line; yet it is probable they have only given us a specimen, and that there are a great number of passages which have a direct reference to Gospel truths, though we may run some hazard in making out the allusion. If St. Paul had not gone before me, I should have hesitated to assert that the prohibition, "Thou shalt not muzzle the ox that treadeth out the corn," was given, not upon the account of oxen, but altogether for our sakes: nor should I without his assistance have found out, that the history of Sarah and Hagar was a designed allegory, to set forth the difference between the Law and Gospel covenants. Therefore, when I hear ministers tracing some other allusions, I cannot be always sure that they push them too far, though perhaps they are not quite satisfactory to *my* judgment; for it may be, they have a farther insight into the meaning of the places than myself. And I think Scriptures may be sometimes used to advantage, by way of accommodation in popular discourses, and in something of a different sense from what they bear in the place where they stand, provided they are not alleged as

proofs, but only to illustrate a truth already proved
or acknowledged. Though Job's friends and Job
himself were mistaken, there are many great
truths in their speeches, which, as such, may, I
think, stand as the foundation of a discourse.
Nay, I either have, or have often intended to
borrow, a truth from the mouth even of Satan,
" Hast thou not set a hedge about him ? " such a
confession extorted from our grand adversary,
placing the safety of the Lord's people, under his
providential care, in a very striking light.

I perfectly agree with you, Madam, that our
religious sensations and exercises are much influenced and tinctured by natural constitution;
and that, therefore, tears and warm emotions on
the one hand, or a comparative dryness of spirit
on the other, are no sure indications of the real
state of the heart. Appearances may agree in
different persons, or vary in the same person,
from causes merely natural : even a change of
weather may have some influence in raising or
depressing the spirits, where the nerves are very
delicate ; and I think such persons are more sus-
ceptive of impressions from the agency of invisible
powers, both good and evil ; an agency which,
though we cannot explain, experience will not
permit us to deny. However, though circum-
stantials rise and fall, the real difference between
nature and grace remains unalterable. That work
of God upon the heart which is sometimes called
a new birth, at others a new creation, is as distinct
from the highest effects of natural principles or
the most specious imitations which education or
resolutions can produce, as light is from darkness,
or life from death. Only he who made the world
can either make a Christian, or support and carry
on his own work. A thirst after God as our portion ; a delight in Jesus, as the only way and

door; a renunciation of self and of the world, so far as it is opposite to the spirit of the Gospel: these, and the like fruits of that grace which bringeth salvation, are not only beyond the power of our fallen nature, but contrary to its tendency; so that we can have no desires of this kind till they are given us from above, and can for a season hardly bear to hear them spoken of, either as excellent or necessary. I am, &c.

LETTER III.

My dear Madam, September 17, 1776.

We are much indebted to you for your kind thoughts of us. Hitherto I feel no uneasiness about what is before me; but I am afraid my tranquillity does not wholly spring from trust in the Lord, and submission to his will, but that a part of it at least is derived from the assurances Mr. W. gave me, that the operation would be neither difficult nor dangerous. I have not much of the hero in my constitution; if in great pains or sharp trials I should ever shew a becoming fortitude, it must be given me from above. I desire to leave all with him, in whose hands my ways are, and who has promised me strength according to my day.

I rejoice that the Lord has not only made you desirous of being useful to others in their spiritual concerns, but has given you in some instances to see, that your desires and attempts have not been in vain. I shall thankfully accept of the commission you are pleased to offer me, and take a pleasure in perusing any papers you may think proper to put into my hands, and offer you my sentiments with that simplicity which I am persuaded will be much more agreeable to you than compliments. Though I know there is in general a delicacy and difficulty in services of this kind, yet with respect to yourself I seem to have nothing to fear.

I have often wished we had more female pens employed in the service of the sanctuary. Though few ladies encumber themselves with the apparatus of Latin and Greek, or engage in voluminous performances; yet, in the article of essay writing, I think many are qualified to succeed better than most men, having a peculiar easiness of style, which few of us can imitate. I remember you once shewed me a paper, together with the corrections and alterations proposed by a gentleman whose opinion you had asked. I thought his corrections had injured it, and given it an air of stiffness which is often observable when learned men write in English. Grammatical rules, as they are called, are wholly derived from the mode of speaking or writing which obtains amongst those who best understand the language; for the language must be supposed established before any grammar can be made for it; and therefore women who, from the course of their education and life, have had an opportunity of reading the best written books, and conversing with those who speak well, though they do not burden themselves with the formality of grammar, have often more skill in the English language than the men who can call every figure of speech by a Latin or Greek name. You may be sure, Madam, I shall not wish your papers suppressed, merely because they were not written by a learned man. Language and style, however, are but the dress. Trifles, however adorned, are trifles still. A person of spiritual discernment would rather be the author of one page written in the humble garb of Bunyan, upon a serious subject, than to be able to rival the sprightliness and elegance of Lady M. W. Montague, unless it could be with a

view to edification. The subjects you propose
are important; and with respect to sacramental
meditations, and all devotional exercises so called,
I perfectly agree with you, that, to be affecting
and useful, they must be dictated rather by the
heart than by the head; and are most likely to
influence others, when they are the fruits and
transcripts of our own experience. So far as I
know, we are but scantily provided with specimens of this sort in print, and therefore I shall
be glad to see an accession to the public stock.
Your other thought of helps to recollection on
Saturday evenings, is, I think, an attempt in
which none have been beforehand with you. So
that, according to the general appearance, I feel
myself disposed to encourage you to do as you
have purposed. On the other hand, if I meet
with any thing, on the perusal of the papers,
which in my view may seem to need alteration, I
will freely and faithfully point it out.

I can almost smile *now*, to think you once
classed me amongst the *Stoics.* If I dare speak
with confidence of myself in any thing, I think I
may lay claim to a little of that pleasing, painful
thing, sensibility. I need not boast of it; for it
has too often been my snare, my sin, and my
punishment. Yet I would be thankful for a spice
of it, as the Lord's gift, and when rightly exercised it is valuable; and I think I should make
but an awkward minister without it, especially
here. Where there is this sensibility in the natural temper, it will give a tincture or cast to our
religious expression. Indeed I often find this
sensibility weakest where it should be strongest,
and have reason to reproach myself that I am no
more affected by the character, love, and sufferings
of my Lord and Saviour, and my own peculiar

personal obligations to him. However, my views
of religion have been such for many years, as I
supposed more likely to make me be deemed an
Enthusiast than a Stoic. A moonlight head-
knowledge derived from a system of sentiments,
however true in themselves, is, in my judgment,
a poor thing : nor, on the other hand, am I an
admirer of those rapturous sallies which are more
owing to a warm imagination, than to a just perception of the power and importance of Gospel
truth. The Gospel addresses both head and heart ;
and where it has its proper effect, where it is received as the word of God, and is closed with the
authority and energy of the Holy Spirit, the understanding is enlightened, the affections awakened and
engaged, the will brought into subjection, and the
whole soul delivered to its impression as wax to the
seal. When this is the case, when the affections
do not take the lead, and push forward with a
blind impulse, but arise from the principles of
Scripture, and are governed by them, the more
warmth the better. Yet in this state of infirmity,
nothing is perfect ; and our natural temperament
and disposition will have more influence upon our
religious sensations than we are ordinarily aware.
It is well to know how to make proper allowances
and abatements upon this head, in the judgment
we form both of ourselves and of others. Many
good people are distressed and alternately elated
by frames and feelings, which perhaps are more
constitutional than properly religious experiences.
I dare not tell you, Madam, what I am ; but I can
tell you what I wish to be. The love of God, as
manifested in Jesus Christ, is what I would wish
to be the abiding object of my contemplation ;
not merely to speculate upon it as a doctrine, but
so to feel it, and my own interest in it, as to have

my heart filled with its effects, and transformed into its resemblance; that, with this glorious Exemplar in my view, I may be animated to a spirit of benevolence, love, and compassion, to all around me; that my love may be primarily fixed upon him who has so loved me, and then, for his sake, diffused to all his children, and to all his creatures. Then, knowing that much is forgiven to me, I should be prompted to the ready exercise of forgiveness, if I have aught against any. Then I should be humble, patient, and submissive under all his dispensations; meek, gentle, forbearing, and kind to my fellow-worms. Then I should be active and diligent in improving all my talents and powers in his service, and for his glory; and live not to myself, but to him who loved me and gave himself for me.   I am, &c.

LETTER IV.

My dear Madam,   Nov. 29, 1776.

I AM persuaded you need not be told, that though there are perhaps supposable extremities in which self would prevail over all considerations, yet in general it is more easy to suffer in our own persons, than in the persons of those whom we dearly love; for through such a medium our apprehensions possibly receive the idea of the trouble enlarged beyond its just dimensions; and it would sit lighter upon us if it were properly our own case, for then we should feel it all, and there would be no room for imagination to exaggerate.

But though I feel grief, I trust the Lord has mercifully preserved me from impatience and murmuring, and that, in the midst of all the pleadings of flesh and blood, there is a something within me

that aims to say, without reserve or exception,
Not my will, but thine be done.

It is a comfortable consideration, that he with
whom we have to do, our great High Priest, who
once put away our sins by the sacrifice of himself,
and now for ever appears in the presence of God
for us, is not only possessed of sovereign authority
and infinite power, but wears our very nature,
and feels and exercises in the highest degree those
tendernesses and commiserations, which I conceive are essential to humanity in its perfect
state. The whole history of his wonderful life
is full of inimitable instances of this kind. His
bowels were moved before his arm was ex-
erted : he condescended to mingle tears with
mourners, and wept over distresses which he intended to relieve. He is still the same in his exalted state ; compassions dwell within his heart.
In a way inconceivable to us, but consistent with
his supreme dignity and perfection of happiness
and glory, he still feels for his people. When Saul
persecuted the members upon earth, the Head
complained from heaven; and sooner shall the
most tender mother sit insensible and inattentive
to the cries and wants of her infant, than the Lord
Jesus be an unconcerned spectator of his suffering
children. No, with the eye, and the ear, and the
heart of a friend, he attends to their sorrows ; he
counts their sighs, puts their tears in his bottle ;
and when our spirits are overwhelmed within us,
he knows our path, and adjusts the time, the measure of our trials, and every thing that is necessary for our present support and seasonable deliverance, with the same unerring wisdom and accuracy as he weighed the mountains in scales and
hills in a balance, and meted out the heavens with
a span. Still more, besides his benevolent, he

has an experimental, sympathy. He knows our sorrows, not merely as he knows all things, but as one who has been in our situation, and who, though without sin himself, endured when upon earth inexpressibly more for us than he will ever lay upon us. He has sanctified poverty, pain, disgrace, temptation, and death, by passing through these states: and in whatever states his people are, they may by faith have fellowship with him in their sufferings, and he will by sympathy and love have fellowship and interest with them in theirs. What then shall we fear, or of what shall we complain; when all our concerns are written upon his heart, and their management, to the very hairs of our head, are under his care and providence; when he pities us more than we can do ourselves, and has engaged his almighty power to sustain and relieve us? However, as he is tender, he is wise also: he loves us, but especially with regard to our best interests. If there were not something in our hearts and our situation that required discipline and medicine, he so delights in our prosperity, that we should never be in heaviness. The innumerable comforts and mercies with which he enriches even those we call darker days, are sufficient proofs that he does not willingly grieve us: but when he sees a need-be for chastisement, he will not withhold it because he loves us; on the contrary, that is the very reason why he afflicts. He will put his silver into the fire to purify it; but he sits by the furnace as a refiner, to direct the process, and to secure the end he has in view, that we may neither suffer too much nor suffer in vain.

                              I am, &c.

LETTER V.

My dear Madam,   December, 1776.

I HAVE often preached to others of the benefit of affliction; but my own path for many years has been so smooth, and my trials, though I have not been without trials, comparatively so light and few, that I have seemed to myself to speak by rote upon a subject of which I had not a proper feeling. Yet the many exercises of my poor afflicted people, and the sympathy the Lord has given me with them in their troubles, has made this a frequent and favourite topic of my ministry among them. The advantages of afflictions, when the Lord is pleased to employ them for the good of his people, are many and great. Permit me to mention a few of them; and the Lord grant that we may all find those blessed ends answered to ourselves, by the trials he is pleased to appoint us.

Afflictions quicken us to prayer. It is a pity it should be so; but experience testifies, that a long course of ease and prosperity, without painful changes, has an unhappy tendency to make us cold and formal in our secret worship; but troubles rouse our spirits, and constrain us to call upon the Lord in good earnest, when we feel a need of that help which we only can have from him.

They are useful, and in a degree necessary, to keep alive in us a conviction of the vanity and unsatisfying nature of the present world, and all its enjoyments; to remind us that this is not our rest, and to call our thoughts upwards, where our true treasure is, and where our conversation ought to be. When things go on much to our wish, our hearts are too prone to say, It is good to be here. It is probable, that had Moses, when he came to invite Israel to Canaan, found them in prosperity, as in the days of Joseph, they would have been very unwilling to remove; but the afflictions they were previously brought into made his message welcome. Thus the Lord, by pain, sickness, and disappointments, by breaking our cisterns and withering our gourds, weakens our attachment to this world, and makes the thought of quitting it more familiar and more desirable.

A child of God cannot but greatly desire a more enlarged and experimental acquaintance with his holy word ; and this attainment is greatly promoted by our trials. The far greater part of the promises in Scripture are made and suited to a state of affliction; and, though we may believe they are true, we cannot so well know their sweetness, power, and suitableness, unless we ourselves are in a state to which they refer. The Lord says, " Call upon me in the day of trouble, and I will deliver." Now, till the day of trouble comes, such a promise is like a city of refuge to an Israelite, who, not having slain a man, was in no danger of the avenger of blood. He had a privilege near him, of which he knew not the use and value, because he was not in the case for which it was provided. But some can say, I not only believe this promise upon the authority of the speaker, but I can set my seal to it: I have been in trouble ; I took this course for relief, and I was not disappointed. The Lord verily heard and delivered me. Thus afflictions likewise give occasion of our knowing and noticing more of the Lord's wisdom, power, and goodness, in supporting and relieving, than we should otherwise have known.

I have not time to take another sheet, must therefore contract my homily. Afflictions evidence to ourselves, and manifest to others, the reality of grace. And when we suffer as Christians, exercise some measure of that patience and submission, and receive some measure of these supports and supplies, which the Gospel requires and promises to believers, we are more confirmed that we have not taken up with mere notions; and others may be convinced that we do not follow cunningly devised fables. They likewise strengthen by exercise our graces : as our limbs and natural powers would be feeble if not called to daily exertion; so the graces of the Spirit would languish, without something was provided to draw them out to use. And, to say no more, they are honourable, as they advance our conformity to Jesus our Lord, who was a man of sorrows for our sake. Methinks, if we might go to heaven without suffering, we should be unwilling to desire it. Why should we ever wish to go by any other path than that which he has consecrated and endeared by his own example? especially as his people's sufferings are not penal; there is no wrath in them : the cup he puts in their hands is very different from that which he drank for their sakes, and is only medicinal to promote their chief good. Here I must stop; but the subject is fruitful, and might be pursued through a quire of paper.

I am, &c.

LETTER VI.

My dear Madam, August, 1778.

Your obliging favour of the 22d from B——, which I received last night, demands an immediate acknowledgment. Many things which would have offered by way of answer, must for the present be postponed ; for the same post brought an information which turns my thoughts to *one* subject. What

shall I say ? Topics of consolation are at hand in
abundance; they are familiar to your mind; and
was I to fill the sheet with them, I could suggest
nothing but what you already know. Then are
they consolatory indeed, when the Lord himself is
pleased to apply them to the heart. This he has
promised, and therefore we are encouraged to expect it. This is my prayer for you : I sincerely
sympathize with you ; I cannot comfort you : but
he can ; and I trust he will. How impertinent
would it be to advise you to forget or suspend the
feelings which such a stroke must excite ! who can
help feeling ! nor is sensibility in itself sinful.
Christian resignation is very different from that
stoical stubbornness which is most easily practised
by those unamiable characters whose regards
centre wholly in self; nor could we in a proper
manner exercise submission to the will of God
under our trials, if we did not feel them. He who
knows our frame is pleased to allow, that afflictions
for the present are not joyous, but grievous. But
to them that fear him he is near at hand, to support
their spirits, to moderate their grief, and in the
issue to sanctify it ; so that they shall come out of
the furnace refined, more humble, and more spiritual. There is, however, a part assigned us : we
are to pray for the help in need ; and we are not
wilfully to give way to the impression of over-
whelming sorrow. We are to endeavour to turn
our thoughts to such considerations as are suited
to alleviate it ; our deserts as sinners, the many
mercies we are still indulged with, the still greater
afflictions which many of our fellow-creatures endure, and, above all, the sufferings of Jesus, that
Man of Sorrows, who made himself intimately
acquainted with grief for our sakes.

When the will of the Lord is manifested to us by

the event, we are to look to him for grace and
strength, and be still to know that he is God, that
he has a right to dispose of us and ours as he pleases,
and that in the exercise of this right he is most certainly good and wise. We often complain of losses ;
but the expression is rather improper. Strictly
speaking, we can lose nothing, because we have
no real property in any thing. Our earthly comforts
are lent us ; and when recalled, we ought to return and resign them with thankfulness to him who
has let them remain so long in our hands. But,
as I said above, I do not mean to enlarge in this
strain : I hope the Lord, the only comforter, will
bring such thoughts with warmth and efficacy upon
your mind. Your wound, while fresh, is painful ;
but faith, prayer, and time, will, I trust, gradually
render it tolerable. There is something fascinating
in grief : painful as it is, we are prone to indulge
it, and to brood over the thoughts and circumstances which are suited (like fuel to fire) to
heighten and prolong it. When the Lord afflicts,
it is his design that we should grieve : but in this,
as in all other things, there is a certain moderation
which becomes a Christian, and which only grace
can teach ; and grace teaches us, not by books or
by hearsay, but by experimental lessons : all beyond this should be avoided and guarded against
as sinful and hurtful. Grief, when indulged and
excessive, preys upon the spirits, injures health,
indisposes us for duty, and causes us to shed tears
which deserve more tears. This is a weeping world.
Sin has filled it with thorns and briars, with crosses
and calamities. It is a great hospital, resounding
with groans in every quarter. It is as a field of
battle, where many are falling around us continually ; and it is more wonderful that we escape so
well, than that we are sometimes wounded. We

must have some share: it is the unavoidable lot of our nature and state ; it is likewise needful in point of discipline. The Lord will certainly chasten those whom he loves, though others may seem to pass for a time with impunity. That is a sweet, instructive, and important passage, Heb. xii. 5—11. It is so plain, that it needs no comment; so full, that a comment would but weaken it. May the Lord inscribe it upon your heart, my dear Madam, and upon mine.   I am, &c.

LETTER VII.

My dear Madam,   November, 1778.

Your obliging favour raised in me a variety of emotions when I first received it, and has revived them this morning while perusing it again. I have mourned and rejoiced with you, and felt pain and pleasure in succession, as you diversified the subject. However, the weight of your grief I was willing to consider as a thing that is past; and the thought that you had been mercifully supported under it, and brought through it, that you were restored home in safety, and that at the time of writing you were tolerably well and composed, made joy, upon the whole, preponderate ; and I am more disposed to congratulate you, and join you in praising the Lord for the mercies you enumerate, than to prolong my condolence upon the mournful parts of your letter. Repeated trying occasions have made me well acquainted with the anxious inquiries with which the busy poring mind is apt to pursue departed friends : it can hardly be otherwise under some circumstances. I have found prayer the best relief. I have thought it very allowable to avail myself to the utmost of every favourable consideration; but I have had the most comfort, when I have been enabled to resign the whole concern into His hands, whose thoughts and ways, whose power and goodness, are infinitely superior to our conceptions. I consider, in such cases, that the great Redeemer can save to the uttermost, and the great Teacher can communicate light, and impress truth, when and how he pleases. I trust the power of his grace and compassion will hereafter triumphantly appear, in many instances, of persons, who, on their dying beds, and in their last moments, have been, by his mercy, constrained to feel the importance and reality of truths which they did not properly understand and attend to in the hour of health and prosperity. Such a salutary change I have frequently, or at least more than once, twice, or thrice, been an eye-witness to, accompanied with such evidence as, I think, has been quite satisfactory. And who can say such a change may not often take place, when the person who is the subject of it is too much enfeebled to give an account to by-standers of what is transacting in his mind! Thus I have encouraged my hope. But the best satisfaction of all is, to be duly impressed with the voice that says, "Be still, and know that I am God." These words direct us, not only to his sovereignty, his undoubted right to do what he will with his own, but to all his adorable and amiable perfections, by which he has manifested himself to us in the Son of his love.

As I am not a Sadducee, the account you give of the music which entertained you on the road, does not put my dependence either upon your veracity or your judgment to any trial. We live upon the confines of the invisible world, or rather, perhaps, in the midst of it. That unseen agents have a power of operating on our minds, at least upon that mysterious faculty we call the imagination, is with me not merely a point of opinion, or even of faith, but of experience. That evil spirits can, when permitted, disturb, distress, and defile us, I know, as well as I know that the fire can burn me: and though their interposition is perhaps more easily and certainly distinguishable, yet, from analogy, I conclude that good spirits are equally willing, and equally able, to employ their kind offices for our relief and comfort. I have formed in my mind a kind of system upon this subject, which, for the most part, I keep pretty much to myself; but I can entrust my thoughts to you as they occasionally offer. I apprehend that some persons (those particularly who rank under the class of nervous) are more open and accessible to these impressions than others, and probably the same person more so at sometimes than others. And though we frequently distinguish between imaginary and real (which is one reason why nervous people are so seldom pitied), yet an impression upon the imagination may, as to the agent that produces it, and to the person that receives it, be as much a reality as any of the sensible objects around him ; though a by-stander, not being able to share in the perception, may account it a mere whim, and suppose it might be avoided or removed by an act of the will. Nor have any a right to withhold their assent to what the Scriptures teach, and many sober persons declare, of this invisible agency, merely because we cannot answer the questions, How ? or Why ? The thing may be certain, though *we* cannot easily explain it; and there may be just and important reasons for it, though we should not be able to assign them. If what you heard, or (which, in my view, is much the same) what you thought you heard, had a tendency to compose your spirit, and to encourage your application to the Lord for help, at the time when you were about to stand in need of especial assistance, then there is a sufficient and suitable reason assigned for it at once, without looking farther. It would be dangerous to make impressions a *rule* of duty; but if they strengthen us and assist us in the performance of what *we know* to be our duty, we may be thankful for them.

You have taken leave of your favourite trees, and the scenes of your younger life, but a few years sooner than you must have done, if the late dispensation had not taken place. All must be left soon: for all below is polluted, and in its best state is too scanty to afford us happiness. If we are believers in Jesus, all we *can* quit is a mere nothing, compared with what we shall obtain. To exchange a dungeon for a palace, earth for heaven, will call for no self-denial when we stand upon the threshold of eternity, and shall have a clearer view than we have now of the vanity of what is passing from us, and the glory of what is before us. The partial changes we meet with in our way through life are designed to remind us of, and prepare us for, the great change which awaits us at the end of it. The Lord grant that we may find mercy of the Lord in that solemn hour.

I am, &c.

FOUR LETTERS

TO

MRS. T****.

LETTER I.

My dear Madam,   March 12, 1774.

MY heart is full, yet I must restrain it. Many thoughts which crowd my mind, and would have vent were I writing to another person, would to you be unseasonable. I write not to remind you of what you have lost, but of what you have, which you cannot lose. May the Lord put a word into my heart that may be acceptable; and may his good Spirit accompany the perusal, and enable you to say with the Apostle, that, as sufferings abound, consolations also abound by Jesus Christ. Indeed I can sympathize with you. I remember too the delicacy of your frame, and the tenderness of your natural spirits; so that were you not interested in the exceeding great and precious promises of the Gospel, I should be ready to fear you must sink under your trial. But I have some faint conceptions of the all-sufficiency and faithfulness of the Lord, and may address you in the king's words to Daniel, "Thy God whom thou servest continually, he will deliver thee." Motives for resignation to his will abound in his word; but it is an additional and crowning mercy, that he has promised to apply and enforce them in time of need. He has said, "My grace shall be sufficient for thee; and as thy day is, so shall thy strength be." This I trust you have already experienced. The Lord is so rich, and so good, that he can by a glance of thought compensate his children for whatever his wisdom sees fit to deprive them of. If he gives them a lively sense of what he has delivered them from, and prepared for them, or of what he himself submitted to endure for their sakes, they find at once light springing up out of darkness : hard things become easy, and bitter sweet. I remember to have read of a good man in the last century (probably you may have met with the story), who, when his beloved and only son lay ill, was for some time greatly anxious about the event. One morning he staid longer than usual in his closet : while he was there his son died. When he came out his family were afraid to tell him ; but, like David, he perceived it by their looks ; and when upon inquiry they said it was so, he received the news with a composure that surprised them. But he soon explained the reason, by telling them, that for such discoveries of the Lord's goodness as he had been favoured with that morning, he could be content to lose a son every day. Yes, Madam, though every stream must fail, the fountain is still full and still flowing. All the comfort you ever received in your dear friend was from the Lord, who is abundantly able to comfort you still ; and he is gone but a little before you. May your faith anticipate the joyful and glorious meeting you will shortly have in a better world. Then your worship and converse together will be to unspeakable advantage, without imperfection, interruption, abatement, or end. Then all tears shall be wiped away, and every cloud removed ; and then you will see, that all your concernments here below (the late afflicting dispensation not excepted), were appointed and adjusted by infinite wisdom and infinite love.

The Lord, who knows our frame, does not expect

or require that we should aim at a Stoical indifference under his visitations. He allows, that afflictions are at present not joyous, but grievous ; yea, he was pleased when upon earth to weep with his mourning friends when Lazarus died. But he has graciously provided for the prevention of that anguish and bitterness of sorrow, which is, upon such occasions, the portion of such as live without God in the world ; and has engaged, that all shall work together for good, and yield the peaceable fruits of righteousness. May he bless you with a sweet serenity of spirit, and a cheerful hope of the glory that shall shortly be revealed.

I intimated, that I would not trouble you with my own sense and share of this loss. If you remember the great kindness I always received from Mr. T**** and yourself, as often as opportunity afforded ; and if you will believe me possessed of any sensibility or gratitude, you will conclude that my concern is not small. I feel likewise for the public. Will it be a consolation to you, madam, to know, that you do not mourn alone ? A character so exemplary as a friend, a counsellor, a Christian, and a minister, will be long and deeply regretted ; and many will join with me in praying, that you, who are most nearly interested, may be signally supported, and feel the propriety of Mrs. Rowe's acknowledgment,

> Thou dost but take the dying lamp away,
> To bless me with thine own unclouded day.

We join in most affectionate respects and condolence. May the Lord bless you and keep you, lift up the light of his countenance upon you, and give you peace.

I am, &c.

LETTER II.

My dear Madam,   April 8, 1775.

I HAVE long and often purposed waiting upon
you with a second letter, though one thing or other
still caused delay ; for though I could not but wish
to hear from you, I was far from making that a
condition of my writing. If you have leisure and
spirits to favour me with a line now and then, it
will give us much pleasure ; but if not, it will be a
sufficient inducement with me to write, to know
that you give me liberty, and that you will receive
my letters in good part. At the same time I must
add, that my various engagements will not permit
me to break in upon you so often as my sincere
affection would otherwise prompt me to do.

I heartily thank you for yours, and hope my soul
desires to praise the Lord on your behalf. I am
persuaded that his goodness to you in supporting
you under a trial so sharp in itself, and in the circumstances that attended it, has been an encouragement and comfort to many. It is in such apparently severe times that the all-sufficiency and
faithfulness of the Lord, and the power and proper
effects of his precious Gospel, are most eminently
displayed. I would hope, and I do believe, that
the knowledge of your case has animated some of
the Lord's people against those anxious fears which
they sometimes feel when they look upon their
earthly comforts with too careful an eye, and their
hearts are ready to sink at the thought. What
should I do, and how should I behave, were the
Lord pleased to take away my desire with a stroke ?
But we see he can supply their absence, and afford
us superior comforts without them. The Gospel
reveals one thing needful, the pearl of great price ;
and supposes, that they who possess this are pro-

vided for against all events, and have ground of
unshaken hope, and a source of never-failing consolation under every change they can meet with
during their pilgrimage state. When his people are
enabled to set their seal to this, not only in theory,
when all things go smooth, but practically, when
called upon to pass through the fire and water;
then his grace is glorified in them and by them;
then it appears, both to themselves and to others,
that they have neither followed cunningly devised
fables, nor amused themselves with empty notions;
then they know in themselves, and it is evidenced
to others, that God is with them of a truth. In this
view a believer, when in some good measure di-
vested from that narrow selfish disposition which
cleaves so close to us by nature, will not only submit to trials, but rejoice in them, notwithstanding
the feelings and reluctance of the flesh.   For if I
am redeemed from misery by the blood of Jesus;
and if he is now preparing me a mansion near himself, that I may drink of the rivers of pleasure at
his right hand for evermore; the question is not (at
least ought not to be), how may I pass through life
with the least inconvenience? but, how may my
little span of life be made most subservient to the
praise and glory of Him who loved me, and gave
himself for me? Where the Lord gives this desire he
will gratify it; and as afflictions, for the most part,
afford the fairest opportunities of this kind, therefore it is, that those whom he is pleased eminently
to honour are usually called, at one time or another, to the heaviest trials; not because he loves to
grieve them, but because he hears their prayers,
and accepts their desires of doing him service in the
world. The post of honour in war is so called, because attended with difficulties and dangers which
but few are supposed equal to; yet generals usually

allot these hard services to their favourites and friends, who on their parts eagerly accept them as tokens of favour and marks of confidence. Should we, therefore, not account it an honour and a privilege, when the Captain of our salvation assigns us a difficult post? since he can and does (which no earthly commander can) inspire his soldiers with wisdom, courage, and strength, suitable to their situation. 2 Cor. xii. 9, 10. I am acquainted with a few who have been led thus into the fore-front of the battle: they suffered much; but I have never heard them say they suffered too much; for the Lord stood by them and strengthened them. Go on, my dear madam : yet a little while Jesus will wipe away all tears from your eyes; you will see your beloved friend again, and he and you will rejoice together for ever.

I am, &c.

LETTER III.

My dear Madam,   October 24, 1775.

THE manner in which you mention Omicron's letters, I hope, will rather humble me than puff me up. Your favourable acceptance of them, if alone, might have the latter effect; but alas! I feel myself so very defective in those things, the importance of which I endeavoured to point out to others, that I almost appear to myself to be one of those who say but do not. I find it much easier to speak to the hearts of others than to my own. Yet I have cause beyond many to bless God, that he has given me some idea of what a Christian ought to be, and I hope a real desire of being one myself; but verily I have attained but a very little way. A friend hinted to me, that the character I have given of C, or Grace in the full ear, must be

from my own experience, or I could not have
written it. To myself, however, it appears otherwise; but I am well convinced, that the state of C
is attainable, and more to be desired than mountains of gold and silver. But I find you complain
likewise; though it appears to me, and I believe
to all that know you, that the Lord has been peculiarly gracious to you, in giving you much of the
Spirit in which He delights, and by which His
name and the power of His Gospel are glorified.
It seems, therefore, that we are not competent
judges either of ourselves or of others. I take it
for granted, that they are the most excellent Christians who are most abased in their own eyes; but
lest you should think upon this ground that I am
something, because I can say so many humiliating
things of myself, I must prevent your over-rating
me, by assuring you, that my confessions rather
express what I know I ought to think of myself,
than what I actually do. Naturalists suppose, that
if the matter of which the earth is formed were
condensed as much as it is capable of, it would
occupy but a very small space; in proof of which
they observe, that a cubical pane of glass, which
appears smooth and impervious to us, must be exceedingly porous in itself; since in every assignable point it receives and transmits the rays of light;
and yet gold, which is the most solid substance
we are acquainted with, is but about eight times
heavier than glass, which is made up (if I may so
say) of nothing but pores. In like manner I conceive, that inherent grace, when it is dilated, and
appears to the greatest advantage in a sinner,
would be found to be very small and inconsiderable, if it was condensed, and absolutely separated
from every mixture. The highest attainments in
this life are very inconsiderable, compared with

what should properly result from our relation and obligations to a God of infinite holiness. The nearer we approach to him, the more we are sensible of this. While we only hear of God as it were by the ear, we seem to be something; but when, as in the oase of Job, he discovers himself more sensibly to us, Job's language becomes ours, and the height of our attainment is, to abhor ourselves in dust and ashes.

I hope I do not write too late to meet you at Bath. I pray that your health may be benefited by the waters, and your soul comforted by the Lord's blessing upon the ordinances, and the converse of his children. If any of the friends you expected to see are still there, to whom we are known, and my name should be mentioned, I beg you to say, we desire to be respectfully remembered to them. Had I wings, I would fly to Bath while you are there. As it is, I endeavour to be with you in spirit. There certainly is a real, though secret, a sweet, though mysterious, communion of saints, by virtue of their common union with Jesus. Feeding upon the same bread, drinking of the same fountain, waiting at the same mercy-seat, and aiming at the same ends, they have fellowship one with another, though at a distance. Who can tell how often the Holy Spirit, who is equally present with them all, touches the hearts of two or more of his children at the same instant, so as to excite a sympathy of pleasure, prayer, or praise, on each other's account? It revives me sometimes in a dull and dark hour to reflect, that the Lord has in mercy given me a place in the hearts of many of his people; and perhaps some of them may be speaking to him on my behalf, when I have hardly power to utter a word for myself. For kind services of this sort I persuade myself I am often indebted to you. O that I were enabled more fervently to repay you in the same way! I can say, that I attempt it : I love and honour you greatly, and your concernments are often upon my mind.

We spent most of a week with Mr. B**** since we returned from London, and he has been once here. We have reason to be very thankful for his connection : I find but few like minded with him, and his family is filled with the grace and peace of the Gospel. I never visit them, but I meet with something to humble, quicken, and edify me. O! what will heaven be, where there shall be all who love the Lord Jesus, and they only ; where all imperfection, and whatever now abates or interrupts their joy in their Lord and in each other, shall cease for ever. There at least I hope to meet you, and spend an eternity with you, in admiring the riches and glory of redeeming love.

We join in a tender of the most affectionate respects. I am, &c.

LETTER IV.

My dear Madam, October 28, 1777.

WHAT can I say for myself, to let your obliging letter remain so long unanswered, when your kind solicitude for us induced you to write ? I am ashamed of the delay. You would have heard from me immediately, had I been at home. But I have reason to be thankful that we were providentially called to London a few days before the fire ; so that Mrs. **** was mercifully preserved from the alarm and shock she must have felt, had she been upon the spot. Your letter followed me hither, and was in my possession more than a week before my return. I purposed writing every

day, but indeed I was much hurried and engaged.
Yet I am not excused : I ought to have saved time
from my meals or my sleep, rather than appear
negligent or ungrateful.   I now seize the first post
I could write by since I came home.   The fire
devoured twelve houses : and it was a mercy, and
almost a miracle, that the whole town was not
destroyed ; which must, humanly speaking, have
been the case, had not the night been calm, as two
thirds of the buildings were thatched.   No lives
were lost ; no person considerably hurt ; and I
believe the contributions of the benevolent will
prevent the loss from being greatly felt.   It was
at the distance of a quarter of a mile from my
house.

Your command limits my attention, at present,
to a part of your letter, and points me out a subject.   Yet at the same time you lay me under a
difficulty.   I would not willingly offend you, and I
hope the Lord has taught me not to aim at saying
handsome things.   I deal not in compliments, and
religious compliments are the most unseemly of
any.   But why might I not express my sense of
the grace of God, manifested in you as well as in
another ?   I believe our hearts are all alike, destitute of every good, and prone to every evil.
Like money from the same mint, they bear the
same impression of total depravity ; but grace
makes a difference, and grace deserves the praise.
Perhaps it ought not greatly to displease you,
that others do, and must, and will think better of
you than you do of yourself.   If I do, how can I
help it, when I form my judgment entirely from
what you say and write ?   I cannot consent, that
you should seriously appoint me to examine and
judge of your state.   I thought you knew, beyond
the shadow of a doubt, what your views and de-

sires are : yea, you express them in your letter, in full agreement with what the Scripture declares of the principles, desires, and feelings of a Christian.   It is true that you feel contrary principles, that you are conscious of defects and defilements; but it is equally true, that you could not be right, if you did not feel these things.   To be conscious of them, and humbled for them, is one of the surest marks of grace; and to be more deeply sensible of them than formerly, is the best evidence of growth in grace.   But when the enemy would tempt us to doubt and distrust, because we are not perfect, then he fights, not only against our peace, but against the honour and faithfulness of our dear Lord.   Our righteousness is in him, and our hope depends, not upon the exercise of grace in us, but upon the fulness of grace and love in him, and upon his obedience unto death.

There is, my dear madam, a difference between the holiness of a sinner and that of an angel. The angels have never sinned, nor have they tasted of redeeming love: they have no inward conflicts, no law of sin warring in their members; their obedience is perfect; their happiness is complete. Yet if I be found among redeemed sinners, I need not wish to be an angel.   Perhaps God is not less glorified by your obedience, and, not to shock you, I will add by mine, than by Gabriel's.   It is a mighty manifestation of his grace indeed, when it can live, and act, and conquer in such hearts as ours ; when, in defiance of an evil nature and an evil world, and all the force and subtilty of Satan, a weak worm is still upheld, and enabled not only to climb, but to thresh the mountains ; when a small spark is preserved through storms and floods. In these circumstances, the work of grace is to be estimated, not merely from its imperfect appearance, but from the difficulties it has to struggle with and overcome; and therefore our holiness does not consist in great attainments, but in spiritual desires, in hungerings, thirstings, and mournings; in humiliation of heart, poverty of spirit, submission, meekness; in cordial admiring thoughts of Jesus, and dependence upon him alone for all we want. Indeed these may be said to be great attainments; but they who have most of them are most sensible that they, in and of themselves, are nothing, have nothing, can do nothing, and see daily cause for abhorring themselves and repenting in dust and ashes.

Our view of death will not always be alike, but in proportion to the degree in which the Holy Spirit is pleased to communicate his sensible influence. We may anticipate the moment of dissolution with pleasure and desire in the morning, and be ready to shrink from the thought of it before night. But though our frames and perceptions vary, the report of faith concerning it is the same. The Lord usually reserves dying strength for a dying hour. When Israel was to pass Jordan, the Ark was in the river; and though the rear of the host could not see it, yet as they successively came forward and approached the banks, they all beheld the Ark, and all went safely over. As you are not weary of living, if it be the Lord's pleasure, so I hope, for the sake of your friends and the people whom you love, he will spare you amongst us a little longer; but when the time shall arrive which he has appointed for your dismission, I make no doubt but he will overpower all your fears, silence all your enemies, and give you a comfortable, triumphant entrance into his kingdom. You have nothing to fear from death; for Jesus, by dying, has disarmed it of its sting, has perfumed the grave, and opened the gates of glory for his believing people. Satan, so far as he is permitted, will assault our peace, but he is a vanquished enemy: our Lord holds him in a chain, and sets him bounds which he cannot pass. He provides for us likewise the whole armour of God, and has promised to cover our heads himself in the day of battle, to bring us honourably through every skirmish, and to make us more than conquerors at last. If you think my short unexpected interview with Mr. C**** may justify my wishing he should know that I respect his character, love his person, and rejoice in what the Lord has done and is doing for him and by him, I beg you to tell him so: but I leave it entirely to you.

We join in most affectionate respects.

I am, &c.

FIVE LETTERS

TO

MR. ****.

─────────

LETTER I.

Dear Sir, March 7, 1765.

Your favour of the 19th February came to my hand yesterday. I have read it with attention, and very willingly sit down to offer you my thoughts. Your case reminds me of my own : my first desires towards the ministry were attended with great uncertainties and difficulties, and the perplexity of my own mind was heightened by the various and opposite judgments of my friends. The advice I have to offer is the result of painful experience and exercise, and for this reason perhaps may not be unacceptable to you. I pray our gracious Lord to make it useful.

I was long distressed, as you are, about what was or was not a proper call to the ministry : it now seems to me an easy point to solve, but perhaps will not be so to you till the Lord shall make it clear to yourself in your own case. I have not room to say so much as I could : in brief, I think it principally includes three things : —

1. A warm and earnest desire to be employed in this service.—I apprehend, the man who is once moved by the Spirit of God to this work, will prefer it, if attainable, to thousands of gold and silver ; so that, though he is at times intimidated by a sense of its importance and difficulty, compared with his own great insufficiency (for it is to be presumed a

call of this sort, if indeed from God, will be accompanied with humility and self-abasement), yet he cannot give it up. I hold it a good rule to inquire in this point, whether the desire to preach is most fervent in our most lively and spiritual frames, and when we are most laid in the dust before the Lord? If so, it is a good sign. But if, as is sometimes the case, a person is very earnest to be a preacher to others, when he finds but little hungerings and thirstings after grace in his own soul, it is then to be feared his zeal springs rather from a selfish principle than from the Spirit of God.

2. Besides this affectionate desire and readiness to preach, there must in due season appear some competent sufficiency as to gifts, knowledge, and utterance. Surely, if the Lord sends a man to teach others, he will furnish him with the means. I believe many have intended well in setting up for preachers, who yet went beyond or before their call in so doing. The main difference between a minister and a private Christian seems to consist in these ministerial gifts, which are imparted to him, not for his own sake, but for the edification of others. But then I say, these are to appear in due season : they are not to be expected instantaneously, but gradually, in the use of proper means. They are necessary for the discharge of the ministry ; but not necessary as pre-requisites to warrant our desires after it. In your case, you are young, and have time before you : therefore, I think you need not as yet perplex yourself with inquiring if you have these gifts already : it is sufficient if your desire is fixed, and you are willing, in the way of prayer and diligence, to wait upon the Lord for them : as yet you need them not.

3. That which finally evidences a proper call is a correspondent opening in Providence, by a gra-

dual train of circumstances pointing out the means, the time, the place, of actually entering upon the work. And till this coincidence arrives, you must not expect to be always clear from hesitation in your own mind. The principal caution on this head is, not to be too hasty in catching at first appearances. If it be the Lord's will to bring you into his ministry, he has already appointed your place and service ; and though you know it not at present, you shall at a proper time. If you had the talents of an angel, you could do no good with them till his hour is come, and till he leads you to the people whom he has determined to bless by your means. It is very difficult to restrain ourselves within the bounds of prudence here, when our zeal is warm, a sense of the love of Christ upon our hearts, and a tender compassion for poor sinners is ready to prompt us to break out too soon ;—— but he that believeth shall not make haste. I was about five years under this constraint : sometimes I thought I must preach, though it was in the streets. I listened to every thing that seemed plausible, and to many things that were not so. But the Lord graciously, and as it were insensibly. hedged up my way with thorns ; otherwise, if I had been left to my own spirit, I should have put it quite out of my power to have been brought into such a sphere of usefulness, as he in his good time has been pleased to lead me to. And I can now see clearly, that at the time I would first have gone out, though my intention was, I hope, good in the main, yet I over-rated myself, and had not that spiritual judgment and experience which are requisite for so great a service. I wish you therefore to take time ; and if you have a desire to enter into the Established Church, endeavour to keep your zeal within moderate bounds, and avoid every thing that might unnecessarily clog your admission with difficulties. I would not have you hide your profession, or to be backward to speak for God ; but avoid what looks like preaching, and be content with being a learner in the school of Christ for some years. The delay will not be lost time ; you will be so much the more acquainted with the Gospel, with your own heart, and with human nature : the last is a necessary branch of a minister's knowledge, and can only be acquired by comparing what passes within us, and around us, with what we read in the word of God.

I am glad to find you have a distaste both for Arminian and Antinomian doctrines ;—but let not the mistakes of others sit too heavy upon you. Be thankful for the grace that has made you to differ ; be ready to give a reason of the hope that is in you with meekness and fear ; but beware of engaging in disputes, without evident necessity, and some probable hope of usefulness. They tend to eat out the life and savour of religion, and to make the soul lean and dry. Where God has begun a real work of grace, incidental mistakes will be lessened by time and experience ; where he has not, it is of little signification what sentiments people hold, or whether they call themselves Arminians or Calvinists.

I agree with you, it is time enough for you to think of Oxford yet ; and that if your purpose is fixed, and all circumstances render it prudent and proper to devote yourself to the ministry, you will do well to spend a year or two in private studies. It would be further helpful, in this view, to place yourself where there is Gospel preaching, and a lively people. If your favourable opinion of this place should induce you to come here, I shall be very ready to give you every assistance in my

power. As I have trod exactly the path you seem
to be setting out in, I might so far perhaps be more
serviceable than those who are in other respects
much better qualified to assist you. I doubt not
but in this, and every other step, you will entreat
the Lord's direction; and I hope you will not forget to pray for,

Sir, your affectionate friend, &c.

LETTER II.

Dear Sir,   June 7, 1767.

I MUST beg you (once for all) to release me from
any constraint about the length or frequency of my
letters Believe that I think of you, and pray for you,
when you do not hear from me. Your correspondence is not quite so large as mine, therefore you
may write the oftener : your letters will be always
welcome ; and I will write to you when I find a leisure hour, and have any thing upon my mind to offer.

You seem sensible where your most observable
failing lies, and to take reproof and admonition concerning it in good part; I therefore hope and believe the Lord will give you a growing victory over
it. You must not expect habits and tempers will be
eradicated instantaneously; but by perseverance
in prayer, and observation upon the experiences of
every day, much may be done in time. Now and
then you will (as is usual in the course of war) lose
a battle; but be not discouraged, but rally your
forces, and return to the fight. There is a comfortable word, a leaf of the tree of life, for healing the
wounds we receive, in 1 John ii. 1. If the enemy
surprises you, and your heart smites you, do not
stand astonished as if there was no help, nor give
way to sorrow as if there was no hope, nor attempt

to heal yourself; but away immediately to the
Throne of Grace, to the great Physician, to the
compassionate High Priest, and tell him all. Satan
knows, that if he can keep us from confession, our
wounds will rankle; but do you profit by David's
experience, Psal. xxxii. 3—5. When we are simple
and open-hearted in abasing ourselves before the
Lord, though we have acted foolishly and ungrate-
fully, he will seldom let us remain long without
affording us a sense of his compassion; for he is
gracious; he knows our frame, and how to bear
with us, though we can hardly bear with ourselves,
or with one another.

The main thing is to have *the heart right with
God:* this will bring us in the end safely through
many mistakes and blunders; but a double mind,
a selfish spirit, that would halve things between
God and the world, the Lord abhors. Though I
have not yet had many opportunities of commending your *prudence,* I have always had a good opinion of your *sincerity* and *integrity:* if I am not mistaken in this, I make no doubt of your doing well.
If the Lord is pleased to bless you, he will undoubtedly make you humble; for you cannot be either
happy or safe, or have any probable hope of abiding
usefulness, without it. I do not know that I have
had any thing so much at heart in my connections
with you, as to impress you with a sense of the necessity and advantages of an humble frame of spirit:
I hope it has not been in vain. O! to be little in our
own eyes! this is the ground-work of every grace;
this leads to a continual dependence upon the Lord
Jesus; this is the spirit which he has promised to
bless; this conciliates us good-will and acceptance
amongst men; for he that abaseth himself is sure to
be honoured. And that this temper is so hard to

attain and preserve, is a striking proof of our depravity. For are we not sinners ? Were we not rebels and enemies before we knew the Gospel ? and have we not been unfaithful, backsliding, and unprofitable ever since ? Are we not redeemed by the blood of Jesus ? and can we stand a single moment except he upholds us ? Have we any thing which we have not received : or have we received any thing which we have not abused ? Why then is dust and ashes proud ?

I am glad you have found some spiritual acquaintance in your barren land. I hope you will be helpful to them, and they to you. You do well to guard against every appearance of evil. If you are heartily for Jesus, Satan owes you a grudge. One way or other he will try to cut you out work, and the Lord may suffer him to go to the length of his chain. But though you are to keep your eye upon him, and expect to hear from him at every step, you need not be slavishly afraid of him : for Jesus is stronger and wiser than he ; and there is a complete suit of armour provided for all who are engaged on the Lord's side.

I am, &c.

LETTER III.

Dear Sir,　　　　　　　　　　　　Oct. 20, 1767.

A CONCERN for the perplexity you have met with, from objections which have been made against some expressions in my printed sermons, and in general against exhorting sinners to believe in Jesus, engages me to write immediately ; otherwise I should have waited a little longer ; for we are now upon the point of removing to the vicarage, and I believe this will be the last letter I

shall write from the old house. I shall chiefly confine myself at present to the subject you propose.

In the first place, I beg you to be upon your guard
against a reasoning spirit. Search the Scriptures ;
and where you can find a plain rule or warrant for
any practice, go boldly on ; and be not discouraged
because you may not be clearly able to answer or
reconcile every difficulty that may either occur to
your own mind, or be put in your way by others.
Our hearts are very dark and narrow ; and the very
root of all apostacy is a proud disposition to question the necessity or propriety of Divine appointments. But the child-like simplicity of faith is
to follow God without reasoning ; taking it for
granted a thing must be right if he directs it, and
charging all seeming inconsistencies to the account of our own ignorance.

I suppose the people that trouble you upon this
head are of two sorts : 1st, those who preach upon
Arminian principles, and suppose a free will in man,
in a greater or less degree, to turn to God when the
Gospel is proposed. These, if you speak to sinners
at large, though they will approve of your doing so,
will take occasion, perhaps, to charge you with
acting in contradiction to your own principles. So
it seems Mr. **** has said. I love and honour
that man greatly, and I beg you will tell him so
from me ; and tell him farther, that the reason why
he is not a Calvinist, is because he misapprehends
our principles. If I had a proper call, I would undertake to prove the direct contrary ; namely, that
to exhort and deal plainly with sinners, to stir them
up to flee from the wrath to come, and to lay hold
of eternal life, is an attempt not reconcileable to
sober reason upon any other grounds than those
doctrines which we are called Calvinists for holding ; and that all the absurdities which are charged

upon us, as consequences of what we teach, are indeed truly chargeable upon those who differ from us in these points. I think this unanswerably proved by Mr. Edwards, in his discourse on the freedom of the will; though the chain of reasoning is so close, that few will give attention and pains to pursue it. As to myself, if I was not a Calvinist, I think I should have no more hope of success in preaching to men, than to horses or cows.

But these objections are more frequently urged by Calvinists themselves; many of them, I doubt not, good men, but betrayed into a curiosity of spirit, which often makes their ministry (if ministers) dry and inefficacious, and their conversation sour and unsavoury. Such a spirit is too prevalent in many professors, that if a man discovers a warm zeal for the glory of God, and is enabled to bear a faithful testimony to the Gospel truths; yea, though the Lord evidently blesses him, they overlook all, and will undervalue a sermon, which upon the whole they cannot but acknowledge to be Scriptural, if they meet with a single sentence contrary to the opinion they have taken up. I am sorry to see such a spirit prevailing. But this I observe, that the ministers who give into this way, though good men and good preachers in other respects, are seldom very useful or very zealous; and those who are in private life, are more ready for dry points of disputation, at least harping upon a string of doctrines, than for experimental and heart-searching converse, whereby one may warm and edify another. Blessed be God, who has kept me and my people from this turn: if it should ever creep in or spread among us, I should be ready to write *Ichabod* upon our assemblies.

I advise you, therefore, to keep close to the Bible and prayer: bring your difficulties to the

Lord, and entreat him to give you and maintain in
you a simple spirit. Search the Scripture. How
did Peter deal with Simon Magus? We have no
right to think worse of any who can hear us, than
the Apostle did of him. He seemed almost to
think his case desperate, and yet he advised him
to repentance and prayer. Examine the same
Apostle's discourse, Acts iii., and the close of St.
Paul's sermon, Acts xiii. The power is all of God;
the means are likewise of his appointment; and he
always is pleased to work by such means as may
shew that the power is his. What was Moses's rod
in itself, or the trumpets that threw down Jericho?
What influence could the pool of Siloam have, that
the eyes of the blind man, by washing in it, should
be opened? or what could Ezekiel's feeble breath
contribute to the making dry bones live? All these
means were exceedingly disproportionate to the
effect; but He who ordered them to be used accompanied them with his power. Yet if Moses had
gone without his rod; if Joshua had slighted the
rams' horns; if the prophet had thought it foolishness to speak to dry bones, or the blind man refused to wash his eyes, nothing could have been
done. The same holds good in the present subject:
I do not reason, expostulate, and persuade sinners,
because I think I can prevail with them, but because the Lord has commanded it. He directs me
to address them as reasonable creatures; to take
them by every handle; to speak to their consciences; to tell them of the terrors of the Lord,
and of his tender mercies; to argue with them
what good they find in sin; whether they do not
need a Saviour; to put them in mind of death,
judgment, and eternity, &c. When I have done all,
I know it is to little purpose, except the Lord
speaks to their hearts; and this to his own, and at

his own time, I am sure he will, because he has promised it. See Isaiah lv. 10, 11 ; Matth. xxviii. 20. Indeed I have heard expressions in the warmth of delivery which I could not wholly approve, and therefore do not imitate. But in general, I see no preaching made very useful for the gathering of souls, where poor sinners are shut out of the discourse. I think one of the closest and most moving addresses to sinners I ever met with, is in Dr. Owen's Exposition of the 130th Psalm, (in my edition) from p. 243 to 276. If you get it and examine it, I think you will find it all agreeable to Scripture; and he was a steady, deep-sighted Calvinist. I wish you to study it well, and make it your pattern. He handles the same point likewise in other places, and shews the weakness of the exceptions taken somewhere at large, but I cannot just now find the passage. Many think themselves quite right, because they have not had their thoughts exercised at large, but have confined themselves to one track. There are extremes in every thing. I pray God to shew you the golden mean.

I am, &c.

LETTER IV.

Dear Sir,   August 30, 1770.

I WOULD steal a few minutes here to write, lest I should not have leisure at home. I have not your letter with me, and therefore can only answer so far as I retain a general remembrance of the contents.

You will, doubtless, find rather perplexity than advantage from the multiplicity of advice you may receive, if you endeavour to reconcile and adopt the very different sentiments of your friends. I think it will be best to make use of them in a full latitude, that is, to correct and qualify them one by another, and to borrow a little from each, without confining yourself entirely to any. You will probably be advised to different extremes : it will then be impossible to follow both ; but it may be practicable to find a middle path between them : and I believe this will generally prove the best and safest method. Only consult your own temper, and endeavour to incline rather to that side to which you are the least disposed, by the ordinary strain of your own inclination ; for on that side you will be in the least danger of erring. Warm and hasty dispositions will seldom move too slow, and those who are naturally languid and cool are as little liable to over-act their part.

With respect to the particulars you instance, I have generally thought you warm and enterprising enough, and therefore thought it best to restrain you ; but I meant only to hold you in, till you had acquired some farther knowledge and observation both of yourself and of others. I have the pleasure to hope (especially of late) that you are become more self-diffident and wary than you was some time ago. And, therefore, as your years and time are advancing, and you have been for a tolerable space under a probation of silence, I can make no objection to your attempting sometimes to speak in select societies ; but let your attempts be confined to such ; I mean where you are acquainted with the people, or the leading part of them, and be upon your guard against opening yourself too much amongst strangers ;—and again, I earnestly desire you would not attempt any thing of this sort in a very public way, which may, perhaps, bring you under inconveniencies, and will be inconsistent with the part you ought to act (in my judgment) from the time you receive Episcopal ordination. You may remember a simile I have sometimes used of green fruit: children are impatient to have it while it is green, but persons of more judgment will wait till it is ripe. Therefore I would wish your exhortations to be brief, private, and not very frequent. Rather give yourself to reading, meditation, and prayer.

As to speaking without notes, in order to do it successfully, a fund of knowledge should be first possessed. Indeed, in such societies as I hope you will confine your attempts to, it would not be practicable to use notes; but I mean, that if you design to come out as a preacher without notes from the first, you must use double diligence in study: your reading must not be confined to the Scriptures; you should be acquainted with church history, have a general view of divinity, as a system, know something of the state of controversies in past times and at present, and indeed of the general history of mankind. I do not mean that you should enter deeply into these things; but you will need to have your mind enlarged, your ideas increased, your style and manner formed; you should read, think, write, compose, and use all diligence to exercise and strengthen your faculties. If you would speak extempore as a clergyman, you must be able to come off roundly, and to fill up your hour with various matter, in tolerable coherence, or else you will not be able to overcome the prejudice which usually prevails amongst the people. Perhaps it may be as well to use some little scheme in the note way, especially at the beginning: but a little trial will best inform you what is most expedient.

Let your backwardness to prayer and reading

the Scripture be ever so great, you must strive
against it. This backwardness, with the doubts
you speak of, are partly from your own evil heart,
but perhaps chiefly temptations of Satan: he
knows, if he can keep you from drawing water out
of the wells of salvation, he will have much advantage. My soul goes often mourning under the
same complaints, but at times the Lord gives me
a little victory. I hope he will over-rule all our
trials to make us more humble, dependent, and to
give us tenderness of spirit towards the distressed.
The exercised and experienced Christian, by the
knowledge he has gained of his own heart, and the
many difficulties he has had to struggle with, ac-
quires a skill and compassion in dealing with
others ; and without such exercise, all our study,
diligence, and gifts in other ways, would leave us
much at a loss in some of the most important parts
of our calling.

You have given yourself to the Lord for the
ministry; his providence has thus far favoured
your views : therefore harbour not a thought of
flinching from the battle, because the enemy
appears in view, but resolve to endure hardship,
as a good soldier of Jesus Christ. Lift up your
banner in his name; trust in him, and he will
support you ; but, above all things, be sure not to
be either enticed or terrified from the privilege of
a Throne of Grace.

Who your enemies are, or what they say, I know
not; for I never conversed with them. Your
friends here have thought you at times harsh and
hasty in your manner, and rather inclining to self-
confidence. These things I have often reminded
you of; but I considered them as blemishes usually
attendant upon youth, and which experience,
temptation, and prayer, would correct. I hope

and believe you will do well. You will have a share in my prayers and best advice; and when I see occasion to offer a word of reproof, I shall not use any reserve.　　　　　　　Yours, &c.

——

LETTER V.

Dear Sir,　　　　　　　　　　　July 25, 1772.

I AM glad to hear you are accommodated at D——, where I hope your best endeavours will not be wanting to make yourself agreeable, by an humble, inoffensive, and circumspect behaviour.

I greatly approve of your speaking from one of the lessons in the afternoon: you will find it a great help to bring you gradually to that habit and readiness of expression which you desire; and you will perhaps find it make more impression upon your hearers than what you read to them from the pulpit. However, I would not discourage or dissuade you from reading your sermons for a time. The chief inconvenience respecting yourself is that which you mention. A written sermon is something to lean upon; but it is best for a preacher to lean wholly upon the Lord. But set off gradually; the Lord will not despise the day of small things: pray heartily that your *spirit* may be right with him, and then all the rest will be well. And keep on writing: if you compose one sermon, and should find your heart enlarged to preach another, still your labour of writing will not be lost. If your conscience bears you witness that you desire to serve the Lord, his promise (now he has brought you into the ministry) of a sufficiency and ability for the work belongs to you as much as to another. Your borrowing help from others may arise from

a diffidence of yourself, which is not blameable;
but it may arise in part likewise from a diffidence
of the Lord, which is hurtful. I wish you may
get encouragement from that word, Exodus iv.
11, 12. It was a great encouragement to me.
While I would press you to diligence in every
rational means for the improvement of your stock
in knowledge, and your ability of utterance, I
would have you remember, that preaching is a
gift. It cannot be learned by industry and
imitation only, as a man may learn to make a
chair or a table : it comes from above ; and if you
patiently wait upon God, he will bestow this
gift upon you, and increase it in you. It will
grow by exercise. To him that hath shall be
given, and he shall have more abundantly. And
be chiefly solicitous to obtain an unction upon
what you *do* say. Perhaps those sermons in
which you feel yourself most deficient, may be
made most useful to others. I hope you will endeavour likewise to be plain and familiar in your
language and manner (though not low or vulgar),
so as to suit yourself, as much as possible, to the
apprehensions of the most ignorant people. There
are, in all congregations, some persons exceedingly ignorant; yet they have precious souls, and
the Lord often calls such. I pray the Lord to
make you wise to win souls. I hope he will.
You cannot be too jealous of your own heart;
but let not such instances as Mr. ****** discourage
you. Cry to Him who is able to hold you up,
that you may be safe, and you shall not cry in
vain. It is indeed an alarming thought, that a
man may pray and preach, be useful and acceptable for a time, and yet be nothing. But
still the foundation of God standeth sure. I have

a good hope, that I shall never have cause to repent the part I have taken in your concerns. While you keep in the path of duty, you will find it the path of safety. Be punctual in waiting upon God in secret. This is the life of every thing, the only way, and the sure way, of maintaining and renewing your strength.

I am, &c.

EIGHT LETTERS

REV. MR. ****.

LETTER I.

Dear Sir,   June 29, 1757.

I ENDEAVOUR to be mindful of you in my
prayers, that you may find both satisfaction and
success, and that the Lord himself may be your
light to discover to you every part of your duty.
I would earnestly press you and myself to be followers of those who have been followers of Christ;
to aim at a life of self-denial; to renounce self-
will, and to guard against self-wisdom. The less
we have to do with the world the better ; and,
even in conversing with our brethren, we have
been, and unless we watch and pray shall often
be, ensnared. Time is precious, and opportunities once gone are gone for ever. Even by reading,
and what we call studying, we may be comparatively losers. The shorter way is to be closely
waiting upon God in humble, secret, fervent
prayer. The treasures of wisdom and knowledge
are in his hands ; and he gives bountifully, without upbraiding. On the other hand, whatever
we may undertake with a sincere desire to promote His glory, we may comfortably pursue :
nothing is trivial that is done for Him. In this
view, I would have you, at proper intervals, pur-

sue your studies, especially at those times when
you are unfit for better work.   Pray for me, that
I may be enabled to break through the snares of
vanity that lie in my way; that I may be crucified with Christ, and live a hidden life by faith in
him who loved me, and gave himself for me.

Adieu.

LETTER II.

Dear Sir,   August 31, 1757.

I wish you much of that spirit which was in the
Apostle, which made him content to become all
things to all men, that he might gain some.   I am
persuaded, that love and humility are the highest
attainments in the school of Christ, and the brightest evidences that he is indeed our Master.   If
any should seem inclined to treat you with less
regard, because you are or have been a Methodist
teacher, you will find forbearance, meekness, and
long-suffering, the most prevailing means to conquer their prejudices.   Our Lord has not only
taught us to expect persecution from the world,
though this alone is a trial too hard for flesh and
blood; but we must look for what is much more
grievous to a renewed mind, to be in some respects
slighted, censured, and misunderstood, even by
our Christian brethren; and that, perhaps, in cases
where we are really striving to promote the glory
of God and the good of souls, and cannot, without
the reproach of our consciences, alter our conduct,
however glad we should be to have their approbation.   Therefore we are required, not only to
resist the world, the flesh, and the devil, but likewise to bear one another's burdens; which plainly
intimates there will be something to be borne with

on all hands; and happy indeed is he that is not offended. You may observe what unjust reports and surmises were received, even at Jerusalem, concerning the Apostle Paul; and it seems he was condemned unheard, and that by many thousands too, Acts xxi. 20, 21; but we do not find he was at all ruffled, or that he sought to retort any thing upon them, though doubtless, had he been so disposed, he might have found something to have charged them with in his turn; but he calmly and willingly complied with every thing in his power to soften and convince them. Let us be followers of this pattern, so far as he was a follower of Christ; for even Christ pleased not himself. How did he bear with the mistakes, weakness, intemperate zeal, and imprudent proposals of his disciples while on earth! and how does he bear with the same things from you and me, and every one of his followers now! and do we, can we think much to bear with each other for his sake? Have we all a full remission of ten thousand talents which we owed him, and were utterly unable to pay; and do we wrangle amongst ourselves for a few pence? God forbid!

If you should be numbered among the regular Independents, I advise you not to offend any of them by unnecessary singularities. I wish you not to part with any truth, or with any thing really expedient; but if the omitting any thing of an indifferent nature will obviate prejudices, and increase a mutual confidence, why should not so easy a sacrifice be made? Above all, my dear friend, let us keep close to the Lord in a way of prayer: He giveth wisdom that is profitable to direct: He is the wonderful counsellor; there is no teacher like Him. Why do the living seek to

the dead? why do we weary our friends and ourselves, in running up and down, and turning over
books for advice? If we shut our eyes upon the
world, and worldly things, and raise our thoughts
upwards in humility and silence, should we not
often hear the secret voice of the Spirit of God
whispering to our hearts, and pointing out to us
the way of truth and peace? Have we not often
gone astray, and hurt either ourselves or our
brethren, for want of attending to this Divine
Instruction? Have we not sometimes mocked
God, by pretending to ask direction from him,
when we had fixed our determination beforehand?
It is a great blessing to know that we are sincere;
and next to this, to be convinced of our insincerity, and to pray against it.

I am, &c.

LETTER III.

Dear Sir,   November 21, 1757.

CAN you forgive so negligent a correspondent?
I am indeed ashamed; but (if that is any good
excuse) I use you no worse than my other friends.
Whenever I write, I am obliged to begin with an
apology; for what with business, and the incidental duties of every day, my time is always
mortgaged before it comes into my hands, especially as I have so little skill in redeeming and
improving it. I long to hear from you, and I long
to see you; and indeed, from the terms of yours,
I expected you here before this; which has been
partly a cause of my delay. I have mislaid your
letter, and cannot remember the particulars: in
general, I remember you were well, and going on
comfortably in your work; which was matter of

joy to me ; and my poor prayers are for you, that
the Lord may own and prosper you more and
more.   The two great points we are called to
pursue in this sinful divided world, are peace and
holiness : I hope you are much in the study of
them.   These are the peculiar characteristics of
a disciple of Jesus ; they are the richest part of
the enjoyments of heaven : and so far as they are
received into the heart, they bring down heaven
upon earth ; and they are more inseparably connected between themselves than some of us are
aware of.   The longer I live, the more I see of
the vanity and the sinfulness of our unchristian
disputes : they eat up the very vitals of religion.
I grieve to think how often I have lost my time
and my temper that way, in presuming to regulate
the vineyards of others, when I have neglected
my own ; when the beam in my own eye has so
contracted my sight, that I could discern nothing
but the mote in my neighbour's.   I am now desirous to choose a better part.   Could I speak
the publican's words with a proper feeling, I wish
not for the tongue of men or angels to fight about
notions or sentiments.   I allow that every branch
of Gospel truth is precious, that errors are abounding, and that it is our duty to bear an honest testimony to what the Lord has enabled us to find
comfort in, and to instruct with meekness such as
are willing to be instructed ; but I cannot see it
my duty, nay, I believe it would be my sin, to
attempt to beat my notions into other people's
heads.   Too often I have attempted it in time
past ; but I now judge, that both my zeal and
my weapons were carnal.   When our dear Lord
questioned Peter, after his fall and recovery, he
said not, Art thou wise, learned, and eloquent ?
nay, he said not, Art thou clear, and sound, and

orthodox ? but this only, " Lovest thou me ? " An
answer to this was sufficient then ; why not now ?
Any other answer we may believe would have
been insufficient then. If Peter had made the most
pompous confession of his faith and sentiments,
still the first question would have recurred,
" Lovest thou me ? " This is a Scripture precedent. Happy the preacher, whoever he be, my
heart and my prayers are with him, who can
honestly and steadily appropriate Peter's answer !
Such a man, I say, I am ready to hear, though he
should be as much mistaken in some points as
Peter afterwards appears to have been in others.
What a pity it is, that Christians in succeeding
ages should think the constraining force of the love
of Christ too weak, and suppose the end better
answered by forms, subscriptions, and questions
of their own devising ! I cannot acquit even those
churches who judge themselves nearest the primi-
tive rule in this respect : alas ! will-worship and
presumption may creep into the best external
forms. But the misfortune both in churches and
private Christians is, that we are too prone rather
to compare ourselves with others, than to judge by
the Scriptures ; and while each can see that they
give not into the errors and mistakes of the opposite party, both are ready to conclude that they
are right ; and thus it happens, that an attachment
to a supposed Gospel-order will recommend a man
sooner and farther to some churches, than an emi-
nency of Gospel practice. I hope you will beware
of such a spirit whenever you publicly assume the
Independent character : this, like a worm at the
root, has nipt the graces, and hindered the usefulness, of many a valuable man ; and those who
change sides and opinions are the most liable to it.
For the pride of our heart insensibly prompts us to

cast about far and near for arguments to justify
our own behaviour, and makes us too ready to hold
the opinions we have taken up to the very extreme,
that those amongst whom we are newly come may
not suspect our sincerity. In a word, let us endeavour to keep close to God, to be much in
prayer, to watch carefully over our hearts, and
leave the busy warm spirits to make the best of
their work. The secret of the Lord is with them
that fear him, and that wait on him continually ;
to these he will shew his covenant, not notionally,
but experimentally. A few minutes of the Spirit's
teaching will furnish us with more real useful
knowledge, than toiling through whole folios of
commentators and expositors : they are useful in
their places, and are not to be undervalued by those
who can perhaps in general do better without
them ; but it will be our wisdom to deal less with
the streams, and be more close in applying to the
fountain head. The Scripture itself, and the Spirit
of God, are the best and the only sufficient expositors of Scripture. Whatever men have valuable
in their writings, they got it from hence ; and the
way is as open to us as to any of them. There is
nothing required but a teachable humble spirit ;
and learning, as it is commonly called, is not necessary in order to this. I commend you to the
grace of God, and remain

Yours, &c.

LETTER IV.

Dear Sir,   January 10, 1760.

I HAVE procured Cennick's sermons ;—they are
in my judgment *sound* and *sweet*. O that you and
I had a double portion of that spirit and unction

which is in them! Come, let us not despair; the fountain is as full and as free as ever:—precious fountain, ever flowing with blood and water, milk and wine. This is the stream that heals the wounded, refreshes the weary, satisfies the hungry, strengthens the weak, and confirms the strong: it opens the eyes of the blind, softens the heart of stone, teaches the dumb to sing, and enables the lame and paralytic to walk, to leap, to run, to fly, to mount up with eagle's wings: a taste of this stream raises earth to heaven, and brings down heaven upon earth. Nor is it a fountain only; it is a universal blessing, and assumes a variety of shapes to suit itself to our wants. It is a sun, a shield, a garment, a shade, a banner, a refuge: it is bread, the true bread, the very staff of life: it is life itself, immortal, eternal life!

> The cross of Jesus Christ, my Lord,
> Is food and medicine, shield and sword.

Take that for your motto; wear it in your heart; keep it in your eye; have it often in your mouth, till you can find something better. The cross of Christ is the tree of life and the tree of knowledge combined. Blessed be God! there is neither prohibition nor flaming sword to keep us back; but it stands like a tree by the highway side, which affords its shade to every passenger without distinction. Watch and pray. We live in a sifting time: error gains ground every day. May the name and love of our Saviour Jesus keep us and all his people! Either write or come very soon to

Yours, &c.

LETTER V.

Dear Sir,   November 15, 1760.

If your visit should be delayed, let me have a
letter. I want either good news or good advice;
to hear that *your* soul prospers, or to receive something that may quicken *my own*. The Apostle says,
"Ye know the grace of our Lord Jesus Christ:"
alas! we know how to say something about it, but
how faint and feeble are our real perceptions of it!
Our love to him is the proof and measure of what
we know of his love to us. Surely, then, we are
mere children in this kind of knowledge, and every
other kind is vain. What should we think of a man
who should neglect his business, family, and all
the comforts of life, that he might study the Chi-
nese language; though he knows beforehand he
should never be able to attain it, nor ever find occasion or opportunity to use it? The pursuit of
every branch of knowledge that is not closely
connected with the one thing needful is no less
ridiculous.

You know something of our friend Mrs. B****.
She has been more than a month confined to her
bed, and I believe her next remove will be to her
coffin. The Lord has done great things for her.
Though she has been a serious exemplary person
all her life, when the prospect of death presented,
she began to cry out earnestly, "What shall I do
to be saved?" But her solicitude is at an end:
she has seen the salvation of God, and now for the
most part rejoices in something more than hope.
This you will account good news, I am sure. Let
it be your encouragement and mine. The Lord's
arm is not shortened, nor is his presence removed:

he is near us still, though we perceive him not.
May he guide you with his eye in all your public
and private concerns, and may he in particular
bless our communications to our mutual advantage!

I remain, &c.

LETTER VI.

Dear Sir,   July 29, 1761.

ARE the quarrels made up? Tell those who
know what communion with Jesus is worth, that
they will never be able to maintain it, if they give
way to the workings of pride, jealousy, and anger.
This will provoke the Lord to leave them dry; to
command the clouds of his grace that they rain
no rain upon them. These things are sure signs
of a low frame, and a sure way to keep it so.
Could they be prevailed upon, from a sense of the
pardoning love of God to their own souls, to forgive each other as the Lord forgives us, freely,
fully, without condition and without reserve, they
would find this like breaking down a stone wall,
which has hitherto shut up their prayers from the
Lord's ears, and shut out his blessing from filling
their hearts. Tell them, I hope to hear that all
animosities, little and big, are buried by mutual
consent in the Redeemer's grave. Alas! the people
of God have enemies enough. Why then will they
weaken their own hands? Why will they help their
enemies to pull down the Lord's work? Why will
they grieve those who wish them well, cause the
weak to stumble, the wicked to rejoice, and bring
a reproach upon their holy profession? Indeed
this is no light matter; I wish it may not lead
them to something worse; I wish they may be

wise in time, lest Satan gain further advantage over them, and draw them to something that shall make them (as David did) roar under the pains of broken bones. But I must break off. May God give you wisdom, faithfulness, and patience : take care that you do not catch an angry spirit yourself, while you aim to suppress it in others ; this will spoil all, and you will exhort, advise, and weep in vain. May you rather be an example and pattern to the flock : and in this view be not surprised if you yourself meet some hard usage ; rather rejoice, that you will thereby have an opportunity to exemplify your own rules, and to convince your people, that what you recommend to them you do not speak by *rote*, but from the experience of your heart. One end why our Lord was tempted was for the encouragement of his poor followers, that they might know him to be a High Priest suited to them, having had a fellow-feeling in their distresses. For the like reason he appoints his ministers to be sorely exercised both from without and within, that they may sympathize with their flock, and know in their own hearts the deceitfulness of sin, the infirmities of the flesh, and the way in which the Lord supports and bears with all that trust in him. Therefore be not discouraged ; usefulness and trials, comforts and crosses, strength and exercise, go together. But remember He has said, " I will never leave thee nor forsake thee : be thou faithful unto death, and I will give thee a crown of life." When you get to heaven, you will not complain of the way by which the Lord brought you   Farewel. Pray for us.

Yours, &c.

LETTER VII.

Dear Sir,　　　　　　　Dec. 14, 1761.

I PRAY the Lord to accompany you ; but cannot help fearing you go on too fast.　If you have
not (as I am sure you ought not) made an absolute
promise, but only conditional, you need not be so
solicitous : depend upon it, when the Lord is
pleased to remove you, he will send one to supply
your place.　I am grieved that your mind is so set
upon a step, which I fear will occasion many inconveniences to a people who have deserved your
best regard.　Others may speak you fairer, but
none wishes you better than myself : therefore I
hope you allow me to speak my mind plainly, and
believe that it is no pleasure to me to oppose your
inclinations.　As to your saying they will take no
denial, it has no weight with me.　Had they asked
what you were exceedingly averse to, you would
soon have expressed yourself so as to convince
them it was to no purpose to urge you ; but they
saw something in your manner or language that
encouraged them ; they saw the proposal was
agreeable to you, that you were not at all unwilling to exchange your old friends for new ones ;
and this is the reason they would take no denial.
If you should live to see those who are most forward in pressing you become the first to discourage you, you will think seriously of my words.

If I thought my advice would prevail, it should
be this : Call the people together, and desire them
(if possible) to forget you ever intended to depart
from them ; and promise not to think of a removal,
till the Lord shall make your way so clear, that
even they shall have nothing reasonable to object
against it.　You may keep your word with your
other friends too ; for when a proper person shall

offer, as likely to please and satisfy the people as yourself, I will give my hearty consent to your removal.

Consider what it is you would have in your office, but maintenance, acceptance, and success. Have you not those where you are? Are you sure of having them where you are going? Are you sure the Spirit of God (without which you will do nothing) will be with you there, as he has been with you hitherto? Perhaps if you act in your own spirit, you may find as great a change as Samson. I am ready to weep when I think what difficulties were surmounted to accomplish your ordination; and now, when the people thought themselves fixed, that you should so soon disappoint them.

Yours, &c.

LETTER VIII.

Dear Sir,   Feb. 15, 1762.

I HAVE been often thinking of you since your removal, and was glad to receive your letter to-day. I hope you will still go on to find more and more encouragement to believe, that the Lord has disposed and led you to the step you have taken. For though I wrote with the greatest plainness and earnestness, and would, if in my power, have prevented it while under deliberation, yet, now it is done, and past recal, I would rather help than dishearten you. Indeed, I cannot say that my view of the affair is yet altered. The best way not to be cast down hereafter, is not to be too sanguine at first. You know there is something pleasing in novelty; as yet you are new to them, and they to you: I pray God that you may find as cordial a regard from them as at present,

when you have been with them as many years as
in the place you came from. And if you have
grace to be watchful and prayful, all will be well;
for we serve a gracious Master, who knows how
to over-rule even our mistakes to his glory and
our own advantage. Yet I observe that when we
do wrong, sooner or later we smart for our indis-
cretion; perhaps many years afterwards. After
we have seen and confessed our fault, and received repeated proofs of pardoning love, as to
the guilt; yet chastisement, to remind us more
sensibly of our having done amiss, will generally
find us out. So it was with David, in the matter
of Uriah: the Lord put away his sin, healed his
broken bones, and restored unto him the light of
his countenance; yet many troubles, in consequence of this affair, followed one upon another,
till at length (many years afterwards) he was driven
from Jerusalem by his own son. So it was with
Jacob: he dealt deceitfully with his brother Esau:
notwithstanding this, the Lord appeared to him and
blessed him, gave him comfortable promises, and
revealed himself to him from time to time; yet,
after an interval of twenty years, his fault was
brought afresh to his remembrance, and his heart
trembled within him when he heard his brother
was coming with armed men to meet him. And
thus I have found it in my own experience: things
which I had forgotten a long while have been
brought to my mind by providential dispensations
which I little expected; but the first rise of which
I have been able to trace far back, and forced to
confess, that the Lord is indeed He that judgeth
the heart and trieth the reins. I hint this for
your caution: you know best upon what grounds
you have proceeded; but if (though I do not
affirm it, I hope otherwise), I say, if you have

acted too much in your own spirit, been too hasty
and precipitate ; if you have not been sufficiently
tender of your people, nor thoughtful of the consequences which your departure will probably in-
volve them in ; if you were impatient under the
Lord's hand, and, instead of waiting his time and
way of removing the trials and difficulties you
found, you have ventured upon an attempt to free
and mend yourself : I say, if any of these things
have mixed with your determinations, something
will fall out to shew you your fault : either you
will not find the success you hope for, or friends
will grow cold, or enemies and difficulties you
dream not of will present themselves, or your
own mind will alter, so as what seems now most
pleasing will afford you little pleasure.   Yet,
though I write thus, I do not mean (as I said before) to discourage you, but that you may be
forewarned, humble, and watchful. If you should
at any time have a different view of things, you
may take comfort from the instances I have mentioned.   The trials of David and Jacob were
sharp ; but they were short, and they proved to
their advantage, put them upon acts of humiliation and prayer, and ended in a double blessing.
Nothing can harm us that quickens our earnestness
and frequency in applying to a Throne of Grace :
only trust the Lord and keep close to him, and all
that befals you shall be for good.   Temptations
end in victory ; troubles prove an increase of consolation ; yea, our very falls and failings tend to increase our spiritual wisdom, to give us a greater
knowledge of Satan's devices, and make us more habitually upon our guard against them. Happy case
of the believer in Jesus ! when bitten by the fiery
serpent he needs not go far for a remedy ; he has
only to look to a bleeding Saviour, and be healed.

I think one great advantage that attends a removal into a new place is, that it gives an easy opportunity of forming a new plan, and breaking off any little habits which we have found inconvenient, and yet perhaps could not so readily lay aside, where our customs and acquaintance had been long formed. I earnestly recommend to you to reflect, if you cannot recollect some things which you have hitherto omitted, which may properly be now taken up; some things formerly allowed, which may now with ease and convenience be laid aside. I only give the hint in general; for I have nothing in particular to charge you with. I recommend to you to be very choice of your time, especially the fore part of the day: let your morning hours be devoted to prayer, reading, and study; and suffer not the importunity of friends to rob you of the hours before noon, without a just necessity: and if you accustom yourself to rise early in the morning, you will find a great advantage. Be careful to avoid losing your thoughts, whether in books or otherwise, upon any subjects which are not of a direct subserviency to your great design, till towards dinner time. The afternoon is not so favourable to study: this is a proper time for paying and receiving visits, conversing among your friends, or unbending with a book of instructive entertainment, such as history, &c., which may increase your general knowledge, without a great confinement of your attention; but let the morning hours be sacred. I think you would likewise find advantage in using your pen more: write short notes upon the Scriptures you read, or transcribe the labours of others; make extracts from your favourite authors, especially those who, besides a fund of spiritual and evangelical matter, have a happy talent of expressing their thoughts in a clear and lively, or pathetic manner : you would find a continued exercise in this way would be greatly useful to form your own style, and help your delivery and memory ; you would become insensibly master of their thoughts, and find it more easy to express yourself justly and clearly.   What we only read we easily lose ; but what we commit to paper is not so soon forgot.   Especially remember (what you well know, but we cannot too often remind each other), that frequent secret prayer is the life of all we do.   If any man lack wisdom, let him ask of God, and it shall be given ; but all our diligence will fail, if we are remiss in this particular.   I am glad it is not thought necessary for you to go to London on this occasion.   I hope you .will not think it necessary upon any other account.   Rather keep close to the work you have undertaken ; and endeavour to avoid any thing that looks like ostentation, or a desire to be taken notice of.   You see I advise you with the freedom of a friend who loves you, and longs to see your work and your soul prosper.

You will, I doubt not, endeavour to promote the practice of frequent prayer in the houses that receive you.   I look upon prayer meetings as the most profitable exercises (excepting the public preaching) in which Christians can engage : they have a direct tendency to kill a worldly trifling spirit, to draw down a Divine blessing upon all our concerns, compose differences, and enkindle (at least to maintain) the flame of Divine love amongst brethren.   But I need not tell you the advantages ; you know them : I only would exhort you ; and the rather as I find in my own case the principal cause of my leanness and unfruitfulness is owing to an unaccountable backwardness to pray.   I can write, or read, or converse, or hear, with a ready will; but prayer is more spiritual and inward than any of these; and the more spiritual any duty is, the more my carnal heart is apt to start from it. May the Lord pour forth his precious spirit of prayer and supplication in both our hearts!

I am not well pleased with the account you give of so many dry bones. It increases my wonder, that you could so readily exchange so much plump flesh and blood as you had about you for a parcel of skeletons. I wish they may not haunt you, and disturb your peace. I wish these same dry bones do not prove thorns in your sides and in your eyes. You say, now you have to pray, and prophesy, and wait for the four winds to come and put life into these bones. God grant that your prayers may be answered: but if I knew a man who possessed a field in a tolerable soil, which had afforded him some increase every year; and if this man, after having bestowed seven years' labour in cultivating, weeding, manuring, fencing, &c. just when he has brought his ground (in his neighbour's judgment) into good order, and might reasonably hope for larger crops than he had ever yet seen, should suddenly forego all his advantages, leave his good seed for the birds to eat, pull up the young fences which cost him so much pains to plant, and all this for the sake of making a new experiment upon the top of a mountain; though I might heartily wish him great suceess, I could not honestly give him great encouragement. You have parted with that for a trifle, which in my eye seems an inestimable jewel; I mean the hearts and affections of an enlightened people. This appears to me one of the greatest honours and greatest pleasures a faithful minister can possess, and which many faithful and eminent ministers have never been able to obtain.   This gave you a vast advantage : your gift was more acceptable there than that of any other person, and more than you will probably find elsewhere.   For I cannot make a comparison between the hasty approbation of a few, whose eyes are but beginning to open, and their affections and passions warm, so that they must, if possible, have the man that first catches their attention ; I say, I cannot think this worthy to be compared to the regard of a people who understood the Gospel, were able to judge of men and doctrines, and had trial of you for so many years. It is indeed much to your honour (it proves that you were faithful, diligent, and exemplary) that the people proved so attached to you ; but that you should force yourself from them, when they so dearly loved you, and so much needed you, this has made all your friends in these parts to wonder, and your enemies to rejoice ; and I, alas ! know not what to answer in your behalf to either.   Say not, " I hate this Micaiah, for he prophesies not good of me, but evil ;" but allow me the privilege of a friend.   My heart is full when I think of what has happened, and · what will probably be the consequence.   In few words, I am strongly persuaded you have taken an unadvised step, and would therefore prepare you for the inconvenience and uneasiness you may probably meet with. And if I am (as I desire I may prove) mistaken, my advice will do no harm ; you will want something to balance the caresses and success you meet with.

We should be very glad to see you, and hope you will take your measures, when you do come, to lengthen your usual stay, in proportion to the difference of the distance.   Pray for us.

I am, &c.

FOUR LETTERS

TO

MRS. P****.

═══════════

LETTER I.

My dear Madam,   May, 1774.

I HAVE had sudden notice, that I may send you a hasty line, to express our satisfaction in hearing that you had a safe though perilous journey. I hope I shall be always mindful to pray, that the Lord may guide, bless, and comfort you, and give you such a manifestation of his person, power, and grace, as may set you at liberty from all fear, and fill you with abiding peace and joy in believing. Remember that Jesus has all power, the fulness of compassion, and embraces with open arms all that come to him for life and salvation.

I know not whether Mrs. ****'s illness was before or since my last. Through mercy she is better again; and I remain so, though death and illness are still walking about the town, O for grace to take warning by the sufferings of others, and set loose to the world, and so number our days as to incline our hearts to the one thing needful! Indeed that one thing includes many things, sufficient to engage the best of our thoughts and the most of our time, if we were duly sensible of their importance; but I may adopt the Psalmist's expression, " My soul cleaveth to the dust." How is it that the truths of which I have the most undoubted conviction, and which are, of all others, the most weighty, should make so little impression

upon me? O I know the cause! It is deeply
rooted. An evil nature cleaves to me; so that
when I would do good, evil is present with me.
It is, however, a mercy to be made sensible of it,
and in any measure humbled for it. Ere long it
will be dropped in the grave; then all complaints
shall cease. That thought gives relief. I shall
not always live this poor dying life: I hope one
day to be all ear, all heart, all tongue: when I
shall see the Redeemer as he is, I shall be like
him. This will be a heaven indeed, to behold his
glory without a veil, to rejoice in his love without
a cloud, and to sing his praises without one jarring
or wandering note, for ever. In the mean time,
may He enable us to serve him with our best.
O that every power, faculty, and talent, were devoted to him! He deserves all we have, and ten
thousand times more if we had it; for he has
loved us, and washed us from our sins in his own
blood. He gave himself for us. In one sense we
are well suited to answer his purpose; for if we
were not vile and worthless beyond expression,
the exceeding riches of his grace would not have
been so gloriously displayed. His glory shines
more in redeeming one sinner, than in preserving
a thousand angels. Poor Mr. **** is still in the
dark valley, but we trust prayer shall yet bring
him out. Mighty things have been done in answer
to prayer; and the Lord's arm is not shortened,
neither is his ear heavy. It is our part to wait till
we have an answer. One of his own hymns says,

> The promise may be long deferr'd,
> But never comes too late.

I suppose you have heard of the death of Mr.
T **** of R ****. This is apparently a heavy
blow. He was an amiable, judicious, candid man,
and an excellent preacher in a great sphere of use-

fulness; and his age and constitution gave hopes that he might have been eminently serviceable for many years. How often does the Lord write vanity upon all our expectations from men! He visited a person ill of a putrid fever, and carried the seeds of infection with him to London, where he died. Mrs. **** is a very excellent and accomplished woman, but exceedingly delicate in her frame and spirits. How can she bear so sudden and severe a stroke! But yet I hope she will afford a proof of the Lord's all-sufficiency and faithfulness. O madam, the Lord our God is a great God! If he frowns, the smiles of the whole creation can afford no comfort; and if he is pleased to smile, he can enable the soul under the darkest dispensations to say, All is well. Yet the flesh will feel, and it ought: otherwise the exercise of faith, patience, and resignation, would be impracticable. I have lost in him one of my most valued and valuable friends: but what is my loss to that of his people!

The Lord bless you and keep you. The Lord increase you more and more, you and your children. The Lord lift up the light of his countenance upon you, and give you his peace. I thank him for leading you to us, but especially for making your visit there in any measure agreeable and profitable to yourself. If I have been an instrument in his hand for your comfort, I have reason to remember it among the greatest favours he has conferred upon me. And now, dear madam, once more farewel. If the Lord spares our lives, I hope we shall see each other again upon earth. But above all, let us rejoice in the blessed Gospel, by which immortality is brought to light, and a glorious prospect opened beyond the grave.

> There sits our Saviour thron'd in light,
> Cloth'd with a body like our own.

There at least, after all the changes and trials of this state, we shall meet to part no more.

I am, &c.

LETTER II.

My dear Madam,   1775.

I SHOULD have been more uneasy at being pre-vented writing immediately, had I any reason to apprehend my advice necessary upon the point you propose, which by this time I suppose is settled, as it should be, without me. I smiled at Miss M****'s disappointment. However, if the Lord favours her with a taste for the library of my proposing, she will be like the merchant-man seeking goodly pearls, and will count all other books but pebbles in comparison of those four volumes, which present us with something new and important whenever we look into them. I shall be much obliged to her if she will commit the third chapter of Proverbs to her memory, and I shall pray the Lord to write it in her heart.

You surprise me when you tell me, that the incident of my birth-day was noticed by those I never saw. Be so good as to return my thanks to my unknown friends, and tell them, that I pray our common Lord and Saviour to bless them abundantly. His people while here are scattered abroad, separated by hills and rivers, and too often by names and prejudices; but by and by we shall all meet where we shall all know and acknowledge each other, and rejoice together for evermore. I have lately read with much pleasure, and I hope with some profit, the history of the Greenland Mission. Upon the whole, it is a glo-rious work. None who love the Lord will refuse to say, it is the finger of God indeed. For my own part, my soul rejoices in it; and I honour the instruments, as men who have hazarded their lives in an extraordinary manner for the sake of the Lord Jesus. Sure I am that none could have sustained such discouragements at first, or have obtained such success afterwards, unless the Lord had sent, supported, and owned them.

I hope we shall have an interest in your prayers. I trust the Lord is yet with us. We have some ripe for the sickle, and some just springing up; some tokens of his gracious presence amongst us; but sin and Satan cut us out abundance of work as individuals, though through mercy as a society we walk in peace.

The toad and spider is an exhibition of my daily experience. I am often wounded, but the Lord is my health. Still I am a living monument of mercy; and I trust that word, " Because I live you shall live also," will carry me to the end. I am poor, weak, and foolish; but Jesus is wise, strong, and abounding in grace. He has given me a desire to trust my all in his hands, and He will not disappoint the expectation which he himself has raised. At present I have but little to say, and but little time to say it in. When you think of this place, I hope you will think and believe, that you have friends here most cordially interested in your welfare, and often remembering you in prayer. May the Lord be your guide and shield, and give you the best desires of your heart. I pray him to establish and settle you in the great truths of his Word. I trust he will. We learn more, and more effectually, by one minute's communication with him through the medium of his written word, than we could from an assembly of divines, or a library of books.

I am, &c.

LETTER III.

My dear Madam,   August, 1775.

It is not owing to forgetfulness that your letter
has been thus long unanswered. It has lain within
my view this fortnight, demanding my first leisure
hour; but affairs of daily occurrence have been
so many and so pressing, that I have been constrained to put it off till now. I trust the Lord,
by his Spirit and providence, will direct and
prosper the settlement of your children. I desire
my love to Miss M****. My idea of her enlarges.
Methinks I see her aspiring to be as tall as her
mamma. I hope likewise, that she increases in
grace and wisdom, as in years and stature; and
that hearing our Lord's flock is a little flock, she
feels an earnest thirst to be one of the happy
number which constitutes his fold.

> There the Lord dwells amongst them upon his own hill,
> With the flocks all around him awaiting his will.

If she has such a desire, I can tell who gave
it her, for I am persuaded it was not born with
her; and where the good husbandman sows, there
will he also reap. Therefore, dear Miss M****,
press forward: knock, and it shall be opened
unto you, for yet there is room. O what a fold!
O what a pasture! O what a Shepherd! Let us
love, and sing, and wonder.

I hope the good people at Bristol, and every
where else, are praying for our sinful, distracted
land, in this dark day. The Lord is angry, the
sword is drawn, and I am afraid nothing but the
spirit of wrestling prayer can prevail for the returning it into the scabbard. Could things have
proceeded to these extremities, except the Lord
had withdrawn his salutary blessing from both
sides? It is a time of prayer. We see the be-

ginning of trouble, but who can foresee the possible consequences? The fire is kindled; but how
far it may spread, those who are above may perhaps know better than we. I meddle not with the
disputes of party, nor concern myself with any
political maxims, but such as are laid down in
Scripture. There I read that righteousness ex-
alteth a nation, and that sin is the reproach, and,
if persisted in, the ruin of any people. Some people are startled at the enormous sum of our national
debt: they who understand spiritual arithmetic
may be well startled if they sit down and compute
the debt of national sin. *Imprimis*, Infidelity:
Item, Contempt of the Gospel: *Item*, The profli-
gacy of manners: *Item*, Perjury: *Item*, The cry
of blood, the blood of thousands, perhaps millions,
from the East Indies. It would take sheets, yea
quires, to draw out the particulars under each of
these heads, and then much would remain untold.
What can we answer, when the Lord saith, " Shall
not I visit for these things? Shall not my soul
be avenged on such a nation as this?" Since we
received the news of the first hostilities in America,
we have had an additional prayer-meeting. Could
I hear that professors in general, instead of
wasting their breath in censuring men and measures, were plying the Throne of Grace, I should
still hope for a respite. Poor New England!
once the glory of the earth, now likely to be visited with fire and sword. They have left their
first love, and the Lord is sorely contending with
them. Yet surely their sins as a people are not
to be compared with ours. I am just so much
affected with these things as to know, that I am
not affected enough. Oh! my spirit is sadly cold
and insensible, or I should lay them to heart in a
different manner: yet I endeavour to give the

alarm as far as I can.   There is one political
maxim which comforts me : " The Lord reigns."
His hand guides the storm ; and he knows them
that are his, how to protect, support, and deliver
them.   He will take care of his own cause; yea,
he will extend his kingdom, even by these formidable methods.   Men have one thing in view ;
He has another, and his counsel shall stand.

The chief piece of news since my last is concerning B. A.   She has finished her course, and
is now with the great multitude who have overcome by the blood of the Lamb, and by the word
of his testimony.   Tuesday the 1st of February
she was in our assembly, was taken ill the next
day, and died while we were assembling the
Tuesday following.   She had an easy dissolution,
retained her senses and her speech till the last
minute, and went without a struggle or a sigh.
She was not in raptures during her illness, but
was composed, and maintained a strong and lively
faith.   She had a numerous levee about her bed
daily, who were all witnesses to the power of
faith, and to the faithfulness of the Lord, enabling
her to triumph over the approaches of death ; for
she was well known and well respected.   She will
be much missed ; but I hope He will answer the
many prayers she put up for us, and raise up
others in her room.   " Blessed are the dead who
die in the Lord."   Blessed are they who know
whom they have believed, and when death comes
can cheerfully rest their hopes on him who died
that we might live. B**** had been long a precious
and honourable woman ; but her hope in the
trying hour rested not in what she had done for
the Lord, but upon what he had done for her ;
not upon the change his grace has wrought in her,
but upon the righteousness he had wrought out

for her by his obedience unto death. This supported her; for she saw nothing in herself but what she was ashamed of. She saw reason to renounce her own goodness, as well as her own sins, as to the point of acceptance with God, and died, as St. Paul lived, determined to know nothing but Jesus Christ and him crucified.

The time when Mr. and Mrs. C**** removed to Scotland drawing near, Mrs. **** is gone to spend a week or two with them, and take her leave. She feels something at parting with a sister, who is indeed a valuable person; and from children they have always lived in the most tender intimacy and uninterrupted friendship. But all beneath the moon (like the moon itself) is subject to incessant change. Alterations and separations are graciously appointed of the Lord, to remind us that this is not our rest, and to prepare our thoughts for that approaching change which shall fix us for ever in an unchangeable state. O Madam! what shall we poor worms render to him who has brought life and immortality to light by the Gospel, taken away the sting of death, revealed a glorious prospect beyond the grave, and given us eyes to see it? Now the reflection, that we must, ere long, take a final farewel of what is most capable of pleasing us upon earth, is not only tolerable, but pleasant. For we know we cannot fully possess our best friend, our chief treasure, till we have done with all below: nay, we cannot till then properly see each other. We are cased up in vehicles of clay, and converse together as if we were in different coaches with the blinds close drawn round. We see the carriage, and the voice tells us that we have a friend within: but we shall know each other better, when death shall open the coach-doors, and hand out the company successively, and lead them into the glorious apartments which the Lord has appointed to be the common residence of them that love him. What an assembly will there be! What a constellation of glory, when each individual shall shine like the sun in the kingdom of their Father! No sins, sorrows, temptations; no veils, clouds, or prejudices, shall interrupt us then. All names of idle distinction (the fruits of present remaining darkness, the channels of bigotry, and the stumbling-block of the world), will be at an end.

The description you give of your present residence pleases me much, and chiefly because it describes and manifests to me something still more interesting, I mean the peaceable situation of your mind. Had he placed you in an Eden some months ago, it would hardly have awakened your descriptive talent. But he whom the winds and seas obey has calmed your mind, and I trust will go on to fill you with all joy and peace in believing. It is no great matter where we are, provided we see that the Lord has placed us there, and that he is with us. I am, &c.

LETTER IV.

1776.

So, my dear Madam, I hope we have found you out, and that this letter will reach you in good time to welcome you in our names to London. We are ready to take it for granted that you will now most certainly make us a visit. Do come as soon, and stay as long, as you possibly can. Methinks you will be glad to get out of the smell and noise as soon as possible. If we did not go to London now and then, we should perhaps forget how people

live there. Especially I pity professors: they are
exposed to as many dangers as people who live in
mines; chilling damps, scorching blasts, epidemical disorders, owing to the impure air.   Such
are the winds of false doctrines, the explosions of
controversy, the blights of worldly conversation,
the contagion of evil custom.   In short, a person
had need have a good constitution of grace, and
likewise to be well supplied with antidotes, to
preserve a tolerable share of spiritual health in
such a situation.

And now, how shall I fill up the rest of the
paper ?   It is a shame for a Christian and a minister to say he has no subject at hand, when the
inexhaustible theme of redeeming love is ever
pressing upon our attention.   I will tell you then,
though you know it, that the Lord reigns.   He
who once bore our sins, and carried our sorrows,
is seated upon a throne of glory, and exercises all
power in heaven and on earth.   Thrones, principalities, and powers, bow before him.   Every
event in the kingdoms of providence and of grace
are under his rule.   His providence pervades and
manages the whole, and is as minutely attentive
to every part as if there were only that single object in his view.   From the tallest archangel to the
meanest ant or fly, all depend on him for their
being, their preservation, and their powers.   He
directs the sparrows where to build their nests,
and to find their food.   He over-rules the rise and
fall of nations, and bends, with an invincible
energy and unerring wisdom, all events; so that
while many intend nothing less, in the issue their
designs all concur and coincide in the accomplishment of his holy will.   He restrains with a
mighty hand the still more formidable efforts of the
powers of darkness; and Satan with all his hosts

cannot exert their malice a hair's-breadth beyond
the limits of his permission. This is he who is the
head and husband of his believing people. How
happy are they whom it is his good pleasure to
bless! How safe are they whom he has engaged
to protect! How honoured and privileged are
they to whom he is pleased to manifest himself,
and whom he enables and warrants to claim him
as their friend and their portion! Having redeemed them by his own blood, he sets a high
value upon them; he esteems them his treasure,
his jewels, and keeps them as the pupil of his eye.
They shall not want; they need not fear: his eye
is upon them in every situation, his ear is open to
their prayers, and his everlasting arms are under
them for their sure support. On earth he guides
their steps, controuls their enemies, and directs all
his dispensations for their good : while in heaven
he is pleading their cause, preparing them a place,
and communicating down to them reviving fore-
tastes of the glory that shall be shortly revealed.
O how is this mystery hidden from an unbelieving
world! Who can believe it, till it is made known
by experience, what an intercourse is maintained
in this land of shadows between the Lord of glory
and sinful worms! How should we praise him
that he has visited us! for we were once blind to
his beauty, and insensible to his love, and should
have remained so to the last, had he not prevented
us with his goodness, and been found of us when
we sought him not.

Mrs. **** presents her love. The bite of the
leech, which I mentioned to you, has confined her
to the house ever since; but I hope she will be
able to go out to-morrow. We were for a while
apprehensive of worse consequences; but the Lord
is gracious : he shews us in a variety of instances

what dependent creatures we are, how blind to events, and how easily the methods which we take to relieve ourselves from a small inconvenience may plunge us into a greater. Thus we learn (happy indeed if we can effectually learn it) that there is no safety but in his protection, and that nothing can do us good but by his blessing. As for myself, I see so many reasons why he might contend with me, that I am amazed he affords me and mine so much peace, and appoints us so few trials. We live as upon a field of battle: many are hourly suffering and falling around us; and I can give no reason why we are preserved, but that he is God, and not man. What a mercy that we are only truly known to him, who is alone able to hear us !

May the Lord bless you and yours: may he comfort you, guide you, and guard you. Come quickly to

Yours, &c.

SIX LETTERS

REV. MR. B****.

_____

LETTER I.

Rev. and dear Sir,   Sept. 14, 1765.

WHEN I was at London in June last your name first reached me, and from that time I have been desirous to wish you success in the name of the Lord. A few weeks ago I received a further account from Mrs. ****, with a volume of your sermons : she likewise gave me a direction where to write, and an encouragement that a letter would not be unacceptable. The latter indeed I did not much need when I had read your book. Though we have no acquaintance, we are already united in the strictest ties of friendship, partakers of the same hope, servants of the same Lord, and in the same part of his vineyard : I therefore hold all apologies needless. I rejoice in the Lord's goodness to you ; I pray for his abundant blessing upon your labours ; I need an interest in your prayers ; I have an affectionate desire to know more concerning you : these are my motives for writing.

Mrs. **** tells me that you have read my Narrative : I need not tell you, therefore, that I am one of the most astonishing instances of the forbearance and mercy of God upon the face of the earth. In the close of it I mention a warm desire I had to the ministry : this the Lord was pleased to keep alive for several years, through a succes-

sion of views and disappointments. At length his
hour came, and my way was made easy. I have
been here about fifteenth months. The Lord has
led me by a way that I little expected, to a pleasant lot, where the Gospel has been many years
known, and is highly valued by many. We have
a large church and congregation, and a considerable number of lively thriving believers, and in
general go on with great comfort and harmony.
I meet with less opposition from the world than
is usual where the Gospel is preached. This burden
was borne by Mr. B**** for ten years; and in that
course of time some of the fiercest opposers were
removed, some wearied, and some softened; so
that we are now remarkably quiet in that respect.
May the Lord teach us to improve the privilege,
and preserve us from indifference. How unspeakable are our obligations to the grace of God!
What a privilege is it to be a believer! They are
comparatively few, and we by nature were no
nearer than others : it was grace, free grace, that
made the difference. What an honour to be a
minister of the everlasting Gospel! These upon
comparison are perhaps fewer still. How wonderful
that one of these few should be sought for among
the wilds of Africa, reclaimed from the lowest state
of impiety and misery, and brought to assure other
sinners, from his own experience, that " there is,
there is forgiveness with him, that he may be
feared." And you, sir, though not left to give
such flagrant proofs of the wickedness of the heart
and the power of Satan, yet owe your present
views to the same almighty grace. If the Lord
had not distinguished you from your brethren, you
would have been now in the character of a minister
misleading the people, and opposing those precious
truths you are now labouring to establish. Not

unto us, O Lord, but unto thy name be the glory!
I shall be thankful to hear from you at your leisure.
Be pleased to inform me whether you received
the knowledge of the truth before or since you
were in orders; how long you have preached the
joyful sound of salvation by Jesus, and what is
the state of things in your parts.

We are called to an honourable service; but it
is arduous. What wisdom does it require to keep
the middle path in doctrines, avoiding the equally
dangerous errors on the right hand and the left!
What steadiness, to speak the truth boldly and
faithfully in the midst of a gainsaying world!
What humility, to stand against the tide of popularity!   What meekness, to endure all things for
the elect's sake, that they may be saved! " Who
is sufficient for these things?" We are not in ourselves, but there is an all-sufficiency in Jesus.
Our enemy watches us close; he challenges and
desires to have us, that he may sift us as wheat:
he knows he can easily shake us if we are left to
ourselves; but we have a Shepherd, a Keeper, who
never slumbers nor sleeps. If he permits us to
be exercised, it is for our good; he is at hand to
direct, moderate, and sanctify every dispensation:
he has prayed for us that our faith may not fail;
and he has promised to maintain his fear in our
hearts, that we may not depart from him.   When
we are prone to wander, he calls us back; when
we say, my feet slip, his mercy holds us up;
when we are wounded, he heals; when we are
ready to faint, he revives. The people of God
are sure to meet with enemies, but especially
the ministers : Satan bears them a double grudge:
the world watches for their halting, and the
Lord will suffer them to be afflicted, that they
may be kept humble, that they may acquire a

sympathy with the sufferings of others, that they may be experimentally qualified to advise and help them, and to comfort them with the comforts with which they themselves have been comforted of God. But the Captain of our salvation is with us : his eye is upon us; his everlasting arm beneath us : in his name therefore may we go on, lift up our banners, and say, "If God be for us, who can be against us ? Nay, in all these things we are more than conquerors, through him that has loved us." The time is short : yet a little while, and he will wipe all tears from our eyes, and put a crown of life upon our heads with his own gracious hand. In this sense, how beautiful are those lines :

> *Temporis illius*
> *Me consolor imagine*
> *Festis quum populus me reducem choris,*
> *Faustisque excipiet vocibus, et Dei,*
> *Pompâ cum celebri, me comitabitur*
> *Augusta ad penetralia.*   Buch. in Ps. xlii.

If any occasions should call you into these parts, my house and pulpit will be glad to receive you. Pray for us, dear sir, and believe me to be

Yours, &c.

LETTER II.

Very dear Sir,   Nov. 2, 1765.

Your letter of the 4th ult. gave me great pleasure. I thank you for the particular account you have favoured me with. I rejoice with you, sympathize with you, and find my heart opened to correspond with unreserved freedom. May the Lord direct our pens, and help us to help each other. The work you are engaged in is great, and your difficulties many; but faithful is he that hath called you, who also will do it. The weapons

which he has now put into your hands are not
carnal, but mighty through God to the pulling
down of strong-holds.   Men may fight, but they
shall not prevail against us, if we are but enabled
to put our cause simply into the Lord's hands,
and keep steadily on in the path of duty.   He
will plead our cause, and fight our battles; he
will pardon our mistakes, and teach us to do
better.   My experience as a minister is but
small, having been but about eighteen months in
the vineyard; but for about twelve years I have
been favoured with an increasing acquaintance
among the people of God, of various ranks and
denominations, which, together with the painful
exercises of my own heart, gave me opportunity
of making observations which were of great use
to me when I entered upon the work myself: and
ever since, I have found the Lord graciously sup-
plying new lights and new strength, as new occurrences arise.   So I trust it will be with you.
I endeavour to avail myself of the examples, advice, and sentiments of my brethren, yet at the
same time to guard against calling any man
master.   This is the peculiar of Christ.   The
best are but men; the wisest may be mistaken;
and that which may be right in another might
be wrong in me, through a difference of circumstances.   The Spirit of God distributes variously,
both in gifts and dispensations; and I would no
more be tied to act strictly by others' rules than
to walk in shoes of the same size.   My shoes
must fit my own feet.

I endeavour to guard against extremes: our
nature is prone to them: and we are liable likewise, when we have found the inconvenience of
one extreme, to revert insensibly (sometimes to
fly suddenly) to the other.   I pray to be led in

the midst of the path. I am what they call a Calvinist; yet there are flights, niceties, and hard sayings, to be found among some of that system, which I do not choose to imitate. I dislike those sentiments against which you have borne your testimony in the note at the end of your preface: but, having known many precious souls in that party, I have been taught, that the kingdom of God is not in names and sentiments, but in righteousness, faith, love, peace, and joy in the Holy Ghost. I should, however, upon some occasions oppose those tenets, if they had any prevalence in my neighbourhood; but they have not: and in general I believe the surest way to refute or prevent error is to preach the truth. I am glad to find you are aware of that spirit of enthusiasm which has so often broken loose and blemished hopeful beginnings, and that the foundation you build upon is solid and Scriptural: this will, I hope, save you much trouble, and prevent many offences. Let us endeavour to make our people acquainted with the Scripture, and to impress them with a high sense of its authority, excellence, and sufficiency. Satan seldom remarkably imposes on ministers or people, except where the word of God is too little consulted or regarded. Another point in which I aim at a medium, is in what is called *prudence.* There is certainly such a thing as Christian prudence, and a remarkable deficiency of it is highly inconvenient. But caution too often degenerates into cowardice; and if the fear of man, under the name of prudence, gets within our guard, like a chilling frost it nips every thing in the bud. Those who trust the Lord, and act openly, with an honest freedom and consistence, I observe he generally bears them out, smooths their way, and makes

their enemies their friends, or at least restrains
their rage; while such as halve things, temporize,
and aim to please God and man together, meet
with double disappointment, and are neither
useful nor respected. If we trust to Him, He will
stand by us; if we regard men, He will leave us
to make the best we can of them.

I have set down hastily what occurred to my
pen, not to dictate to you, but to tell you how I have
been led, and because some expressions in your
letter seemed to imply that you would not be
displeased with me for so doing. As to books, I
think there is a medium here likewise. I have
read too much in time past; yet I do not wholly
join with some of our brethren, who would restrain
us entirely to the word of God. Undoubtedly
this is the fountain; here we should dwell; but a
moderate and judicious perusal of other authors
may have its use; and I am glad to be beholden to
such helps, either to explain what I do not understand, or to confirm me in what I do. Of these,
the writings of the last age afford an immense
variety.

But, above all, may we, dear sir, live and feed
upon the precious promises, John xiv. 16, 17, 26;
and xvi. 13—15. There is no teacher like Jesus,
who by his Holy Spirit reveals himself in his
word to the understanding and affections of his
children. When we thus behold his glory in the
Gospel glass, we are changed into the same image.
Then our hearts melt, our eyes flow, our stammer-
ing tongues are unloosed. That this may be your
increasing experience, is the prayer of, dear sir,

Yours, &c.

LETTER III.

Dear Sir,   Jan. 21, 1766.

YOUR letters give me the sincerest pleasure. Let us believe that we are daily thinking of and praying for each other, and write when opportunity offers, without apologies. I praise the Lord that he has led you so soon to a settled judgment in the leading truths of the Gospel. For want of this, many have been necessitated with their own hands to pull down what, in the first warm emotions of their zeal, they had laboured hard to build. It is a mercy, likewise, to be enabled to acknowledge what is excellent in the writings or conduct of others, without adopting their singularities, or discarding the whole on account of a few blemishes. We should be glad to receive instruction from all, and avoid being led by the *ipse dixit* of any. *Nullius jurare in verbum* is a fit motto for those who have one master, even Christ. We may grow wise apace in opinions, by books and men; but vital, experimental knowledge can only be received from the Holy Spirit, the great instructor and comforter of his people. And there are two things observable in his teaching: 1. That he honours the means of his own appointment, so that we cannot expect to make any great progress without diligence on our parts: 2. That he does not teach all at once, but by degrees. Experience is his school; and by this I mean the observation and improvement of what passes within us and around us in the course of every day. The word of God affords a history in miniature of the heart of man, the devices of Satan, the state of the world, and the method of grace: and the most instructing and affecting commentary on it, to an enlightened mind, may be gathered from what we see, feel, and hear from day to day. *Res, ætas, usus, semper aliquid apportent novi:* and no knowledge in spiritual things but what we acquire in this way, is properly our own, or will abide the time of trial. This is not always sufficiently considered. We are ready to expect that others should receive upon our word, in half an hour's time, those views of things which have cost us years to attain. But none can be brought forward faster than the Lord is pleased to communicate inward light. Upon this ground controversies have been multiplied among Christians to little purpose; for plants of different standings will be *(cæteris paribus)* in different degrees of forwardness. A young Christian is like a green fruit: it has perhaps a disagreeable austerity, which cannot be corrected out of its proper course; it wants time and growth: wait a while, and, by the nourishment it receives from the root, together with the action of the sun, wind, and rain in succession from without, it will insensibly acquire that flavour and maturity for the want of which an unskilful judge would be ready to reject it as nothing worth. We are favoured with many excellent books in our tongue; but I with you agree in assigning one of the first places (as a teacher) to Dr. Owen. I have just finished his Discourse on the Holy Spirit, which is an epitome, if not the master-piece, of his writings. I should be glad to see the republication you speak of; but I question if the booksellers will venture upon it: I shall perhaps mention it to my London friends. As to Archbishop Leighton, besides his Select Works, there are two octavo volumes, published at Edinburgh in the year 1748, and since reprinted at London. They contain a valuable Commentary on St. Peter's First Epistle, and Lectures on Isa. vi., Ps. xxxix. cxxx. iv., and

a part of Rom. xii. I have likewise a small quarto,
in Latin, of his Divinity Lectures, when professor
at Edinburgh : the short title is *Prælectiones Theo-
logiæ.* Mine was printed in London 1698. I
believe this book is scarce : I set the highest value
upon it. He has wonderfully united the simplicity of the Gospel with all the captivating beauties
of style and language. Bishop Burnet says he
was the greatest master of the Latin tongue he
ever new ; of which, together with his compass
of learning, he has given proof in his Lectures :
yet, in his gayer dress, his eminent humility and
spirituality appear to no less advantage than when
clad in plain English. I think it may be said to
be a diamond set in gold. I could wish it trans-
lated, if it was possible (which I almost question)
to preserve the beauty and spirit of the original.

Edwards on Free Will I have read with pleasure,
as a good answer to the proud reasoners in their
own way ; but a book of that sort cannot be generally read : where the subject matter is unpleasing,
and the method of treating it requires more attention than the Athenian spirit of the times will
bear, I wonder not if it is uncalled for ; and am
afraid we shall not see him upon Original Sin, if
it depends upon the sale of the other. This answer to Dr. Taylor, which you speak of, is not a
MS., but has been already printed at Boston.

You send us good news indeed, that two more
of your brethren are declaring on the Gospel side.
The Lord confirm and strengthen them, add yet
to your numbers, and make you helps and comforts to each other. Surely he is about to spread
his work. Happy those whom he honours to be
fellow-workers with him. Let us account the
disgrace we suffer for his Name's sake to be
our great honour. Many will be against us ; but

there are more for us : all the praying souls on earth, all the glorified saints in heaven, all the angels of God, yea, the God of angels himself, all are on our side.   Satan may rage, but he is a chained enemy : men may contradict and fight, but they cannot prevail.   Two things we shall especially need, courage and patience, that we neither faint before them, nor upon any provocation act in their spirit.   If we can pity and pray for them, return good for evil, make them sensible that we bear them a hearty good-will, and act as the disciples of Him who wept for his enemies, and prayed for his murderers—in this way we shall find the Lord will plead our cause, soften opposers, and by degrees give us a measure of outward peace.   Warmth and imprudence have often added to the necessary burden of the cross. I rejoice that the Lord has led you in a different way ; and I hope your doctrine and example will make your path smoother every day : you find it so in part already.   As the Lord brings you out a people, witnesses for you to the truth of his word, you will find advantage in bringing them often together.   The interval from Sabbath to Sabbath is a good while, and affords time for the world and Satan to creep in.   Intermediate meetings for prayer, &c., when properly conducted, are greatly useful.   I could wish for larger sheets and longer leisure; but I am constrained to say adieu, in our dear Lord and Saviour.

Yours, &c.

LETTER IV.

Dear Sir,   Dec. 12, 1767.

THIS is not intended as an answer to your last acceptable letter, but an occasional line, in conquence of the account Mr. T**** has given me of your late illness. I trust this dispensation will be useful to you; and I wish the knowledge of it may be so to me. I am favoured with an unusual share of health, and an equal flow of spirits. If the blow you have received should be a warning to me, I shall have cause to be thankful. I am glad to hear you are better; I hope the Lord has no design to disable you from service, but rather (as he did Jacob) to strengthen you by wounding you; to maintain and increase in you that conviction which, through grace, you have received, of the vanity and uncertainty of every thing below; to give you a lively sense of the value of health and opportunities; and to add to the treasury of your experience new proofs of his power and goodness, in supporting, comforting, and healing you; and likewise to quicken the prayers of your people for you, and to stir them up to use double diligence in the present improvement of the means of grace, while by this late instance they see how soon and suddenly you might have been removed from them.

I understand you did not feel that lively exercise of faith and joy which you would have hoped to have found at such a season: but let not this discourage you from a firm confidence, that, when the hour of dismission shall come, the Lord will be faithful to his gracious promise, and give you strength sufficient to encounter and vanquish your last enemy. You had not this strength lately, because you needed it not: for though you might think yourself near to death, the Lord intended to restore you: and he permitted you to feel weakness, that you might know your strength does not consist in grace received, but in his fulness, and his promise to communicate from himself as your occasions require. Oh, it is a great thing to be strong in the grace that is in Christ Jesus! but it is a hard lesson: it is not easy to understand it in theory; but, when the Lord has taught us so far, it is still more difficult to reduce our knowledge to practice. But this is one end he has in view in permitting us to pass through such a variety of inward and outward exercises, that we may cease from trusting in ourselves, or in any creature or frame or experiences, and be brought to a state of submission and dependence upon him alone. I was once visited something in the same way, seized with a fit of the apoplectic kind, which held me near an hour, and left a disorder in my head which quite broke the scheme of life I was then in, and was, consequently, one of the means the Lord appointed to bring me into the ministry; but I soon perfectly recovered. From the remembrance Mrs. **** has of what she then suffered, she knows how to sympathize with Mrs. B**** in her share of your trial. And I think dear Mr. **** some years since had a sudden stroke on a Christmas-day, which disabled him from duty for a time. To him and to me these turns were only like the caution which Philip of Macedon ordered to be repeated to him every morning; Remember thou art a man. I hope it will be no more to you, but that you shall live to praise him, and to give many cause to praise him on your behalf. Blessed be God, we are in safe hands: the Lord himself is our keeper; nothing befals us but what is adjusted by his wisdom

and love.   Health is his gift; and sickness, when
sanctified, is a token of love likewise.   Here we
may meet with many things which are not joyous,
but grievous to the flesh; but he will in one way
or other sweeten every bitter cup, and ere long
he will wipe away all tears from our eyes.   Oh that
joy, that crown, that glory, which awaits the
believer! Let us keep the prize of our high calling
in view, and press forward in the name of Jesus the
Redeemer, and he will not disappoint our hopes.

I am but just come off from a journey, am weary,
and it grows late; must therefore break off.   When
you have leisure and strength to write, oblige me
with a confirmation of your recovery, for I shall
be something anxious about you.

I am, &c.

LETTER V.

My dear Friend,   March 14, 1775.

I THOUGHT you long in writing, but am afraid
I have been longer.   A heavy family affliction
called me from home in December, which put me
out of my usual course, and threw me behind-
hand in my correspondence; yet I did not suspect
the date of your last letter was so old by two
months as I find it.   Whether I write more frequently or more seldom, the love of my heart to
you is the same; and I shall believe the like of
you; yet, if it can be helped, I hope the interval
will not be so long again on either side.   I am
glad that the Lord's work still flourishes in your
parts, and that you have a more comfortable prospect at home than formerly: and I was pleased
with the acceptance you found at S——; which
I hope will be an earnest of greater things.   I
think affairs in general, with respect to this land,

have a dark appearance; but it is comfortable to observe, that, amidst the aboundings of iniquity, the Lord is spreading his Gospel; and that, though many oppose, yet in most places whither the word is sent, great numbers seem disposed to hear. I am going (if the Lord please) into Leicestershire on Friday. This was lately such a dark place as you describe your country to be, and much of it is so still; but the Lord has visited three of the principal towns with Gospel light. I have a desire of visiting these brethren in the vineyard, to bear my poor testimony to the truths they preach, and to catch, if I may, a little fire and fervour among them. I do not often go abroad; but I have found a little excursion now and then (when the way is made plain) has its advantages, to quicken the spirits, and enlarge the sphere of observation. On these accounts, the recollection of my N—— journey gives me pleasure to this day; and very glad should I be to repeat it; but the distance is so great, that I consider it rather as desirable than practicable.

My experiences vary as well as yours: but possibly your sensations, both of the sweet and of the bitter, may be stronger than mine. The enemy assaults me more by sap than storm; and I am ready to think I suffer more by languor than some of my friends do by the sharper conflicts to which they are called. So likewise, in those seasons which comparatively I call my best hours, my sensible comforts are far from lively. But I am in general enabled to hold fast my confidence, and to venture myself upon the power, faithfulness, and compassion of that adorable Saviour to whom my soul has been directed and encouraged to flee for refuge. I am a poor, changeable, inconsistent creature; but he deals graciously with me: he does not leave me wholly to myself; but I have such daily proofs of the malignity and efficacy of the sin that dwelleth in me, as ought to cover me with shame and confusion of face, and make me thankful if I am permitted to rank with the meanest of those who sit at his feet. That I was ever called to the knowledge of his salvation, was a singular instance of his sovereign grace; and that I am still preserved in the way, in defiance of all that has arisen from within and from without to turn me aside, must be wholly ascribed to the same sovereignty: and if, as I trust, he shall be pleased to make me a conqueror at last, I shall have peculiar reason to say, Not unto me, not unto me, but unto thy name, O Lord, be the glory and the praise!

> How oft have sin and Satan strove
> To rend my soul from thee, my God!
> But everlasting is thy love,
> And Jesus seals it with his blood.

The Lord leads me, in the course of my preaching, to insist much on a life of communion with himself, and of the great design of the Gospel to render us conformable to him in love; and as, by his mercy, nothing appears in my outward conduct remarkably to contradict what I say, many, who only can judge by what they see, suppose I live a very happy life. But, alas! if they knew what passes in my heart, how dull my spirit is in secret, and how little I am myself affected by the glorious truths I propose to others, they would form a different judgment. Could I be myself what I recommend to them, I should be happy indeed. Pray for me, my dear friend, that, now the Lord is bringing forward the pleasing spring, he may favour me with a spring season in my soul; for indeed I mourn under a long winter.

I am, &c.

LETTER VI.

My dear Friend,   April 16, 1772.

I HOPE the Lord has contracted my desires and aims almost to the one point of study, the knowledge of his truth. All other acquisitions are transient, and comparatively vain. And yet, alas! I am a slow scholar; nor can I see in what respect I get forward, unless that every day I am more confirmed in the conviction of my own emptiness and inability to all spiritual good. And as, notwithstanding this, I am still enabled to stand my ground, I would hope, since no effect can be without an adequate cause, that I have made some advance, though in a manner imperceptible to myself, towards a more simple dependence upon Jesus as my all in all. It is given me to thirst and to taste, if it is not given me to drink abundantly; and I would be thankful for the desire. I see and approve the wisdom, grace, suitableness, and sufficiency of the Gospel salvation; and since it is for sinners, and I am a sinner, and the promises are open, I do not hesitate to call it mine. I am a weary, laden soul; Jesus has invited me to come, and has enabled me to put my trust in him. I seldom have an uneasy doubt, at least not of any continuance, respecting my pardon, acceptance, and interest in all the blessings of the New Testament. And, amidst a thousand infirmities and evils under which I groan, I have the testimony of my conscience, when under the trial of his word, that my desire is sincerely towards him, that I choose no other portion, that I allowedly serve no

other master. When I told our friend —— lately
to this purpose, he wondered, and asked, " How
is it possible, that, if you can say these things, you
should not be always rejoicing ? " Undoubtedly I
derive from the Gospel a peace at bottom, which
is worth more than a thousand worlds ; but so it
is—I can only speak for myself—though I rest and
live upon the truths of the Gospel, they seldom
impress me with a warm and lively joy. In
public, indeed, I sometimes seem in earnest and
much affected ; but even then it appears to me
rather as a part of the gift entrusted to me for the
edification of others, than as a sensation which is
properly my own. For when I am in private, I am
usually dull and stupid to a strange degree, or the
prey to a wild and ungoverned imagination ; so
that I may truly say, when I would do good, evil,
horrid evil, is present with me. Ah, how different
is this from sensible comfort! and if I was to compare myself to others, to make their experience
my standard, and was not helped to retreat to the
sure word of God as my refuge, how hard should
I find it to maintain a hope that I had either part
or lot in the matter! What I call my good times,
are when I can find my attention in some little
measure fixed to what I am about ; which indeed is
not always, nor frequently, my case in prayer, and
still seldomer in reading the Scripture. My judgment embraces these means as blessed privileges,
and Satan has not prevailed to drive me from
them ; but in the performance I too often find
them tasks ; feel a reluctance when the seasons return, and am glad when they are finished. O what
a mystery is the heart of man! what a warfare is
the life of faith! (at least in the path the Lord is
pleased to lead me.) What reason have I to lie
in the dust as the chief of sinners, and what cause

for thankfulness that salvation is wholly of grace! Notwithstanding all my complaints, it is still true that Jesus died and rose again; that he ever liveth to make intercession, and is able to save to the uttermost. But, on the other hand, to think of that joy of heart in which some of his people live, and to compare it with that apparent deadness and want of spirituality which I feel, this makes me mourn. However, I think there is a Scriptural distinction between faith and feeling, grace and comfort: they are not inseparable, and perhaps, when together, the degree of the one is not often the just measure of the other. But though I pray that I may be ever longing and panting for the light of his countenance, yet I would be so far satisfied, as to believe the Lord has wise and merciful reasons for keeping me so short of the comforts which he has taught me to desire and value more than the light of the sun.

I am, &c.

NINE LETTERS

REV. MR. R****.

LETTER I.

Dear Sir, Jan. 16, 1772.

Iт is true I was apprehensive from your silence that I had offended you; but when your letter came it made me full amends: and now I am glad I wrote as I did, though I am persuaded I shall never write to you again in the same strain. I am pleased with the spirit you discover; and your bearing so well to be told of the mistakes I pointed out to you, endears you more to me than if you had not made them. Henceforward I can converse freely with you, and shall be glad when I have the opportunity.

As to your view of justification, I did not oppose it: I judge for myself, and I am willing others should have the same liberty. If we hold the *Head* and love the Lord, we *agree* in him, and I should think my time ill employed in disputing the point with you. I only meant to except against the positive manner in which you had expressed yourself. My end is answered, and I am satisfied. Indeed, I believe the difference between a *judicious* Supra-lapsarian, and a *sound* Sub-lapsarian, lies more in a different way of expressing their sentiments than is generally thought. At the close of Halyburton's Insufficiency of Natural Religion, he has an Inquiry into the Nature of Regeneration and Justification, wherein he proposes a scheme, in which, if I mistake not, the moderate of both parties might safely unite. I have used the epithets *judicious* and *sound*, because, as I acknowledge some of the one side are not quite *sound*, so I think some on the other side are not so *judicious* as I could wish; that is, I think they do not sufficiently advert to the present state of human nature, and the danger which may arise from leading those who are weak in faith and judgment into inquiries and distinctions evidently beyond the line of their experience, and which may be hurtful; because, admitting them to be true when properly explained, they are very liable to be misunderstood. To say nothing of Mr. Hussey (in whose provisions I have frequently found more bones than meat, and seasoned with much of an angry and self-important spirit), I have observed passages in other writers, for whom I have a higher esteem, which, to say the least, appear to me paradoxical and hard to be understood; though perhaps I can give my consent to them, if I had such restrictions and limitations as the authors would not refuse. But plain people are easily puzzled. And though I know several in the Supra-lapsarian scheme, at whose feet I am willing to sit and learn, and have found their preaching and conversation savoury and edifying; yet I must say I have met with many who have appeared to be rather wise than warm, rather positive than humble, rather captious than lively, and more disposed to talk of speculations than experience. However, let us give ourselves to the study of the word, and to prayer; and may the great Teacher make every Scriptural truth food to our souls. I desire to grow in knowledge, but I want nothing which bears that name that has not a direct tendency to make sin more hateful, Jesus more precious to my soul; and at the same time to animate me to a diligent use of every appointed means, and an unreserved regard to every branch of duty. I think the Lord has shewn me in a measure there is a consistent sense running through the whole Scripture, and I desire to be governed and influenced by it all. Doctrines, precepts, promises, warnings, all have their proper place and use: and I think many of the inconveniences which obtain in the present day, spring from separating those things which God hath joined together, and insisting on some parts of the word of God almost to the exclusion of the rest.

I have filled my paper with what I did not intend to say a word of when I began, and must leave other things which were more upon my mind for another season. I thank you for saying you pray for me. Continue that kindness; I both need it and prize it.

I am, &c.

LETTER II.

Dear Sir, July 31, 1773.

I RECEIVED your sorrowful epistle yesterday; and in order to encourage you to write, I answer it to-day.

The ship was safe when Christ was in her, though he was *really* asleep. At present I can tell you good news, though you know it; He is wide awake, and his eyes are in every place. You and I, if we could be pounded together, might perhaps make two tolerable ones. You are too anxious, and I am too easy in some respects. Indeed I cannot be too easy, when I have a right thought that all is safe in his hands; but if your anxiety makes you pray, and my composure makes me careless, you have certainly the best of it.   However, the ark is fixed upon an immoveable foundation; and if we think we see it totter, it is owing to a swimming in our heads. Seriously, the times look dark and stormy, and call for much circumspection and prayer; but let us not forget that we have an infallible Pilot, and that the power and wisdom and honour of God are embarked with us.   At Venice they have a fine vessel, called the *Bucentaur*, in which, on a certain day of the year, the doge and nobles embark, and go a little way to sea, to repeat the foolish ceremony of marriage between the republic and the Adriatic (in consequence of some lying, antiquated pope's bull, by which the banns of matrimony between Venice and the Gulf were published in the dark ages), when, they say, a gold ring is very gravely thrown overboard.   Upon this occasion, I have been told, when the honour and government of Venice are shipped on board the Bucentaur, the pilot is obliged by his office to take an oath that he will bring the vessel safely back again, *in defiance of winds and weather.*   Vain mortals!   If this be true, what an instance of God's long-suffering is it, that they have never yet sunk as lead in the mighty waters!   But my story will probably remind you, that Jesus has actually entered into such an engagement in behalf of his church.   And well he may; for both wind and weather are at his command, and he can turn the storm into a calm in a moment.   We may therefore safely and confidently leave the government upon his shoulders. Duty is our part; the care is his.

A revival is wanted with us as well as with you; and I trust some of us are longing for it.

We are praying and singing for one; and I send you, on the other side, a hymn, that you (if you like it) may sing with us. Let us take courage: though it may seem marvellous in our eyes, it is not so in the Lord's. He changed the desert into a fruitful field, and bid dry bones live. And if he prepare our heart to pray, he will surely incline his ear to hear.

The miscarriages of professors are grievous; yet such things must be; how else could the Scriptures be fulfilled? But there is one who is able to keep *us* from falling. Some who have distressed us perhaps never were truly changed; how then could they stand? We see only the outside. Others who are sincere are permitted to fall for our instruction, that we may not be high-minded, but fear. However, he that walketh humbly walketh surely.

Believe me, &c.

LETTER III.

Dear Sir, Feb. 22, 1774.

Your letter by last post surprised and grieved me. We knew nothing of the subject, though Mrs. **** remembers, when **** was here, a hint or two was dropped which she did not understand; but no name was mentioned.

This instance shews the danger of leaning to impressions. Texts of Scripture brought powerfully to the heart are very desirable and pleasant, if their tendency is to humble us, to give us a more feeling sense of the preciousness of Christ, or of the doctrines of grace; if they make sin more hateful, enliven our regard to the means, or increase our confidence in the power and faithfulness of God. But if they are understood as inti-

mating our path of duty in particular circumstances, or confirming us in purposes we may
have already formed, not otherwise clearly warranted by the general strain of the word, or by
the leadings of Providence, they are for the most
part insnaring, and always to be suspected. Nor
does their coming into the mind at the time of
prayer give them more authority in this respect.
When the mind is intent upon any subject, the
imagination is often watchful to catch at any
thing which may seem to countenance the favourite
pursuit. It is too common to ask counsel of the
Lord when we have already secretly determined
for ourselves: and in this disposition we may
easily be deceived by the sound of a text of Scripture, which, detached from the passage in which
it stands, may seem remarkably to tally with our
wishes. Many have been deceived this way; and
sometimes, when the event has shewn them they
were mistaken, it has opened a door for great distress, and Satan has found occasion to make them
doubt even of their most solid experiences.

I have sometimes talked to **** upon this subject, though without the least suspicion of any
thing like what has happened. As to the present
case, it may remind us all of our weakness. I
would recommend prayer, patience, much tenderness towards her, joined with faithful expostulation.
Wait a little while, and I trust the Lord who loves
her will break the snare. I am persuaded, in her
better judgment, she would dread the thoughts of
doing wrong; and I hope and believe the good
Shepherd, to whom she has often committed her
soul and her ways, will interpose to restore and
set her to rights. * * * * * * * * *
* * * * * * * * * * * * * *
* * * * * * I am sorry you think any of

whom you have hoped well are going back; but
be not discouraged. I say again, pray, and wait,
and hope the best. It is common for young professors to have a slack time; it is almost necessary, that they may be more sensible of the weakness and deceitfulness of their hearts, and be more
humbled in future, when the Lord shall have
healed their breaches, and restored their souls.
We join in love to you and yours. Pray for us.

I am, &c.

LETTER IV.

Dear Sir,   Feb. 3, 1775.

IT would be wrong to make you wait long for
an answer to the point you propose in your last.
It is an important one. I am not a casuist by
profession, but I will do my best. Suppose I
imitate your laconic manner of stating the question and circumstances.

I doubt not but it is very lawful at your age to
think of marriage, and, in the situation you describe, to think of money likewise. I am glad
you have no person, as you say, *fixedly in view;*
in that case, advice comes a post or two too late.
But your expression seems to intimate, that there
is one *transiently in view.* If it be so, since you
have no settlement, if she has no money, I cannot
but wish she may pass on till she is out of sight
and out of mind. I see this will not do; I must
get into my own grave way about this grave business. I take it for granted, that my friend is free
from the love of filthy lucre; and that money will
never be the turning point with you in the choice
of a wife. Methinks I hear you think, If I wanted
money, I would either dig or beg for it; but to
preach or marry for money, that be far from me.

I commend you. However, though the love of money be a great evil, money itself, obtained in a fair and honourable way, is desirable, upon many accounts, though not for its own sake. Meat, clothes, fire, and books, cannot easily be had without it: therefore, if these be necessary, money which procures them must be a necessary like-wise. If things were otherwise than you repre-sent them, if you were able to provide for a wife yourself, then I would say, Find a gracious girl (if she be not found already) whose person you like, whose temper you think will suit; and then, with your father and mother's consent (without which I think you would be unwilling to move), thank the Lord for her, marry her, and account her a valuable portion, though she should not have a shilling. But while you are without income or settlement, if you have thoughts of marriage, I hope they will be regulated by a due regard to consequences. They who set the least value upon money have in some respects the most need of it. A generous mind will feel a thousand pangs in strait circumstances, which some unfeeling hearts would not be sensible of. You could perhaps endure hardships alone, yet it might pinch you to the very bone to see the person you love ex-posed to them. Besides, you might have a John, a Thomas, and a William, and half a dozen more to feed (for they must all eat); and how this could be done without a competency on one side or the other, or so much on both sides as will make a competency when united, I see not. Besides, you would be grieved not to find an occasional shilling in your pocket to bestow upon one or other of the Lord's poor, though you should be able to make some sort of a shift for those of your own house.

But is it not written, "The Lord will provide?"

It is : but it is written again, " Thou shalt not tempt the Lord thy God." Hastily to plunge ourselves into difficulties, upon a persuasion that he will find some way to extricate us, seems to me a species of tempting him.

Therefore I judge, *it is so far lawful for you to have a regard to money in looking out for a wife,* that it would be wrong, that is, in other words, *unlawful,* for you to omit it, supposing you have a purpose of marrying in your present situation.

Many serious young women have a predilection in favour of a minister of the Gospel ; and I believe among such, one or more may be found as spiritual, as amiable, as suitable to make you a good wife, with a tolerable fortune to boot, as another who has not a penny. If you are not willing to trust your own judgment in the search, entreat the Lord to find her for you. He chose well for Isaac and Jacob ; and you, as a believer, have warrant to commit your way to him, and many more express promises than they had for your encouragement. He knows your state, your wants, what you are at present, and what use he designs to make of you. Trust in him, and wait for him : prayer, and faith, and patience, are never disappointed. I commend you to his blessing and guidance. Remember us to all in your house.

I am, &c.

LETTER V.

Dear Sir,   May 28, 1775.

* * * * * * * * * * * * *
* * * * * * * You must not expect a long letter this morning : we are just going to court, in hopes of seeing the King, for he has

promised to meet us. We can say he is mindful of his promise; and yet is it not strange that though we are all in the same place, and the King in the midst of us, it is but here and there one (even of those who love him) can see him at once? However, in our turns we are all favoured with a glimpse of him, and have had cause to say, How great is his goodness! How great is his beauty! We have the advantage of the queen of Sheba; a more glorious object to behold, and not so far to go for the sight of it. If a transient glance exceeds all that the world can afford for a long continuance, what must it be to dwell with him? If a day in his courts be better than a thousand, what will eternity be in his presence? I hope the more you see, the more you love; the more you drink, the more you thirst; the more you do for him, the more you are ashamed you can do so little; and that the nearer you approach to your journey's end, the more your pace is quickened. Surely, the power of spiritual attraction should increase as the distance lessens. O that heavenly loadstone! may it so draw us that we may not creep, but run. In common travelling the strongest become weary if the journey be very long; but in the spiritual journey we are encouraged with a hope of going on from strength to strength. *Instaurabit iter vires,* as Johnson expresses it. No road but the road to heaven can thus communicate refreshment to those who walk in it, and make them more fresh and lively when they are just finishing their course than when they first set out.

I am, &c.

LETTER VI.

Dear Sir,   April 18, 1776.

ARE you sick, or lame of your right hand, or
are you busy in preparing a folio for the press,
that I hear nothing from you? You see by the
excuses I would contrive I am not willing to suppose you have forgotten me, but that your silence
is rather owing to a *cannot* than a *will not*.

I hope your soul prospers. I do not ask you
if you are always filled with sensible comfort:
but do you find your spirit more bowed down to
the feet and will of Jesus, so as to be willing to
serve him for the sake of serving him, and to
follow him, as we say, through thick and thin; to
be willing to be any thing or nothing, so that he
may be glorified? I could give you plenty of
good advice upon this head; but I am ashamed
to do it, because I so poorly follow it myself. I
want to live with him by the day, to do all for
him, to receive all from him, to possess all in
him, to live all to him, to make him my hiding-
place and my resting-place. I want to deliver
up that rebel Self to him in chains; but the rogue,
like Proteus, puts on so many forms, that he slips
through my fingers: but I think I know what I
would do if I could fairly catch him.

My soul is like a besieged city: a legion of
enemies without the gates, and a nest of restless
traitors within, that hold a correspondence with
them without; so that I am deceived and counteracted continually. It is a mercy that I have
not been surprised and overwhelmed long ago:
without help from on high it would soon be over
with me. How often have I been forced to cry
out, O God, the heathen are got into thine inheritance; thy holy temple have they defiled,

and defaced all thy work! Indeed it is a miracle
that I still hold out. I trust, however, I shall be
supported to the end, and that my Lord will at
length raise the siege, and cause me to shout
deliverance and victory

Pray for me, that my walls may be strengthened and wounds healed. We are all pretty
well as to the outward man, and join in love to
all friends.

I am, &c.

LETTER VII.

Dear Sir,   July 6, 1776.

I WAS abroad when your letter came, but employ the first post to thank you for your confidence. My prayers (when I can pray) you
may be sure of: as to advice, I see not that
the case requires much. Only be a quiet child,
and lie patiently at the Lord's feet. He is the
best friend and manager in these matters, for he
has a key to open every heart * * * * *
* * * * * * * * * * * * * * *
* * * * * * * * * * * I should
not have taken Mr. Z****'s letter for a denial,
as it seems you did. Considering the years of
the parties, and other circumstances, a prudent
parent could hardly say more, if he were inclined to favour your views. To me you seem
to be in a tolerably fair way; but I know in
affairs of this kind Mr. Self does not like suspense,
but would willingly come to the point at once:
but Mr. Faith (when he gets liberty to hold up
his head) will own, that, in order to make our
temporal mercies wear well, and to give us a
clearer sense of the hand that bestows them, a
waiting and a praying time are very season-

able. Worldly people expect their schemes to run upon all-fours, as we say, and the objects of their wishes to drop into their mouths without difficulty ; and if they succeed, they of course burn incense to their own drag, and say, This was my doing ; but believers meet with rubs and disappointments, which convince them, that if they obtain any thing, it is the Lord must do it for them. For this reason I observe, that he usually brings a death upon our prospects, even when it is his purpose to give us success in the issue. Thus we become more assured that we did not act in our own spirits, and have a more satisfactory view that his providence has been concerned in filling up the rivers and removing the mountains that were in our way. Then when he has given us our desire, how pleasant is it to look at it and say, This I got, not by my own sword, and my own bow ; but I wrestled for it in prayer, I waited for it in faith, I put it into the Lord's hand, and from his hand I received it.

You have met with the story of one of our kings (if I mistake not) who wanted to send a nobleman abroad as his ambassador, and he desired to be excused on account of some affairs which required his presence at home : the king answered, " Do you take care of my business, and I will take care of yours." I would have you think the Lord says thus to you. You were sent into the world for a nobler end than to be pinned to a girl's apron-string ; and yet if the Lord sees it not good for you to be alone, he will provide you a help-mate. I say, if he sees the marriage state best for you, he has the proper person *already* in his eye ; and though she were in Peru or Nova-Zembla, he knows how to bring you together. In the mean time, go thou and

preach the Gospel.   Watch in all things; endure
afflictions; do the work of an Evangelist; make
full proof of your ministry: and when the thoughts
rise in your mind (for you have no door to shut
them quite out), run with them to the Throne of
Grace, and commit them to the Lord.   Satan will
perhaps try to force them upon you unseasonably
and inordinately; but if he sees they drive you
to prayer, he will probably desist, rather than be
the occasion of doing you so much good.   Believe
likewise, that as the Lord has the appointment of
the person, so He fixes the time.   His time is
like the time of the tide; all the art and power
of man can neither hasten nor retard it a moment:
it must be waited for; nothing can be done without it, and, when it comes, nothing can resist it.
It is unbelief that talks of delays: faith knows
that, properly, there can be no such thing.   The
only reason why the Lord seems to delay what
he afterwards grants is, that the best hour is not
yet come.   I know you have been enabled to
commit and resign your all to his disposal.   You
did well.   May He help you to stand to the surrender.   Sometimes He will put us to the trial,
whether we mean what we say.   He takes his
course in a way we did not expect; and then,
alas! how often does the trial put us to shame!
Presently there is an outcry raised in the soul
against his management: this is wrong, that unnecessary, the other has spoiled the whole plan;
in short, all these things are against us.   And
then we go into the pulpit, and gravely tell the
people how wise and how good he is; and preach
submission to his will, not only as a duty, but a
privilege!   Alas, how deceitful is the heart!   Yet
since it is and will be so, it is necessary we should

know it by experience. We have reason, however, to say, He is good and wise; for he bears with our perverseness, and in the event shews us that if he had listened to our murmurings, and taken the methods we would have prescribed to him, we should have been ruined indeed, and that He has been all the while doing us good in spite of ourselves.

If I judge right, you will find your way providentially opened more and more; and yet it is possible, that when you begin to think yourself sure, something may happen to put you in a panic again. But a believer, like a sailor, is not to be surprised if the wind changes, but to learn the art of suiting himself to all winds for the time; and though many a poor sailor is shipwrecked, the poor believer shall gain his port. O it is good sailing with an infallible Pilot at the helm, who has the wind and weather at his command!

I have been much abroad, which of course puts things at sixes and sevens at home. If I did not love you well, I could not have spared so much of the only day I have had to myself for this fortnight past. But I was willing you should know that I think of you and feel for you, if I cannot help you.

I have read Mr. ****'s book. Some things I think strongly argued; in some he has laid himself open to a blow, and I doubt not but he will have it. I expect answers, replies, rejoinders, &c. &c. and say with Leah, *Gad, a troop cometh.* How the wolf will grin to see the sheep and the shepherds biting and worrying one another! And well he may. He knows that contentions are a surer way to weaken the spirit of love, and stop the progress of the Gospel, than his old stale method of fire and sword. Well, I trust we shall be of one heart and one mind when we get to heaven at least.

Let who will fight, I trust neither water nor fire shall set you and me at variance. We unite in love to you. The Lord is gracious to us, &c.

I am, &c.

LETTER VIII.

Dear Sir,   —— 1776.

I DO not often serve your letters so; but this last I burnt, believing you would like to have it out of danger of falling into improper hands. When I saw how eagerly the flames devoured the paper, how quickly and entirely every trace of the writing was consumed, I wished that the fire of the love of Jesus might as completely obliterate from your heart every uneasy impression which your disappointment has given you. *   *   *   *
*   *   *   *   *   *   *   *   *   *   *   *
*   *   *   *   *   *   *   *   *   * Surely when he crosses our wishes it is always in mercy, and because we short-sighted creatures often know not what we ask, nor what would be the consequences if our desires were granted.

Your pride, it seems, has received a fall by meeting a repulse. I know Self does not like to be mortified in these affairs; but if you are made successful in wooing souls for Christ, I hope that will console you for meeting a rebuff when only wooing for yourself. Besides, I would have you pluck up your spirits. I have two good old proverbs at your service: "There is as good fish in the sea as any that are brought out of it;" and, "If one won't another will, or wherefore serves the market?" Perhaps all your difficulties have arisen from this, that you have not yet seen the right person : if so, you have reason to be thankful that the Lord would not let you take the wrong, though you unwittingly would have done it if you could.   Where the right one lies hid I know not ; but upon a supposition that it will be good for you to marry, I may venture to say,

Ubi ubi est, diu celari non potest.

The Lord in his providence will disclose her, put her in your way, and give you to understand, This is she.   Then you will find your business go forward with wheels and wings, and have cause to say, His choice and time were better than your own.

Did I not tell you formerly, that if you would take care of his business he will take care of yours? I am of the same mind still.   He will not suffer them who fear Him and depend upon Him to want any thing that is truly good for them.   In the mean while, I advise you to take a lodging as near as you can to Gethsemane, and to walk daily to mount Golgotha, and borrow (which may be had for asking) that telescope which gives a prospect into the unseen world.   A view of what is passing within the vail has a marvellous effect to compose our spirits, with regard to the little things that are daily passing here.   Praise the Lord, who has enabled you to fix your supreme affection upon Him who is alone the proper and suitable object of it, and from whom you cannot meet a denial or fear a change.   He loved you first, and He will love you for ever ; and if He be pleased to arise and smile upon you, you are in no more necessity of begging for happiness to the prettiest creature upon earth, than of the light of a candle on Midsummer noon.

Upon the whole, I pray and hope the Lord will sweeten your cross, and either in kind or in kindness make you good amends. Wait, pray, and believe, and all shall be well. A cross we must have somewhere; and they who are favoured with health, plenty, peace, and a conscience sprinkled with the blood of Jesus, *must* have more causes for thankfulness than grief. Look round you, and take notice of the very severe afflictions which many of the Lord's own people are groaning under, and your trials will appear comparatively light.—Our love to all friends.

I am, &c.

LETTER IX.

Dear Sir,   June 3, 1777.

It seems I must write something about the small-pox, but I know not well what: having had it myself, I cannot judge how I should feel if I were actually exposed to it. I am not a professed advocate for inoculation: but if a person who fears the Lord should tell me, I think I can do it in faith, looking upon it as a salutary expedient, which he in his providence has discovered, and which therefore appears my duty to have recourse to, so that my mind does not hesitate with respect to the lawfulness, nor am I anxious about the event; being satisfied, that whether I live or die, I am in that path in which I can cheerfully expect his blessing; I do not know that I could offer a word by way of dissuasion.

If another person should say, My times are in the Lord's hands; I am now in health, and am not willing to bring upon myself a disorder, the consequences of which I cannot possibly foresee,

If I am to have the small-pox, I believe he is the
best judge of the season and manner in which I
shall be visited, so as may be most for his glory
and my own good; and therefore I choose to
wait his appointment, and not to rush upon even
the possibility of danger without a call. If the
very hairs of my head are numbered, I have no
reason to fear that, supposing I receive the small-
pox in a natural way, I shall have a single pimple
more than he sees expedient; and why should I
wish to have one less? Nay, admitting, which
however is not always the case, that inoculation
might exempt me from some pain and inconvenience, and lessen the apparent danger, might
it not likewise, upon that very account, prevent
my receiving some of those sweet consolations
which I humbly hope my gracious Lord would
afford me, if it were his pleasure to call me to
a sharp trial? Perhaps the chief design of this
trying hour, if it comes, may be to shew me more
of his wisdom, power, and love, than I have ever
yet experienced. If I could devise a mean to
avoid the trouble, I know not how great a loser I
may be in point of grace and comfort. Nor am
I afraid of my face: it is now as the Lord, has
made it, and it will be so after the small-pox.
If it pleases him, I hope it will please me. In
short, though I do not censure others, yet, as to
myself, inoculation is what I dare not venture
upon. If I did venture, and the issue should not
be favourable, I should blame myself for having
attempted to take the management out of the
Lord's hands, into my own; which I never did
yet in other matters, without finding I am no
more able than I am worthy to choose for myself.
Besides, at the best, inoculation would only

secure me from *one* of the innumerable natural evils the flesh is heir to: I should still be as liable as I am at present to a putrid fever, a bilious cholic, an inflammation in the bowels, or in the brain, and a thousand formidable diseases which are hovering round me, and only wait his permission to cut me off in a few days or hours: and therefore I am determined, by his grace, to resign myself to his disposal. Let me fall into the hands of the Lord (for his mercies are great), and not into the hands of men.

If a person should talk to me in this strain, most certainly I could not say, Notwithstanding all this, your safest way is to be inoculated.

We preach and hear, and I hope we know something of faith, as enabling us to intrust the Lord with our souls: I wish we had all more faith to intrust him with our bodies, our health, our provision, and our temporal comforts likewise. The former should seem to require the strongest faith of the two, How strange is it, that when we think we can do the *greater*, we should be so awkward and unskilful when we aim at the *less?* Give my love to your friend. I dare not advise: but if she can quietly return at the usual time, and neither run intentionally into the way of the small-pox, nor run out of the way, but leave it simply with the Lord, I shall not blame her. And if you will mind your praying and preaching, and believe that the Lord can take care of her without any of your contrivances, I shall not blame you: nay, I shall praise him for you both. My prescription is to read Dr. Watts, Psalm cxxi., every morning before breakfast, and pray it over till the cure is effected. *Probatum est.*

Hast thou not giv'n Thy word,
    To save my soul from death?
And I can trust my Lord
    To keep my mortal breath.
        I'll go and come,
        Nor fear to die,
        Till from on high
        Thou call me home.

Adieu! pray for

Yours, &c.

THREE LETTERS

MISS TH****.

LETTER I.

My dear Madam,

LET what has been said on the subject of acquaintance, &c. suffice. It was well meant on my side, and well taken on yours. You may perhaps see that my hints were not wholly unnecessary, and I ought to be satisfied with your apology, and am so. The circumstance of your being seen at the playhouse has nothing at all mysterious in it, as you say you have not been there these six or seven years : it was neither more nor less than a mistake. I heard you had been there within these two years : I am glad to find I was misinformed. I think there is no harm in your supposing, that of the many thousands who frequent public diversions some may, in other respects, be better than yourself; but I hope your humble and charitable construction of their mistake will not lead you to extenuate the evil of those diversions in themselves. For though I am persuaded that a few, who know better what to do with themselves, are, for want of consideration, drawn in to expose themselves in such places ; yet I am well satisfied, that if there is any practice in this land sinful, attendance on the playhouse is properly and eminently so. The theatres are fountains and means of vice; I had almost said, in the same manner and degree as the ordinances of the Gospel

are the means of grace: and I can hardly think
there is a Christian upon earth who would dare to
be seen there, if the nature and effects of the
theatre were properly set before them.   Dr. Wi-
therspoon of Scotland has written an excellent
piece upon the stage, or rather against it, which I
wish every person who makes the least pretence
to fear God had an opportunity of perusing.   I
cannot judge much more favourably of Ranelagh,
Vauxhall, and all the innumerable train of dissi-
pations, by which the god of this world blinds the
eyes of multitudes, lest the light of the glorious
Gospel should shine in upon them.   What an
awful aspect upon the present times have such
texts as Isa. xxii. 12—14. iii. 12, Amos vi. 3—6,
James iv. 4.   I wish you, therefore, not to plead
for any of them, but use all your influence to
make them shunned as pest-houses, and dangerous
nuisances to precious souls; especially if you
know any who you hope in the main are seriously
disposed, who yet venture themselves in those
purlieus of Satan, endeavour earnestly and faithfully to undeceive them.

The time is short; eternity at the door; was
there no other evil in these vain amusements than
the loss of precious time (but, alas! their name is
legion), we have not leisure in our circumstances
to regard them.   And, blessed be God! we need
them not.   The Gospel opens a source of purer,
sweeter, and more substantial pleasures: we are
invited to communion with God : we are called to
share in the theme of angels; the songs of heaven,
and the wonders of redeeming love are laid open
to our view.   The Lord himself is waiting to be
gracious, waiting with promises and pardons in
his hands.   Well then may we bid adieu to the
perishing pleasures of sin ; well may we pity those

who can find pleasure in those places and parties where he is shut out; where his name is only mentioned to be profaned; where his commandments are not only broken, but insulted; where sinners proclaim their shame as in Sodom, and attempt not to hide it; where, at best, wickedness is wrapt up in a disguise of delicacy, to make it more insinuating; and nothing is offensive that is not grossly and unpolitely indecent.

I sympathize with all your complaints; but if the Lord is pleased to make them subservient to the increase of your sanctification, to wean you more and more from this world, and to draw you nearer to himself, you will one day see cause to be thankful for them, and to number them amongst your choicest mercies. A hundred years hence it will signify little to you whether you were sick or well the day I wrote this letter.

We thank you for your kind condolence. There is a pleasure in the pity of a friend; but the Lord alone can give true comfort. I hope he will sanctify the breach, and do us good. Mrs. **** exchanges forgiveness with you about your not meeting in London; that is, you forgive her not coming to you, and she forgives you entertaining a suspicious thought of her friendship (though but for a minute) on account of what she was really unable to do.

I am, &c.

LETTER II.

My dear Madam,   September 1, 1767.

I SHALL not study for expressions to tell my dear friend how much we were affected by the news that came last post. We had, however, the pleasure to hear that your family was safe. I hope this will find you recovered from the hurry of spirits you must have been thrown into, and that both you and your papa are composed under the appointment of Him who has a right to dispose of his own as he pleases; for we know that, whatever may be the second causes and occasions, nothing can happen to us but according to the will of our heavenly Father. Since what is past cannot be recalled, my part is now to pray, that this, and every other dispensation you meet with, may be sanctified to your soul's good; that you may be more devoted to the God of your life, and have a clearer sense of your interest in that kingdom which cannot be shaken, that treasure which neither thieves nor flames can touch, that better and more enduring substance which is laid up for believers, where Jesus their Head and Saviour is. With this in view, you may take joyfully the spoiling of your goods.

I think I can feel for my friends; but for such as I hope have a right to that promise, that all things shall work together for their good, I soon check my solicitude, and ask myself, Do I love them better, or could I manage more wisely for them, than the Lord does? Can I wish them to be in safer or more compassionate hands than in his? Will he who delights in the prosperity of his servants, afflict them with sickness, losses, and alarms, except he sees there is need of these things? Such thoughts calm the emotions of my mind. I sincerely condole you; but the command is, to rejoice always in the Lord. The visitation was accompanied with mercy; not such a case as that of the late Lady Molesworth, which made every one's ears to tingle that heard it. Nor is yours such a case as of some, who in almost every great fire lose their all, and perhaps have no knowledge of God to support them.

Though our first apprehensions were for you, we almost forgot you for a moment when we thought of your next-door neighbour, and the circumstance she was in, so unfit to bear either a fright or a removal. We shall be in much suspense till we hear from you. God grant that you may be able to send us good news, that you are all well, at least as well as can be expected after such a distressing scene. If what has happened should give you more leisure, or more inclination, to spend a little time with us, I think I need not say we shall rejoice to receive you.

I am, &c.

LETTER III.

My dear Madam,   September 3, 1767.

THE vanity of all things below is confirmed to us by daily experience. Amongst other proofs, one is, the precariousness of our intimacies; and what little things, or rather what nothings, will sometimes produce a coolness, or at least a strangeness, between the dearest friends. How is it that our correspondence has been dropt, and that, after having written two letters since the fire, which removed you from your former residence, I should be still disappointed in my hopes of an answer? On our parts I hope there has been no abatement of regard; nor can I charge you with any thing but remissness. Therefore, waving the past, and all apologies on either side, let me beg you to write soon, to tell us how it is with you, and how you have been supported under the various changes you have met with since we saw you last. I doubt not but you have met with many exercises. I pray that they may have been sanctified to lead you nearer to the Lord, the fountain of all consolation, who is the only refuge in time of troubles, and whose gracious presence is abundantly able to make up every deficiency and every loss. Perhaps the reading of this may recal to your mind our past conversations, and the subjects of the many letters we have exchanged. I know not in what manner to write after so long an interval. I would hope your silence to us has not been owing to any change of sentiments, which might make such letters as mine less welcome to you. Yet when you had a friend, who I think you believed very nearly interested himself in your welfare, it seems strange, that in a course of two years you should have nothing to communicate. I cannot suppose you have forgotten me; I am sure I have not forgotten you; and therefore I long to hear from you soon, that I may know how to write; and should this likewise pass unanswered, I must sit down and mourn over my loss.

As to our affairs, I can tell you the Lord has been and is exceedingly gracious to us: our lives are preserved, our healths continued, and abundance of mercies and blessings on every side; but especially we have to praise him that he is pleased to crown the means and ordinances of his grace with tokens of his presence. It is my happiness to be fixed amongst an affectionate people, who make an open profession of the truth as it is in Jesus, and are enabled, in some measure, to shew forth its power in their lives and conversation. We walk in peace and harmony. I have reason to say, the Lord Jesus is a good

Master, and that the doctrine of free salvation, by faith in his name, is a doctrine according to godliness: for, through mercy, I find it daily effectual to the breaking down the strong holds of sin, and turning the hearts of sinners from dead works to serve the living God. May the Lord give my dear friend to live in the power and consolation of his precious truth!

I am, &c.

SEVEN LETTERS

TO

* * * * * *

LETTER I.

March 18, 1767.

I CAN truly say, that I bear you upon my heart and in my prayers. I have rejoiced to see the beginning of a good and gracious work in you; and I have confidence in the Lord Jesus, that he will carry it on and complete it; and that you will be amongst the number of those who shall sing redeeming love to eternity. Therefore fear none of the things appointed for you to suffer by the way; but gird up the loins of your mind, and hope to the end. Be not impatient, but wait humbly upon the Lord. You have one hard lesson to learn, that is, the evil of your own heart: you know something of it, but it is needful that you should know more; for the more we know of ourselves, the more we shall prize and love Jesus and his salvation. I hope what you find in yourself by daily experience will humble you, but not discourage you: humble you it should, and I believe it does. Are not you amazed sometimes that you should have so much as a hope, that, poor and needy as you are, the Lord thinketh of you? But let not all you feel discourage you; for if our Physician is almighty, our disease cannot be desperate; and if he casts none out that come to him, why should you fear? Our sins are many, but his mercies are more: our sins are great, but his righteousness is greater: we are weak, but he is power. Most of our complaints are owing to unbelief, and the remainder of a legal spirit; and these evils are not removed in a day. Wait on the Lord, and he will enable you to see more and more of the power and grace of our High Priest. The more you know him, the better you will trust him: the more you trust him, the better you will love him; the more you love him, the better you will serve him. This is God's way: you are not called to buy, but to beg; not to be strong in yourself, but in the grace that is in Christ Jesus. He is teaching you these things, and I trust he will teach you to the end. Remember, the growth of a believer is not like a mushroom, but like an oak, which increases slowly indeed but surely. Many suns, showers, and frosts, pass upon it before it comes to perfection; and in winter, when it seems dead, it is gathering strength at the root. Be humble, watchful, and diligent in the means, and endeavour to look through all, and fix your eye upon Jesus, and all shall be well. I commend you to the care of the good Shepherd, and remain, for his sake, Yours, &c.

LETTER II.

May 31, 1769.

I WAS sorry I did not write as you expected, but I hope it will do now. Indeed I have not forgotten you; you are often in my thoughts, and seldom omitted in my prayers. I hope the Lord will make what you see and hear while abroad profitable to you, to increase your knowledge, to strengthen your faith, and to make you from henceforth well satisfied with your situation. If

I am not mistaken, you will be sensible, that though there are some desirable things to be met with in London preferable to any other place, yet, upon the whole, a quiet situation in the country, under one stated ministry, and in connection with one people, has the advantage. It is pleasant now and then to have opportunity of hearing a variety of preachers, but the best and greatest of them are no more than instruments: some can please the ear better than others, but none can reach the heart any farther than the Lord is pleased to open it. This he shewed you upon your first going up; and I doubt not but your disappointment did you more good than if you had heard with all the pleasure you expected.

The Lord was pleased to visit me with a slight illness in my late journey. I was far from well on the Tuesday, but supposed it owing to the fatigue of riding, and the heat of the weather; but the next day I was taken with a shivering, to which a fever succeeded. I was then near sixty miles from home. The Lord gave me much peace in my soul, and I was enabled to hope he would bring me safe home, in which I was not disappointed: and though I had the fever most part of the way, my journey was not unpleasant. He likewise strengthened me to preach twice on Sunday; and at night I found myself well, only very weary, and I have continued well ever since. I have reason to speak much of his goodness, and to kiss the rod, for it was sweetened with abundant mercies. I thought that had it been his pleasure I should have continued sick at Oxford, or even have died there, I had no objection. Though I had not that joy and sensible comfort which some are favoured with, yet I was quite free from pain, fear, and care, and felt myself sweetly composed to his will, whatever it might be. Thus he fulfils his promise in making our strength equal to our day; and every new trial gives us a new proof how happy it is to be enabled to put our trust in Him.

I hope, in the midst of all your engagements, you find a little time to read his good word, and to wait at his mercy-seat. It is good for us to draw nigh to Him. It is an honour that He permits us to pray; and we shall surely find he is a God hearing prayer. Endeavour to be diligent in the means; yet watch and strive against a legal spirit, which is always aiming to represent him as a hard master, watching, as it were, to take advantage of us. But it is far otherwise. His name is Love: He looks upon us with compassion; He knows our frame, and remembers that we are but dust; and when our infirmities prevail, He does not bid us despond, but reminds us that we have an Advocate with the Father, who is able to pity, to pardon, and to save to the uttermost. Think of the names and relations he bears. Does he not call himself a Saviour, a Shepherd, a Friend, and a Husband? Has he not made known unto us his love, his blood, his righteousness, his promises, his power, and his grace, and all for our encouragement? Away then with all doubting, unbelieving thoughts; they will not only distress your heart, but weaken your hands. Take it for granted upon the warrant of his word, that you are his, and he is yours; that he has loved you with an everlasting love, and therefore in loving-kindness has drawn you to himself; that he will surely accomplish that which he has begun, and that nothing which can be named or thought of shall ever be able to separate you from him. This persuasion will give you strength for the battle; this is the shield which

will quench the fiery darts of Satan; this is the
helmet which the enemy cannot pierce. Whereas
if we go forth doubting and fearing, and are afraid
to trust any farther than we can feel, we are weak
as water, and easily overcome. Be strong, therefore, not in yourself, but in the grace that is in
Christ Jesus. Pray for me, and believe me to be

Your's &c.

LETTER III.

March 14.

I THINK you would hardly expect me to write
if you knew how I am forced to live at London.
However, I would have you believe I am as
willing to write to you, as you are to receive my
letters. As a proof, I try to send you a few lines
now, though I am writing to you and talking to
Mrs. **** both at once! and this is the only season
I can have to change a few words with her. She
is a woman of a sorrowful spirit: she talks and
weeps. I believe she would think herself happy
to be situated as you are, notwithstanding the
many advantages she has at London. I see daily,
and I hope you have likewise learnt, that places,
and outward circumstances cannot, of themselves,
either hinder or help us in walking with God. So
far as he is pleased to be with us, and to teach us
by his Spirit, wherever we are we shall get
forward; and if he does not bless us and water us
every moment, the more we have of our own
wishes and wills, the more uneasy we shall make
ourselves.

One thing is needful; an humble, dependent
spirit, to renounce our own wills, and give up
ourselves to his disposal without reserve. This
is the path of peace: and it is the path of safety;

for he has said, The meek he will teach his way,
and those who yield up themselves to him he will
guide with his eye. I hope you will fight and
pray against every rising of a murmuring spirit,
and be thankful for the great things which he has
already done for you. It is good to be humbled
for sin, but not to be discouraged ; for though we
are poor creatures, Jesus is a complete Saviour ;
and we bring more honour to God by believing in
his name, and trusting his word of promise, than
we could do by a thousand outward works.

I pray the Lord to shine upon your soul, and to
fill you with all joy and peace in believing. Remember to pray for us, that we may be brought
home to you in peace.

I am, &c.

LETTER IV.

London, Aug. 19, 1775.

You see I am mindful of my promise ; and glad
should I be to write something that the Lord may
be pleased to make a word in season. I went
yesterday into the pulpit very dry and heartless.
I seemed to have fixed upon a text, but when I
came to the pinch, it was so shut up that I could
not preach from it. I had hardly a minute to
choose, and therefore was forced to snatch at that
which came first upon my mind, which proved
2 Tim. i. 12. Thus I set off at a venture, having
no resource but in the Lord's mercy and faithfulness ; and indeed what other can we wish for ?
Presently my subject opened, and I know not
when I have been favoured with more liberty.
Why do I tell you this ? Only as an instance
of his goodness, to encourage you to put your

strength in him, and not to be afraid, even when you feel your own weakness and insufficiency most sensibly. We are never more safe, never have more reason to expect the Lord's help, than when we are most sensible that we can do nothing without him. This was the lesson Paul learnt,—to rejoice in his own poverty and emptiness, that the power of Christ might rest upon him. Could Paul have done any thing, Jesus would not have had the honour of doing all. This way of being saved entirely by grace, from first to last, is contrary to our natural wills : it mortifies self, leaving it nothing to boast of; and, through the remains of an unbelieving, legal spirit, it often seems discouraging. When we think ourselves so utterly helpless and worthless, we are too ready to fear that the Lord will therefore reject us ; whereas, in truth, such a poverty of spirit is the best mark we can have of an interest in his promises and care.

How often have I longed to be an instrument of establishing you in the peace and hope of the Gospel! and I have but one way of attempting it, by telling you over and over of the power and grace of Jesus. You want nothing to make you happy, but to have the eyes of your understanding more fixed upon the Redeemer, and more enlightened by the Holy Spirit to behold his glory. Oh, he is a suitable Saviour! He has power, authority, and compassion to save to the uttermost. He has given his word of promise, to engage our confidence ; and he is able and faithful to make good the expectations and desires he has raised in us. Put your trust in him; believe (as we say) through thick and thin, in defiance of all objections from within and without. For this, Abraham is recommended as a pattern to us. He overlooked all difficulties: he ventured and hoped even against hope, in a case which, to appearance, was desperate; because he knew that He who had promised was also able to perform.

Your sister is much upon my mind. Her illness grieves me: were it in my power I would quickly remove it: the Lord can, and I hope will, when it has answered the end for which he sent it. I trust he has brought her to us for good, and that she is chastised by him that she may not be condemned with the world. I hope, though she says little, she lifts up her heart to him for a blessing. I wish you may be enabled to leave her, and yourself, and all your concerns, in his hands. He has a sovereign right to do with us as he pleases; and if we consider what we are, surely we shall confess we have no reason to complain: and to those who seek him, his sovereignty is exercised in a way of grace. All shall work together for good: every thing is needful that he sends; nothing can be needful that he withholds. Be content to bear the cross; others have borne it before you. You have need of patience; and if you ask, the Lord will give it: but there can be no settled peace till our will is in a measure subdued. Hide yourself under the shadow of his wings; rely upon his care and power; look upon him as a physician who has graciously undertaken to heal your soul of the worst of sicknesses, sin. Yield to his prescriptions, and fight against every thought that would represent it as desirable to be permitted to choose for yourself. When you cannot see your way, be satisfied that he is your leader. When your spirit is overwhelmed within you, he knows your path: he will not leave you to sink. He has appointed seasons of refreshment, and you shall find he does not forget you. Above all, keep close to the Throne of Grace. If we seem to get no good by attempting to draw near him, we may be sure we shall get none by keeping away from him. I am, &c.

LETTER V.

I PROMISED you another letter, and now for the performance. If I had said, It may be, or, Perhaps I will, you would be in suspense; but if I promise, then you expect that I will not disappoint you, unless something should render it impossible for me to make my word good. I thank you for your good opinion of me, and for thinking I mean what I say; and I pray that you may be enabled more and more to honour the Lord, by believing his promise : for he is not like a man, that should fail or change, or be prevented by any thing unforeseen from doing what he has said. And yet we find it easier to trust to worms than to the God of truth. Is it not so with you? And I can assure you it is often so with me. But here is the mercy, that his ways are above ours as the heavens are higher than the earth. Though we are foolish and unbelieving, he remains faithful : he will not deny himself. I recommend to you especially that promise of God, which is so comprehensive that it takes in all our concernments, —I mean, that all things shall work together for good. How hard is it to believe, that not only those things which are grievous to the flesh, but even those things which draw forth our corruptions, and discover to us what is in our hearts, and fill us with guilt and shame, should in the issue work for our good! Yet the Lord has said it. All your pains and trials, all that befals you in your own person, or that affects you upon the account of others, shall in the end prove to your advantage. And your peace does not depend upon any change of circumstances which may appear desirable, but in having your will bowed to the Lord's will, and made willing to submit all to his disposal and management. Pray for this, and wait patiently for him, and he will do it. Be not surprised to find yourself poor, helpless, and vile; all whom he favours and teaches will find themselves so. The more grace increases, the more we shall see to abase us in our own eyes; and this will make the Saviour and his salvation more precious to us. He takes his own wise methods to humble you, and to prove you; and I am sure he will do you good in the end.

I am, &c.

LETTER VI.

September 16, 1775.

WHEN you receive this, I hope it will give you pleasure to think, that, if the Lord be pleased to favour us with health, we shall all meet again in a few days. I have met with much kindness at London, and many comforts and mercies: however, I shall be glad to return home. There my heart lives, let my body be where it will. I long to see all my dear people, and I shall be glad to see you.—I steal a little time to write another line or two, more to satisfy you than for any thing particular I have to say I thank you for your letter. I doubt not but the Lord is bringing you forward, and that you have a good right to say to your soul, Why art thou cast down and disquieted? hope thou in God; for I shall yet praise him. An evil heart, an evil temper, and the many crosses we meet with in passing through an evil world, will cut us out trouble : but the Lord has provided a balm for every wound, a cordial for every care : the fruit of all is to take away sin, and the end of all will be eternal life in glory. Think of these words ; put them in the balance of the sanctuary ; and then throw all your trials into the opposite scale, and you will find there is no proportion between them. Say then, "Though he slay me I will trust in him ;" for, when he has fully tried me, I shall come forth like gold. You would have liked to have been with me last Wednesday. I preached at Westminster Bridewell. It is a prison and house of correction. The bulk of my congregation were housebreakers, highwaymen, pick-pockets, and poor unhappy women, such as infest the streets of this city, sunk in sin, and lost to shame. I had a hundred or more of these before me. I preached from 1 Tim. i. 15 ; and began with telling them my own story : this gained their attention more than I expected. I spoke to them near an hour and a half. I shed many tears myself, and saw some of them shed tears likewise. Ah! had you seen their present condition, and could you hear the history of some of them, it would make you sing, " O to grace how great a debtor!" By nature they were no worse than the most sober and modest people ; and there was doubtless a time when many of them little thought what they should live to do and suffer. I might have been, like them, in chains, and one of them have come to preach to me, had the Lord so pleased. I am, &c.

LETTER VII.

Oct. 10, 1777.

I AM just come from seeing A**** N****. The people told me she is much better than she was, but she is far from being well. She was brought to me into a parlour, which saved me the painful task of going to inquire and seek for her among the patients. My spirits always sink when I am within those mournful walls, and I think no money could prevail on me to spend an hour there every day. Yet surely no sight upon earth is more suited to teach one thankfulness and resignation. Surely I have reason, in my worst times, to be thankful that I am out of hell, out of Bedlam, out of Newgate. If my eyes were as bad as yours, and my back worse, still I hope I should set a great value upon this mercy, that my senses are preserved. I hope you will think so too. The Lord afflicts us at times: but it is always a thousand times less than we deserve, and much less than many of our fellow-creatures are suffering around us. Let us therefore pray for grace to be humble, thankful, and patient.

This day twelvemonth I was under Mr. W****'s knife : there is another cause for thankfulness, that the Lord inclined me to submit to the operation, and brought me happily through it. In short, I have so many reasons for thankfulness, that I cannot count them. I may truly say they are more in number than the hairs of my head. And yet, alas! how cold, insensible, and ungrateful! I could make as many complaints as you ; but I find no good by complaining, except to him who is able to help me. It is better for you and me to be admiring the compassion and fulness

of grace that is in our Saviour, than to dwell
and pore too much upon our own poverty and vileness.   He is able to help and save to the uttermost: there I desire to cast anchor, and wish you
to do so likewise.   Hope in God, for you shall
yet praise him.

I am, &c.

FIVE LETTERS

MR. C****.

====

LETTER I.

Dear Sir,   January 16, 1775.

THE death of a near relative called me from home in December, and a fortnight's absence threw me so far behind-hand in my course, that I deferred acknowledging your letter much longer than I intended. I now thank you for it. I can sympathize with you in your troubles; yet, knowing the nature of our calling, that, by an unalterable appointment, the way to the kingdom lies through many tribulations, I ought to rejoice, rather than otherwise, that to you it is given, not only to believe, but also to suffer. If you escaped these things, whereof all the Lord's children are partakers, might not you question your adoption into his family? How could the power of grace be manifest, either to you, in you, or by you, without afflictions? How could the corruptions and devastations of the heart be checked without a cross? How could you acquire a tenderness and skill in speaking to them that are weary, without a taste of such trials as they also meet with? You could only be a hearsay witness to the truth, power, and sweetness of the precious promises, unless you have been in such a situation as to need them, and to find their suitableness and sufficiency. The Lord has given you a good desire to serve him in the Gospel, and he is now training you for that service. Many things, yea, the most important things, belonging to the Gospel ministry, are not to be learned by books and study, but by painful experience. You must expect a variety of exercises; but two things he has promised you,—that you shall not be tried above what he will enable you to bear, and that all shall work together for your good. We read somewhere of a conceited orator, who declaimed upon the management of war in the presence of Hannibal, and of the contempt with which Hannibal treated his performance. He deserved it; for how should a man who had never seen a field of battle be a competent judge of such a subject? Just so, were we to acquire no other knowledge of the Christian warfare than what we could derive from cool and undisturbed study, instead of coming forth as able ministers of the New Testament, and competently acquainted with the τα νοηματα, with the devices, the deep-laid counsels and stratagems of Satan, we should prove but mere declaimers. But the Lord will take better care of those whom he loves and designs to honour. He will try, and permit them to be tried, in various ways. He will make them feel much in themselves, that they may know how to feel much for others, according to that beautiful and expressive line,

Haud ignara mali, miseris succurrere disco.

And as this previous discipline is necessary to enable us to take the field in a public capacity with courage, wisdom, and success, that we may lead and animate others in the fight, it is equally necessary for our own sakes, that we may obtain and preserve the grace of humility, which I perceive with pleasure he has taught you to set a high value upon. Indeed, we cannot value it too highly; for we can be neither comfortable, safe, nor habitually useful, without it. The root of pride lies deep in our fallen nature, and, where the Lord has given natural and acquired abilities, it would grow apace, if he did not mercifully watch over us, and suit his dispensations to keep it down. Therefore I trust he will make you willing to endure hardships, as a good soldier of Jesus Christ. May he enable you to behold him with faith holding out the prize, and saying to you, Fear none of those things that thou shalt suffer; be thou faithful unto death, and I will give thee a crown of life.

We sail upon a turbulent and tumultuous sea; but we are embarked on a good bottom, and in a good cause, and we have an infallible and almighty Pilot, who has the winds and weather at his command, and can silence the storm into a calm with a word whenever he pleases. We may be persecuted, but we shall not be forsaken; we may be cast down, but we cannot be destroyed. Many will thrust sore at us that we may fall, but the Lord will be our stay.

I am sorry to find you are quite alone at Cambridge; for I hoped there would be a succession of serious students to supply the place of those who are transplanted to shine as lights in the world. Yet you are not alone; for the Lord is with you, the best counsellor and the best friend. There is a strange backwardness in us (at least in me) fully to improve that gracious intimacy to which he invites us. Alas! that we so easily wander from the fountain of life to hew out cisterns for ourselves; and that we seem more attached to a few drops of his grace in our fellow-creatures, than to the fulness of grace that is in himself. I think nothing gives me a more striking sense of my depravity than my perverseness and folly in this respect: yet he bears with me, and does me good continually.

I am, &c.

━━━

LETTER II.

Dear Sir, March, 1776.

I KNOW not the length of your college terms, but hope this may come time enough to find you still resident. I shall not apologize for writing no sooner, because I leave other letters of much longer date unanswered that I may write so soon. It gave me particular pleasure to hear that the Lord helped you through your difficulties, and succeeded your desires. And I have sympathized with you in the complaints you make of a dark and mournful frame of spirits afterwards. But is not this, upon the whole, right and salutary, that, if the Lord is pleased at one time to strengthen us remarkably in answer to prayer, he should leave us at another time, so far as to give us a real sensibility that we were supported by his power, and not our own? Besides, as you feel a danger of being elated by the respect paid you, was it not a merciful and seasonable dispensation that made you feel your own weakness, to prevent your being exalted above measure? The Lord, by withdrawing his smiles from you, reminded you that the smiles of men are of little value, otherwise perhaps you might have esteemed them too highly. Indeed, you scholars that know the Lord are singular instances of the power of his grace; for (like the young men in Dan. iii.) you live in the very midst of the fire. Mathematical studies in particular have such a tendency to engross and fix the mind to the contemplation of cold and unin-

teresting truth, and you are surrounded with so
much intoxicating applause if you succeed in your
researches, that for a soul to be kept humble and
alive in such a situation, is such a proof of the
Lord's presence and power as Moses had when
he saw the bush unconsumed in the midst of the
flames. I believe I had naturally a turn for the
mathematics myself, and dabbled in them a little
way; and though I did not go far, my head,
sleeping and waking, was stuffed with diagrams
and calculations. Every thing I looked at that
exhibited either a right line or a curve, set my
wits a wool-gathering. What then must have
been the case had I proceeded to the interior
arcana of speculative geometry? I bought my
namesake's *Principia;* but I have reason to be
thankful that I left it as I found it, a sealed book,
and that the bent of my mind was drawn to something of more real importance before I understood
it. I say not this to discourage you in your pursuits: they lie in your line and path of duty; in mine
they did not. As to your academics, I am glad
that the Lord enables you to shew those among
whom you live, that the knowledge of his Gospel
does not despoil you either of diligence or acumen.
However, as I said, you need a double guard of
grace, to preserve you from being either puffed
up or deadened by those things, which, considered
in any other view than *quoad hoc*, to preserve your
rank and character in the University while you
remain there, are, if taken in the aggregate, little
better than a *splendidum nihil.* If my poor people
at ——— could form the least conception of what
the learned at Cambridge chiefly admire in each
other, and what is the intrinsic reward of all their
toil, they would say (supposing they could speak
Latin) *Quam suave istis suavitatibus carere!* How

gladly would some of them, if such mathematical and metaphysical lumber could by any means get into their heads, how gladly would they drink at Lethe's stream to get it out again! How many perplexities are they freed from by their happy ignorance, which often pester those to their lives' end who have had their natural proneness to vain reasoning sharpened by academical studies!

LETTER III.

Dear Sir,   May 18, 1776.

Though I wished to hear from you sooner, I put a candid interpretation upon your silence; was something apprehensive for your health, but felt no disposition to anger. Let our correspondence be free from fetters. Write when you please, and when you can: I will do the like. Apologies may be spared on both sides. I am not a very punctual correspondent myself, having so many letters to write, and therefore have no right to stand upon punctilios with you.

I sympathize with you in your sorrow for your friend's death. Such cases are very distressing! But such a case might have been our own. Let us pray for grace to be thankful for ourselves, and submit every thing in humble silence to the sovereign Lord, who has a right to do as he pleases with his own. We feel what happens in our own little connections; but—O the dreadful mischief of sin!—instances of this kind are as frequent as the hours, the minutes, perhaps the moments of every day: and though we know but one in a million, the souls of others have an equal capacity for endless happiness or misery. In this situation the Lord has honoured us with a call to warn our

fellow-sinners of their danger, and to set before
them his free and sure salvation; and if he is
pleased to make us instrumental of snatching but
one as a brand out of the fire, it is a service of
more importance than to be the means of preserving a whole nation from temporal ruin. I congratulate you upon your admission into the ministry, and pray him to favour you with a single eye
to his glory, and a fresh anointing of his Holy
Spirit, that you may come forth as a scribe well
instructed in the mysteries of his kingdom, and
that his word in your mouth may abundantly
prosper.

I truly pity those who rise early and take late
rest and eat the bread of carefulness, with no
higher prize and prospect in view than the obtaining of academical honours. Such pursuits will
ere long appear (as they really are) vain as the
sports of children. May the Lord impress them
with a noble ambition of living to and for him.
If these adventurers, who are labouring for pebbles
under the semblance of goodly pearls, had a discovery of the Pearl of great price, how quickly
and gladly would they lay down their admired
attainments, and become fools that they might be
truly wise! What a snare have you escaped!
You would have been poorly content with the
name of a mathematician or a poet, and looked
no farther, had not He visited your heart and enlightened you by his grace. Now I trust you
account your former gain but loss, for the excellency of the knowledge of Jesus Christ the Lord.
What you have attained in the way of literature
will be useful to you, if sanctified, and chiefly so
by the knowledge you have of its insufficiency to
any valuable purpose in the great concerns of
walking with God and winning souls.

I am pleased with your fears lest you should not be understood in your preaching. Indeed, there is a danger of it. It is not easy for persons of quick parts duly to conceive how amazingly ignorant and slow of apprehension the bulk of our congregations generally are. When our own ideas are clear, and our expressions proper, we are ready to think we have sufficiently explained ourselves; and yet, perhaps, nine out of ten (especially of those who are destitute of spiritual light) know little more of what we say than if we were speaking Greek. A degree of this inconvenience is always inseparable from written discourses. They cast our thoughts into a style, which, though familiar to ourselves, is too remote from common conversation to be comprehended by narrow capacities; which is one chief reason of the preference I give, *cæteris paribus*, to extempore preaching. When we read to the people, they think themselves less concerned in what is offered than when we speak to them point-blank. It seems a good rule, which I have met with somewhere, and which perhaps I have mentioned to you, to fix our eyes upon some one of the auditory whom we judge of the least capacity: if we can make *him* understand, we may hope to be understood by the rest. Let those who seek to be admired for the exactness of their compositions enjoy the poor reward they aim at: it is best for Gospel preachers to speak plain language. If we thus singly aim at the glory of our Master and the good of souls, we may hope for the accompanying power of his Spirit, which will give our discourses a weight and energy that Demosthenes had no conception of.

I can give you no information of a curacy in a better situation. But either the Lord will provide you one, or I trust he will give you usefulness and a competency of health and spirits where you are. He who caused Daniel to thrive upon pulse, can make you strong and cheerful even in the Fens, if he sees that best for you. All things obey him, and you need not fear but he will enable you for whatever service he has appointed you to perform.

This letter has been a week in hand: many interruptions from without, and indispositions within. I seem to while away my life, and shall be glad to be saved upon the footing of the thief upon the cross, without any hope or plea but the power and grace of Jesus, who has said, I will in nowise cast out. Adieu.

Pray for yours, &c.

LETTER IV.

Dear Sir,   Sept. 10, 1777.

I WAS glad to hear from you at last, not being willing to think myself forgotten. I supposed you were ill. It seems, by your account, that you are far from well: but I hope you are as well as you ought to be; that is, as well as the Lord sees it good for you to be. I say, I hope so: for I am not sure that the length and vehemence of your sermons, which you tell me astonish many people, may not be rather improper and imprudent, considering the weakness of your constitution; at least, if this expression of yours be justly expounded by a report which has reached me, that the length of your sermons is frequently two hours, and the vehemence of your voice so great that you may be heard far beyond the church-walls. Unwilling should I be to damp your zeal; but I feel unwilling likewise, that by excessive, unnecessary exertions you should wear away at once, and preclude your own usefulness. This concern is so much upon my mind that I begin with it, though it makes me skip over the former part of your letter; but when I have relieved myself upon this point, I can easily skip back again. I am perhaps the more ready to credit the report, because I know the spirits of you nervous people are highly volatile. I consider you as mounted upon a fiery steed, and provided you use due management and circumspection, you travel more pleasantly than we plodding folks upon our sober, phlegmatic nags ; but then, if instead of pulling the rein you plunge in the spurs, and add wings to the wind, I cannot but be in pain for the consequences. Permit me to remind you of the Terentian adage, *ne quid nimis.* The end of speaking is to be heard ; and if the person farthest from the preacher can hear, he speaks loud enough. Upon some occasions a few sentences of a discourse may be enforced with a voice still more elevated, but to be uncommonly loud from beginning to end is hurtful to the speaker, and I apprehend nowise useful to the hearer. It is a fault which many inadvertently give into at first, and which many have repented of too late : when practice has rendered it habitual, it is not easily corrected. I know some think that preaching very loudly and preaching with power are synonimous expressions ; but your judgment is too good to fall in with that prejudice. If I was a good Grecian I would send you a quotation from Homer, where he describes the eloquence of Nestor, and compares it, if I remember right, not to a thunderstorm or hurricane, but to a fall of snow, which, though pressing, insinuating, and penetrating, is soft and gentle. You know the passage : I think the simile is beautiful and expressive.

Secondly (as we say), as to long preaching. There is still in being an old-fashioned instrument called an hour-glass, which in days of yore, before clocks and watches abounded, used to be the measure of many a good sermon, and I think it a tolerable stint. I cannot wind up my ends to my own satisfaction in a much shorter time, nor am I pleased with myself if I greatly exceed it. If an angel was to preach for two hours, unless his hearers were angels likewise, I believe the greater part of them would wish he had done. It is a shame it should be so: but so it is ; partly through the weakness and partly through the wickedness of the flesh, we can seldom stretch our attention to spiritual things for two hours together without cracking it, and hurting its spring : and when weariness begins, edification ends. Perhaps it is better to feed our people like chickens, a little and often, than to cram them like turkeys, till they cannot hold one gobbet more. Besides, overlong sermons break in upon family concerns, and often call off the thoughts from the sermon to the pudding at home, which is in danger of being over-boiled. They leave likewise but little time for secret or family religion, which are both very good in their place, and are entitled to a share in the Lord's day. Upon the preacher they must have a bad effect, and tend to wear him down before his time : and I have known some, by over-acting at first, have been constrained to sit still and do little or nothing for months or years afterwards. I rather recommend to you the advice of your brother Cantab, Hobson the carrier, So to set out that you may hold out to your journey's end.

Now, if Fame with her hundred mouths has brought me a false report of you, and you are not guilty of preaching either too long or too loud, still I am not willing my remonstrance may stand for nothing. I desire you will accept it, and thank me for it as a proof of my love to you, and likewise of the sincerity of my friendship; for if I had wished to flatter you, I could easily have called another subject.

I have one more report to trouble you with, because it troubles me; and therefore you must bear a part of my burden. Assure me it is false, and I will send you one of the handsomest letters I can devise by way of thanks. It is reported then (but I will not believe it till you say I must), that you stand upon your tiptoes, upon the point of being whirled out of our vortex, and hurried away, comet-like, into the regions of eccentricity: in plain English, that you have a hankering to be an itinerant. If this be true, I will not be the first to tell it in St. John's college, or to publish it on the banks of Cam, lest the mathematicians rejoice, and the poets triumph. But to be serious; for it is a serious subject; let me beg you to deliberate well, and to pray earnestly before you take this step. Be afraid of acting in your own spirit, or under a wrong impression: however honestly you mean, you may be mistaken. The Lord has given you a little charge; be faithful in it, and in his good time he will advance you to a greater: but let his providence evidently open the door to you, and be afraid of moving one step before the cloud and pillar. I have had my warm fits and desires of this sort in my time; but I have reason to be thankful that I was held in with a strong hand. I wish there were more itinerant preachers. If a man has grace and zeal, and but little fund, let him go and diffuse the substance of a dozen sermons over as many counties; but you have natural and acquired abilities, which qualify you for the more difficult, and, in my judgment, not less important, station of a parochial minister. I wish you to be a burning, shining, steady light. You may perhaps have less popularity; that is, you will be less exposed to the workings of self and the snares of Satan, if you stay with us; but I think you may live in the full exercise of your gifts and graces, be more consistent with your voluntary engagements, and have more peace of mind, and humble intercourse with God, in watching over a flock which he has committed to you, than, by forsaking them, to wander up and down the earth without a determined scope.

Thus far I have been more attentive to the *utile* than the *dulce.* I should now return to join you in celebrating the praises of poetry, and the other subjects of your letter; but time and paper fail together. Let me hear from you soon, or I shall fear I have displeased you, which, fond as I am of poetry, would give me more pain than I ever found pleasure in reading Alexander's Feast. Indeed I love you; I often measure over the walks we have taken together; and when I come to a favourite stile, or such a favourite spot upon the hill-top, I am reminded of something that passed, and say, or at least think, *Hic stetit* C ****. Your's, &c.

LETTER V.

Dear Sir,

By your flying letter from London, as well as by your more particular answer to my last, I judge that what I formerly wrote will answer no other end than to be a testimony of my fidelity and friendship. I am ready to think you were so far determined before you applied to the bishop, as to be rather pleased than disappointed by a refusal which seemed to afford you liberty to preach at large. As your *testimonium* was not countersigned, the consequence was no other than might have been expected: yet I have been told (how true I know not), that the bishop would have passed over the informality, if you had not, unasked by him, avowed yourself a Methodist. I think, if you had been unwilling to throw hindrances in your own way, the most perfect simplicity would have required no more of you than to have given a plain and honest answer to such questions as he might think proper to propose. You might have assisted Mr. **** for a season without being in full orders; and you may still, if you are not resolved at all events to push out. He wrote to me about you, and you may easily judge what answer I gave. I have heard from him a second time, and he laments that he cannot have you. I likewise lament that you cannot be with him. I think you would have loved him; and I hoped his acquaintance might not have proved unuseful to you.

If you have not actually passed the Rubicon, if there be yet room for deliberation, I once more entreat you to pause and consider. In many respects I ought to be willing to learn from you; but in one point I have a little advantage of you: I am some years older, both in life and in profession; and in this difference of time perhaps I have learned something more of the heart, the world, and the devices of Satan, than you have had opportunity for. I hope I would not damp

your zeal, but I will pray the Lord to direct it
into the best channel for permanent usefulness : I
say permanent.   I doubt not that you would be
useful in the itinerant way; but I more and more
observe great inconveniences follow in that way.
Where you make a gathering of people, others
will follow you ; and if they all possessed your
spirit, and had your disinterested views, it might
be well.   But, generally, an able preacher only
so far awakens people to a desire to hear, as exposes them to the incursions of various winds of
doctrine, and the attempts of injudicious pre-
tenders, who will resemble you in nothing but
your eagerness to post from place to place.   From
such measures, in time, proceed errors, parties,
contentions, offences, enthusiasm, spiritual pride,
and a noisy ostentatious form of godliness, but
little of that power and life of faith which shews
itself by humility, meekness, and love.

A parochial minister, who lives among his
people, who sees and converses with them frequently, and exemplifies his doctrine in their
view by his practice, having knowledge of their
states, trials, growth, and dangers, suits himself
to their various occasions, and, by the blessing
of God, builds them up, and brings them forward
in faith and holiness.   He is instrumental in
forming their experience; he leads them to a
solid, orderly, Scriptural knowledge of Divine
things.   If his name is not in so many mouths as
that of the itinerant, it is upon the hearts of the
people of his charge.   He lives with them as a
father with his children.   His steady consistent
behaviour silences in some measure the clamours
of his enemies; and the Lord opens him doors of
occasional usefulness in many places, without

provoking our superiors to discountenance other young men who are seeking orders.

I now wish I had taken larger paper, for I have not room for all I would say. I have no end to serve. I am of no party. I wish well to irregulars and itinerants who love and preach the Gospel. I am content that they should labour that way, who have not talents nor fund to support the character and fill up the office of a parochial minister. But I think you are qualified for more important service. If you had patient faith to wait a while for the Lord's opening, I doubt not but you might yet obtain priest's orders. We are hasty, like children; but God often appoints us a waiting time. Perhaps it requires as much or more grace to wait than to be active; for it is more trying to self. After all, whatever course you take, I shall love you, pray for you, and be glad to see you.

I am, &c.

EIGHT LETTERS

MRS. ****.

=======

LETTER I.

My dear Madam,   July—1764.

THE complaints you make are inseparable from
a spiritual acquaintance with our own hearts: I
would not wish you to be less affected with a
sense of in-dwelling sin. It becomes us to be
humbled into the dust: yet our grief, though it
cannot be too great, may be under a wrong direction; and if it leads us to impatience or distrust,
it certainly is so.

Sin is the sickness of the soul, in itself mortal
and incurable, as to any power in heaven or earth
but that of the Lord Jesus only. But he is the
great, the infallible Physician. Have we the privilege to know his name? Have we been enabled
to put ourselves into his hand? We have then
no more to do but to attend his prescriptions, to
be satisfied with his methods, and to wait his
time. It is lawful to wish we were well; it is
natural to groan, being burdened: but still he
must and will take his own course with us; and,
however dissatisfied with ourselves, we ought still
to be thankful that he has begun his work in us,
and to believe that he will also make an end.
Therefore while we mourn, we should likewise
rejoice; we should encourage ourselves to expect
all that he has promised; and we should limit
our expectations by his promises. We are sure,

that when the Lord delivers us from the guilt and
dominion of sin, he could with equal ease free us
entirely from sin, if he pleased. The doctrine of
sinless perfection is not to be rejected, as though
it were a thing simply impossible in itself, for
nothing is too hard for the Lord, but because it is
contrary to that method which he has chosen to
proceed by. He has appointed that sanctification
should be effected, and sin mortified, not at once
completely, but by little and little ; and doubtless
he has wise reasons for it.   Therefore, though we
are to desire a growth in grace, we should, at the
same time, acquiesce in his appointment, and not
be discouraged or despond, because we feel that
conflict which his word informs us will only terminate with our lives.

Again, some of the first prayers which the Spirit
of God teaches us to put up, are for a clearer sense
of the sinfulness of sin, and our vileness on account
of it.   Now, if the Lord is pleased to answer your
prayers in this respect, though it will afford you
cause enough for humiliation, yet it should be received likewise with thankfulness, as a token for
good.   Your heart is not worse than it was formerly, only your spiritual knowledge is increased :
and this is no small part of the growth in grace,
which you are thirsting after, to be truly humbled,
and emptied, and made little in your own eyes.

Farther ; the examples of the saints recorded in
Scripture prove (and indeed of the saints in general), that the greater measure any person has of
the grace of God in truth, the more conscientious
and lively they have been; and the more they
have been favoured with assurances of the Divine
favour, so much the more deep and sensible their
perception of indwelling sin and infirmity has always been : so it was with Job, Isaiah, Daniel,

and Paul. It is likewise common to overcharge ourselves. Indeed we cannot think ourselves worse than we really are; yet some things which abate the comfort and alacrity of our Christian profession are rather impediments than properly sinful, and will not be imputed to us by Him who knows our frame, and remembers that we are but dust. Thus, to have an infirm memory, to be subject to disordered, irregular, or low spirits, are faults of the constitution, in which the *will* has no share, though they are all burthensome and oppressive, and sometimes needlessly so, by our charging ourselves with guilt on their account. The same may be observed of the unspeakable and fierce suggestions of Satan, with which some persons are pestered, but which shall be laid to him from whom they proceed, and not to them who are troubled and terrified because they are forced to feel them.—Lastly, It is by the experience of these evils within ourselves, and by feeling our utter insufficiency, either to perform duty or to withstand our enemies, that the Lord takes occasion to shew us the suitableness, the sufficiency, the freeness, the unchangeableness of his power and grace. This is the inference St. Paul draws from his complaints, Rom. vii. 25; and he learnt it upon a trying occasion from the Lord's own mouth, 2 Cor. xii. 8, 9.

Let us then, dear madam, be thankful and cheerful; and while we take shame to ourselves, let us glorify God, by giving Jesus the honour due to his name. Though we are poor, he is rich: though we are weak, he is strong; though we have nothing, he possesses all things. He suffered for us: he calls us to be conformed to him in sufferings. He conquered in his own person, and he will make each of his members more than con-

querors in due season. It is good to have one
eye upon ourselves; but the other should ever be
fixed on him who stands in the relation of Saviour,
Husband, Head, and Shepherd. In him we have
righteousness, peace, and power. He can con-
troul all that we fear; so that if our path should
be through the fire or through the water, neither
the flood shall drown us, nor the flame kindle
upon us, and ere long he will cut short our conflicts, and say, Come up hither. " Then shall our
grateful songs abound, and every fear be wiped
away." Having such promises and assurances,
let us lift up our banner in his name, and press on
through every discouragement.

With regard to company that have not a savour
of the best things, as it is not your choice, I would
advise you (when necessary) to bear it as a cross:
we cannot suffer by being where we ought to be,
except through our own impatience; and I have
an idea, that when we are providentially called
amongst such (for something is due to friends and
relations, whether they walk with us or no), that
the hours need not be wholly lost: nothing can
pass but may be improved; the most trivial conversation may afford us new views of the heart,
new confirmation of Scripture, and renew a sense
of our obligations to distinguishing grace, which
has made us in any degree to differ. I would wish
when you go amongst your friends, that you do
not confine your views to getting safe away from
them without loss, but entertain a hope that
you may be sent to do some of them good. You
cannot tell what effect a word or a look may have,
if the Lord is pleased to bless it. I think we may
humbly hope, that while we sincerely desire to
please the Lord, and to be guided by him in all
things, he will not suffer us to take a journey, or

hardly to make a short visit, which shall not answer some good purpose to ourselves or others, or both.   While your gay friends affect an air of raillery, the Lord may give you a secret witness in their consciences ; and something they observe in you, or hear from you, may set them on think-ing perhaps after you are gone, or after the first occasion has entirely slipped your memory; Eccles. xi. 1.   For my own part, when I consider the power, the freedom of Divine Grace, and how sovereign the Lord is in the choice of the instru-ments and means by which he is pleased to work, I live in hopes from day to day of hearing of won-ders of this sort.   I despair of nobody : and if I sometimes am ready to think such or such a person seems more unlikely than others to be brought in, I relieve myself by a possibility that that very person, and for that very reason, may be the first instance.   The Lord's thoughts are not like ours : in his love and in his ways there are heights which we cannot reach, depths which we cannot fathom, lengths and breadths beyond the ken of our feeble sight.   Let us then simply depend upon Him, and do our little best, leaving the event in his hand.

I cannot tell if you know any thing of Mrs. ****.   In a letter I received yesterday she writes thus:—"I am at present very ill with some disorder in my throat, which seems to threaten my life ; but death or life, things present or things to come, all things are mine, and I am Christ's, and Christ is God's.   O glorious privilege! precious founda-tion of soul-rest and peace, when all things about us are most troublous!   Soon we shall be at home with Christ, where sin, sorrow, and death have no place ; and in the mean time our beloved will lead us through the wilderness.   How safe, how

joyous are we, may we be, in the most evil case!"
—If these should be some of the last notes of this
swan, I think them worth preserving. May we
not with good reason say, Who would not be a
Christian? The Lord grant that you and I, madam,
and yours and mine, may be happy in the same
assurance, when we shall have death and eternity
near in view. I am, &c.

LETTER II.

My dear Madam, Sept. — 1764.

Your welfare I rejoice in; your warfare I
understand something of. St. Paul describes his
own case in few words, "Without were fightings, within were fears." Does not this comprehend all you would say? And how are you to
know experimentally either your own weakness,
or the power, wisdom, and grace of God, seasonably and sufficiently afforded, but by frequent and
various trials? How are the graces of patience,
resignation, meekness, and faith, to be discovered
and increased but by exercise? The Lord has
chosen, called, and armed us for the fight; and
shall we wish to be excused? Shall we not rather
rejoice that we have the honour to appear in such
a cause, under such a Captain, such a banner,
and in such company? A complete suit of armour
is provided, weapons not to be resisted, and precious balm to heal us if haply we receive a wound,
and precious ointment to revive us when we are
in danger of fainting. Further, we are assured of
the victory beforehand; and, O what a crown is
prepared for every conqueror, which Jesus, the
righteous Judge, the gracious Saviour, shall place
upon every faithful head with his own hand! Then

let us not be weary and faint, for in due season
we shall reap. The time is short; yet a little
while, and the struggle of indwelling sin, and the
contradiction of surrounding sinners, shall be
known no more. You are blessed, because you
hunger and thirst after righteousness; He whose
name is *Amen* has said you shall be filled. To
claim the promise is to make it our own; yet it
is becoming us to practise submission and patience, not in temporals only, but also in spirituals. We should be ashamed and grieved at our
slow progress, so far as it is properly chargeable
to our remissness and miscarriage; yet we must
not expect to receive every thing at once, but
wait for a gradual increase; nor should we forget
to be thankful for what we may account a little,
in comparison of the much we suppose others
have received. A little grace, a spark of true
love to God, a grain of living faith, though small
as mustard-seed, is worth a thousand worlds.
One draught of the water of life gives interest in,
and earnest of, the whole fountain. It becometh
the Lord's people to be thankful; and to acknowledge his goodness in what we have received, is
the surest as well as the pleasantest method of
obtaining more. Nor should the grief, arising
from what we know and feel of our own hearts,
rob us of the honour, comfort, and joy, which
the word of God designs us, in what is there
recorded of the person, offices, and grace of
Jesus, and the relations he is pleased to stand
in to his people: Psal. xxiii. 1; Isa. liv. 5; Cant.
v. 16; John xv. 15; 1 John ii. 1; John xv. 1;
Jer. xxiii. 5; 1 Cor. i. 30; Matt. i. 21—23.
Give me leave to recommend to your consideration Psal. lxxxix. 15—18. These verses may be
called the Believer's Triumph: though they are

nothing in themselves, yet having all in Jesus, they may rejoice in his name all the day. The Lord enable us so to do! The joy of the Lord is the strength of his people: whereas unbelief makes our hands hang down, and our knees feeble, dispirits ourselves, and discourages others; and though it steals upon us under a semblance of humility, it is indeed the very essence of pride. By inward and outward exercises the Lord is promoting the best desire of your heart, and answering your daily prayers. Would you have assurance? The true solid assurance is to be obtained no other way. When young Christians are greatly comforted with the Lord's love and presence, their doubts and fears are for that season at an end. But this is not assurance; so soon as the Lord hides his face they are troubled, and ready to question the very foundation of hope. Assurance grows by repeated conflict, by our repeated experimental proof of the Lord's power and goodness to save; when we have been brought very low and helped, sorely wounded and healed, cast down and raised again, have given up all hope, and been suddenly snatched from danger, and placed in safety; and when these things have been repeated to us and in us a thousand times over, we begin to learn to trust simply to the word and power of God, beyond and against appearances: and this trust, when habitual and strong, bears the name of assurance; for even assurance has degrees.

You have good reason, madam, to suppose, that the love of the best Christians to an unseen Saviour is far short of what it ought to be. If your heart be like mine, and you examine your love to Christ by the warmth and frequency of your emotions towards him, you will often be in a sad suspense whether or no you love him at all. The best mark to judge, and which he has given us for that purpose, is to inquire if his word and will have a prevailing, governing influence upon our lives and temper. If we love him, we do endeavour to keep his commandments: and it will hold the other way; if we have a desire to please him, we undoubtedly love him. Obedience is the best test; and when, amidst all our imperfections, we can humbly appeal concerning the sincerity of our views, this is a mercy for which we ought to be greatly thankful. He that has brought us to will, will likewise enable us to do, according to his good pleasure. I doubt not but the Lord whom you love, and on whom you depend, will lead you in a sure way, and establish and strengthen and settle you in his love and grace. Indeed he has done great things for you already. The Lord is your Shepherd; a comprehensive word. The sheep can do nothing for themselves: the Shepherd must guide, guard, feed, heal, recover. Well for us that our Shepherd is the Lord Almighty. If his power, care, compassion, fulness, were not infinite, the poor sheep would be forsaken, starved, and worried. But we have a Shepherd full of care, full of kindness, full of power, who has said, I will seek that which was lost, and bind up that which was broken, and bring again that which was driven away, and will strengthen that which was sick. How tender are these expressions, and how well fulfilled! His sheep feed in the midst of wolves, yet are preserved safe; for, though they see him not, his eye and his heart are upon them. Do we wonder that Daniel was preserved in the lion's den? Why, it is a common case. Which of God's children have not cause to say, "My soul is among lions?" But the Angel of the Covenant stops their mouths, or only permits them to gape and roar, to shew their teeth, and what they would do if they might; but they may not, they shall not, bite and tear us at their own will. Let us trust him, and all shall be well.

As to daily occurrences, it is best to believe that a daily portion of comforts and crosses, each one the most suitable to our case, is adjusted and appointed by the hand which was once nailed to the cross for us; that where the path of duty and prudence leads, there is the best situation we could possibly be in at that juncture. We are not required to afflict ourselves immoderately for what is not in our power to prevent, nor should any thing that affords occasions for mortifying the spirit of self be accounted unnecessary.

I am, &c.

LETTER III.

1768.

I HAVE been some time hoping to hear from you; but Mr. **** was here last Saturday, and informed me that you were ill, or had been so very lately. This intelligence prompted me to write as soon as I could find leisure. I think the Lord has seen fit to visit you with much indisposition of late; I say *He* has seen fit, for all our trials are under his immediate direction, and we are never in heaviness without a *need-be*. I trust he does and will give you strength equal to your day, and sweeten what would be otherwise bitter with the essence of his precious love. I hope soon to hear that you are restored to health, and that you have found cause to praise him for the rod.

How happy is the state of a believer, to have a sure promise that all shall work together for good in the end, and in the mean time a sure refuge where to find present relief, support, and protection! How comfortable is it, when trouble is near, to know that the Lord is near likewise, and to commit ourselves and all our cares simply to him, believing that his eye is upon us, and his ear open to our prayers. Under the conduct of such a Shepherd we need not fear: though we are called to pass through fire and water, through the valley of the shadow of death, he will be with us, and will shew himself mighty on our behalf. It seems almost needless to say, that we were very happy in the company of **** : the only inconvenience was, that it renewed the pain it always gives me to part with them. Though the visit was full as long as I could possibly expect, it seemed very short. This must be the case while we are here : our pleasures are short, interrupted, and mixed with troubles : this is not, cannot be our rest. But it will not be always the case : we are travelling to a better world, where every evil and imperfection shall cease; then we shall be for ever with the Lord, and with each other. May the prospect of this blessed hope set before us revive our fainting spirits, and make us willing to endure hardships as good soldiers of Jesus Christ! Here we must often sow in tears, but there we shall reap in joy, and all tears shall be wiped from our eyes for ever. I hope the conversation of friends whom I so greatly love and honour afforded me not only pleasure but profit: it left a savour upon my mind, and stirred up my languid desires after the Lord. I wish I could say the good effect has remained with me to this hour; but, alas! I am a poor creature, and have had many causes of humiliation since. But, blessed be God! amidst all my changes I find the foundation stands sure; and I am seldom or never left to doubt either of

the Lord's love to me, or the *reality* of the desires
he has given me towards himself: though when I
measure my love by the degree of its exercise, or
the fruits it produceth, I have reason to sit down
ashamed as the chief of sinners and the least of
all saints. But in Him I have righteousness and
peace, and in Him I must and will rejoice.

I would willingly fill up my sheet, but feel a
straitness in my spirit, and know not what further
to say. O for a ray of Divine light to set me at
liberty, that I might write a few lines worth reading, something that might warm my heart and
comfort *yours!* Then the subject must be Jesus;
but of him what can I say that you do not know?
Well; though you know him, you are glad to hear
of him again and again. Come then, magnify the
Lord with me, and let us exalt his name together.
Let us adore him for his love, that love which has
a height, and depth, and length, and breadth, beyond the grasp of our poor conceptions; a love that
moved him to empty himself, to take on him the
form of a servant, and to be obedient unto death,
even the death of the cross; a love that pitied us
in our lost estate, that found us when we sought
him not, that spoke peace to our souls in the day
of our distress; a love that bears with all our
present weakness, mistakes, backslidings, and
shortcomings; a love that is always watchful,
always ready to guide, to comfort, and to heal; a
love that will not be wearied, cannot be conquered,
and is incapable of changes; a love that will in the
end prevail over all opposition, will perfect that
which concerns us, and will not leave us till it has
brought us perfect in holiness and happiness, to
rejoice in his presence in glory. The love of
Christ: it is the wonder, the joy, the song of
angels; and the sense of it shed abroad in our

hearts makes life pleasant and death welcome. Alas! what a heart have I that I love him no better! But I hope he has given me a desire to make him my all in all, and to account every thing loss and dross that dares to stand in competition with him. I am, &c.

LETTER IV.

1769.

I FOUND this morning among my unanswered letters one from you, but hope I left it among them by mistake. I am willing, however, to be on the sure side, and would rather write twice than be too long silent. I heard of your being laid on the bed of affliction, and of the Lord's goodness to you there, and of his raising you up again. Blessed be his name! he is all-sufficient and faithful; and though he cause grief, he is sure to shew compassion in supporting and delivering. Ah! the evil of our nature is deeply rooted and very powerful, or such repeated, continual corrections and chastisements would not be necessary; and were they not necessary, we should not have them. But such we are, and therefore such must be our treatment; for though the Lord loves us with a tenderness beyond what the mother feels for her sucking child, yet it is a tenderness directed by Infinite Wisdom, and very different from that weak indulgence which in parents we call fondness, which leads them to comply with their children's desires and inclinations, rather than to act with a steady view to their true welfare. The Lord loves his children, and is very indulgent to them so far as they can safely bear it, but he will not spoil them. Their sin-sickness requires medicines, some of which are very unpalatable; but when the case calls for such, no short-sighted entreaties of ours can excuse us from taking what he prepares for our good. But every dose is prepared by his own hand, and not one is administered in vain, nor is it repeated any oftener than is needful to answer the purposed end. Till then, no other hand can remove what he lays upon us; but when his merciful design is answered, he will relieve us himself; and in the mean time he will so moderate the operation, or increase our ability to bear, that we shall not be overpowered. It is true, without a single exception, that all his paths are mercy and truth to them that fear him. His love is the same, when he wounds as when he heals, when he takes away as when he gives : we have reason to thank him for *all*, but *most for the severe*.

I received a letter from you which mentions dear Mrs. ****'s case, a very trying one; but in this likewise we see the Lord's faithfulness. Our own experience, and all that we observe of his dealings with others, may convince us that we need not be afraid to intrust ourselves and our dearest concerns in his hands; for he can and will make every thing work for good.

How little does the world know of that intercourse which is carried on between heaven and earth; what petitions are daily presented, and what answers are received at a Throne of Grace! O the blessed privilege of prayer! O the wonderful love, care, attention, and power of · our great Shepherd! His eye is always upon us; when our spirits are almost overwhelmed within us, he knoweth our path. His ear is always open to us: let who will overlook and disappoint us, he will not. When means and hope fail, when every thing looks dark upon us, when we seem shut up on

every side, when we are brought to the lowest
ebb, still our help is in the name of the Lord who
made heaven and earth.   To him all things are
possible; and before the exertion of his power,
when he is pleased to arise and work, all hindrances
give way and vanish, like a mist before the sun.
And he can so manifest himself to the soul, and
cause his goodness to pass before it, that the hour
of affliction shall be the golden hour of the greatest
consolation.   He is the fountain of life, strength,
grace and comfort, and of his fulness his children
receive according to their occasions : but this is
all hidden from the world; they have no guide in
prosperity, but hurry on as they are instigated by
their blinded passions, and are perpetually mul-
tiplying mischiefs and miseries to themselves;
and in adversity they have no resource, but must
feel all the evil of affliction, without inward support, and without deriving any advantage from it.
We have therefore cause for continual praise.
The Lord has given us to know his name as a
resting-place and a hiding-place, a sun and a
shield. Circumstances and creatures may change;
but he will be an unchangeable friend.   The way
is rough, but he trod it before us, and is now with
us in every step we take; and every step brings
us nearer to our heavenly home.   Our inheritance
is surely reserved for us, and we shall be kept for
it by his power through faith.   Our present
strength is small, and without a fresh supply
would be quickly exhausted; but he has engaged
to renew it from day to day; and he will soon
appear to wipe all tears from our eyes; and then
we shall appear with him in glory.

I am very sorry if our friend Mr. **** appears
to be aiming to reconcile things that are incompatible.   I am indeed afraid that he has been for

some time under a decline; and, as you justly observe, we meet with too many instances to teach us, that they who express the warmest zeal at their first setting out do not always prove the most steady and thriving afterwards; yet I am willing to hope, in this case, that he will revive and flourish again. Sometimes the Lord permits those whom he loves to wander from him for a season; and when his time comes to heal their backslidings, they walk more humbly, thankfully, and fruitfully afterwards, from a sense of his abounding mercy, and the knowledge they have by experience acquired of the deceitfulness and ingratitude of their hearts. I hope and pray it will be so with him. However, these things for the present are grievous; and usually, before the Lord heals such breaches, he makes his people sensible, that it is an evil and bitter thing to forsake him when he led them by the way.

Indeed London is a dangerous and ensnaring place to professors. I account myself happy that my lot is cast at a distance from it. It appears to me like a sea, wherein most are tossed by storms, and many suffer shipwreck. In this retired situation, I seem to stand upon a cliff; and, while I pity those whom I cannot help, I hug myself in the thoughts of being safe upon the shore. Not that we are without our trials here; the evil of our own hearts, and the devices of Satan, cut us out work enough; but we are happily screened from many things which must be either burdensome or hurtful to those who live in the way of them; such as political disputes, winds of doctrine, scandals of false professors, parties for and against particular ministers, and fashionable amusements, in some measure countenanced by the presence of persons in other respects exemplary. In this view, I often think of our dear friend's expression, upon a certain occasion, of the difference between London and country grace. I hold it in a two-fold sense. By London grace, when genuine, I understand grace in a very advanced degree. The favoured few who are kept alive to God, simple-hearted, and spiritually minded (I mean especially in genteel life), in the midst of such snares and temptations, appear to me to be the first-rate Christians of the land : I adore the power of the Lord in them, and compare them to the young men who walked unhurt in the midst of the fire. In another sense, the phrase *London grace* conveys no great idea to me. I think there is no place in the kingdom where a person may set up for a professor upon a smaller stock. If people can abstain from open immoralities, if they will fly to all parts of the town to hear sermons, if they can talk about the doctrines of the Gospel, if they have something to say upon that useless question, Who is the best preacher ? if they can attain to a speaking acquaintance with some of an acknowledged character, then they expect to pass muster. I am afraid there are many who, upon no better evidences than these, deceive both themselves and others for a course of years. Though I feel not in a writing cue to-day, I have almost filled the sheet somehow ; and if a line or a word may be a means of suggesting a seasonable and comfortable thought to you, I have my end. Through mercy, we are all pretty well. My soul is kept alive as it were by miracle. I feel much inward warfare ; the enemy thrusts sore at me, that I may fall ; and I have abundant experience of the evil and deceitfulness of my heart : but the Lord is gracious, and, in the midst of all conflicts, I have a peace springing from the knowledge of his power and grace, and a consideration that I have been helped to commit myself to him.

I am, &c.

LETTER V.

WE are much obliged to you for your late visit; and I am glad to find that the Lord is pleased to give you some tokens of his presence when you are with us, because I hope it will encourage you to come again. I ought to be very thankful that our Christian friends in general are not wholly disappointed of a blessing when they visit us.

I hope the Lord will give me an humble sense of what I am, and that broken and contrite frame of heart in which he delights. This is to me the chief thing. I had rather have more of the mind that was in Christ, more of a meek, quiet, resigned, peaceful, and loving disposition, than to enjoy the greatest measure of sensible comforts, if the consequence should be (as perhaps it would) spiritual pride, self-sufficiency, and a want of that tenderness to others which becomes one who has reason to style himself the chief of sinners. I know indeed that the *proper* tendency of sensible consolations is to humble; but I can see, that, through the depravity of human nature, they have not always that effect. And I have been sometimes disgusted with an apparent want of humility, an air of self-will and self-importance, in persons of whose sincerity I could not at all doubt. It has kept me from envying them those pleasant frames with which they have sometimes been favoured; for I believe Satan is never nearer us than at some times when we think ourselves nearest the Lord.

What reason have we to charge our souls in David's words! " My soul, wait thou *only* upon God." A great stress should be laid upon that word *only*. We dare not entirely shut him out of our regards, but we are too apt to suffer something to share with him. This evil disposition is deeply fixed in our hearts; and the Lord orders all his dispensations towards us with a view to rooting it out; that, being wearied with repeated disappointments, we may at length be compelled to betake ourselves to Him alone. Why else do we experience so many changes and crosses? why are we so often in heaviness? We know that He delights in the pleasure and prosperity of his servants; that He does not willingly afflict or grieve his children: but there is a necessity on our parts, in order to teach us that we have no stability in ourselves, and that no creature can do us good but by His appointment. While the people of Israel depended upon Him for food, they gathered up the manna every morning in the field: but when they would hoard it up in their houses, that they might have a stock within themselves, they had it without his blessing, and it proved good for nothing; it soon bred worms, and grew offensive. We may often observe something like this occurs, both in our temporal and spiritual concerns. The Lord gives us a dear friend to our comfort; but ere long we forget that the friend is only the channel of conveyance, and that all the comfort is from himself. To remind us of this, the stream is dried up, the friend torn away by death, or removed far from us, or perhaps the friendship ceases, and a coolness insensibly takes place, we know not *how* or *why*: the true reason is, that when we rejoiced amiss in our gourd, the

Lord, for our good, sent a worm to the root of it. Instances of this kind are innumerable ; and the great inference from them all is, Cease from man, cease from creatures, for wherein are they to be accounted of? My soul, wait thou *only*, *only* upon the Lord, who is (according to the expressive phrase, Heb. iv. 13.) he with whom we have to do for soul and body, for time and eternity. What thanks do we owe, that though we have not yet attained perfectly this great lesson, yet we are admitted into that school where alone it can be learnt; and though we are poor, slow scholars, the great and effectual Teacher to whom we have been encouraged and enabled to apply, can and will bring us forward? He communicates not only instructions, but capacities and powers. There is none like him; He can make the blind to see, the deaf to hear, and the dumb to speak : and how great is his condescension and patience! how does He accommodate himself to our weakness, and teach us as we are able to bear! Though all are very dunces when He first receives them, not one was ever turned out as *incapable:* for He makes them what He would have them to be. O that we may set Him always before us, and consider every dispensation, person, thing, we meet in the course of every day, as messengers from Him, each bringing us some *line of instruction* for us to copy into that day's experience! Whatever passes within us or around us may be improved (when he teaches us how) as a perpetual commentary upon his good word. If we converse and observe with this view, we may learn something every moment, wherever the path of duty leads us, in the streets as well as in the closet, and from the conversation of those who know not

God (when we cannot avoid being present at it), as well as from those who do.

Separation of dear friends is, as you observed, hard to flesh and blood; but grace can make it tolerable.   I have an abiding persuasion that the Lord can easily give more than ever he will take away.   Which part of the alternative must be my lot, or when, he only knows; but in general I can rely on him to appoint the time, the manner; and I trust his promise of strength suited to the day shall be made good.   Therefore I can for the most part rejoice, that all things are in the hand and under the direction of him who knows our frame, and has himself borne our griefs, and carried our sorrows, in his own body.   A time of weeping must come, but the morning of joy will make amends for all.   Who can expound the meaning of that one expression, " An exceeding, and eternal weight of glory ? "   The case of unconverted friends is still more burdensome to think of ; but we have encouragement and warrant to pray and to hope.   He who called *us* can easily call others: and he seldom lays a desire of this sort very closely and warmly upon the hearts of his people, but when it is his gracious design, sooner or later, to give an answer of peace.   However, it becomes us to be thankful for ourselves, and to bow our anxieties and reasonings before his sovereign will, who doth as he pleases with his own.

Methinks winter is your summer.   You have been, like the bee, collecting from many flowers ; I hope you will carry good store of honey home with you.   May you find the Lord there, and he can easily supply the failure of means and creatures.   We cannot be in any place to so much advantage as where the call of duty leads.   What we cannot avoid may we cheerfully submit to, and not indulge a vain thought that we could choose a better situation for ourselves (all things considered) than he has chosen for us.

When we have opportunity of enjoying many ordinances, it is a mercy to be able to prize and improve them; but when he cuts us short for a season, if we wait upon him, we shall do well without them. Secret prayer, and the good word, are the chief *wells* from whence we draw the water of salvation. These will keep the soul alive when creature-streams are cut off; but the richest variety of public means, and the closest attendance upon them, will leave us lean and pining in the midst of plenty, if we are remiss and formal in the other two. I think David never appears in a more lively frame of mind than when he wrote the 42d, 63d, and 84th Psalms, which were all penned in a dry land, and at a distance from the public ordinances.

I am, &c.

LETTER VI.

1772.

I HAD been wishing to hear from you, that I might know where to write. I hope I can assure you of a friendly sympathy with you in your trials. I can in some measure guess at what you feel, from what I have seen and felt myself in cases where I have been nearly concerned. But my compassion, though sincere, is ineffectual: if I can pity, I cannot relieve. All I can do is, as the Lord enables me, to remember you both before him. But there is one whose compassion is infinite. The love and tenderness of ten thousand earthly friends, of ten thousand mothers towards their sucklings, if compared with his, are less than a drop of water to the ocean ; and his power is infinite too. Why then do our sufferings continue, when he is so compassionate, and could remove them with a word? Surely, if we cannot give the particular reasons (which yet he will acquaint us with hereafter, John xiii. 7), the general reason is at hand : He afflicts not for his own pleasure, but for our profit ; to make us partakers of his holiness, and because he loves us.

> Judge not the Lord by feeble sense,
>   But trust him for his grace :
> Behind a frowning providence
>   He hides a smiling face.

I wish you much comfort from David's thought, Psal. cxlii. 3 : " When my spirit was overwhelmed within me, thou knewest my path." The Lord is not withdrawn to a great distance, but his eye is upon you, and he sees you not with the indifference of a mere spectator ; but he observes with attention, he knows, he considers your path : yea, he appoints it, and every circumstance about it is under his direction. Your trouble began at the hour he saw best : it could not come before, and he has marked the degree of it to a hair's breadth, and the duration to a minute. He knows likewise how your spirit is affected ; and such supplies of grace and strength, and in such seasons as he sees needful, he will afford. So that when things appear darkest, you shall still be able to say, Though chastened, not killed. Therefore, hope in God, for you shall yet praise him.

I shall pray that the Bath waters may be beneficial ; and that the waters of the sanctuary there may be healing and enlivening to you all. Our all-sufficient God can give seasons of refreshment in the darkest hours, and break through the thickest clouds of outward affliction or distress. To you it is given not only to believe in Jesus, but to suffer for his sake : for so we do, not only when we are called to follow him to imprisonment or death, but when he enables us to bear afflictive dispensations with due submission and patience. Then he is glorified : then his grace and power are manifested in us. The world, so far as they know our case, have a proof before them that our religion is not merely notional, but that there is a power and reality in it. And the Lord's people are encouraged by what they see of his faithfulness to ourselves. And there are more eyes upon us still. We are a spectacle to the universe, to angels as well as to men. Cheer up : the Lord has put you in your present trying situation, that you may have the fairer opportunity of adorning your profession of the Gospel; and though you suffer much, he is able to make you abundant amends. Nor need I remind you that he has suffered unspeakably more for you : he drank for your sake a cup of unmixed wrath, and only puts into your hand a cup of affliction mixed with many mercies.

The account you gave of the poor man detained in the inn was very affecting. Such scenes are or should be instructive, to teach us resignation under the trials we must meet with every day. For not only are we visited less than our iniquities have deserved, but much less than many of our fellow-creatures daily meet with. We need not look about far or long to find others in a worse situation than ourselves. If a fit of the gout or cholic is so grievous and so hard to bear, what do we owe to him who delivered us from that place of unutterable torment, where there is weeping, wailing, and gnashing of teeth for ever, without hope or respite? And if we cannot help interesting ourselves in the groans of a stranger, how ought the groans of Jesus to be as it were continually sounding in our ears? What are all other sufferings compared to his? And yet he endured them freely. He needed not to have borne them, if he would have left us to perish; but such was his love, he died that we might live, and endured the fiercest agonies that he might open to us the gate of everlasting peace and happiness. How amazingly perverse is my heart, that I can be more affected with a melancholy story in a newspaper concerning persons I never saw, than with all that I read of his bitter passion in the garden and on the cross, though I profess to believe he endured it all for me! Oh, if we could always behold him by faith as evidently crucified before our eyes, how would it compose our spirits as to all the sweets and bitters of this poor life! What a banner would it prove against all the snares and temptations whereby Satan would draw us into evil; and what a firm ground of confidence would it afford us amidst the conflicts we sustain from the working of unbelief and indwelling sin! I long for more of that faith which is the substance of things hoped for, and the evidence of things not seen, that I may be preserved humble, thankful, watchful, and dependent. To behold the glory and the love of Jesus is the only effectual way to participate of his image.

We are to set out to-night from the Interpreter's house towards the hill *Difficulty*, and hope to be favoured with a sight of the cross by the way. To stand at the foot of it with a softened heart and melting eyes; to forget our sins, sorrows, and burdens, while we are wholly swallowed up in the contemplation of Him who bore our sins in his own body upon the tree, is certainly the most desirable situation on this side the grave. To speak of it, and to see it by the light of the Spirit, are widely different things : and though we cannot always enjoy this view, yet the remembrance of what we have seen is an excellent means of encouragement to mount the hill, and to face the lions.

I believe I shall hardly find leisure to fill my paper this time. It is now Saturday evening, and growing late. I am just returned from a serious walk, which is my usual manner of closing the week when the weather is fine. I endeavour to join in heart with the Lord's ministers and people, who are seeking a blessing on to-morrow's ordinances. At such times I especially remember those friends with whom I have gone to the house of the Lord in company, consequently you are not forgot. I can venture to assure you, that if you have a value for our prayers, you have a frequent share in them, yea, are loved and remembered by many here; but as we are forgetful creatures, I hope you will always refresh our memory, and quicken our prayers, by a yearly visit. In the morning I shall think of you again. What a multitude of eyes and hearts will be directed to our Redeemer to-morrow! He has a numerous and necessitous family; but he is rich enough to supply them all, and his tender compassions extend to the meanest and most unworthy. Like the sun, he can cheer and enlighten thousands and millions at once, and give to each as bountifully as if there were no more to partake of his favour. His best blessings are not diminished by being shared among many. The greatest earthly monarch would soon be poor if he was to give a little (though but a little) to all his subjects; but Jesus has unsearchable, inexhaustible riches of grace to bestow. The innumerable assembly before the Throne have been all supplied from his fulness; and yet there is enough and to spare for us also, and for all that shall come after us. May he give us an eager appetite, a hunger and thirst that will not be put off with any thing short of the bread of life; and then we may confidently open our mouths wide, for he has promised to fill them.

I am, &c.

LETTER VII.

1773.

SINCE I wrote last, the Lord has been gracious to us here. He crowned the last year with his goodness, and renews his benefits to us every day. He has been pleased to bless the preaching of his Gospel amongst us, both to consolation and conviction; and several are, I hope, earnestly seeking him, who were lately dead in trespasses and sins. Dear Mr. **** was released from all his complaints the 25th of November. A few days before his death he was enabled to speak more intelligibly than usual for about a quarter of an hour, and expressed a comfortable hope, which was a great satisfaction to us; for though we had not the least doubt of his being built upon the Rock, it was to us an answer to prayer that he could again speak the language of faith; and much prayer had been made on this account, especially that very evening. After that night he spoke little, and hardly took any notice, but continued chiefly drowsy till he died. I preached his funeral sermon from Lam. iii. 31—33. Mrs. L****'s complaint grows worse and worse: she

suffers much in her body, and has much more
perhaps to suffer; but her consolations in the
Lord abound. He enables her to maintain faith,
patience, and submission, in an exemplary manner; and shews us, in his dealings with her, that
he is all-sufficient and faithful to those who put
their trust in him.—I am glad to hear that you
had comfortable seasons while at Bath. It is
indeed a great mercy that God's ordinances are
established in that place of dissipation; and I hope
many who go there with no higher view than to
drink the Bath waters, will be brought to draw
with joy the waters of life from those wells of salvation. He does nothing in vain; and when he
affords the means, we may confidently hope he
will bestow the blessing. The dissipation of
spirit you complain of, when you are in a strange
place, is, I suppose, felt by most, if not by all, who
can be satisfied in no place without some token of
the Lord's presence. I consider it rather as an
infirmity than a sin, strictly speaking; though all
our infirmities are sinful, being the effects of a
depraved nature. In our present circumstances
new things excite new ideas, and when our usual
course of life is broken in upon, it disjoints and
unsettles our thoughts. It is a proof of our weakness: it may and ought to be lamented; but I
believe we shall not get the better of it, till we
leave the mortal body to moulder into dust.
Perhaps few suffer more inconvenience from this
article than myself; which is one reason why I
love home, and seldom leave it without some reluctance: and it is one reason why we should love
heaven, and long for the hour when, at liberty
from all encumbrance, we shall see the Lord without a vail, and serve him without distraction. The
Lord, by his providence, seconds and confirms the

declarations of his word and ministry.   Much we
read and much we hear concerning the emptiness,
vanity, and uncertainty of the present state.
When our minds are enlightened by his Holy
Spirit, we receive and acknowledge what his
word declares to be truth : yet if we remain long
without changes, and our path is very smooth,
we are for the most part but faintly affected with
what we profess to believe.   But when some of
our dearest friends are taken from us, the lives of
others threatened, and we ourselves are brought
low with pain and sickness, then we not only *say*
but *feel* that this must not, cannot be our rest.
You have had several exercises of this kind of late
in your family ; and I trust you will be able to set
your seal to that gracious word, That though afflictions in themselves are not joyous, but grievous,
yet in due season they yield the peaceful fruits of
righteousness.   Various and blessed are the fruits
they produce.   By affliction prayer is quickened,
for our prayers are very apt to grow languid and
formal in a time of ease.   Affliction greatly helps
us to understand the Scriptures, especially the
promises ; most of which being made to times of
trouble, we cannot so well know their fulness,
sweetness, and certainty, as when we have been
in the situation to which they are suited, have
been enabled to trust and plead them, and found
them fulfilled in our own case.   We are usually
indebted to affliction as the means or occasion of
the most signal discoveries we are favoured with
of the wisdom, power, and faithfulness of the Lord.
These are best observed by the evident proofs we
have that he is near to support us under trouble,
and that he can and does deliver us out of it.
Israel would not have seen so much of the
Lord's arm outstretched in their behalf, had not

Pharoah oppressed, opposed, and pursued them. Afflictions are designed likewise for the manifestation of our sincerity to ourselves and to others. When faith endures the fire, we know it to be of the right kind ; and others, who see we are brought safe out, and lose nothing but the dross, will confess that God is with us of a truth; Dan. iii. 27, 28. Surely this thought should reconcile us to suffer, not only with patience but with cheerfulness, if God may be glorified in us. This made the Apostle rejoice in tribulation, that the power of Christ might be noticed, as resting upon him, and working mightily in him. Many of our graces likewise cannot thrive or shew themselves to advantage without trials ; such as resignation, patience, meekness, long-suffering. I observe some of the London porters do not appear to be very strong men; yet they will trudge along under a burden which some stouter people could not carry so well: the reason is, that they are accustomed to carry burdens, and by continual exercise their shoulders acquire a strength suited to their work. It is so in the Christian life : activity and strength of grace is not ordinarily acquired by those who sit still and live at ease, but by those who frequently meet with something which requires a full exertion of what power the Lord has given them. So again, it is by our own sufferings we learn to pity and sympathize with others in their sufferings : such a compassionate disposition, which excites our feelings for the afflicted, is an eminent branch of the mind which was in Christ. But these feelings would be very faint, if we did not in our experience know what sorrows and temptations mean. Afflictions do us good likewise, as they make us more acquainted with what is in our own hearts, and thereby promote humiliation and self-abasement. There are abominations which, like nests of vipers, lie so quietly within, that we hardly suspect they are there till the rod of affliction rouses them: then they hiss and shew their venom. This discovery is indeed very distressing; yet, till it is made, we are prone to think ourselves much less vile than we really are, and cannot so heartily abhor ourselves and repent in dust and ashes.

But I must write a sermon rather than a letter, if I would enumerate all the good fruits which, by the power of sanctifying grace, are produced from this bitter tree. May we, under our several trials, find them all revealed in ourselves, that we may not complain of having suffered in vain. While we have such a depraved nature, and live in such a polluted world; while the roots of pride, vanity, self-dependence, self-seeking, are so strong within us; we need a variety of sharp dispensations to keep us from forgetting ourselves, and from cleaving to the dust.

I am, &c.

LETTER VIII.

1774.

THE very painful illness which Mrs. **** so long endured) had doubtless not only prepared you to expect the news of her dismission, but made you more willing to resign her. You are bereaved of a valuable friend : but life in her circumstances was burdensome; and who can be sorry to consider her now as freed from all suffering, and possessed of all happiness? But, besides this, I trust the Lord has favoured you with an habitual sense of the wisdom and propriety of all his appointments; so that when his will is manifested

by the event, you are enabled to say, " All is
well." " I was dumb, and opened not my mouth,
because thou didst it." She is gone a little before
you; and, after a few more changes, you will
meet her again to unspeakable advantage, and
rejoice together before the Throne for ever. There
every tear will be wiped away, and you shall
weep no more. The Lord could have prevented
the cause of her great sufferings; but I doubt not
he afflicted her in wisdom and mercy : he could
easily have restored her to health; but the time
was hastening when he purposed to have her with
him where he is, that she might behold his glory,
and have all the desires he put into her heart
abundantly satisfied. Precious in his sight is the
death of his saints, and every circumstance under
the direction of Infinite Wisdom. His sovereignty
forbids us to say, Why hast thou done this ? And
his love assures us that he does all things well.
I have lost a friend likewise : I believe I may say
few persons, not immediately related to her, could
value her more highly than myself; and though
of late years I could not have the pleasure of her
company, it was a constant satisfaction to me to
know I had such a friend.

Mr. T****'s sickness and death followed immediately upon this stroke. I doubt not but you
have been much affected with this dispensation
likewise. But here again we have the same
strong hold to retreat to : The Lord has done it.
What a pleasing prospect of increasing usefulness
is now interrupted ! How many will mourn his
loss ! Yet we are sure the work which the Lord
had appointed him was finished. They who
loved his ministry, and were profited by it, are
left apparently destitute; but Jesus, the good
Shepherd, is able to take care of his own, and will

fulfil his promise to them all. He has said, Verily they shall be fed.

We have had trying and dying times here : half my time almost has been taken up with visiting the sick. I have seen death in a variety of forms, and have had frequent occasion of observing how insignificant many things, which are now capable of giving us pain or pleasure, will appear, when the soul is brought near to the borders of eternity. All the concerns which relate solely to this life, will then be found as trivial as the traces of a dream from which we are awakened. Nothimg will then comfort us but the knowledge of Jesus and his love; nothing grieve us but the remembrance of our unfaithful carriage to him, and what poor returns we made to his abundant goodness. The Lord forbid that this thought should break our peace! No; faith in his name may forbid our fear, though we shall see and confess we have been unprofitable servants. There shall be no condemnation to them that are in him: but surely shame and humiliation will accompany us to the very threshold of heaven, and ought to do so. I surely shall then be more affected than I am now with the coolness of my love, the faintness of my zeal, the vanity of my heart, and my undue attachment to the things of time. O these clogs, fetters, vales, and mountains, which obstruct my course, darken my views, slacken my pace, and disable me in service! Well it is for me that I am not under the law, but under grace.

To-morrow is the Sabbath. I am usually glad when it returns, though it seldom finds me in that frame of mine which I would desire. But it is my happiness to live amongst many who count the hours from one ordinance to another. I know they pray that I may be a messenger of peace,

and an instrument of good to their souls; and I
have cause to hope their prayers are in a measure
answered. For their sakes, as much as my own,
I am glad to go up to the house of the Lord. O
that in watering others I may be also watered
myself! I have been praying that to-morrow may
be a day of power with you and with us, and with
all that love Jesus in sincerity; that we may see
his glory, and taste his love in the sanctuary!
When it is thus, the Sabbath is a blessed day indeed, an earnest of heaven. There they keep an
everlasting sabbath, and cease not night or day
admiring the riches of redeeming love, and adoring
Him who washed his people from their sins in his
own blood. To have such imperfect communion
with them as is in this state attainable in this
pleasing exercise, is what alone can make life
worth the name. For this I sigh and long, and
cry to the Lord to rend the vail of unbelief, scatter
the clouds of ignorance, and break down the walls
which sin is daily building up to hide him from my
eyes. I hope I can say, My soul is athirst for
God, and nothing less than the light of his countenance can satisfy me. Blessed be his Name for
the desire: it is his own gift, and he never gives
it in vain. He will afford us a taste of the water
of life by the way; and ere long we shall drink
abundantly at the fountain-head, and have done
with complaint for ever. May we be thankful for
what we receive, and still earnestly desirous of
more.

I am, &c.

FIVE LETTERS

TO

MISS D****.

LETTER I.

My dear Miss,   August — 1772.

THE Lord brought us home in peace.   My visit to **** was agreeable, and I shall often think of it with pleasure ; though the deadness and dryness of my own spirit, a good part of the time I was there, proved a considerable abatement.   I am eager enough to converse with the Lord's people, when at the same time I am backward and indisposed to communion with the Lord himself.   The two evils charged upon Israel of old, a proneness to forsake the fountain of living waters, and to trust to broken cisterns (which can do me no good unless he supplies them), run through the whole of my experience abroad and at home.   A few drops of grace in my fellow-worms endear them to me exceedingly.   If I expect to see any Christian friends, I count the hours till we meet : I promise myself great benefit ; but if the Lord withdraws his influence, the best of them prove to me but clouds without water.   It was not, however, wholly so with me all the time I staid with my friends ; but I suffer much in learning to depend upon the Lord alone : I have been at this lesson many a long year ; but am so poor and dull a scholar, that I have not yet made any tolerable progress in it.   I think I received some instruction and advantage where I little expected it : I

mean, at **Mr. Cox's** Museum. The efforts of his
ingenuity amazed me, while at the same time
I was struck with their insignificance. His fine
things were curious beyond all I had any idea of;
and yet what are they better than toys and amusements, suited to the taste of children!   And notwithstanding the variety of their motions, they
were all destitute of life.   There is unspeakably
more wisdom and contrivance in the mechanism
of a butterfly or a bee, that flies unnoticed in the
fields, than in all his apparatus put together. But
the works of God are disregarded, while the
feeble imitations of them which men can produce
gain universal applause.

If you and I could make self-moving dragons
and elephants, what would it profit us?   Blessed
be God, that he has given us some glimpses of his
wisdom and love ! by which our hearts, more hard
and lifeless by nature than the stones in the street,
are constrained and enabled to move upwards,
and to seek after the Lord.   He has given us in
his word a greater treasure than all that we ever
beheld with our eyes, and a hope which shall flourish when the earth and all its works shall be
burnt up.   What will all the fine things of men's
device be worth in that day ?

I think the passage you refer to in Mr. ****
justly exceptionable.   His intention is good, and
the mistake he would censure very dangerous ;
but he might have explained himself more clearly.
I apprehend he and you do not mean the same
thing by being in the dark.   It is not an uncomfortable, but a careless, frame which he would
censure.   They who walk in darkness and see no
light, and yet are exhorted to stay themselves
upon God, Isa. l. 10, are said to hearken to the
voice of his servant.   Though they cannot see the

Lord, they are seeking and mourning after him, and waiting in the use of means, and warring against sin.   Mr. **** had another set of people in view, who trust in the notions of Gospel truth, or some past convictions and comforts; though at present they give no evidence of spiritual desires, but are worldly in their spirit and conversation; talk of trusting in the Lord; account it a weakness to doubt of their state, and think all is well, because they profess to believe the doctrines of grace.   In a word, it is the darkness of sin and sloth, not the occasional darkness of an exercised soul, against which his observation is pointed. Or if, indeed, he meant more than this, we are not obliged to believe him.   Remember your privilege; you have the Bible in your hands, and are not bound to follow books or preachers any farther than what they deliver agrees with the Oracles of Truth.   We have great reason to be thankful for the instructions and writings of spiritual men, but they are all fallible even as ourselves.   One is our master, even Christ: what he says, we are to receive implicitly; but we do not owe implicit subjection to the best of our fellow-creatures.   The Bereans were commended that they would not take even the Apostle Paul upon trust, but searched the Scriptures to see whether these things were so.   May the Lord give us a spirit of humility and discernment in all things.

I am, &c.

LETTER II.

May 4, 1773.

METHINKS it is high time to ask you how you do, to thank you for your last letter, and to let you know, that though necessity makes me slack in writing, yet I can and do often think of you My silence has been sometimes owing to want of leisure ; and sometimes when I could have found leisure, my harp has been out of tune, and I had no heart to write. Perhaps you are ready to infer, by my sitting down to write at last, that my harp is now well tuned, and I have something extraordinary to offer: beware of thinking so, lest you should be sadly disappointed. Should I make myself the subject, I could give you at present but a mournful ditty. I suppose you have heard I have been ill : through mercy, I am now well. But indeed I must farther tell you, that when I was sick I was well; and since the Lord has removed my illness, I have been much worse. My illness was far from violent in itself, and was greatly sweetened by a calm submissive frame the Lord gave me under it. My heart seemed more alive to him then than it has done since my cough, fever, and deafness have been removed. Shall I give you another bit of a riddle ; that, notwithstanding the many changes I pass through, I am always the same? This is the very truth : " In me, that is, in my flesh, dwelleth no good thing ;" so that if sometimes my spirit is in a measure humble, lively, and dependent, it is not I am grown better than I was, but the Lord is pleased to put forth his gracious power in my weakness ; and when my heart is dry and stupid, when I can find no pleasure in waiting upon God, it is not because I am worse than I was before, but only the Lord sees it best that I should feel, as well as say, what a poor creature I am. My heart was once like a dungeon, out of the reach of day, and always dark : the Lord by his grace has been pleased to make this dungeon a room, by putting windows in it; but I need not tell you,

that though windows will transmit the daylight
into a room, they cannot supply the want of it.
When the day is gone, windows are of little use :
when the day returns, the room is enlightened by
them again. Thus, unless the Lord shines, I
cannot retain to-day the light I had yesterday ;
and though his presence makes a delightful difference, I have no more to boast of in myself at one
time than another ; yet when it is dark, I am
warranted to expect the return of light again.
When he is with me, all goes on pleasantly : when
he withdraws, I find I can do nothing without him.
I need not wonder that I find it so ; for it must be
so of course, if I am what I confess myself to be,
a poor, helpless, sinful creature in myself. Nor
need I be over-much discouraged, since the Lord
has promised to help those who can do nothing
without him, not those who can make a tolerable
shift to help themselves. Through mercy, he does
not so totally withdraw, as to leave me without
any power or will to cry for his return. I hope
he maintains in me at all times a desire of his presence ; yet it becomes me to wait for him with
patience, and to live upon his faithfulness, when I
can feel nothing but evil in myself.

In your letter, after having complained of your
inability, you say you converse with many who
find it otherwise, who can go whenever they will
to the Father of mercies with a child-like confidence, and never return without an answer—an
answer of peace. If they only mean that they are
favoured with an established faith, and can see
that the Lord is always the same, and that their
right to the blessings of the covenant is not at all
affected by their unworthiness, I wish you and I
had more experience of the same privilege. In
general, the Lord helps me to aim at it, though I

find it sometimes difficult to hold fast my confidence. But if they speak absolutely with respect to their frames, that they not only have something to support them under their changes, but meet with no changes that require such support, I must say it is well that they do not live here; if they did, they would not know how to pity us, and we should not know how to understand them. We have an enemy at **** that fights against our peace, and I know not one amongst us but often groans under the warfare. I advise you not to be troubled by what you hear of other folk's experience, but keep close to the written word, where you will meet with much to encourage you, though you often feel yourself weary and heavy laden. For my own part, I like that path best which is well beaten by the footsteps of the flock, though it is not always pleasant and strewed with flowers. In *our* way we find some hills, from whence we can cheerfully look about us; but we meet with deep valleys likewise, and seldom travel long upon even ground.

I am, &c.

LETTER III.

1775.

I am satisfied with your answer to my question: we are not proper judges of each other's circumstances; and I am in some measure weaned from judging hastily, that what would not be convenient for me must therefore necessarily be wrong for another. However, my solicitude for your welfare made me venture to drop a hint, as I was persuaded you would take it in good part. Indeed all situations and circumstances (supposing them not sinful in themselves, and that we are lawfully placed in them) are nearly alike. In London, *I* am in a crowd; in the country, I am sure there is a crowd to *me*. To what purpose do I boast of retirement, when I am pestered by a legion in every place? How often, when I am what I call alone, may my mind be compared to a puppet-show, a fair, a Newgate, or any of those scenes where folly, noise, and wickedness most abound? On the contrary, sometimes I have enjoyed sweet recollection and composure where I could have hardly expected it. But still, though the power be all of the Lord, and we of ourselves can do nothing, it is both our duty and our wisdom to be attentive to the use of appointed means on the one hand, and, on the other, watchful against those things which we find by experience have a tendency to damp our fervour, or to dissipate our spirits. A comfortable intimacy with a fellow-worm cannot be maintained without a certain delicacy and circumspection, a studiousness in improving opportunities of pleasing, and in avoiding what is known to be offensive. For though love will make large allowances for involuntary mistakes, it cannot easily brook a slight. We act thus as it were by instinct towards those whom we dearly love, and to whom we feel ourselves greatly obliged :. and happy are they who are most influenced by this sentiment in their walk before the Lord. But, alas! here we are chargeable with such inconsistencies as we should be greatly ashamed of in common life. And well it is for us that the Lord's thoughts and ways are above ours, and that he is infinite in mercy as well as in power; for surely our dearest friends would have been weary of us, and have renounced us long ago, had we behaved to them as we have too

often done to him. He is God and not man, and
therefore he still waits to be gracious, though we
have too often trifled with him. Surely we may
well say with the prophet, " Who is a God like
unto thee, that pardoneth iniquity! " His tenderness and forbearance towards his own people
(whose sins, being committed against love, and
light, and experience, are more aggravated than
others) is astonishing indeed. But, oh! may the
times past suffice to have grieved his Spirit; and
may we be enabled from henceforth to serve him
with a single eye and a simple heart, to be faithful
to every intimation of his will, and to make him
our All in all!

Mr. **** has been here, and I have been with
him at **** since his return. We seem glad to be
together when we can. When I am with him, I
feel quite at home and at ease, and can tell him (so
far as I dare tell a creature) all that is in my heart;
a plain proof, that union of spirit depends no more
upon an exact uniformity of sentiment, than on a
uniformity of prayers: for in some points of doctrine we differ considerably ; but I trust I agree
with him in the views I have of the excellency,
suitableness, and sufficiency of the Saviour, and
of his right to reign without a rival in the hearts
of his redeemed people. An experimental knowledge of Jesus, as the deliverer from *sin* and *wrath*,
and the author of eternal life and salvation to all
who are enabled to believe, is a sufficient ground
for union of heart: in this point, all who are
taught of God are of one mind. But an eager
fighting for or against those points which are
usually made the subjects of controversy, tends
to nourish pride and evil tempers in ourselves, and
to alienate our hearts from those we hope to spend

an eternity with.   In heaven we shall neither be Dissenters, Moravians, nor Methodists; neither Calvinists nor Arminians; but followers of the Lamb, and children of the kingdom.   There we shall hear the voice of war no more.

We are still favoured with health and many temporal blessings.   My spiritual walk is not so smooth as my outward path: in public, I am mercifully supported; in secret, I most sensibly feel my own vileness and weakness: but through all the Lord is gracious.

I am, &c.

LETTER IV.

January 10, 1775.

THERE is hardly any thing in which the Lord permits me to meet with more disappointment, than in the advantage I am ready to promise myself from creature-converse.   When I expect to meet any of my Christian friends, my thoughts usually travel much faster than my body: I anticipate the hour of meeting, and my imagination is warmed with expectation of what I shall say, and what I shall hear; and sometimes I have had seasons for which I ought to be more thankful than I am.   It is pleasant indeed when the Lord favours us with a happy hour, and is pleased to cause our hearts to burn within us while we are speaking of his goodness.   But often it is far otherwise with me. I carry with me a dissipation of spirit, and find that I can neither impart nor receive.   Something from within or from without crosses my schemes, and when I retire I seem to have gained nothing but a fresh conviction, that we can neither help nor be helped, unless the Lord himself is pleased to help us. With his presence in our hearts, we might be comfortable and happy if shut up in one of the cells of Newgate : without it, the most select company, the most desirable opportunities, prove but clouds without water.

I have sometimes thought of asking you, whether you find that difference between being abroad and at home that I do ? But I take it for granted that you do not ; your connections and intimacies are, I believe, chiefly with those who are highly favoured of the Lord, and if you can break through or be upon your guard against the inconveniences which attend frequent changes and much company, you must be very happy in them. But I believe, considering my weakness, the Lord has chosen wisely and well for me, in placing me in a state of retirement, and not putting it in my power, were it ever so much my inclination, to be often abroad. As I stir so seldom, I believe when I do it is not, upon the whole, to my disadvantage ; for I meet with more or less upon which my reflections afterwards may, by his blessing, be useful to me, though at the time my visits most frequently convince me how little wisdom or skill I have in improving time and opportunities. But were I to live in London, I know not what might be the consequence. Indeed I need not puzzle myself about it, as my call does not lie there ; but I pity and pray for those who do live there ; and I admire such of them as, in those circumstances which appear so formidable to me, are enabled to walk simply, humbly, and closely with the Lord. They remind me of Daniel, unhurt in the midst of lions, or of the bush which Moses saw, surrounded with flames, yet not consumed, because the Lord was there. Some such I do know, and I hope you are one of the number.

This is certain, that if the light of God's countenance, and communion with him in love, afford
the greatest happiness we are capable of, then
whatever tends to indispose us for this pursuit, or
to draw a vail between him and our souls, must
be our great loss.   If we walk with him, it must
be in the path of duty, which lies plain before us
when our eye is single, and we are waiting with
attention upon his word, Spirit, and providence.
Now, wherever the path of duty leads we are safe;
and it often does lead and place us in such circumstances as no other consideration would make us
choose.   We were not designed to be mere re-
cluses, but have all a part to act in life.   Now, if
I find myself in the midst of things disagreeable
enough in themselves to the spiritual life; yet if,
when the question occurs, What dost thou here?
my heart can answer, I am here by the will of
God; I believe it to be, all things considered, my
duty to be here at this time, rather than elsewhere. If, I say, I am tolerably satisfied of this,
then I would not burden and grieve myself about
what I cannot avoid or alter, but endeavour to
take all such things up with cheerfulness, as a
part of my daily cross; since I am called, not
only to do the will of God, but to suffer it: but if
I am doing my own will rather than his, then I
have reason to fear, lest I should meet with either
a snare or a sting at every step.   May the Lord
Jesus be with you!

I am, &c.

LETTER V.

Dear Madam,   April 13, 1776.

I AM rather of the latest to present my congra-
tulation to you and Mr. **** on your marriage, but
I have not been unmindful of you. My heart has
repeatedly wished you all that my pen can express,
that the new relation in which the providence of
God has placed you may be blessed to you in
every respect, may afford you much temporal
comfort, promote your spiritual progress, and enlarge your sphere of usefulness in the world and
in the church.

By this time I suppose visits and ceremonies
are pretty well over, and you are beginning to be
settled in your new situation. What an important
period is a wedding-day! What an entire change
of circumstances does it produce! What an influence it has upon every day of future life! How
many cares, inquietudes, and trials, does it expose
us to, which we might otherwise have avoided!
But they who love the Lord, and are guided by
his word and providence, have nothing to fear;
for in every state, relation, and circumstance in
life, he will be with them, and will surely do
them good. His grace, which is needful in a
single, is sufficient for a married, life. I sincerely
wish Mr. **** and you much happiness together;
that you may be mutually helps meet, and assist
each other in walking as fellow-heirs of the hope
of eternal life. Your cares and trials I know must
be increased; may your comforts be increased
proportionally! They will be so, if you are enabled heartily and simply to entreat the Lord to
keep your heart fixed near to himself. All the
temporal blessings and accommodations he pro-

vides to sweeten life, and make our passage
through this wilderness more agreeable, will fail
and disappoint us, and produce us more thorns
than roses, unless we can keep sight of his hand
in bestowing them, and hold and use the gifts in
some due subserviency to what we owe to the
Giver. But, alas! we are poor creatures, prone
to wander, prone to admire our gourds, cleave to
our cisterns, and think of building tabernacles,
and taking our rest in this polluted world. Hence
the Lord often sees it necessary, in mercy to his
children, to embitter their sweets, to break their
cisterns, send a worm to their gourds, and draw a
dark cloud over their pleasing prospects. His word
tells us, that all here is vanity, compared with
the light of his countenance; and if we cannot or
will not believe it upon the authority of his word,
we must learn it by experience. May he enable
you to settle it in your hearts, that creature-
comforts are precarious, insufficient, and insnaring;
that all good comes from his hand, and that
nothing can do *us* good, but so far as he is pleased
to make it the instrument of communicating, as
a stream, that goodness which is in him as a
fountain. Even the bread which we eat, without
the influence of his promise and blessing, would
no more support us than a stone; but his blessing
makes every thing good, gives a tenfold value to
our comforts, and greatly diminishes the weight
of every cross.

The ring upon your finger is of some value as
gold; but this is not much: what makes it chiefly
valuable to you is, that you consider it as a pledge
and token of the relation you bear to him who
gave it you. I know no fitter emblem of the light
in which we should consider all those good things

which the Lord gives us richly to enjoy. When every thing we receive from him is received and prizèd as a fruit and pledge of his covenant-love, then his bounties, instead of being set up as rivals, and idols to draw our hearts from him, awaken us to fresh exercises of gratitude, and furnish us with fresh motives of cheerful obedience every hour.

Time is short, and we live in a dark and cloudy day. When iniquity abounds, the love of many waxes cold; and we have reason to fear the Lord's hand is lifted up in displeasure at our provocations. May he help us to set loose all below, and to be found watching unto prayer for grace to keep our garments undefiled, and to be faithful witnesses for him in our places! O! it is my desire for myself and for all my dear friends, that whilst too many seem content with half profession, a name to live, an outward attachment to ordinances and sentiments and parties, we may be ambitious to experience what the glorious Gospel is capable of effecting, both as to sanctification and consolation, in this state of infirmity; that we may have our loins girded up, our lamps burning, and, by our simplicity and spirituality, constrain those who know us to acknowledge that we have been with Jesus, have sat at his feet, and drank of his spirit.

I am, &c.

THREE LETTERS

MRS. H****.

LETTER I.

LONG and often I have thought of writing to you: now the time is come. May the Lord help me to send a word in season! I know not how it may be with you, but *he* does; and to him I look to direct my thoughts accordingly. I suppose you are still in the school of the cross, learning the happy art of extracting *real* good out of *seeming* evil, and to grow tall by stooping. The *flesh* is a sad unto-ward dunce in this school: but grace makes the spirit willing to learn by suffering; yea, it cares not what it endures, so sin may be mortified, and a conformity to the image of Jesus be increased. Surely when we see the most and the best of the Lord's children so often in heaviness, and when we consider how much he loves them, and what he has done and prepared for them, we may take it for granted that there is a need-be for their suf-ferings. For it would be easy to his power, and not a thousandth part of what his love intends to do for them, should he make their whole life here, from the hour of their conversion to their death, a continued course of satisfaction and comfort, without any thing to distress them from within or without. But were it so, should we not miss many advantages? In the first place, we should

not then be very conformable to our Head, nor be
able to say, As he was, so are we in this world.
Methinks a believer would be ashamed to be so
utterly unlike his Lord. What! the Master *always*
a man of sorrow and acquainted with grief, and
the servant *always* happy and full of comfort!
Jesus despised, reproached, neglected, opposed,
and betrayed; and his people admired and ca-
ressed: *he* living in the want of all things, and
they filled with abundance: *he* sweating blood for
anguish, and *they* strangers to distress: how un-
suitable would these things be! How much better
to be called to the honour of filling up the measure
of his sufferings! A cup was put into his hand on
our account, and his love engaged him to drink it
for us. The wrath which it contained he drank
wholly himself; but he left us a little affliction to
taste, that we might pledge him and remember
how he loved us, and how much more he endured
for us than he will ever call us to endure for him.
Again, how could we without sufferings manifest
the nature and truth of Gospel-grace? What place
should we then have for patience, submission,
meekness, forbearance, and a readiness to forgive,
if we had nothing to try us either from the hand
of the Lord or from the hand of men. A Christian
without trials would be like a mill without wind
or water: the contrivance and design of the wheel-
work within-side would be unnoticed and unknown, without something to put it in motion
from without. Nor would our graces grow, unless
they were called out to exercise: the difficulties
we meet with not only prove but strengthen the
graces of the Spirit. If a person was always to
sit still, without making use of legs or arms, he
would probably wholly lose the power of moving
his limbs at last; but by walking and working he

becomes strong and active.   So, in a long course
of ease, the powers of the new man would certainly languish; the soul would grow soft, indolent, cowardly, and faint; and therefore the Lord
appoints his children such dispensations as make
them strive, and struggle, and pant : they must
press through a crowd, swim against a stream,
endure hardships, run, wrestle, and fight; and
thus their strength grows in the using.

By these things likewise they are made more
willing to leave the present world, to which we
are prone to cleave too closely in our hearts when
our path is very smooth.   Had Israel enjoyed
their former peace and prosperity in Egypt, when
Moses came to invite them to Canaan, I think
they would hardly have listened to him.   But the
Lord suffered them to be brought into great
trouble and bondage, and then the news of deliverance was more welcome; yet still they were
but half willing, and they carried a love to the
flesh-pots of Egypt with them into the wilderness.
We are like them : though we say this world is
vain and sinful, we are too fond of it; and though
we hope for true happiness only in heaven, we
are often well content to stay longer here.   But
the Lord sends afflictions one after another to
quicken our desires, and to convince us that this
cannot be our rest.   Sometimes if you drive a
bird from one branch of a tree, he will hop to
another a little higher, and from thence to a third;
but if you continue to disturb him, he will at last
take wing, and fly quite away.   Thus we, when
forced from one creature-comfort, perch upon
another, and so on; but the Lord mercifully follows
us with trials, and will not let us rest upon any :
by degrees our desires take a nobler flight, and
can be satisfied with nothing short of himself; and

we say, To depart and be with Jesus is best of
all.

I trust you find the name and grace of Jesus
more and more precious to you : his promises
more sweet, and your hope in them more abiding ;
your sense of your own weakness and unworthiness daily increasing ; your persuasion of his all-
sufficiency to guide, support, and comfort you,
more confirmed. You owe your growth in these
respects, in a great measure, to his blessing upon
those afflictions which he has prepared for you
and sanctified to you. May you praise him for
all that is past, and trust him for all that is to
come. I am, &c.

LETTER II.

Though I have the pleasure of hearing of you,
and sending a remembrance from time to time, I
am willing by this opportunity to direct a few
lines to you, as a more express testimony of my
sincere regard.

I think your experience is generally of the fearful, doubting cast. Such souls, however, the
Lord has given particular charge to his ministers
to comfort. He knows our infirmities, and what
temptations mean ; and, as a good Shepherd, he
expresses a peculiar care and tenderness for the
weak of the flock, Isa. xl. 4. But how must I
attempt your comfort? Surely not by strengthening a mistake to which we are all too liable, by
leading you to look into your own heart for (what
you will never find there) something in yourself
whereon to ground your hopes, if not wholly, yet
at least in part. Rather let me endeavour to lead
you out of yourself : let me invite you to look

unto Jesus.   Should we look for light in our own
eyes, or in the sun ? Is it indwelling sin distresses
you?   Then I can tell you (though you know it)
that Jesus died for sin and sinners.   I can tell
you, that his blood and righteousness are of infinite value; that his arm is almighty, and his
compassions infinite : yea, you yourself read his
promises every day, and why should you doubt
their being fulfilled ? If you say you do not question their truth, or that they are accomplished to
many, but that you can hardly believe they belong
to you ; I would ask, what evidence you would
require ? A voice or an angel from heaven you do
not expect.   Consider, if many of the promises
are not expressly directed to those to whom they
belong.   When you read your name on the super-
scription of this letter, you made no scruple to
open it : why then do you hesitate at embracing
the promises of the Gospel ; where you read that
they are addressed to those who mourn, who
hunger and thirst after righteousness, who are
poor in spirit, &c., and cannot but be sensible that
a gracious God has begun to work these dispositions in your heart.   If you say, that though you
do at times mourn, hunger, &c., you are afraid you
do it not enough, or not aright : consider, that
this sort of reasoning is very far from the spirit
and language of the Gospel ; for it is grounded
on a secret supposition, that in the forgiveness of
sin, God has a respect to something more than
the atonement and mediation of Jesus ; namely,
to some previous good qualifications in a sinner's
heart, which are to share with the blood of Christ
in the honour of salvation.   The enemy deceives
us in this matter the more easily, because a pro-
pensity to the covenant of works is a part of our
natural depravity.   Depend upon it, you will

never have a suitable and sufficient sense of the evil of sin, and of your share in it, so long as you have any sin remaining in you. We must see Jesus as he is, before our apprehensions of any spiritual truth will be complete. But if we know that we must perish without Christ, and that he is able to save to the uttermost, we know enough to warrant us to cast our souls upon him, and we dishonour him by fearing that when we do so he will disappoint our hope. But if you are still perplexed about the high points of election, &c. I would advise you to leave the disposal of others to the great Judge: and as to yourself, I think I need not say much to persuade you, that if ever you are saved at all, it must be in a way of free and absolute grace. Leave disputes to others; wait upon the Lord, and he will teach you all things, in such degree and time as he sees best. Perhaps you have suffered for taking things too much upon trust from men. " Cease from man, whose breath is in his nostrils." One is your master, even Christ. Study and pray over the Bible; and you may take it as a sure rule, that whatever sentiment makes any part of the word of God unwelcome to you is justly to be suspected. Aim at a cheerful spirit. The more you trust God, the better you will serve him. While you indulge unbelief and suspicion, you weaken your own hands and discourage others. Be thankful for what he has shewn you, and wait upon him for more: you shall find he has not said, " Seek ye my face" in vain.—I heartily commend you to his grace and care.

I am, &c.

LETTER III.

At length, and without farther apology for my silence, I sit down to ask you how you fare? Afflictions, I hear, have been your lot; and if I had not heard so, I should have taken it for granted: for I believe the Lord loves you; and as many as he loves he chastens. I think you can say afflictions have been good for you, and I doubt not but you have found strength according to your day; so that though you may have been sharply tried, you have not been overpowered. For the Lord has engaged his faithfulness for this to all his children, that he will support them in all their trials: so that the fire shall not consume them, nor the floods drown them, 1 Cor. x. 13; Isa. xliii. 2.

If you can say thus much, cannot you go a little further, and add, in the Apostle's words, " None of these things move me, neither count I my life dear. I rather glory in my infirmities, that the power of Christ may rest upon me; yea, doubtless, I count all things loss and of no regard, for the excellency of the knowledge of Christ Jesus my Lord; for when I am weak, then I am strong ?" Methinks I hear you say, God, who comforteth those who are cast down, has comforted my soul, and as my troubles have abounded my consolations in Christ have abounded also. He has delivered, he does deliver, and in him I trust that he will yet deliver me. Surely you can set your seal to these words. The Lord help you then to live more and more a life of faith, to feed upon the promises, and to rejoice in the assurance that all things are yours, and shall surely work for your good.

If I guess right at what passes in your heart, the name of Jesus is precious to you; and this is a sure token of salvation, and that of God. You could not have loved him, if he had not loved you first. He spoke to *you*, and said, "Seek my face," before your heart cried to *him*, "Thy face, O Lord, will I seek." But you complain, "Alas! I love him so little." That very complaint proves that you love him a great deal: for if you loved him but a little, you would think you loved him enough. A mother loves her child a great deal, yet does not complain for not loving it more; nay, perhaps she hardly thinks it possible. But such an infinite object is Jesus, that they who love him better than parents or child, or any earthly relation or comfort, will still think they hardly love him at all; because they see such a vast disproportion between the utmost they can give him, and what in himself he deserves from them. But I can give you good advice and good news: love him as well as you can now, and ere long you shall love him better. O when you see him as he is, then I am sure you will love him indeed! If you want to love him better now while you are here, I believe I can tell you the secret how this is to be attained: *trust him.* The more you trust him, the better you will love him. If you ask farther, How shall I do to trust him? I answer, *Try him:* the more you make trial of him, the more your trust in him will be strengthened. Venture upon his promises; carry them to him, and see if he will not be as good as his word. But, alas! Satan and unbelief work the contrary way. We are unwilling to try him, and therefore unable to trust him; and what wonder, then, that our love is faint, for who can love at uncertainties?

If you are in some measure thankful for what you have received, and hungering and thirsting for more, you are in the frame I would wish for myself; and I desire to praise the Lord on your behalf.—Pray for us. We join in love to you.

I am, &c.

TWO LETTERS

TO

MISS P****

LETTER I.

August 17, 1776.

Iт is indeed natural to us to wish and to plan; and it is merciful in the Lord to disappoint our plans, and to cross our wishes. For we cannot be safe, much less happy, but in proportion as we are weaned from our own wills, and made simply desirous of being directed by his guidance. This truth (when we are enlightened by his word) is sufficiently familiar to the judgment; but we seldom learn to reduce it into practice, without being trained awhile in the school of disappointment. The schemes we form look so plausible and convenient, that when they are broken we are ready to say, What a pity! We try again, and with no better success: we are grieved, and perhaps angry, and plan out another, and so on: at length, in a course of time, experience and observation begin to convince us, that we are not more able than we are worthy to choose aright for ourselves. Then the Lord's invitation to cast our cares upon him, and his promise to take care of us, appear valuable; and when *we* have done planning, *his* plan in our favour gradually opens, and he does more and better for us than we could either ask or think. I can hardly recollect a single plan of mine, of which I have not since seen reason to be satisfied, that, had it taken place in season and circumstance just as I proposed, it would, humanly speaking, have proved my ruin; or, at least, it would have deprived me of the greater good the Lord had designed for me. We judge of things by their present appearances, but the Lord sees them in their consequences: if we could do so likewise, we should be perfectly of his mind; but as we cannot, it is an unspeakable mercy that he will manage for us, whether we are pleased with his management or not; and it is spoken of as one of his heaviest judgments, when he gives any person or people up to the way of their own hearts, and to walk after their own counsels.

Indeed, we may admire his patience towards us. If we were blind, and reduced to desire a person to lead us, and should yet pretend to dispute with him, and direct him at every step, we should probably soon weary him, and provoke him to leave us to find the way by ourselves if we could. But our gracious Lord is long-suffering and full of compassion: he bears with our frowardness, yet he will take methods both to shame and to humble us, and to bring us to a confession that he is wiser than we. The great and unexpected benefit he intends us, by all the discipline we meet with, is to tread down our wills, and bring them into subjection to his. So far as we attain to this, we are out of the reach of disappointment: for when the will of God can please us, we shall be pleased every day, and from morning to night; I mean, with respect to his dispensations. O the happiness of such a life! I have an idea of it; I hope I am aiming at it; but surely I have not attained it. Self is active in my heart, if it does not absolutely reign there. I profess to believe that one thing is needful and sufficient, and yet my thoughts are prone to wander after a hundred more. If it be true, that the light of his countenance is better than life, why am I solicitous about any thing else? If he be all-sufficient, and gives me liberty to call him *mine,* why do I go a begging to creatures for help? If he be about my path and bed; if the smallest, as well as the greatest, events in which I am concerned are under his immediate direction; if the very hairs of my head are numbered; then my care (any farther than a care to walk in the paths of his precepts, and to follow the openings of his providence) must be useless and needless, yea indeed sinful and heathenish, burdensome to myself, and dishonourable to my profession. Let us cast down the load we are unable to carry; and if the Lord be our Shepherd, refer all, and trust all to him. Let us endeavour to live to him and for him to-day, and be glad that to-morrow, with all that is behind it, is in his hands.

It is storied of Pompey, that when his friends would have dissuaded him from putting to sea in a storm, he answered, It is necessary for me to sail, but it is not necessary for me to live. O pompous speech, in Pompey's sense! He was full of the idea of his own importance, and would rather have died than have taken a step beneath his supposed dignity. But it may be accommodated with propriety to a believer's case. It becomes us to say, It is not necessary for me to be rich, or what the world accounts wise; to be healthy, or admired by my fellow-worms; to pass through life in a state of prosperity and outward comfort;—these things may be, or they may be otherwise, as the Lord in his wisdom shall appoint: but it is necessary for me to be humble and spiritual, to seek communion with God, to adorn my profession of the Gospel, and to yield submissively to his disposal, in whatever way, whether of service or suffering, he shall be pleased to call me to glorify him in the world. It is not necessary for me to live long, but highly expedient that whilst I do live I should live to him. Here then I would bound my desires; and here, having his word both for my rule and my warrant, I am secured from asking amiss. Let me have his presence and his Spirit, wisdom to know my calling, and opportunities and faithfulness to improve them; and as to the rest, Lord, help me to say, What thou wilt, when thou wilt, and how thou wilt.

I am, &c.

LETTER II.

Dear Madam,

WHAT a poor, uncertain, dying world is this! What a wilderness in itself! How dark, how desolate, without the light of the Gospel and the knowledge of Jesus! It does not appear so to us in a state of nature, because we are then in a state of enchantment, the magical lantern blinding us with a splendid delusion.

> Thus in the desert's dreary waste,
> By magic pow'r produc'd in haste,
>   As old romances say,
> Castles and groves, and music sweet,
> The senses of the trav'ller cheat,
>   And stop him in his way:

But while he gazes with surprize,
The charm dissolves, the vision dies;
  'Twas but enchanted ground.
Thus, if the Lord our spirit touch,
The world, which promis'd us so much,
  A wilderness is found.

It is a great mercy to be undeceived in time; and though our gay dreams are at an end, and we awake to every thing that is disgustful and dismaying, yet we see a highway through the wilderness, a powerful Guard, an infallible Guide at hand to conduct us through; and we can discern, beyond the limits of the wilderness, a better land, where we shall be at rest and at home. What will the difficulties we met by the way then signify? The remembrance of them will only remain to heighten our sense of the love, care, and power of our Saviour and Leader. O how shall we then admire, adore, and praise him, when he shall condescend to unfold to us the beauty, propriety, and harmony of the whole train of his dispensations towards us, and give us a clear retrospect of all the way and all the turns of our pilgrimage!

In the mean while, the best method of adorning our profession, and of enjoying peace in our souls, is simply to trust him, and absolutely to commit ourselves and our all to his management. By casting our burdens upon him, our spirits become light and cheerful; we are freed from a thousand anxieties and inquietudes, which are wearisome to our minds, and which, with respect to events, are *needless* for us, yea, *useless*. But though it may be easy to speak of this trust, and it appears to our judgment perfectly right and reasonable, the actual attainment is a great thing; and especially

so to trust the Lord not by fits and starts, sur-
rendering one day and retracting the next, but to
abide by our surrender, and go habitually trusting,
through all the changes we meet, knowing that
his love, purpose, and promise are unchangeable.
Some little faintings perhaps none are freed from ;
but I believe a power of trusting the Lord in good
measure at all times, and living quietly under the
shadow of his wing, is what the promise warrants
us to expect, if we seek it by diligent prayer ; if
not all at once, yet by a gradual increase.   May
it be your experience and mine!

I am, &c.

FOURTEEN LETTERS

TO THE

REV. MR. B****.

LETTER I.

Dear and Rev. Sir,   January 27, 1778.

I CALL you *dear* because I love you, and I shall continue to style you *Reverend* as long as you dignify me with that title.   It is indeed a pretty sounding epithet, and forms a striking contrast in the usual application.   The inhabitants of the moon (if there be any) have perhaps no idea how many Reverend, Right Reverend, and Most Reverend sinners we have in Europe.   And yet you *are* reverend; and I revere you, because I believe the Lord liveth in you, and has chosen you to be a temple of his presence, and an instrument of his grace.

I hope the two sermons you preached in London were made useful to others, and the medicines you took there were useful to yourself.   I am glad to hear you are safe at home, and something better. Cheerful spring is approaching; then I hope the barometer of your spirits will rise.   But the presence of the Lord can bring a pleasanter spring than April, and even in the depth of winter.

At present it is January with me, both within and without.   The outward sun shines and looks pleasant; but his beams are faint, and too feeble to dissolve the frost.   So is it in my heart: I have many bright and pleasant beams of truth in my view, but cold predominates in my frost-bound

spirit, and they have but little power to warm
me. I could tell a stranger sometning about
Jesus that would perhaps astonish him : such a
glorious person ! such wonderful love ! such humiliation ! such a death ! and then what he is now
in himself, and what he is to his people ! What
a sun ! what a shield ! what a root ! what a life !
what a friend ! My tongue can run on upon these
subjects sometimes ; and could my heart keep
pace with it, I should be the happiest fellow in
the country. Stupid creature ! to know these
things so well, and yet be no more affected with
them ! Indeed I have reason to be upon ill terms
with myself ! It is strange that pride should ever
find any thing in my experience to feed upon ; but
this completes my character for folly, vileness,
and inconsistence, that I am not only poor, but
proud : and though I am convinced I am a very
wretch, and nothing before the Lord, I am prone
to go forth among my fellow-creatures as though
I were wise and good.

You wonder what I am doing ; and well you
may : I am sure you would if you lived with me.
Too much of my time passes in busy idleness, too
much in waking dreams. I aim at something ;
but hindrances from within and without make it
difficult for me to accomplish any thing. I dare
not say I am absolutely idle, or that I wilfully
waste much of my time. I have seldom one hour
free from interruption. Letters come that must
be answered, visitants that must be received,
business that must be attended to. I have a good
many sheep and lambs to look after, sick and
afflicted souls, dear to the Lord ; and therefore
whatever stands still, these must not be neglected.
Amongst these various avocations, night comes
before I am ready for noon and the week closes,

when, according to the state of my business, it should not be more than Tuesday. O precious, irrecoverable time! O that I had more wisdom in redeeming and improving thee! Pray for me, that the Lord may teach me to serve him better.

I am, &c.

LETTER II.

Dear Sir, April 28, 1778.

I was not much disappointed at not meeting you at home. I know how difficult it is to get away from ******, if you are seen in the street after breakfast. The horse-leech has three daughters, saying, "Give, give:" the cry there is, "Preach, preach." When you have told them all, you must tell them more, or tell it them over again. Whoever will find tongue, they will engage to find ears. Yet I do not blame this importunity: I wish you were teased more with it in your own town; for though undoubtedly there are too many, both at N**** and here, whose religion lies too much in hearing, yet in many it proceeds from a love to the truth, and to the ministers who dispense it. And I generally observe, that they who are not willing to hear a stranger (if his character is known) are indifferent enough about hearing their own minister.

I beg you to pray for me. I am a poor creature, full of wants. I seem to need the wisdom of Solomon, the meekness of Moses, and the zeal of Paul, to enable me to make full proof of my ministry. But, alas! you may guess the rest.

Send me the way to Christ. I am willing to be a debtor to the wise and unwise, to doctors and shoe-makers, if I can get a hint, or a *Nota Bene* from any one, without respect to parties.

When a house is on fire, Churchmen, Dissenters, Methodists, Papists, Moravians, and Mystics, are all welcome to bring water. At such times, nobody asks, "Pray friend, whom do you hear?" or, "What do you think of the five points?" &c. &c.

I am, &c.

LETTER III.

My dear Friend,   July 7, 1778.

I KNOW not that I have any thing to say worth postage, though perhaps, had I seen you before you set off, something might have occurred which will not be found in my letter. Yet I write a line, because you bid me, and are now in a far foreign country. You will find Mr. **** a man to your tooth, but he is in Mr. W******'s connection. So I remember venerable Bede, after giving a high character of some contemporarary, kicks his full pail of milk down, and reduces him almost to nothing, by adding in the close to this purpose; " But, unhappy man, he did not keep Easter our way!" A fig for all connections, say I, and say you, but that which is formed by the bands, joints, and ligaments the Apostle speaks of, Eph. iv. 16, *et alibi.* Therefore I venture to repeat it, that Mr. ****, though he often sees and hears Mr. W******, and I believe loves him well, is a good man : and you will see the invisible mark upon his forehead, if you examine him with your spiritual spectacles.

Now, methinks, I do pity you: I see you melted with heat, stifled with smoke, stunned with noise. Ah! what a change from the brooks, and bushes, and birds, and green fields, to which you had lately access. Of old they used to retire into the deserts for mortification. If I was to set myself a moderate penance, it might be to spend a fortnight in London in the height of summer. But I forget myself: I hope the Lord is with you, and then all places are alike. He makes the dungeon and the stocks comfortable, Acts xvi.; yea, a fiery furnace, and a lion's den. A child of God in London seems to be in all these trying situations; but Jesus can preserve his own. I honour the grace of God in those few (comparatively few, I fear,) who preserve their garments undefiled in that Sardis. The air is filled with infection; and it is by special power and miraculous preservation they enjoy spiritual health, when so many sicken and fall around them on the right hand and on the left. May the Lord preserve you from the various epidemical soul diseases which abound where you are, and be your comfort and defence from day to day.

Last week we had a lion in town. I went to see him. He was wonderfully tame; as familiar with his keeper, as docile and obedient as a spaniel. Yet the man told me he had his surly fits, when they durst not touch him. No looking-glass could express my face more justly than this lion did my heart. I could trace every feature: as wild and fierce by nature; yea, much more so; but grace has in some measure tamed me. I know and love my Keeper, and sometimes watch his looks that I may learn his will. But, oh! I have my surly fits too; seasons when I relapse into the savage again, as though I had forgotten all.

I am, &c.

LETTER IV.

My dear Friend,   July 13, 1778.

As we are so soon to meet, as I have nothing very important to communicate, and many things occur which might demand my time ; I have no other plea to offer, either to you or myself, for writing again, but because I love you.

I pity the unknown considerable minister, with whom you smoked your morning pipe. But we must take men and things as we find them : and when we fall in company with those from whom we can get little other good, it is likely we shall at least find occasion for the exercise of patience and charity towards them, and of thankfulness to him who hath made us to differ. And these are good things, though perhaps the occasion may not be pleasant. Indeed, a Christian, if in a right spirit, is always in his Lord's school, and may learn either a new lesson, or how to practise an old one, by every thing he sees or hears, provided he does not wilfully tread upon forbidden ground. If he were constrained to spend a day with the poor creatures in the common side of Newgate, though he could not talk with them of what God has done for his soul, he might be more sensible of his mercy, by the contrast he would observe around him. He might rejoice for himself, and mourn over them, and thus perhaps get as much benefit as from the best sermon he ever heard.

It is necessary, all things taken together, to have connection more or less with narrow-minded people. If they are, notwithstanding their pre-judices, civil to us, they have a right to some civility from us. We may love them, though we cannot admire them, and pick something good

from them, notwithstanding we see much to
blame. It is perhaps the highest triumph we can
obtain over bigotry, when we are able to bear
with bigots themselves. For they are a set of
troublesome folks, whom Mr. Self is often very
forward to exclude from the comprehensive candour and tenderness which he professes to exercise
towards those who differ from him.

I am glad your present home (a believer should
be always at home) is pleasant; the rooms large
and airy; your host and hostess kind and spiritual;
and, upon the whole, all things as well as you
could expect to find them, considering where you
are. I could give you much such an account of
my usual head-quarters in the city; but still
London is London. I do not wish you to live
there, for my own sake as well as yours: but if
the Lord should so appoint, I believe he can make
you easy there, and enable me to make a tolerable
shift without you. Yet I certainly should miss
you; for I have no person in this neighbourhood
with whom my heart so thoroughly unites in
spirituals, though there are many whom I love.
But conversation with most Christians is something like going to court; where, except you are
dressed exactly according to a prescribed standard,
you will either not be admitted, or must expect to
be heartily stared at. But you and I can meet
and converse *sans contrainte*, in an undress, without fear of offending, or being accounted offenders,
for a word out of place, and not exactly in the
pink of the mode.

I know not how it is: I think my sentiments
and experience are as orthodox and Calvinistical
as need be; and yet I am a sort of speckled bird
among my Calvinist brethren. I am a mighty

good Churchman, but pass amongst such as a Dissenter in prunella. On the other hand, the Dissenters (many of them I mean) think me defective, either in understanding or in conscience, for staying where I am. Well! there is a middle party, called Methodists; but neither do my dimensions exactly fit with them. I am somehow disqualified for claiming a full brotherhood with any party. But there are a few among all parties who bear with me and love me, and with this I must be content at present. But so far as they love the Lord Jesus, I desire, and by his grace I determine (with or without their leave) to love them all. Party-walls, though stronger than the walls of Babylon, must come down in the general ruin, when the earth and all its works shall be burnt up, if no sooner.

I am, &c.

LETTER V.

My dear Sir,   July, 1778.

I was glad to hear that you were again within a few miles of me; and I would praise the Lord, who led you out and brought you home in safety, and preserved all in peace while you were abroad, so that you found nothing very painful to imbitter your return. Many go abroad well, but return no more. The affectionate wife, the prattling children, listen for the well-known sound of papa's foot at the door; but they listen in vain: a fall or a fever has intercepted him, and he is gone far, far away. Some leave all well when they go from home; but how changed, how trying, the scene when they come back! In their absence the Lord has taken away the desire of their eyes with a stroke; or perhaps ruffians have plundered

and murdered their family in the dead of the
night, or the fire devoured their habitation.

Ah! how large and various is the list of evils
and calamities with which sin has filled the world!
You and I and ours escape them: we stand,
though in a field of battle, where thousands fall
around us, because the Lord is pleased to keep
us. May He have the praise, and may we only
live to love and serve him.

Mrs. **** has been very ill, and my heart often
much pained while you have been absent. But
the Lord has removed his hand: she is much
better, and I hope she will be seen in his house
to-morrow. I have few trials in my own person;
but when the Lord afflicts her, I feel it. It is a
mercy that he has made us *one;* but it exposes
us to many a pain, which we might have missed
if we cared but little for each other. Alas! there
is usually an ounce of the golden calf, of idolatry
and dependence, in all the warm regard we bear
to creatures. *Hinc illæ lachrymæ!* for this reason,
our sharpest trials usually spring from our most
valued comforts.

I cannot come to you; therefore you must come
hither speedily. Be sure to bring Mr. B****
with you. I shall be very glad to see him, and I
long to thank him for clothing my book. It looks
well on the outside, and I hope to find it sound
and savoury. I love the author, and that is a
step towards liking the book. For where we
love, we are generally tender, and favourably take
every thing by the best handle, and are vastly full
of candour: but if you are prejudiced against the
man, the poor book is half condemned before we
open it. It had need be written well; for it will
be read with a suspicious eye, as if we wished to
find treason in every page. I am glad I diverted

and profited you by calling you a speckled bird. I can tell you, such a bird in this day, that wears the full colour of no sect or party, is *rara avis;* if not quite so scarce as the phœnix, yet to be met with but here and there.   It is impossible I should be all of a colour, when I have been a debtor to all sorts ; and, like the jay in the fable, have been beholden to most of the birds in the air for a feather or two.   Church and Meeting, Methodist and Moravian, may all perceive something in my coat taken from them.   None of them are angry with me for borrowing from *them ;* but then, why could I not be content with *their* colour, without going amongst other flocks and coveys, to make myself such a motley figure ?   Let them be angry ; if I have culled the best feathers from all, then surely I am finer than any.

I am, &c.

LETTER VI.

Dear Sir,   August, 1778.

If the Lord affords health ; if the weather be tolerable; if no unforeseen change takes place ; if no company comes in upon me to-night, (which sometimes unexpectedly happens,) with these provisos, Mr. S**** and I have engaged to travel to **** on Monday next, and hope to be with you by or before eleven o'clock.

In such a precarious world, it is needful to form our plans at two days' distance, with precaution and exceptions, James iv. 13.   However, if it be the Lord's will to bring us together, and if the purposed interview be for his glory and our good, then I am sure nothing shall prevent it. And who in his right wits would wish either to visit or be visited upon any other terms ?   O ! if we could but be pleased with his will, we might be pleased from morning to night, and every day in the year.

Pray for a blessing upon our coming together. It would be a pity to walk ten miles to pick straws, or to come with our empty vessels upon our heads, saying, " We have found no water."

I am, &c.

LETTER VII.

My dear Friend, October, 1778.

YOUR letters are always welcome; the last doubly so, for being unexpected. If you never heard before of a line of your's being useful, I will tell you for once, that I get some pleasure and instruction whenever you write to me. And I see not but your call to letter-writing is as clear as mine, at least when you are able to put pen to paper.

I must say something to your queries about 2 Sam. xiv. I do not approve of the scholastic distinctions about inspiration, which seem to have a tendency to explain away the authority and certainty of one half of the Bible at least. Though the penmen of Scripture were ever so well informed of some facts, they would, as you observe, need express, full, and infallible inspiration, to teach them which the Lord would have selected and recorded for the use of the church, amongst many others which to themselves might appear equally important.

However, with respect to historical passages, I dare not pronounce positively that any of them are, even in the literal sense, unworthy of the wisdom of the Holy Ghost, and the dignity of inspiration. Some, yea, many of them, have often appeared trivial to me; but I check the thought, and charge it to my own ignorance and temerity. It must have some importance, because I read it in God's book.   On the other hand, though I will not deny that they may all have a spiritual and mystical sense, (for I am no more qualified to judge of the deep things of the Spirit, than to tell you what is passing this morning at the bottom of the sea,) yet if, with my present modicum of light I should undertake to expound many passages in a mystical sense, I fear such a judge as you would think my interpretations fanciful and not well supported.   I suppose I should have thought the Bible complete, though it had not informed me of the death of Rebekah's nurse, or where she was buried. But some tell me that Deborah is the law, and that by the oak I am to understand the cross of Christ : and I remember to have heard of a preacher who discovered a type of Christ crucified in Absalom hanging by the hair on another oak. I am quite a mole when compared with these eagle-eyed divines ; and must often content myself with plodding upon the lower ground of *accommodation* and *allusion ;* except when the New-Testament writers assure me what the mind of the Holy Ghost was, I can find the Gospel with more confidence in the history of Sarah and Hagar, than in that of Leah and Rachel; though, without Paul's help, I should have considered them both as family squabbles, recorded chiefly to illustrate the general truth, that vanity and vexation of spirit are incident to the best men, in the most favoured situations.   And I think there is no part of Old-Testament history from which I could not (the Lord helping me) draw observations, that might be suitable to the pulpit, and profitable to his people ; so I might perhaps from Livy or Tacitus

But then, with the Bible in my hands, I go upon sure grounds : I am certain of the facts I speak from, that they really did happen. I may likewise depend upon the springs and motives of actions, and not amuse myself and my hearers with speeches which were never spoken, and motives which were never thought of, till the historian rummaged his pericranium for something to embellish his work. I doubt not but were you to consider Joab's courtly conduct only in a literal sense, how it tallied with David's desire, and how gravely and graciously he granted himself a favour, while he professed to oblige Joab ; I say in this view you would be able to illustrate many important scriptural doctrines, and to shew that the *passage* is important to those who are engaged in studying the anatomy of the human heart.

I am, &c.

LETTER VIII.

My dear Friend,   October 27, 1778.

I HAVE been witness to a great and important revolution this morning, which took place while the greatest part of the world was asleep. Like many state-revolutions, its first beginnings were almost undiscernible; but the progress, though gradual, was steady, and the event decisive. A while ago darkness reigned. Had a man then dropped, for the first time, into our world, he might have thought himself banished into a hopeless dungeon. How could he expect light to rise out of such a state ? And when he saw the first glimmering of dawn in the east, how could he promise himself that it was the forerunner of such a glorious sun as has since arisen ! With what wonder would such a new-comer observe the bounds of his view enlarging, and the distinctness of objects increasing from one minute to another; and how well content would he be to part with the twinklings of the stars, when he had the broad day all around him in exchange! I cannot say this revolution is extraordinary, because it happens every morning; but surely it is astonishing, or rather it would be so, if man was not astonishingly stupid.

Such strangers once were we. Darkness, gross darkness, covered us. How confined were our views! And even the things which were within our reach we could not distinguish. Little did we then think what a glorious day we were appointed to see; what an unbounded prospect would ere long open before us! We knew not that there was a Sun of Righteousness, and that he would dawn, and rise, and shine upon our hearts. And as the idea of what we see now was then hidden from us, so at present we are almost equally at a loss how to form any conception of the stronger light and brighter prospects which we wait and hope for. Comparatively we are in the dark still: at the most, we have but a dim twilight, and see nothing clearly; but it is the dawn of immortality, and a sure presage and earnest of glory.

Thus, at times, it seems a darkness that may be felt broods over your natural spirits; but when the day-star rises upon your heart, you see and rejoice in his light. You have days as well as nights; and after a few more vicissitudes, you will take your flight to the regions of everlasting light, where your sun will go down no more. Happy you, and happy I, if I shall meet you there, as I trust I shall. How shall we love, and sing, and wonder, and praise the Saviour's name!

Last Sunday a young man died here of extreme old age, at twenty-five. He laboured hard to ruin a good constitution, and unhappily succeeded ; yet amused himself with the hopes of recovery almost to the last. We have a sad knot of such poor creatures in this place, who labour to stifle each other's convictions, and to ruin themselves and associates, soul and body. How industriously is Satan served! I was formerly one of his most active under-tempters. Not content with running the broad way myself, I was indefatigable in enticing others ; and, had my influence been equal to my wishes, I would have carried all the human race with me. And doubtless some have perished, to whose destruction I was greatly instrumental, by tempting them to sin, and by poisoning and hardening them with principles of infidelity ; and yet I was spared. When I think of the most with whom I spent my unhappy days of ignorance, I am ready to say, "I only am escaped alive to tell thee." Surely I have not half the activity and zeal in the service of Him who snatched me as a brand out of the burning, as I had in the service of his enemy. Then the whole stream of my endeavours and affections went one way ; now my best desires are continually crossed, counteracted, and spoiled, by the sin which dwelleth in me : then the tide of a corrupt nature bore me along ; now I have to strive and swim against it. The Lord cut me short of opportunities, and placed me where I could do but little mischief; but had my abilities and occasions been equal to my heart, I should have been a Voltaire and a Tiberius in one character, a monster of profaneness and licentiousness. "O to grace how great a debtor!" A common drunkard or profligate is a petty sinner to what I was. I had the ambition of a Cæsar or an Alexander, and wanted to rank in wickedness among the foremost of the human race. When you have read this, praise the Lord for his mercy to the chief of sinners, and pray that I may have grace to be faithful. But I have rambled. I meant to tell you, that on Sunday afternoon I preached from *Why will ye die?* Ezek. xxxii. 10, 11. I endeavoured to shew poor sinners, that if they died, it was because they *would,* and if they *would,* they *must.* I was much affected for a time : I could hardly speak for weeping, and some wept with me. From some, alas! I can no more draw a tear or a relenting thought, than from a millstone.

I am, &c.

LETTER IX.

My dear Friend,   Nov. 27, 1778.

You are a better expositor of Scripture than of my speeches, if you really inferred from my last that I think you shall die soon. I cannot say positively you will not die soon, because life at all times is uncertain : however, according to the doctrine of probabilities, I think, and always thought, you bid fair enough to outlive me. The gloomy tinge of your weak spirits led you to consider yourself much worse in point of health than you appear to me to be.

In the other point I dare be more positive, that, die when you will, you will die in the Lord. Of this I have not the least doubt ; and I believe you doubt of it less, if possible, than I, except in those darker moments when the atrabilious humour prevails.

I heartily sympathize with you in your complaints ; but I see you in safe hands. The Lord loves you, and will take care of you. He who raises the dead, can revive your spirits when you are cast down. He who sets bounds to the sea, and says " Hitherto shalt thou come, and no further," can limit and moderate that gloom which sometimes distresses you. He knows why he permits you to be thus exercised. I cannot assign the reasons, but I am sure they are worthy of his wisdom and love, and that you will hereafter see and say, He has done all things well. If I was as wise as your philosopher, I might say a great deal about a melancholy complexion; but I love not to puzzle myself with second causes, while the first cause is at hand, which sufficiently accounts for every phenomenon in a believer's experience. Your constitution, your situation, your temper, your distemper, all that is either comfortable or painful in your lot, is of his appointment. The hairs of your head are all numbered: the same power which produced the planet Jupiter is necessary to the production of a single hair, nor can one of them fall to the ground without his notice, any more than the stars can fall from their orbits. In providence, no less than in creation, he is *Maximus in minimis*. Therefore fear not ; only believe. Our sea may sometimes be stormy, but we have an infallible Pilot, and shall infallibly gain our port.

I am, &c.

LETTER X.

My dear Friend, Feb. 23, 1779.

On Saturday, and not before, I heard you had been ill. Had the news reached me sooner, I should have sent you a line sooner. I hope you will be able to inform me that you are now better, and that the Lord continues to do you good by every dispensation he allots you. Healing and wounding are equally from his hand, and equally tokens of his love and care over us. I have but

little affliction in my own person, but I have been
oftened chastened of late by proxy. The Lord, for
his people's sake, is still pleased to give me health
and strength for public service: but, when I need
the rod, he lays it upon Mrs. ****. In this way
I have felt much without being disabled or laid
aside. But he has heard prayer for her likewise,
and for more than a fortnight past she has been
comfortably well. I lay at least one half of her
sickness to my own account. She suffers for me,
and I through her. It is, indeed, touching me in
a tender part. Perhaps if I could be more wise,
watchful, and humble, it might contribute more
to the re-establishment of her health than all the
medicine she takes.

I somehow neglected to confer with you about
the business of the fast day. The last of my three
sermons, when I had, as I expected, the largest
congregation, was a sort of historical discourse,
from Deut. xxxii. 15; in which, running over the
leading national events from the time of Wickliff,
I endeavoured to trace the steps and turns by
which the Lord has made us a fat and thriving
people, and in the event blessed us, beyond his
favourite Jeshurun of old, with civil and religious
liberty, peace, honour, and prosperity, and Gospel
privileges. How fat we were when the war ter-
minated in the year 1763, and how we have
kicked and forsaken the Rock of our salvation of
late years! Then followed a sketch of our present
state and spirit as a people, both in a religious
and political view. I started at the picture while
I drew it, though it was a very inadequate representation. We seemed willing to afflict our souls
for one day, as Dr. Louth reads, Isa. lviii. 5. But
the next day things returned into their former
channel: the fast and the occasion seemed pre-

sently forgotten, except by a few simple souls, who are despised and hated by the rest for their preciseness, because they think sin ought to be lamented every day in the year.

Who would envy Cassandra her gift of prophecy upon the terms she had it; that her declarations, however true, should meet with no belief or regard? It is the lot of Gospel ministers, with respect to the bulk of their hearers. But blessed be the grace which makes a few exceptions! Here and there, one will hear, believe, and be saved. Every one of these is worth a world; and our success with a few should console us for all our trials.

Come and see us as soon as you can, only not to-morrow, for I am then to go to T****. My Lord, the Great Shepherd, has one sheep there, related to the fold under my care. I can seldom see her, and she is very ill. I expect she will be soon removed to the pasture above. Our love to Mrs. B****.

Believe me yours, &c.

LETTER XI.

My dear Friend,   April 23, 1779.

MAY I not style myself a friend, when I remember you after the interval of several weeks since I saw you, and through a distance of three-score miles? But the truth is, you have been neither absent nor distant from my heart a day. Your idea has travelled with me; you are a kind of familiar, very often before the eye of my mind. This, I hope, may be admitted as a proof of friendship.

I know the Lord loves you, and you know it likewise: every affliction affords you a fresh proof of it. How wise his management in our trials! How wisely adjusted in season, weight, continuance, to answer his gracious purposes in sending them! How unspeakably better to be at his disposal than at your own! So you say; so you think; so you find. You trust in him, and shall not be disappointed. Help me with your prayers, that I may trust him too, and be at length enabled to say without reserve, " What thou wilt, when thou wilt, how thou wilt." I had rather speak these three sentences from my heart, in my mother-tongue, than be master of all the languages in Europe.

I am yours, &c.

LETTER XII.

My dear Friend,   Aug. 19, 1779.

AMONG the rest of temporal mercies, I would be thankful for pen, ink, and paper, and the convenience of the post, by which means we can waft a thought to a friend when we cannot get at him. My will has been good to see you; but you must accept the will for the deed. The Lord has not permitted me.

I have been troubled of late with the rheumatism in my left arm. Mine is a sinful, vile body, and it is a mercy that any part of it is free from pain. It is virtually the seat and subject of all diseases; but the Lord holds them, like wild beasts in a chain, under a strong restraint. Was that restraint taken off, they would rush upon their prey from every quarter, and seize upon every limb, member, joint, and nerve, at once. Yet, though I am a sinner, and though my whole texture is so frail and exposed, I have enjoyed for a number of years an almost perfect exemption both from pain and sickness. This is wonderful indeed, even in my own eyes.

But my soul is far from being in a healthy state. There I have laboured, and still labour, under a complication of diseases; and, but for the care and skill of an infallible Physician, I must have died the death long ago. At this very moment my soul is feverish, dropsical, paralytic. I feel a loss of appetite, a disinclination both to food and to medicine : so that I am alive by miracle : yet I trust I shall not die, but live, and declare the works of the Lord. When I faint he revives me again. I am sure he is able, and I trust he has promised to heal me: but how inveterate must my disease be, that is not yet subdued, even under his management!

Well, my friend, there is a land where the inhabitants shall no more say, " I am sick." Then my eyes will not be dim, nor my ear heavy, nor my heart hard.

> One sight of Jesus as he is,
> Will strike all sin for ever dead.

Blessed be his name for this glorious hope! May it cheer us under all our present uneasy feelings, and reconcile us to every cross. The way must be right, however rough, that leads to such a glorious end.

O for more of that gracious influence, which in a moment can make the wilderness-soul rejoice and blossom like the rose! I want something which neither critics nor commentators can help me to. The Scripture itself, whether I read it in Hebrew, Greek, French, or English, is a sealed book in all languages, unless the Spirit of the Lord is present to expound and apply. Pray for me. No prayer seems more suitable to me than that of the Psalmist: "Bring my soul out of prison, that I may praise thy name."

I am, &c.

LETTER XIII.

My dear Friend,   August 28, 1779.

I want to hear how you are. I hope your
complaint is not worse than when I saw you. I
hope you are easier, and will soon find yourself
able to move about again. I should be sorry, if,
to the symptoms of the stone, you should have
the gout superadded in your right hand; for then
you will not be able to write to me.

We go on much as usual; sometimes very
poorly, sometimes a little better: the latter is
the case to-day. My rheumatism continues; but
it is very moderate and tolerable. The Lord
deals gently with us, and gives us many proofs
that he does not afflict willingly.

The days speed away apace; each one bears
away its own burden with it, to return no more.
Both pleasures and pains that are past are gone
for ever. What is yet future will likewise be
soon past. The end is coming. O to realize the
thought, and to judge of things now in some
measure suitable to the judgment we shall form
of them, when we are about to leave them all!
Many things which now either elate or depress
us, will then appear to be trifles light as air.

One thing is needful: to have our hearts united
to the Lord in humble faith; to set him always
before us; to rejoice in him as our Shepherd and
our portion; to submit to all his appointments,
not of necessity, because he is stronger than we,
but with a cheerful acquiescence, because he is
wise and good, and loves us better than we do
ourselves; to feed upon his truth; to have our
understandings, wills, affections, imaginations,
memory, all filled and impressed with the great
mysteries of redeeming love; to do all for him,

to receive all from him, to find all in him. I have mentioned many things, but they are all comprised in one, a life of faith in the Son of God. We are empty vessels in ourselves, but we cannot remain empty. Except Jesus dwells in our hearts, and fills them with his power and presence, they will be filled with folly, vanity, and vexation.

I am, &c.

LETTER XIV.

My dear Friend,   October 26, 1779.

BEING to go out of town to-day, I started up before light to write to you, and hoped to have sent you a long letter; when, behold! I could not get at any paper. I am now waiting for a peep at Mr. B**** at his lodgings, who came to town last night; and I shall write as fast as I can till I see him.

I feel for you a little in the same way as you feel for yourself. I bear a friendly sympathy in your late sharp and sudden trial. I mourn with that part of you which mourns: but at the same time I rejoice in the proof you have, and which you give, that the Lord is with you of a truth. I rejoice on your account, to see you supported and comforted, and enabled to say, " He has done all things well." I rejoice on my own account. Such instances of his faithfulness and all-sufficiency are very encouraging. We must all expect hours of trouble in our turn. We must all feel in our concernments the vanity and uncertainty of creature comforts. What a mercy is it to know from our own past experience, and to have it confirmed to us by the experience of others, that the Lord is good, a strong hold in the day of trouble, and that he knoweth them that trust in him.

Creatures are like candles; they waste while they afford us a little light, and we see them extinguished in their sockets one after another. But the light of the sun makes amends for them all. The Lord is so rich that he easily can, so good that he certainly will, give his children more than he ever will take away. When his gracious voice reaches the heart, "It is I, be not afraid; be still, and know that I am God;" when he gives us an impression of his wisdom, power, love, and care, then the storm which attempts to rise in our natural passions is hushed into a calm; the flesh continues to feel, but the spirit is made willing, and something more than submission takes place,—a sweet resignation and acquiescence, and even a joy that we have any thing which we value, to surrender to his call.

Yours, &c.

SIX

DISCOURSES (OR SERMONS),

AS INTENDED FOR THE PULPIT.

Στύλος και έδραιωμα της άληθειας, και όμολογουμένως μέγα έςι
τὸ της έυσεβειας μυςηριον· Θεὸς έφανερωθη έν σαρκι·—

PREFACE.

THE following Discourses were drawn up about twelve months since, when I expected a speedy opportunity of delivering them from the pulpit. As the views I then had are now over-ruled, I take this method of laying them before the public ; that those who have thought proper to foretel the part I would have acted, and the doctrine I would have taught, if my desires had taken place, may be either satisfied or silenced.

Yet I should not have thought it worth my while to give either myself or others this trouble, merely for my own vindication. Attempts of this kind usually imply too much of a man's importance to himself, to be either acceptable or successful. Or, at best, it can be a point of no great moment to my real happiness, what the few persons to whom my little name is known are pleased to say or think of me. Nothing but great inattention to our true circumstances can afford us leisure either to censure others, or to justify ourselves, unless when the interests of religion or morality are evidently concerned. A few years will fix and determine our characters beyond all possibility of mistake ; and till then it would be vain to hope for it.

The true reasons therefore of this publication are, the importance of the subjects treated of ; and the probability that, upon this occasion, many persons who have not yet considered them with the attention they deserve, may be induced (some from a motive of friendship, and others from curiosity) to read what might appear in my name, the rather for being mine.

Had I wrote with a design to print, I should have chosen to put my sentiments in another form : and perhaps a desire to avoid the censure of severe critics would have made me more solicitous about expression and method. But as I profess to publish not what I might, but what I really would have spoken, I could not allow myself to deviate from my first draught, except in a few places where I thought the sense entangled, ambiguous, or defective. For the same reason, I am forced to decline the judgment and correction of my friends; the advantages of which, as well as my own great need of them, I have more than once experienced.

If there is found in some places a coincidence of thought or expression, I hope it will be excused; as I had not the least apprehension, at the time of composing, that what I designed for distinct and separate occasions, would ever appear abroad in one view.

In a word, so far as these essays are mine, I entreat a candid perusal; and that those who read them, in order to form their judgment of the author, do not make their estimate from a sentence here and there, but have the patience to read them throughout. So far as what they contain is agreeable to Scripture, reason, and experience, an apology would be impertinent. In this case they deserve attention. Every particle of truth is valuable in itself, by whatever means or instruments it may be conveyed to us; and like a torch displays itself by its own light, without any relation to the hand that bears it.

Liverpool,
January 1, 1760.

DISCOURSES (OR SERMONS).

SERMON I.

ON THE DECEITFULNESS OF THE HEART.

JER. xvii. 9, 10.

The heart is deceitful above all things, and desperately wicked: who can know it? I the Lord search the heart, I try the reins, even to give every man according to his ways, and according to the fruit of his doings.

THE prophet Jeremiah had a hard task. He was appointed to inculcate unwelcome truths upon a vain insensible people. He had the grief to find all his expostulations and warnings, his prayers and tears, had no other effect than to make them account him their enemy, and to draw reproach and persecution upon himself. He lived to see the accomplishment of his own predictions; to see the land of his nativity desolated, the city destroyed, the people almost extirpated, and the few who remained, transported into a distant country, to end their days in captivity.

Those who have resolved, honestly and steadily, to declare the word of the Lord, have, in all ages, found a part of his trial: the message they have had to deliver has been disagreeable and disregarded. It is no hard matter to frame discourses that shall meet with some degree of general approbation; nor is it difficult to foresee the reception which plain truth must often meet with: but those who undertake a charge must perform it; and ministers are bound to declare to the people every thing that regards their welfare, whether they will hear, or whether they will forbear. If the watchman sees the danger coming, and does not blow the trumpet, to give the most public notice possible, he is answerable for all the evils that may follow. This is applied as a caution to the prophet Ezekiel; and, undoubtedly, every one who administers in holy things is concerned in it. " So thou, O son of man, I have set thee a watchman unto the house of Israel : therefore thou shalt hear the word at my mouth, and warn them from me. When I say unto the wicked man, O wicked man, thou shalt surely die ; if thou dost not speak to warn the wicked from his way, that wicked man shall die in his iniquity, but his blood will I require at thine hand ;" Ezek. xxxiii. Let this awful passage plead our excuse, if, at any time, we seem too urgent, or too plain, in our discourses. Too plain or urgent we cannot be. Our business is most important : opportunities are critical and precious. It is at the hazard of our souls if we speak deceitfully ; and at the hazard of yours if we speak in vain.

In the preceding verses, the prophet gives us a striking image of the opposition between the righteous and the wicked, in their present state, their hopes, and their end. The one is compared to a tree; the other to heath and stubble ; the one, *planted* by streams of water ; the other, *exposed* on the salt burning desert : the one, green, flourishing, and full of fruit; the other, parched and withering : the hope of the one, fixed on the Lord, the all-sufficient Almighty God ; the rash dependence of the other, on a frail feeble arm of flesh. Suitable to this difference is their end : the one, blessed, provided against all evil, so that he shall not be careful in the year of drought; the other, cursed, and cut off from the expectation of any amendment. " He shall not see when good cometh." The immediate design was, perhaps, to shew the Jews, that there was no way to avert the judgments of God, and to avoid the impending evils which threatened them, but by returning to the Lord, who had begun to smite, and who alone was able to heal them. But this they refused. They preferred their own contrivances: " they leaned upon an arm of flesh;" sometimes upon Egypt, sometimes upon Assyria: one while presuming upon force; another while upon cunning. They were fruitful in expedients; and, when one broken cistern failed them, had recourse to another. But the prophet denounces the curse of God both on them and their supports, subjoining the words of my text; which may be understood, either as a farther proof of what he had said, or an assigned cause of that obstinacy and perverseness he had complained of: " The heart is deceitful above all things, and desperately wicked: who can know it? "

But, without confining the words to the first occasion of their delivery, I shall consider them, as teaching us a doctrine, abundantly confirmed by many other passages of Scripture, " That the heart is deceitful and desperately wicked:" which I shall endeavour to illustrate in a plain familiar way. I shall, secondly, from the next verse, enforce this observation, That the heart (bad as it is) is incessantly under the Divine inspection and examination: " I the Lord search the heart and try the reins." I shall, thirdly, consider the issue and design of this inquest; that "every man" may, in the end, receive " according to his ways, and

according to the fruit of his doings." And may
the Lord enable us so to try and examine ourselves
here, that hereafter we may be found unblameable
and without rebuke before him, through Jesus
Christ our Lord.

1. The heart is here characterized, first, As deceitful, and that above or in all things: second,
As desperately wicked: in so dangerous, so deplorable a state, as is not to be conceived or found
out. "Who can know it?" The word in the original [אנש], which we translate *desperately wicked*,
signifies a mortal, incurable disease; a disease
which, seizing on the vitals, affects and threatens
the whole frame; and which no remedy can reach.
This idea leads us to that first transgression,
whereby man, departing from God, fatally destroyed his soul's health, and sunk into that state
so pathetically described by Isaiah, chap. i. "The
whole head is sick;" all the powers of the understanding disordered: "and the whole heart faint;"
all the springs of the affections enfeebled. "From
the sole of the foot, even unto the head, there is
no soundness, but wounds, bruises, and putrefying
sores;" the evil growing worse continually, and
no help or helper at hand: "they have not been
closed nor bound up, nor mollified with ointment." In consequence of this deep-rooted disorder, the heart is deceitful;—that is, it deceives
and fails us in every instance: it promises more
than it can perform: it misleads us with vain desires; and mocks us with unsuccessful efforts: like
the faint attempts of a sick man, to perform those
actions which require a state of sound health and
strength. That this is indeed the case, will, I think,
appear from the following particulars; to which
I entreat your attention.

Scripture and reason do jointly assure us, that

all we see is the work of an Almighty Being :—
the heavens and the earth, the sun, moon, and stars,
and even the grass and flowers of the field, loudly
proclaim the presence, the power, the wisdom, and
the goodness of God : yet behold the extreme *insensibility* of man.   The wisest of our species, in
those places where Divine revelation was not
known, ever mistook the *effect* for the *cause;* and
ascribed that honour to the creature which is due
only to the Creator.   This was the very best of the
case ; for, in general, they sunk still lower, to worship stocks and stones : nay, to the eternal reproach of the natural understanding in the things of
God, the more civilized any nation was, the more
renowned for arts and arms, the farther they were
removed from those they termed *barbarians,* so
much the more vile and contemptible the idolatry
they established generally proved.   The wisdom
of the Egyptians paid divine honours to cats, mon-
keys, and the vilest reptiles.   The fine taste of the
Greeks consecrated those for gods, who, if they
had lived amongst men, would have been deemed
the pests of society ; gods who were, professedly,
both *patterns* and *patrons* of the most shameful vices.
The prowess of the Romans established altars to
fear and paleness.   So deeply were they infatuated,
so totally lost to common sense, that the Apostle
Paul's worst enemies could find no more plausible
accusation against him, in one of the politest
cities then in the world, than that he had ventured
to affirm, " they were no gods who were made
with hands."

Thus stood the case with Heathens : let us now
come nearer home.   It is to be feared, the greatest
difference between them and the generality of us
called *Christians,* is, that we do not partake in
their gross *outward* idolatry.   In other respects,

our insensibility is perhaps as much greater than theirs, as our superior knowledge renders it more inexcusable. We acknowledge a God ; that there is but one ; that he is the cause of all things ; that in him we live, and move, and have our being. Had the poor Heathens known this, we may judge, by their application to their mistaken worship, it would have had some influence on their practice. But what numbers of " us " live altogether as " without God in the world." I come not here to make invectives ; let conscience judge, and give evidence accordingly. What do we think of the perpetual *presence of God* around us, and within us ? We know that he is acquainted with all our thoughts, words, and actions ; yet are we not more effectually restrained and awed by the presence of our fellow-worms, than by the regard of that Eye which is ten thousand times brighter than the sun ? How are we affected by the *works of God?* Has not the appearance of a fine day, or the beauty of an extensive prospect, a force to *extort* a sense of satisfaction from every one ? but how few are there of us that can realize and acknowledge the hand of the glorious Author of these things ? How *seldom* and how *faintly*, do we adopt the reflection of David ? "When I consider the heavens, the work of THY fingers, the moon and stars which THOU hast ordained ; Lord, what is man that thou shouldst be mindful of him ? " Ps. viii. What is our judgment of the *word of God*, that glorious message of love, in which he has pointed out to us the way of salvation ? Is not this book the least read, the least admired, and the least understood, of any ? We are presently affected, we enter with all our spirit into the moving incidents (as we term them) of a romance or tragedy, though we know they are not founded on truth, nor have any relation to ourselves; but we can read the history of Jesus Christ, his life and doctrines, his death and passion, with indifference, though we say, all he spoke, or did, or suffered, was for our sakes. What are our thoughts *of that eternity* to which we are posting, and to which, for aught we know, a few hours may introduce us? Is it not in the power of the meanest trifle that occurs, to hide this important point from our view? It were easy to multiply particulars; but are not these sufficient to shew the deceitfulness, the desperate wickedness, of the heart? Let me add one more: the judgments of God are now abroad in the world for these things. We have warnings all around us. We know that many fruitful lands in our neighbourhood are, in a manner, turned into a wilderness, for the sins of the inhabitants. Every post brings us tidings of some new desolation, and we cannot tell how soon the case may be our own; but we have neither sympathy for our fellow-creatures, nor concern for ourselves. We hear, we pity, we forget, in the same instant. But these things are remote. Is then what we *see* and *feel* more laid to heart? Our friends and acquaintance are taken from amongst us daily; some of them suddenly, in the midst of their warmest pursuits, or just upon the accomplishment of their most favourite schemes: we drop an unmeaning tear, and fly to every officious vanity for relief. Perhaps we are visited ourselves, and brought down to the borders of the grave: but, even against this, we are, for the most part, proof; or, if we feel a slight impression, it gradually wears off with the disease; and we return, as soon as we recover, to our former follies with redoubled ardour.

This is a slight view of the *insensibility* of the

human heart. Let us now consider its *ingratitude.*
The Israelites were a sample of all mankind in this
respect. God visited them, in Egypt, in the midst
of their affliction. Without any application on
their part, he undertook and effected their deliverance : he brought them from among their enemies
" with a high hand, and a stretched-out arm :"
he led them safely through the wilderness : he
screened them with a cloud, from the piercing
beams of the sun : he gave them light by night,
in a pillar of fire : he fed them with bread from
heaven, and caused streams to flow in the sandy
desert : he made a covenant with them, and chose
them for his peculiar people : he destroyed all
their enemies before them ; and, at length, put
them in the full and peaceable possession of a
land flowing with milk and honey. Interwoven
with the history of God's gracious dealings with
them, we have an account of their behaviour towards *him ;* which was a continual series of rebellion, perverseness, murmuring, and disobe-
dience. And are we better than they ? In no wise.
If we had leisure to consider the natural, civil, and
religious advantages we enjoy as a nation, it
would appear that *we* likewise have long been a
peculiarly favoured people. The eye of the Lord
our God has been upon us continually for good ;
and we have reason to say, " He has not dealt
so with any nation." The history of all ages and
countries, affords us no instance of national prosperity that can be compared, either for degree or
continuance, with what we have enjoyed since the
Revolution : nor would it be easy, I fear, to find a
parallel, in any history, of our great ingratitude.
What I have said in the former article will necessarily infer this : for it is impossible that those who
have so little sensibility, either of the value of the

gifts of God, or of his hand in bestowing them, can be grateful.   The *seat* of gratitude is in the heart; the *proof* appears in the words and actions.   Now, what are the prevailing subjects of conversation amongst us?   Are the great things that God has done for us, the high obligations we are under to him, the comforts of our holy religion, and the nature of that blessed hope set before us by the Gospel, in the number?   On the contrary, is not the least hint of these things in company, for the most part, received with reserve, if not with con- tempt and disgust?   " Out of the abundance of the heart the mouth speaketh."   God, and the things of God, have little place there; but levity, detraction, ill temper, and, not seldom, profane- ness and obscenity, in our discourses, too plainly discover the nature of the fountain from whence they flow.   And if we look upon the actions of men in general, they are but of a piece with their words: engrossed by business, or enslaved to pleasure, for a season, all upon the stretch in amassing treasures; and then, perhaps, as restless and eager to dissipate them.   Whatever passion rules them for the time, or whatever changes they may admit in their schemes, it is too plain, that a principle of gratitude to God, and a conscious de- sire to please him, has little influence either in forming or executing their plans.   If these things are so, we have another instance of the deceitful- ness and desperate wickedness of the heart: it is full of the blackest ingratitude.

Need any thing be added to these two charges? Have we not said enough to confirm the prophet's assertion?   If not, we can name a third particular, if possible, more absurd and inexcusable than either of the former.   Man is not only insensible of the greatest part of those things which most con-

cern him, and ungrateful and disobedient to his
Maker and Preserver, his best and only friend, but
he is *proud* too.   Though he has nothing but what
he has received, has received nothing but what he
has perverted and mismanaged, and must render a
strict account of his mismanagement, yet he is
proud.   We have already seen his blindness and
baseness; there wanted only pride to make him
a monster indeed.   And need we spend time to
prove this?   No.   *This*, at least, is an universal
evil.   Any man may easily perceive it in every man
but himself; and every *thinking* man may perceive
it working within himself incessantly.   Whether
we are alone or in company, whether with friends
or enemies, with those above us or those below us,
pride will insinuate.   Nay, in the immediate presence of God, when we come together to implore
his mercy, while the most humbling confessions
are upon our lips, and we are charging ourselves
as most miserable, helpless sinners, even here
pride will find us out.   Those must be great
strangers to themselves, who are not sensible of
this.   Now, " why is dust and ashes proud ?"
proud of our failings ! proud of our infirmities ! Is
it not from hence, because the heart is deplorably
diseased, desperately wicked, and deeply deceitful ?

I shall pursue this point no farther.   I shall not
attempt to enumerate, at present, those " evil
thoughts, murders, adulteries, fornications, thefts,
and blasphemies," Mark vii. 21, which our Lord
assures us do perpetually " proceed from the
heart."   I chose to insist on insensibility, ingratitude, and pride; because these are the vices
which, in common life, we most condemn, are
willing to think ourselves most free from, and can
the least bear to be charged with.   And it must be

allowed, that, between man and man, there is often the appearance of much generosity, gratitude, and condescension. But what will it avail us, that we stand upon some tolerable terms towards each other in these respects, if we are guilty before God? "The Lord seeth not as man seeth," 1 Sam. xvi.: he cannot be deceived or put off with a fair appearance; for he "searcheth the heart, and trieth the reins." This is the next point to be considered.

II. That the heart, with all its workings and all its faults, is incessantly under the Divine inspection and examination: "I, the Lord, search the heart, and try the reins." The *heart* and *reins,* as distinguished in Scripture phrase, signify those different powers of the mind, the affections, and the thoughts. The words *search* and *try* have an emphasis in the original, which cannot be reached without a paraphrase, if at all.

The Lord *searches* [חקר] the heart: he traces, investigates, the inmost principles of our souls to their first rise, with (if I may so speak) a mathematical accuracy. He *tries* [בחן] the reins: he watches every rising thought; he brings it to the test of his most pure law: he examines it with the utmost exactness; as a refiner essays his metals, with a purpose to reject whatever is inferior to the prescribed standard. To form a more just idea of this scrutiny, let us ask ourselves, how we could bear to be obliged to declare aloud, in full company, every thought which passes through our minds every wish and desire of which we are conscious, without the least reserve or exception? I am persuaded there are few people so lost to shame, but, if they were brought to this trial, they would rather choose to die than comply with it. Some things they would perceive, especially upon such a provocation, which they could hardly, upon any terms, prevail with themselves to express. The Lord has mercifully kept us from the knowledge of each other's hearts, any farther than we are willing to disclose ourselves : for was every man compelled to speak all he thinks, there would be an end of society ; and man would no more venture to dwell with man, than with tygers and bears. We know what mischief one ungoverned tongue may some-times occasion : now, the tongue can do no evil, any farther than as it is an instrument of disclosing the hidden things of the heart ; yet it is but a small part of these the worst tongue is capable of disclosing. What then would be the case, if all our hearts were open, all our desires known to one another ? What a mixture of confusion, and defiance, shame, rage, fear, and contempt, would overspread every countenance ! and yet thus we are exposed to the searching eye of a pure and holy God. The Lord knows the thoughts of man's heart, that they are vain. He long ago declared the re-sult of his observation. " God saw the wicked-ness of man was great in the earth ; and that every imagination of the thoughts of his heart was only evil continually ;" Gen. vi. And, though the world was drowned for this, matters were not mended afterwards : for, upon a second survey, the judg-ment amounts to the same. " The Lord looked down from heaven upon the children of men, to see if there were any that did understand, and seek God. They are all gone aside ; they are altogether become filthy ; there is none that doeth good, no, not one. Their throat is an open se-pulchre : with their tongues they have used de-ceit ; the poison of asps is under their lips," Ps. xiv., Isa. lix. Compare Rom. iii. How it was in our blessed Saviour's time we have already ob-

served; and neither Scripture nor experience give
us reason to hope it has been better since, or is
now.   The Apostle Paul has assured us, " That,
in the last days (a character which it is likely co-
incides with our days), perilous times shall come.
For men shall be lovers of their own selves, covet-
ous, boasters, proud, blasphemers, disobedient to
parents, unthankful, unholy, without natural affection, truce-breakers, false accusers, incontinent,
fierce, despisers of those that are good, traitors,
heady, high-minded, lovers of pleasure more than
lovers of God: having a form of godliness, but
denying the power thereof." 2 Tim. iii.   Surely,
I say, if these are marks of the *last days,* they
must be already commenced.   However, we
see, upon the whole, how vile and hateful our
hearts must appear in the sight of a heart-searching God.

III. One thing more we have to consider: That
the Lord does not observe the heart of man with
the indifference of a mere spectator, but as an impartial and inflexible Judge; " that he may give
every man according to his ways, and according
to the fruit of his doings."   This was the third
particular to be spoken to.

But, alas! what can be said to this?   Is it
not sufficient to fill our souls with astonishment,
and to cause *all faces to gather blackness;* to hear,
that the Lord has purposed to render to every man
according to his works; and that he sits Judge,
not only upon outward actions, but examines the
very thoughts and intents of the heart?   Dare any
of *us* abide the issue of such a trial?   Which of us
will presume to say, I am clean?   To what purpose
can any of us plead, I have not committed adultery,
if God charges us with every inordinate desire,
with every offence of the eye?   What will it

avail, that we have never assaulted the life of our neighbour, if every angry word, every degree of ill-will or revenge, is considered as murder in God's sight? It will not suffice to say, I am no thief or extortioner, unless we can clear ourselves of the most distant wish of possessing what was the property of another. If we are sure that we have not forsworn ourselves, but have performed to the Lord our oaths, it is only thus far well, that we shall not be condemned for open and actual perjury. But if we have at any time mentioned, or even *thought* of, the name of God, without the highest habitual reverence, we have taken his name in vain; and he has declared he will not hold us guiltless. That this is no gloss of my inventing, but the very words of truth, the declaration of Him by whom we must be one day judged, the fifth chapter of Matthew will inform you. There a wanton glance is styled adultery; an angry expression censured as murder; and to speak unadvisedly, even of the hairs of our head, is deemed a branch of profane swearing. And why? Because all these spring from the heart, which is " naked and open," without either covering or concealment, " in the sight of him with whom we have to do;" Heb. iv. This is thought uncomfortable doctrine, and not without reason, could we go no farther. For there is nothing in heaven or in earth, in time or eternity, that affords the least glimpse of comfort to fallen man, if either God is strict to mark what is amiss, or if he, trusting in himself, presumes to plead with his Maker. The Divine law requires perfect, unremitted, unsinning obedience: it denounces a curse upon the least failure. " Cursed is every one that continueth not in all things which are written in the book of the law to do them;" Gal. iii. 10;

every one, without exception of person or circumstance, *that continueth not*, from the beginning to the end of life, *in all things*, great and small, *to do them*, τον ποιησαι αυτα, to finish them, to do them completely, without any defect either in matter or manner.   Most uncomfortable doctrine indeed, were there no remedy provided!   For the law of God is as eternal and unchangeable as his nature: it must not, it cannot be attempered or brought down to our capacities; neither can the penalty be evaded: for the God of truth has said, has sworn, that " the soul that sinneth shall die," Ezek. xviii. 4.   Here then we must receive " a sentence of death in ourselves," 2 Cor. i. 9.   Here, " every mouth must be stopped, and all the world become guilty before God," Rom. iii. 19.   Here we must say with the Apostle, " Therefore, by the deeds of the law, there shall be no flesh justified in his sight," Gal. ii. 16; " for by the law is the knowledge of sin," Rom. iii. 20.   O that we could all sincerely say so; that we were brought to this, to feel and confess our lost, undone estate, and our utter inability to save ourselves!   then, with joy, should I proceed to what I have had in my eye all along.   For with what view have I said so much upon so disagreeable a subject?   Why have I attempted to lay open some of the depths of the heart?   but that I might more fully illustrate the wonderful grace and goodness of God, vouchsafed to us in the Gospel; and, at the same time, shew the utter impossibility, not of being saved at all, but of finding salvation in any other way than that which God has appointed.   For, behold!   " God has so loved the world," John iii., that he sent his Son to accomplish that for us, " which the law could not do through the weakness of our flesh," Rom. viii.   Jesus Christ

performed perfect obedience to the law of God in
our behalf: He died, and satisfied the penalty due
to our sins : He arose from the grave as our representative : He is entered into heaven as our forerunner.   " He has received gifts for men, even
for the rebellious," Psalm lxviii. He is "exalted"
on high, to " bestow repentance and remission of
sins," Acts v., on all that seek to him.   He has
established his ordinances for this purpose : He
has commanded his people, not to "neglect assembling themselves together."   He has charged
his ministers, at such seasons, to declare first
the guilty, deplorable condition of mankind, and
then to proclaim the glad tidings of salvation,
" by faith which is in him."   He has promised to
be with them in this work to the end of the world.
He has promised, that where his word is faithfully
preached, he will accompany it " with a spirit
and power," that shall bear down all opposition.
He has promised, that while we are speaking to
the ear, he will, by his secret influence, apply it
to the heart, and open it to receive and embrace
the truth spoken, as in the case of Lydia.   Who
would venture to preach a doctrine so unpalatable
to the carnal mind, as Jesus Christ, and him crucified ?   Who would undertake so ungrateful a
task, as to depreciate that noble creature *man,*
and arraign him publicly of insensibility, ingratitude, pride, and deceit ; were it not that we have,
first, a *command,* and that at our peril, to speak
plain ; and, secondly, a *promise* that we shall not
speak in vain ?   Not that we can expect to be
universally received : the time *is* come, when
many " will not endure sound doctrine," 2 Tim.
iv. 3 ; but some there will be, whom God is
pleased to save by the *foolishness of preaching,* so
called.   Some such I would hope are in this as-

sembly.   To such I say, Think not to satisfy the
Divine justice by any poor performances of your
own ; think not to cleanse or expiate the evil of
your hearts by any of your own inventions ; but,
" behold the Lamb of God, which taketh away
the sin of the world," John i. 29.   He died, that
you may live : He lives, that you may live for
ever.   Put, therefore, your trust in the Lord ; for
with him is plenteous redemption.   His sufferings
and death are a complete final propitiation for sin.
" He is able to save to the uttermost ;" and he is
as willing as he is able.   It was *this* brought him
down from heaven; for *this* he emptied himself
of all glory, and submitted to all indignity.   His
humiliation expiates our pride; his perfect love
atones for our ingratitude ; his exquisite tenderness pleads for our insensibility.   Only believe ;
commit your cause to him by faith and prayer.
As a *Priest,* he shall make atonement for your
sins, and present your persons and your services
acceptable before God.   As a *Prophet,* he shall
instruct you in the true wisdom, which maketh
wise to salvation : he shall not only cause you to
know his commandments, but to love them too :
he shall write them in your hearts.   As a *King,*
he shall evermore mightily defend you against
all your enemies.   He shall enable you to withstand temptations, to support difficulties, to break
through all opposition.   He shall supply you
with every thing you need, for this life or a better,
out of the unsearchable riches of his grace.   He
shall strengthen you to overcome all things ; to
endure to the end : and then he shall give you a
place in his kingdom; a seat near his throne ; a
crown of life ; a crown of glory ; incorruptible,
undefiled, and that fadeth not away.

SERMON II.

ON THE SAVIOUR, AND HIS SALVATION.

1 Tim. i. 15.

This is a faithful saying, and worthy of all acceptation, that Christ Jesus came into the world to save sinners; of whom I am chief.

THOUGH the Apostle Paul has written largely and happily upon every branch of Christian doctrine and practice; and, with respect to his writings, as well as his preaching, could justly assert, " that he had not shunned to declare the whole counsel of God;" yet there are two points which seem to have been (if I may so speak) his favourite topics, which he most frequently repeats, most copiously insists on, and takes every occasion of introducing. The one is, to display the honours, power, and faithfulness of the Lord Jesus Christ; the other, to make known the great things God had done for his own soul. How his heart was filled and fired with the first of these, is evident from almost every chapter of his Epistles. When he speaks of that mystery of godliness, " God manifested in the flesh," and the exceeding grace and love declared to a lost world, through him, the utmost powers of language fall short of his purpose. With a noble freedom he soars beyond the little bounds of criticism; and, finding the most expressive words too weak and faint for his ideas, he forms and compounds new ones, heaps one hyperbole upon another; yet, after his most laboured essays to do justice to his subject, he often breaks off in a manner that shews he was far from being satisfied with all he could say.

This reflection is most obvious to those who can read him in the *original:* but no disadvantages of a translation can wholly confine that inimitable ardour with which he seems to pour his whole soul into his words, when he is speaking of his Lord and Saviour. And he who can read the first chapters of his Epistles to the Ephesians, Colossians, and Hebrews, the second to the Philippians, or many similar passages, with indifference, must be, I say, not merely a person of small devotion, but of little taste and sensibility.

And how deeply his mind was impressed with the mercies he had received in his conversion and call, is equally conspicuous. He takes every occasion to aggrandize the goodness of God to himself; to exaggerate and deplore the guilt and misery of his former life, in which he once trusted; and to lament the small returns he was able to make for such blessings ; even when he could say, without boasting, that he had " laboured more abundantly " than the most diligent and zealous of his fellow-servants.

A powerful abiding sense of these two points upon the Apostle's mind, have given rise to many sudden, lively, and beautiful digressions in the course of his writings. The context to the passage I have read is of this kind. Having incidentally spoken of the Gospel in the 11th verse, he is suddenly struck with the reflection of his own misery while ignorant of it, and the wonderful goodness of God, in affording him the knowledge of salvation, and honouring him, who was before a blasphemer, with a commission to publish the same glad tidings to others. This thought suspends his argument, and fills his heart and mouth with praise. And having acknowledged, that " the grace of our Lord was exceeding abundant " towards himself, he subjoins the words of the text, for an encouragement to others; assuring us, that his case was not so peculiar, but that multitudes might be partakers with him in the same hope of mercy.

The words easily resolve into two parts:

First, A short, but comprehensive proposition, including the purport of the whole Gospel, " that Jesus Christ came into the world to save sinners."

Secondly, A commendation of this doctrine in a two-fold respect " as a faithful saying," and as " worthy of all acceptation;" each of these illustrated by the instance of himself; when he adds, " of whom I am chief."

I. The Apostle well knew the different reception the Gospel would meet in the world; that many poor guilty souls, trembling under a sense of sin and unworthiness, would very hardly be persuaded, that such sinners as they could be saved at all. To these he recommends it as " a faithful saying," founded upon the immutable counsel, promise, and oath of God, that Jesus Christ came into the world to save *sinners;* sinners in general; " the chief of sinners;" such as he represents himself to have been. He knew, likewise, that many others, from a mistaken opinion of their own goodness, or a mistaken dependence on something of their own choosing, would be liable to undervalue this faithful saying. For the sake of these, he adds, " it is worthy of all acceptation." None are so bad but the Gospel affords them a ground of hope: none are so good as to have any just ground of hope without it. There was a time when St. Paul could have made a fair profession of himself likewise: he could say, " circumcised on the eighth day, of the stock of Israel, of the tribe of Benjamin, an Hebrew of the

Hebrews; as to the law, a Pharisee; as to the righteousness which is by the law, blameless ;" Phil. iii. But he has been since taught to " count all things but loss for the excellency " of the knowledge of Christ," and is content to style himself *the chief of sinners.*

Having thus attempted to shew the design and meaning of the words, I propose, something more at large, to unfold the proposition, and point out some of those important and extensive truths it contains. I say, *some of them ;* for it is not possible that either men or angels can fully sound the depth of this one sentence, " that Jesus Christ came into the world to save sinners." I shall afterwards *infer*, and *enforce* the other part of the text, that it is indeed " a faithful saying, and worthy of all acceptation." And may He, who came into the world to procure salvation for sinners, and is now exalted on high to bestow it, accompany the whole with his promised blessing.

The tenor of the proposition readily suggests three inquiries. First, Who this person is, here spoken of, Jesus Christ ? Second, What is meant by the salvation he is said to have undertaken ? Third, By what means he effected it ?

Let us, *first*, speak of this gracious, this wonderful person, Jesus Christ. We already bear his name as professed Christians ; and we speak of him as *our Master*, and *our Lord :* and so far we say well. But, as he has told us, many will call him *Lord* at the great day, to whom he will profess, " I never knew you whence you are; depart;" so it is to be feared there are many *now*, that outwardly acknowledge him, who neither know *whence* he is nor *who* he is. Though we have Moses and the prophets, the apostles and evangelists, continually with us ; though it is the imme-

diate aim and intent of all their writings, in every
history, promise, prophecy, type, ceremony, and
law, to set *Him* before our eyes ; and though there
is hardly an image in the material creation but is
adopted by the Scriptures to shadow forth his
excellency; ignorance of Jesus Christ, and what
he has done for his people, is the great cause that
religion appears so *low* and *contemptible* to some,
and is found so *tedious* and *burdensome* by others.
Let us therefore attend *to the record God has given
of his Son ;* for I propose in this article to say
little of my own, but to lay before you the express, powerful, indubitable testimony of holy
Scripture.

And here we are taught, first, *That Jesus Christ
is God.* The first words of St. John's Gospel are
full to this point : " In the beginning " (that is, at
the commencement of time and things, when as
yet nothing else existed,) " was the Word, and the
Word was with God, and the Word was God."
To prevent a possibility of mistake, and to confirm
the eternity of this Divine Word in the strongest
manner, it is immediately added, " the same was
in the beginning with God. All things were made
by him." And lest this likewise should be either
contested or misunderstood, it is guarded by an
universal negative, " without him was not any
thing made that was made." Further, to prevent,
if possible, the surmise, that, in these glorious
words, the Eternal Word acted with a deputed
power only, the Apostle subjoins, " In him was
life," life essentially ; and from him, as the fountain, life and light proceeded to his creatures :
" In him was life, and that life was the light of
men." To this agrees the declaration of St. Paul :
" For by him were all things created that are in
heaven, and that are in earth, visible and invisible,

whether thrones, or dominions, or principalities, or powers : all things were created by him and for him;" *(by* his power and wisdom, *for* his glory and pleasure). " And he is before all things, and by him all things consist," Col. i.   Elsewhere he speaks of him expressly, as " over all God, blessed for ever ; who upholdeth all things by the word of his power; the same yesterday, to-day, and for ever."   It were easy to enlarge this way; but I shall content myself with observing this general proof of the Divinity of Christ, that the Scriptures, which were given to make us wise to salvation, do ascribe to him the names of God, particularly *Jehovah ;* the essential attributes of God, such as *Eternity, Omnipresence, Omnipotence ;* the peculiar works of God, as *Creation, Providence, Redemption,* and *Forgiveness of Sin ;* and, finally, command us to pay him those *Divine* honours, and to rely on him with that *absolute dependence,* which would be idolatry if referred any where below the Supreme Majesty of heaven and earth.

Again, we learn from Scripture, that *Christ* is truly and properly *Man.*   This is indeed wonderful! therefore styled " the great mystery of godliness ;" 1 Tim. iii.   But that He, of whom we have begun to speak, is the very person who came into the world to save sinners, we have abundant proof.   The Apostle John, whose testimony we have already cited, says, a few verses lower, John i. 14, " And the Word " (that glorious Word, which was God with God) " was made flesh, and dwelt amongst us, and we beheld his glory," (that is, we, his disciples, whose eyes were spiritually enlightened, for the world in general saw nothing of it,) " as the glory of the only begotten of the Father, full of grace and truth."   In other places it is said, " Himself took our infirmities and bore our sicknesses; Matth. viii. 17; and was in all points tempted as we are, yet without sin;" Heb. iv. 15. " As the children are partakers of flesh and blood, he also, himself, likewise took part of the same;" Heb. ii. 14. " In the fulness of time, God sent forth his Son, made of a woman;" Gal. iv. Many are the mistakes of mortals, and wide the extremes into which mistaken mortals run! Some have rashly ventured to deny our Lord's Divinity; some have wildly and fancifully explained away his Humanity; but may we, through grace, abide by the Scriptural truth, and be directed in the midst of the path of judgment.

From this mystical union of the divine and human nature in one person, the Scripture speaks of him, thirdly, under the character of a *Mediator*, the " one Mediator between God and man." To this idea the names *Jesus Christ*, which are as ointment poured forth, direct us in their original import. The former, which signifies the *Saviour*, pointing out the success and efficacy of his undertaking; the latter, which is the same with *Messiah*, or the *Anointed*, expressing both his Divine appointment thereto, and the complete supply of all grace and power, wherewith he was filled for the discharge of it. Thus much for the person spoken of.

We proceed, in the next place, to consider the design of his appearance in the world : " to save sinners." And as the idea of *deliverance* presupposes a state of *distress*, it will be necessary previously to inquire into the condition of those whom he came to save; which is indeed emphatically implied in the appellation given them, *sinners.* Man having broken that law under which he was created, and with which his happiness was closely connected, fell under accumulated ruin. The image of God, in which he was formed, was de-

faced, and a far different image set up in his heart,
even of him who had seduced him from his alle-
giance; darkness in the understanding, rebellion
in the will, sensuality in the affections; the justice
of God threatening a penalty he could neither satisfy nor sustain; the commandments of God still
challenging an obedience he had no longer any
power to yield. The very gifts and bounties of
God, with which he was encompassed, designed
not only for his comfort, but his instruction, to
lead him, as by so many steps, to their gracious
Author, became eventually the occasions of withdrawing him farther from his duty, and increasing,
as well as aggravating, his ingratitude. Thus stood
man towards his Maker. With regard to his
fellow-creatures, self-love and inordinate desires
having raised a variety of interfering interests in
the breasts of all, peace withdrew from the earth.
Every man's heart and hand was set against his
neighbour; and violence, rage, envy, and confusion, overspread the world. Nor could he be
easier in himself; hurried by restless desires towards things either unsatisfying or unattainable,
haunted with cares, tortured with pains, tired
with opposition, shocked with disappointment;
conscience, like the hand that appeared in Bel-
shazzar's feast, Daniel v., writing bitter things
against him, when outward circumstances allowed
a short repose: and vanity, like a worm, destroy-
ing the root of every flower that promised the
fairest bloom of success. Behold a few outlines
of the picture of fallen man! Miserable in his life,
more miserable in the continual dread of losing
such a life; miserable, most of all, that neither his
fancy can feign, nor his fear conceive, the consequences of the death he dreads,—which will introduce him to the immediate presence, to the *tribunal,* of an incensed, almighty, ever-living God!

Such was the state from which Jesus Christ came to save us. He came to restore us to the favour of God; to reconcile us to ourselves, and to each other; to give us peace and joy in life, hope and triumph in death, and after death glory, honour, and immortality. For he came, not merely to repair, and to restore, but to exalt; not only, " that we might have life," the life we had forfeited, but " that we might have it more abundantly," John x.; that our happiness might be more exalted, our title more firm, and our possession more secure, than the state of Adam in paradise could boast, or than his posterity could have attained unto, if he had continued unsinning upon the tenor of the first covenant.

Now, could we suppose it possible, that a set of innocent beings, without any default of their own, had sunk into a state of misery, we must confess it would have been great grace and favour in the Lord Jesus to save them. But let us not forget the stress laid in the text upon the word *sinners.* He came to save, not the *unfortunate,* but the *ungodly;* Rom. v. How then should every heart glow with love to him, who hath thus loved us! If any of *us* can hear or speak of this subject with indifference or disgust, it is to be feared we are quite strangers to the *nature,* or the *necessity,* of that salvation with which God has graciously visited his people. Let us no more usurp the sacred words of *generosity, sensibility,* or *gratitude,* if this astonishing instance of Divine goodness leaves us cold and unimpressed; especially if to this we join the consideration of the third point I proposed to speak of, By what means Jesus Christ effected this salvation for sinners.

In the passage before us, it is only said, that he *came into the world* on this account; which teaches us, *this* was the sole design of his advent; and that,

coming on set purpose for this, he would leave
nothing undone that was necessary to accomplish
it.   He emptied himself of that divine glory and
honour he possessed with the Father from eternity.
" He bowed the heavens, and came down" to our
earth ; and that not with an external glory, as a
celestial messenger, to constrain the attention and
homage of mankind, " but was made of a woman,"
Gal. iv. ; not of high and noble extraction in the
judgment of men, " but in the form of a servant ;"
born in a stable, laid in a manger, brought up in
an obscure and contemptible place, and reputed
no higher than the Son of a carpenter.   " He was
despised and rejected of men : there was no form
or comeliness in him," Isa. liii., to attract a general
regard : on the contrary, " he came to his own,
and his own received him not," John i.   Farther,
as he was made of a woman, " he was made under
the law ;" the one in order to the other ; for this
was the way Divine Wisdom had appointed, and
which Divine Justice required, to make salvation
possible to sinners.   Eternal Truth had pronounced
tribulation, wrath, and anguish, upon every soul
of man that doth evil.   All men, in every age and
place, " had corrupted their ways before God ;"
yet his mercy had designed, " that where sin had
abounded,   grace   should   much   more   abound,"
Rom. viii.   Jesus Christ was the grand expedient,
in whom " mercy and truth met together," Psalm
lxxxv., and the inflexible *righteousness* of God was
brought to correspond and harmonize with the
peace of sinful man.   That justice might be satisfied, truth vindicated, and sinners saved, " God
so loved a lost world," that, when no inferior
means could avail, when none in heaven or earth
were *willing*, or *worthy*, or *able*, to interpose, " he
gave his only-begotten Son," John iii.   Jesus
Christ, the brightness of the Father's glory, and

express image of his person, " so loved the world,"
that he assumed our nature, undertook our cause,
bore our sins, sustained our deserved punishment ;
and, having done and suffered all that the case
required, he is now gone before, "to prepare a
place," John xiv., for all that believe in him and
obey him. Man lay under a double incapacity
for happiness ; he could neither keep the law of
God in future, nor satisfy for his past breach and
contempt of it. To obviate the former, Jesus
Christ performed a perfect unsinning obedience in
our stead. To remove the latter, he became " the
propitiation of our sins ;" yielded up his life as a
prey into the hands of murderers, and poured
forth his precious blood, in drops of sweat in the
garden, in streams from his side upon the cross.
For this he endured the fiercest temptations of the
devil, the scorn, rage, and malice of men, and
drank the bitter cup of the wrath of God, when it
pleased the Father to bruise him, and make his
soul an offering for sin. His love carried him
through all ; and when he had finally overcome
the sharpness of death, he opened the kingdom of
heaven to all believers. In few words, he lived
and died for us when upon earth : nor is he unmindful of us in heaven, but lives and intercedes
on our behalf. He continually executes the offices
of Prophet, Priest, and King, to his people ; instructing them by his word and Spirit ; presenting their persons and prayers, acceptable to God
through his merits ; defending them, by his power,
from all their enemies, ghostly and bodily ; and
ordering, by his providence, all things to work
together for their good, till at length they are
brought home, to be with him where he is, and to
behold his glory.

II. From what has been said, we may justly
infer, in the first place, that " this is," as the

Apostle styles it, " a faithful saying." When man first fell, God, " in the midst of judgment remembering mercy," declared, unsought and undesired, " that the Seed of the woman should bruise the serpent's head;" Gen. iii. In every succeeding age, he confirmed his purpose by types, promises, prophecies, and oaths. At length, in the fulness of time, Christ, " the Desire of all nations," came into the world, fulfilled all that had been foretold, and encouraged every humble penitent sinner to come unto him, that they might have life, pardon, and peace. To doubt, or to deny, his readiness to save, is, so far as in us lies, to " make the word of God of none effect;" it is " to charge God foolishly," as though, like the heedless unskilful builder in the Gospel, he had begun to build that which was not to be finished. If, after all that is set before us, it is possible for any soul to miss salvation that sincerely desires it, and seeks it in God's appointed way, it must be because the Lord Jesus Christ either *cannot* or *will not* save them. That he cannot, is flatly false; for " all power is his in heaven and in earth ;" Matth. xxviii.; and it is particularly said, that " he is able to save to the uttermost all that come unto God by him ;" Heb. vii. : and that he will not, is as false; for he himself hath said, " Whosoever cometh unto me, 1 will in nowise cast out." John vi.

We may infer, secondly, that this doctrine is not only faithful, but " worthy of all acceptation." And here, methinks, I could begin anew. A point so much mistaken by some, and neglected by most, rather requires a whole, or many discourses, than to be passed over in few words. The most high and wise God has esteemed the redemption of mankind so precious, " that he spared not his only Son ;" Rom. viii.—And are there any amongst us, in a

land of Gospel light and liberty, where the words
of wisdom are sounding in our ears every day, that
dare make light of this message, just give it a
hearing, and return to their farms, their merchandise, and their diversions, as though this unspeakable grace of God called for no return? Alas!
" How shall we escape, if we neglect this salvation?" Heb. ii. " He that despised Moses' law
died without mercy." It was dangerous, it was
destructive, to refuse him that spoke upon earth;
take heed how you trifle with Him " that speaketh
from heaven!" To such as neglect this, " there
remains no other sacrifice for sin, but a certain
fearful looking for of fiery indignation that shall
devour the adversaries;" Heb. x. Let none of us
think it is well with us, merely because we were
born and educated in a Christian country, have
means of instruction in our hands, and enjoy frequent opportunities of presenting ourselves before
God in public worship. To thousands these, so far
from being advantages, will greatly aggravate
their condemnation, and point the sting of the
never-dying worm. Better were it for us to have
been inhabitants of Tyre and Sidon, Luke x.; yea
of Sodom and Gomorrah, than to appear in judgment with no better plea than this. Neither let us
speak peace to ourselves, because we are not so bad
as others, but perhaps live decently and comfortably, are useful in society, and perform many things
that are commonly called *good works*. If these works
spring from a true love of God, if they are framed
according to the rule of his word, if they are performed by faith in Christ Jesus our Lord, they are
undoubtedly good, and shall be rewarded before
men and angels: if otherwise, you have already
your reward, in the complacence of your own
minds, and the approbation of friends and acquaint-

ance. The Christianity of the New Testament imports more than all this. It is, to believe in Jesus
Christ; so to believe in him, as to obey him in all
his commands, to trust him in all his dispensations,
to walk in his steps, copying out the bright example
of his love, meekness, patience, self-denial, and active zeal for the glory of God, and the good of mankind. It is, from a consciousness of our utter inability to perform these great things, to depend
continually upon the promised aid and direction of
his Holy Spirit, to seek this assistance by frequent
fervent prayer, to offer up ourselves daily as living
sacrifices unto God;—and, finally, when we have
done all, to be deeply sensible of our unworthiness
of the least of his mercies, to confess ourselves
unprofitable servants, and to place all our hopes
upon this faithful saying, " That Jesus Christ
came into the world to save sinners."

Thus, from the consideration of the person of the
Lord Jesus Christ, the greatness of our misery by
nature, and the wonderful things he has done and
suffered for our redemption, we may learn the
complete security of that salvation he has provided,
the extreme danger of neglecting it, and the folly
and presumption of attempting to establish a
righteousness of our own, independent of Him
" who is appointed of God unto us, wisdom,
righteousness, sanctification, and redemption;"
1 Cor. i. In setting these things before you plainly
and faithfully, I trust I have delivered my own
soul. Time is short, life is precarious, and perhaps, to some, this may be the last opportunity of
the kind that may be afforded them : God grant
we may be wise in time, that, " to-day, while it is
called to-day," we may hear his voice. Then we
shall understand more of the text than words can
teach us; then we shall experience " a peace which

passeth all understanding," Phil. iv.; " a joy" which "a stranger intermeddleth not with," Prov. xiv.; and a hope " full of glory," which shall be completed in the endless possession of those " pleasures which are at the right hand of God," Psalm xvi.; where sin, and its inseparable attendant sorrow, shall cease for ever; where "there shall be no more grief, or pain, or fear," Rev. xxi.; but every tear shall be wiped from every eye.

SERMON III.

ON THE CHRISTIAN NAME,

Acts xi. 26, latter part.

—And the disciples were called Christians first at Antioch.

The evangelist Luke, having contributed his appointed part to the history of our Lord and Saviour Jesus Christ, proceeds, in the book we style *the Acts of the Apostles,* to inform us of the state and behaviour of those faithful followers he left behind him on earth, when he ascended, in the name and behalf of his people, to that heaven from whence his love had brought him down. We are informed, that the gracious promises he had made while he was yet with them, began soon to take place; for, " when the day of Pentecost was fully come," Acts ii., the Holy Spirit descended powerfully upon them, qualified them for preaching the Gospel to the whole world, and gave them an earnest of success, in making their first essay the happy means of converting about " three thousand souls."

The first believers, who " were of one heart and one soul, who continued stedfastly in the Apostle's doctrine, and had all things in common," would probably have been well content to have lived together in Jerusalem, till death had successively transplanted them to the Jerusalem which is above. But this was not to be their rest; and their Lord, who had appointed them to be " the salt of the earth," and " the light of the world," Matth. v., made use of the rage of their enemies to effect that separation which those who are united by the grace of God are often so loth to yield to. Little did Herod and the Jews consider what would be the consequence of the persecution they raised against the church of Christ: but persecutors are always blind, and counteract their own designs. So here; for we are told, that those whom they scattered abroad, "went every where preaching the word." Thus, the word of the Lord " ran and was glorified ;" their bitterest enemies contributing to push it forward, till, in a few years, it was published " from sea to sea, and from the river to the ends of the earth." Psalm lxxii.

For a while these faithful followers of the Lamb were known only by particular names, according to the different humours of different places ; *Nazarenes, Galileans, the people of that way, pestilent fellows*, and the like : but at length, when they grew more numerous, when their societies were regularly formed, and their enemies universally alarmed, they began to bear a more general and emphatical name. St. Luke has informed us, that this was the case in fact, and has likewise told us where it first obtained ; and as I suppose he did not this without some design, I shall endeavour to draw some observations for our use and direction, from this remark in the text, that " the disciples were called Christians first at Antioch :" which I shall divide into two; thus—That the first general name by which the disciples were distinguished from the world, and united among themselves, was that of

Christians; and, secondly, That this took place at Antioch. Thus the propositions lie in the text; but, in treating of each, it may be more convenient to invert this order, and consider the latter as previous to the other.

Now, if we consider the state of the city of Antioch, *before, at the time,* and *since* the event which is here recorded; from each of these views we may gather some lesson of instruction for ourselves; which ought to be our view in all we read, but especially when we read those books " which are able to make us wise unto salvation," and where no one sentence is insignificant. But let us not forget, with all we read and hear concerning religion, to mingle our frequent prayers to the great Author and Fountain of all grace, for that aid and assistance of his Holy Spirit, without which we can do nothing to advantage.

Antioch, the capital of Syria, built about three hundred years before Christ, had been long the most flourishing city of the East: the most remarkable circumstance of its ancient state, as suiting our present purpose, was its having been the seat and residence of Antiochus, the most cruel and inveterate enemy of the church and people of God ; the most direct and eminent type of that Antichrist who was afterwards to appear in the world ; spoken of expressly by prophecy in Daniel, chap. xi.; the completion of which you may see at large in the First Book of Maccabees, in Josephus, and more briefly in the 79th and 80th Psalms. But behold the wisdom, the power, and the providence of God! When his people were brought low, he helped them : he set those bounds to the rage of the adversary which could not be broken through ; and, at length, in his appointed time, he erected *this* first general standard of the Gospel, upon the very spot where his grand enemy had so long encamped, and from whence his pernicious counsels and enterprises had so far proceeded. The application of this is very suitable to the times in which we now live. We see a powerful combination against the Protestant interest. Our enemies are many and mighty : their designs, we have reason to believe, are deep laid, and their efforts unwearied. Once and again our hopes have been almost swallowed up : and though we, through the singular goodness of God, have hitherto escaped, the storm has fallen heavy upon our brethren abroad. What may be the *immediate* issue of the present threatening appearances, we know not : but we may encourage ourselves from the experience of past ages, as well as from the sure promises of Scripture, that however " the kings of the earth may assemble, and the rulers take counsel together," Psalm ii., God " has a hook in their nose, and a bridle in their jaws," Isa. xxxvii. ; and all their force and policy shall at last bring about what they least desire and intend—the welfare and glory of God's church. He that caused the Christian name to go forth first at Antioch, where the truth of God had been most eminently and successfully opposed, can likewise introduce a temper and worship *truly Christian*, in those places which at present seem destitute of either. And for this it is our duty continually to pray.

Again ; if we consider the state of Antioch at the time the disciples were first called *Christians* there, we may learn how to form a judgment of our profession. This city was then luxurious and dissolute to a proverb, even in Asia, where luxury and effeminacy were universally prevalent. Whether this name was assumed by the disciples, or imposed by their enemies, we cannot doubt but that, in common repute, it was a term of the most

extreme reproach and ignominy. Nor can I suppose the worst appellations any sect in succeeding
ages has been doomed to bear, have implied half
of that contempt which an inhabitant of Antioch
or Daphne expressed when he called a man a
Christian. If we imagine a set of people, who, at
this time, in France, should style themselves the
disciples of the late Damien, and be called after
his name, we may perhaps form some idea of what
the people of Antioch understood by the word
Christian. The Apostle assures us, that he and
his brethren were " accounted the filth and off-
scourings of all things," 1 Cor. iv. ὡς περικαθαρματα
τοῦ κοσμου — παντων περιψημα. He has chosen two
words of the most vile and despicable signification ;
which, I believe, no *two* words in our language
will fully express. The outward state of things
is since changed, and the external profession of
Christianity is now no reproach; but let us not
imagine the nature of things is changed too. It
was then received as a maxim, that " all who will
live godly in Christ Jesus, must suffer persecution," 2 Tim. iii. ; and it is a truth still, founded
upon Scripture, and confirmed by experience. If
we know nothing of it in our own cases, it is because our tempers and manners have hitherto been
too conformable to that wicked world which in
our baptisms we were engaged to renounce. I
shall have occasion to speak farther upon this
point before I close : in the mean time, here is a
test to examine ourselves by. If we could not
glory in the Christian name, under the same circumstances as the disciples bore it at Antioch, we
are as yet unworthy of it. Let conscience judge.

Once more : Antioch, the city where the Gospel
once so flourished that from thence the whole
Christian church received that name by which it
is still called, *is now no more.* It has been a heap

of ruins more than five hundred years. The light of the Gospel has been long withdrawn: gaiety and festivity are likewise forgot. Slavery, imposture, and barbarism, have blotted out the resemblance, and even the remembrance, of what it once was. O that our *yet* happy land could from hence take a timely warning! Our privileges are great; perhaps greater, all things considered, than any nation has possessed since the days of Solomon. Our preservation hitherto has been wonderful: often have we been in extreme danger, but have always found deliverance at hand. Yet let us not be high-minded; our sins and aggravations (it is to be feared) have been, and still are, very great likewise; and God, we see, is no more a respecter of places than of persons. Antioch is ruined, Rev. iii.; Philadelphia, which received so honourable a testimony from the mouth of the Lord himself, has been long since destroyed. Let us beware of boasting; let us not presume too much on what we are; nor say, " The temple of the Lord, the temple of the Lord is here," Jer. vii.; we are the bulwark of the Protestant interest, and none can hurt us. If the Lord is with us, it is true; if we " walk worthy of the vocation wherewith we are called," we are safe; but, if otherwise, we know not how soon God may visit us with his heavy judgments, war, famine, discord, or pestilence, till we become a warning to others, as others are now proposed warnings to us. Our liberties, our properties, our religion, are in God's hands: may he incline our hearts to true repentance, lest at length these blessings should be taken from us, and given to a people that will bring forth more fruit.

There is an ambiguity in the original word χρηματισαι, which our translation renders *called :* for, though that is the more general sense it bears in heathen writers, wherever it occurs in the New Testament, except in this passage, and in Rom. vii. 3, it signifies to be taught or warned by a revelation from Heaven. Thus it is spoken of Joseph and the Wise Men, Matth. ii.; Simeon, Luke ii.; Cornelius, Acts x.; Noah, Heb. xi.; and elsewhere. It does not therefore appear quit certain from the text, whether the disciples chose this name for themselves, or the wits of the time fixed it upon them as a mark of infamy; or, lastly, whether it was by the special direction of the Spirit of God that they assumed it. But I incline to the latter supposition; partly, because, in those happy days, it was the practice and the privilege of the disciples to ask, and to receive, direction from on High, in almost every occurrence; but, chiefly, on account of the excellent instructions couched under this emphatical name, sufficient to direct and to animate those who were to be known by it, in their duty to each other, to God, and to the world. Some of these I propose to infer from the other proposition contained in the text, that the first name by which the followers of the Gospel were generally known, was that of *Christians*.

Hitherto, as they were separated from the world, so they had been divided among themselves; and so strong were the prejudices subsisting between the members of the same body, that we find, in the beginning of this chapter, some of one party contended with the Apostle Peter only for eating with those of another. Hence we read the phrases, *we of the Jews, they of the Gentiles.* But henceforward they are taught to blend and lose the greater distinction of *Jew* and *Gentile*, and the lesser divisions of Paul, Apollos, and Cephas, in a denomination derived from Him who alone was worthy to be their Head, and who was equally "rich in mercy to all that call upon him" in every place.

And as they thus were taught union and affection among themselves, so their relation to God, the way of their access to him, and their continual dependence upon him, were strongly implied in this name. A Christian is the child of God by faith in Christ: he draws near to God in the name of Christ: he is led and supported by the Spirit of Christ: Christ is the Alpha and Omega, the beginning and the ending, of the faith, hope, and love of every believer. *From him* alone every good desire proceeds: *by him* alone every good purpose is established: *in him* alone any of our best performances are acceptable. Let us beware (it is a necessary caution in these days) of a Christianity without Christ. I testify to you in plain words, that this is no better than a house without a foundation, a tree without a root, a body without a head, a hope without hope; a delusion, which, if persisted in, will end in irremediable destruction: "for other foundation can no man lay, than that which is laid, Christ Jesus;" he is the cornerstone, "chosen of God and precious." Alas! for those who are offended with him in whom God is well pleased! but those who trust in him shall never be ashamed. This is another important lesson comprised in the word *Christian.*

Nor is this all; but in the name of *Christian* they *might*, and we *may*, read the terms upon which we are to stand with the world. If I was asked what the words *Platonist* or *Pythagorean* signified, I should say they expressed certain persons, who embraced the sentiments, submitted to the institutions, and imitated the conduct of Pythagoras and Plato; and, in order to describe them farther, I need do no more than give an account of the lives and writings of their respective masters. Could I thus, in some distant, unknown country, where the name of Christianity had been only heard of, have an opportunity of declaring the history, the doctrines, and the laws, of Jesus Christ; how he lived, how he taught, how he *died*, and upon what account; what usage he himself received from the world, and what he taught his followers to expect after he should leave them: if I should then describe the lives and the treatment of his most eminent servants, who lived immediately after him, and shew, " that as he was, so were they in the world," 1 John iv. ; that, pursuing his pattern, they found exactly the same opposition;—would not the inhabitants of such a country conclude, even as the Scripture has assured us, that the temper of Christianity, and the temper of the world, must be exactly opposite; and that, as it is said, " Whoever will be a friend of the world is an enemy of God," James iv. ; so whoever had boldness to profess himself a friend of God, must necessarily be an enemy to the world, and would be sure to find the world, and all in it, at sworn enmity with him? But if I should farther tell them, that though the same laws, the same warnings, and the same examples, still subsist; yet that fierce opposition I have spoken of is at length nearly over, so that none are better pleased with the world, or more agreeable to it, than many of those who speak most honourably of the Christian name : would not these people immediately infer, that one of these contending powers must have yielded to the triumphant genius of the other? that either the whole world were become such Christians as those who were first styled so at Antioch, or that modern Christians must be, for the most part, so only by profession, and have neither right nor pretence to their ancient spirit? And

could we suppose farther, that, after this information, some of these remote people were to land at
Dover, and make the tour of this kingdom, can
you think they would be long in determining which
of these is indeed the case ?

Numbers are deceived by restricting many passages in the New Testament to the times in which
they were delivered, though it seems to have been
the great care of the Apostles to prevent, if possible, our making this mistake. St. John, having
expressly said, " If any man love the world, the
love of the Father is not in him," immediately
explains what he means by the world ; namely,
" the lust of the flesh, the lust of the eye, and the
pride of life," 1 John ii. If high distinction, vain
shew, and sensual pleasure make no part of the
world at this day, I must allow that we have no
part in the Apostle's decision, nor any cause to
observe his caution : but if these things are as
highly prized, as eagerly, and almost as universally
pursued, now in Britain, as they were sixteen
hundred years since at Rome and Antioch, surely
we bear the name of Christians in vain ; if our
hopes and fears, our joys and sorrows, our comforts
and our cares, are not very different from those of
the generality among whom we live. " If any
man," says St. Paul, " have not the spirit of Christ,
he is none of his," Rom. viii. Now, whatever
more is meant by the phrase of " having the spirit
of Christ," it must certainly mean thus much at
least ; a disposition and turn of mind in some degree conformable to the mind that was in Christ
Jesus, to be evidenced by a life and conversation
suitable to his precepts and example. " He was
holy, harmless, undefiled, separate from sinners :
he went about doing good," Heb. vii. He was
gentle and compassionate, meek and patient under

the greatest provocations : so active for the glory
of God, that his zeal, by a strong and lively figure,
is said to have " eaten him up," John ii. ; so affected with the worth of souls, that he wept over
his bitterest enemies ; so intent on his charitable
designs towards men, that an opportunity of helping or instructing them, was as meat and drink
when he was hungry, John iv., and made him
forget weariness and pain ; so full of devotion
towards God, that when the day had been wholly
consumed in his labours of love, he would frequently redeem whole nights for prayer ! Luke vi.
But I must stop. No pen can describe, no heart
conceive, the life of the Son of God in the flesh !
Yet, in all these things he was our great Exemplar ;
and no profession or appellation can benefit us,
unless we are of those who copy closely and carefully after him. For thus saith the beloved Apostle, " He that saith he abideth in him, ought
himself so to walk even as he walked. He that
saith, I know him, and keepeth not his commandments, is a liar, and the truth is not in him,"
1 John ii.

I shall conclude with a short address to three
sorts of persons. And, first, If there are any such
here (would to God this part of my labour may
prove needless), I would recommend this subject
to the consideration of those who have *almost*, if not
altogether, cast off the honourable name into which
they were baptized ; who, trusting to what they
call the light of nature, and the powers of human
reason, venture to determine the fitness of things by
their own standard, and declare in their words, as
well as by their actions, " they will not have this
man to rule over them," Luke xix. Is not this
an unaccountable event upon your plan, that the
name which first went out from Antioch, under

the greatest disadvantages, should so soon overspread the world, without arts or arms, without
any force, or any motive of an external kind? Is
it possible, that any kind or degree of enthusiasm
could influence, not a *few,* at one time, or in one
place, but *multitudes,* of all ages, sexes, tempers,
and circumstances, to embrace a profession which,
in proportion to the strictness wherewith it was
followed, was always attended with reproach and
suffering? Those places which were most noted
for opposition to this way, have been long since
buried in the dust: but a succession of those
whom the world counted "not worthy to live,"
and "of whom the world was not worthy," Acts
xxv., Heb. xi., has always subsisted, and still subsists. Had you lived in those days when Jesus
Christ assured a company of poor disregarded
fishermen, that neither the power nor the policy
of the world, nor "the gates of hell should ever
prevail against them," Matth. xvi., you might
have been less inexcusable in refusing to believe
him. But now—when you have the accomplishment of this promise before your eyes, and well
know (for you are book-read) what various attempts
have been made, with what steadiness and formidable appearances they have been for a while carried on, to render these words vain, but how at
length all such attempts have totally failed, and
ended in the confusion and ruin of those who engaged in them—what tolerable reason can you
assign for the part you act? Does the tendency
of the Gospel displease you? Is it an enemy to
that virtue you are so fond—to talk of? On the
contrary, we are ready to put it to the proof, that
here are not only the sublimest maxims of true
virtue, but that the practice, or even the real love

of virtue, are quite unattainable upon any other
scheme; and that the most specious pretences,
independent of this, are no more than great
"swelling words of vanity," 2 Pet. ii.—I speak
the more freely upon this point, because I speak
from experience. I was once as you are. I verily
thought that I "ought to do" (or at least that I
might do) "many things against Jesus of Nazareth," Acts xxvi. None ever went farther than I,
according to the limits of my years and capacity,
in opposing the truths of the Gospel. But the
mercy of God spared me; and his providence
having led me through various changes and circumstances of life, in each of which I had a still
deeper conviction of my former errors, has at length
given me this opportunity to tell you (O that I could
speak it to your hearts!) "that at the name of
Jesus every knee," sooner or later, "must bow,"
Phil. ii.; before him every heart must either bend
or break: that he is full of mercy, love, and pardon, to all that submit themselves to him; but that
ere long, he shall be "revealed from heaven in
flaming fire, to execute judgment, and to convince
ungodly sinners of all the hard speeches they have
spoken against him," Jude.—I would, 2dly, address those who, while they *profess to believe* in the
Lord Jesus, do, *in their works*, manifestly *deny him*,
Tit. i. This is, if possible, a worse case than
the other: yet how frequent! You believe that
Jesus Christ came into the world, both to be a
propitiation for sin, and also to give us an example
of a godly life, and yet continue contentedly in
the practice of those sins for which he poured forth
his soul, in the pursuit of those vices which the
Gospel disallows, and in the indulgence of those
desires which your own consciences condemn.

Think, I entreat you, of these words in the 50th Psalm : " Unto the wicked God saith, What hast thou to do, that thou shouldst take my covenant into thy mouth ; seeing thou hatest instruction, and castest my words behind thee ? "   This question is now proposed to our consciences, that we may be aware in time of the danger of insincerity; and not " perish with a lie in our right hands," Isa. xliv.   If we cannot answer it now, what shall we say in that awful hour when God shall speak it in ten thousand thunders, to all who, in this life, presumed to mock him with an empty outside worship, " drawing near him with their lips, when their hearts were far from him ? " Isa. xxix.   For the day is at hand, " the day of the Lord," when God shall bring " every hidden thing to light;" when every man's work shall be tried and weighed ; *tried* in the fire of His purity, *weighed* in the balance of His righteousness ; and as the issue proves, so must the consequence abide to all eternity : a trial and a scrutiny which no flesh could abide, were it not for the interposing merits of Jesus Christ, our Saviour and our Judge.   But he has already told us, that he will then own none but those who were faithfully devoted to his service here.   To the urgent cries and strongest pleas of others, he will give no other answer, but " I know you not ; I never knew you," Matth. vii. ; " depart from me, ye accursed, into everlasting fire," Matth. xxv.— What will it then avail to plead our privileges, when, if this be all, we may read our doom already ? " And that servant who knew his master's will, and prepared not himself, neither did according to his will, shall be beaten with many stripes : for unto whomsoever much is given, of him much shall be required ; and to whom men have committed much, of him they will ask the more.   O con-

sider this, ye that forget God, lest he tear you in
pieces, and there be none to deliver." Luke xii.;
Psalm l.

Finally, Let those who through grace have attained to worship God "in spirit and in truth," be
careful to adorn and hold fast their profession.
"You see your calling, brethren:" let the name
of Christian always remind you of your high obligation to, and continual dependence upon, the
Author of your faith.   Use it as a means to animate and regulate your whole behaviour; and if,
upon some occasions, you find undeserved ill offices,
or unkind constructions, wonder not at it: thus it
must and will be, more or less, to all who would
" exercise themselves in keeping a conscience void
of offence," Acts xxiv. Yet be careful to model
your actions by the rule of God's word. Our Lord
says, "Blessed are ye when men revile you, and
say all manner of evil against you, falsely, for my
sake," Matth. v.   Observe, first, the evil spoken
of you, must be false and groundless; and, 2dly,
the cause must be " for the sake of Christ," and
not for any singularities of your own, either in
sentiment or practice, which you cannot clearly
maintain from Scripture. It is a great blessing
when the innocence and simplicity of the dove is
happily blended with true wisdom. It is a mercy
to be kept from giving unnecessary offence in these
times of division and discord. Endeavour that a
principle of love to God, and to mankind for his
sake, may have place in all your actions; this
will be a secret, seasonable, and infallible guide,
in a thousand incidents, where particular rules
cannot reach. "Be sober, be vigilant;" "continue
instant in prayer;" and in a little while all your conflicts shall terminate in conquest, faith shall give
place to sight, and hope to possession. Yet a little

while, and " Christ, who is our life, shall appear,"
Col. iii., to vindicate his truth, to put a final end
to all evil and offence; and then *we also*, even all
who have loved him, and waited for him, " shall
appear with him in glory." Isa. xxv.

SERMON IV.

ON ALL THINGS BEING GIVEN US WITH CHRIST.

ROM. viii. 32.

*He that spared not his own Son, but delivered him up
for us all, how shall he not with him also freely give us
all things?*

VARIOUS have been the disputes and various the
mistakes of men, concerning the things of God.
Too often, amidst the heat of fierce contending
parties, truth is injured by both sides, befriended
by neither.   Religion, the pretended cause of our
many controversies, is sometimes wholly unconcerned in them: I mean, that " pure religion and
undefiled," that " wisdom which, coming from
above," abounds with proof of its Divine original,
being " pure, peaceable, gentle, and easy to be entreated, full of mercy and good works, without
partiality, and without hypocrisy," James iii.
Religion is a serious and a personal concern.   It
arises from a right knowledge of God and ourselves; a sense of the great things he has done
for fallen man; a persuasion, or at least a well-
grounded hope, of our own interest in his favour;
and a principle of unbounded love to *him who* thus
first loved us.   It consists in an entire surrender of
ourselves, and our all, to God; in setting him

continually before us, as the object of our desires, the scope and inspector of our actions, and our only refuge and hope in every trouble: finally, in making the goodness of God to us the motive and model of our behaviour to our fellow-creatures; to love, pity, relieve, instruct, forbear, and forgive them, as occasions offer, because we ourselves both need and experience these things at the hand of our heavenly Father. The two great points to which it tends, and which it urges the soul, where it has taken place, incessantly to press after, are, *communion* with God, and *conformity* to him; and as neither of these can be fully attained in this life, it teaches us to pant after a better; to withdraw our thoughts and affections from temporal things, and fix them on that eternal state, where we trust our desires shall be abundantly satisfied; and the work begun by *grace* shall be crowned with *glory*.

Such is the religion of the Gospel. This the life and doctrine of our Lord, and the writings of his Apostles, jointly recommend. An excellent abridgment of the whole we have in this eighth chapter to the Romans, describing the state, temper, practice, privileges, and immoveable security, of a true Christian. Every verse is rich in comfort and instruction, and might, without violence, afford a theme for volumes; particularly, that which I have read may be styled *evangelium evangelii;* a complete and comprehensive epitome of whatever is truly worthy our knowledge and our hope. The limits of our time are too narrow to admit any previous remarks on the context, or indeed to consider the subject according to the order of an exact division: therefore I shall not at present use any artificial method; but, taking the words as they lie, I shall offer a few practical observations, which seem naturally and immediately to arise from the perusal of them, making such improvement as may occur as I go along. And may the Father of mercies, who has put this treasure into our hands, favour us with his gracious presence and blessing.

I. From the words, " He spared not his own Son," we may observe, in one view, the wonderful goodness and inflexible severity of God. So great was his goodness, that, when man was by sin rendered incapable of *any* happiness, and obnoxious to *all* misery; incapable of restoring himself, or of receiving the least assistance from any power in heaven or in earth; God spared not his only begotten Son, but, in his unexampled love to the world, gave him, who alone was able to repair the breach. Every gift of God is good : the bounties of his common providence are very valuable; that he should continue life, and supply that life with food, raiment, and a variety of comforts, to those who by rebellion had forfeited all, was wonderful: but what are all inferior blessings, compared to this unspeakable gift of the Son of his love? Abraham had given many proofs of his love and obedience before he was commanded to offer up Isaac upon the altar; but God seems to pass by all that went before, as of small account in comparison of this last instance of duty : " Now I know that thou fearest God, seeing thou hast not withheld thy son, thine only son, from me," Gen. xxii. Surely we likewise must say, " In this was manifested the love of God to us, because he gave his Son, his only Son, to be the life of the world." But all comparison fails: Abraham was bound in duty, bound by gratitude; neither was it a freewill offering, but by the express command of God; but to us the mercy was undesired, as well as un-

deserved. " Herein is love; not that we loved
God ;" on the contrary, we were enemies to him,
and in rebellion against him, " but that he loved
us, and sent his Son to be the propitiation of our
sins," the sins we had committed against himself.
My friends, ought not this love to meet a return?
Is it not most desirable to be able to say, with the
Apostle, upon good grounds, " We love him, because he first loved us?" Should it not be our
continual inquiry, " What shall we render to the
Lord for all his benefits?" especially for this, which
is both the crown and the spring of all the rest!
Are we cold and unaffected at this astonishing proof
of Divine love? and are not our hearts grieved and
humbled at our own ingratitude? Then are we
ungrateful and insensible indeed!

The justice and severity of God is no less conspicuous than his goodness in these words : as he
spared not to give his Son for our sakes, so, when
Christ appeared in our nature, undertook our
cause, and was charged with our sins, though he
was the Father's well-beloved Son, " he was not
spared." He drank the bitter cup of the wrath of
God to the very dregs : he bore all the shame, sorrow, and pain, all the distress of body and mind,
that must otherwise have fallen upon our heads.
His whole life, from the manger to the cross, was
one series of humiliation and suffering; John xviii.
Observe him in the world, despised, vilified, persecuted even to death, by unreasonable and wicked
men; ridiculed, buffeted, spit upon; and at length
nailed to the accursed tree! Consider him in the
wilderness, Luke iv., given up to the power and
assaulted by the temptations of the devil! Behold
him in the garden, Luke xxii., and say, " Was
ever sorrow like unto his sorrow, wherewith the
Lord afflicted him in the day of his fierce anger ?"

How inconceivable must that agony be, which caused his blood to forsake its wonted channels, and start from every pore of his body! Behold him, lastly, upon the cross, Matth. xxvii., suffering the most painful and ignominious death; suspended between two thieves; surrounded by cruel enemies, who made sport of his pangs; derided by all that passed by! Attend to his dolorous cry, expressive of an inward distress beyond all we have yet spoken of, "My God, my God, why hast thou forsaken me!" St. Paul reminds the Galatians, that, by his preaching among them, Jesus Christ had been "evidently set forth crucified before their eyes," Gal. iii. Would it please God to bless my poor words to the like purpose, you would see a meaning you never yet observed in that awful passage, "Tribulation, and wrath, and anguish upon every soul of man that doth evil," Rom. ii.; for the punishment due to the sins of all that shall stand at the last day on the right hand of God met and centred in Christ, the Lamb of expiation; nor was the dreadful weight removed till he, triumphant in death, pronounced "It is finished," John xix. Let us not think of this as a matter of speculation only; our lives, our precious souls, are concerned in it. Let us infer from hence, how "fearful a thing it is to fall into the hands of the living God," Heb. x. The Apostle Peter, 2 Pet. ii., admonishes those to whom he wrote from the fearful example of the angels who sinned, and of the old world; where the same word is used as in my text, ουκ εφεισατο, "he spared them not;" that is, he punished them to the utmost; he did not afford them the least mitigation. It is a frequent figure of speech, by which much more is understood than is or can be expressed. Much more then may we say, if God "spared not his

Son, what shall be the end of those who obey not
the Gospel?" 1 Pet. iv. If the holy Jesus was
thus dealt with, when he was only accounted a
sinner by imputation, where shall the impenitent
and the ungodly appear? " If these things were
done in the green tree, what shall be done in the
dry?" Luke xxiii. The punishment of sin in the
soul in a future state is twofold : the *wrath of God*
in all its dreadful effects, typified by fire unquench-
able, Mark ix. ; and *the stings of conscience*, represented by a worm that never dies. Our Lord endured the former ; but the other, perhaps, could
have no place in him, who was absolutely perfect
and sinless. But if the *prospect* of *one* made him
amazed and sorrowful beyond measure, what con-
sternation must the *concurrence* of *both* raise in the
wicked, when they shall hear and feel their irrevocable doom ! May we have grace so to reflect
on these things, that we may flee for safety to the
hope set before us, to Jesus Christ, the only and
the sure *refuge from* that approaching *storm*, which
" shall sweep away all the workers of iniquity as
a flood," Isa. xxiii.

II. Here, as in a glass, we may see the evil of
sin. The bitter fruits of sin are indeed visible
every where. Sin is the cause of all the labour,
sickness, pain, and grief under which the whole
creation groans. Sin often makes man a terror
and a burden, both to himself and those about him.
Sin occasions discord and confusion in families,
cities, and kingdoms. Sin has always *directed* the
march, and *ensured* the *success*, of those instruments
of Divine vengeance whom we style *mighty conquerors*. Those ravagers of mankind, who spread
devastation and horror far and wide, and ruin more
in a few days than ages can repair, have only afforded so many melancholy proofs of the malignity

of sin.   For this, a shower of flaming brimstone
fell upon a whole country; for this, an overwhelm-
ing deluge destroyed a whole world; for this,
principalities and powers were cast from heaven,
and are reserved under *chains* of *darkness,* 2 Pet. ii.,
to a more dreadful doom.   But none of these
things, nor all of them together, afford such a
conviction of the heinous nature and destructive
effects of sin, as we may gather from these words,
" He spared not his own Son."

III.   Here we may likewise see the value of the
human soul.   We ordinarily judge of the worth of
a thing by the price which a wise man, who is acquainted with its intrinsic excellency, is willing to
give for it.   Now, the soul of man was of such
estimation in the sight of God, who made it, that,
when it was sinking into endless ruin, " he spared
not his own Son, but freely delivered him for our
ransom."   Two things especially render the soul
thus important in the view of Infinite Wisdom: first,
the capacity he had given it ; for " he formed it
for himself," Isa. xliii., capable of knowing, serving,
and enjoying God; and, by consequence, incapable of happiness in any thing beneath him ; for
nothing can satisfy any being but the attainment
of its proper end : and, secondly, the duration he
had assigned it, beyond the limits of time, and the
existence of the material world.   The most excellent and exalted being, if only the creature of a
day, would be worthy of little regard*.   On the
other hand, immortality itself would be of small
value to a creature that could rise no higher than
the pursuits of animal life.   But in the soul of man
the capability of complete happiness or exquisite
misery, and that for ever, make it a prize worthy
the contention of different worlds.   For this an

---

* Vid. Young's Night Thoughts, 7th Night.

open intercourse was maintained between heaven
and earth, till at length the Word of God appeared
" in the likeness of sinful flesh," that, in our nature, he might encounter and subdue the sworn
enemy of our species. All that has been transacted
in the kingdoms of providence and grace, from the
beginning of the world, has been in subserviency to
this grand point, the redemption of the deathless
soul. And is it so—and shall there be found
among us numbers utterly insensible of their natural dignity; that dare disparage the plan of Infinite Wisdom, and stake those souls for trifles,
which nothing less than the blood of Christ could
redeem ? There is need to use great plainness of
speech ; the matter is of the utmost weight; be not
therefore offended that I would warn you against
"the deceitfulness of sin." Suffer not your hearts
to be entangled in the vanities of the world ; either
they will fail, and disappoint you in life, or at least
you must leave them behind you when you die.
You must enter an invisible unknown state, where
you cannot expect to meet any of those amusements or engagements which you now find so necessary to pass away the tedious load of time that
hangs upon your hands. You, to whom a few hours
of leisure are so burdensome, have you considered
how you shall be able to support an eternity ? You
stand upon a brink, and all about you is uncertainty. You see, of your acquaintance, some or
other daily called away—some who are as likely to
live as yourselves. You know not but you may
be the very next. You cannot be certain, but
" this very night your soul may be required of
you," Luke xii. Perhaps a few hours may introduce you into the presence of that God whom
you have been so little desirous to please. And
can you, in such a situation, sport and play, with

as little concern as the lamb already marked out
to bleed to-morrow ? Oh ! it is strange ! How
fatally has the god of this world blinded your
eyes ! and how dreadful must your situation be in
death, if death alone can undeceive you !

IV. Lastly, We may gather from these words
the certainty of the Gospel salvation. God himself
delivered up his Son for us all. He declared
himself well pleased with him, Matth. iii., as our
Surety, upon his first entrance on his work ; and
testified his acceptance of his undertaking, in that
he raised him from the dead, and received him
into heaven as our Advocate. Now, " if God
himself be thus for us, who can be against us ? "
Rom. viii. If he who only has right to judge us
is pleased to justify us, " who can lay any thing
to our charge ? If Christ who died " for our sins,
and is risen on our behalf, has engaged to " inter-
cede for us, who shall condemn ? " " There is
now no condemnation to them that are in Christ
Jesus." Nor is this all ; but every thing we stand
in need of is fully provided ; and we may well
argue, as the Apostle has taught us elsewhere,
" If when we were enemies we were reconciled to
God by the death of his Son, much more, being
reconciled, we shall be saved by his life," Rom.v. ;
or, as in the passage before us, " He that spared
not his own Son, but delivered him up for us all,"
when we were alienated from him, " how shall he
not with him freely give us all things," now he has
taught us to pray, and given us his own promises
to plead for all we ask ? This brings me to the
second clause of the text ; only it may be proper,
before I enter upon it, to subjoin two cautions, to
prevent mistakes from what has been already said.

1st, Let us remember that all is *free gift*. He

gave his Son; he *gives* all things with him. The
Gospel allows no place for merit of our own in any
respect. There was no moving cause in us, unless
our misery may be deemed such. Our deliverance, in its rise, progress, and accomplishment,
must be ascribed to grace alone; and he that
would glory, must " glory in the Lord." 1 Cor. i.

2d, Let us observe the Apostle's phrase. He
says, not absolutely for all, but for *us* all ; that is,
those who are described in the former part of the
chapter, " who are led by the Spirit of God, who
walk not after the flesh, who are delivered from the
bondage of corruption," who have liberty to call
God, " Abba, Father," and prove their relation by
following him as " dear children." Christ is " the
author of eternal salvation to those only who obey
him," Heb. v. It cannot be otherwise, since a
branch of that salvation is to deliver us " from our
sins," and " the present evil world," Gal. i.; to
" purify us from dead works, to serve the living
God." " Be not deceived, God will not be
mocked ; whatsoever a man soweth, that shall he
reap. He that soweth to the flesh, shall," notwithstanding all that Christ has done or suffered,
yea so much the rather, " of the flesh reap corruption." Gal. vi.

The text, having declared that God spared not
his Son for our sakes, proceeds to infer, that " with
him he will assuredly give us all things." Here
we may take notice, first, that the words *all things*
must be limited to such as are needful and good
for us. It may be said of many of our desires,
" Ye know not what ye ask," Matth. xx.: in
such cases, the best answer we can receive is a
denial. For those blessings which God has promised absolutely to give, such as pardon, grace,

and eternal life, we cannot be too earnest or explicit in our prayers; but in temporal things we should be careful to ask nothing but with submission to the Divine will. The promises, it is true, appertain to " the life that now is, as well as that which is to come," 1 Tim. iv. " Whether Paul, or Apollos, or Cephas, or life, or death, or things present, or things to come; all are ours, if we are Christ's," 1 Cor. iii. But the particular *modus* of these things God has reserved in his own hands, to bestow them as best shall suit our various tempers, abilities, and occasions. And well for us that it is so: for we should soon ruin ourselves if left to our own choice: like children who are fond to meddle with what would hurt them, but refuse the most salutary medicines, if unpalatable; so we often pursue, with earnestness and anxiety, those things which, if we could obtain them, would greatly harm, if not destroy, us. Often, too, with a rash and blind impatience, we struggle to avoid or escape those difficulties which God sees fit to appoint for the most gracious and merciful purposes —to correct our pride and vanity, to exercise and strengthen our faith, to wean us from the world, to teach us a closer dependence upon himself, and to awaken our desires after a better inheritance.

Again; as God, by his promise freely to give us all things, has not engaged to comply with the measure of our unreasonable short-sighted wishes; so neither has he confined himself as to the time or manner of bestowing his gifts. The blessing we seek, though perhaps not wholly improper, may be at present unseasonable: in this case, the Lord will suspend it till he sees it will afford us the comfort and satisfaction he intends us by it; and then we shall be sure to have it. Sometimes it is

withheld to stir us up to fervency and importunity in our prayers, sometimes to make it doubly
welcome and valuable when it comes. So likewise as to the manner. We ask one good thing,
and he gives us an equivalent in something else;
and when we come to weigh all things, we see
cause to say his choice was best. Thus David
acknowledges: " In the day that I called, thou
didst answer me, and strengthenedst me with
strength in my soul," Ps. cxxxviii. David asked
for deliverance from trouble; the Lord gave him
strength to bear it; and he allows his prayer was
fully answered. A parallel case the Apostle re-
cords: he besought the Lord thrice, 2 Cor. xii.,
for the removal of that trial which he calls " a
thorn in the flesh;" the answer he received was,
" My grace is sufficient for thee." Such an assurance was more valuable than the deliverance
he sought could be. Sometimes we seek a thing
in a way of our own, by means and instruments of
our own devising. God crosses our feeble purposes, that he may give us the pleasure of receiving it immediately from himself. It were easy to
enlarge on this head: let it suffice to know, our
concerns are in his hands who " does all things
well;" and who will, and does, appoint " all to
work together for our good."

From the latter clause, thus limited and explained, many useful directions might be drawn.
I shall only mention two or three, and conclude.

1st, Since we are told, that God freely gives us
all things, let us learn to see and acknowledge his
hand in all we have, and in all we meet with.
When Jacob was returning to Canaan after a long
absence, Gen. xxxii., the fear of his brother Esau
occasioned him to divide his family and substance

into separate companies; and, comparing his present situation with the poor condition in which he had been driven from home, twenty years before, he breaks out into this act of praise, " I am not worthy, O Lord, of all thy mercies; for with my staff I passed over this Jordan, and now I am become two bands ! " How pious and how cheering was this reflection! And afterwards, Gen. xxxiii., when his brother Esau asked him concerning his sons, " They are the children (said he) which God has graciously given thy servant." Such a deep and abiding persuasion of the Most High God, ordering, and over-ruling all our concerns, would, like the light, diffuse a lustre and a beauty upon every thing around us. To consider every comfort of life as an effect and proof of the Divine favour towards us, would, like the feigned alchymist's stone, turn all our possessions to gold, and stamp a value upon things which a common eye might judge indifferent. Nor is this more than the truth : " The hairs of our head are all numbered," Matth. x. The eye of Divine Providence is upon every " sparrow of the field ;" nor can we properly term any circumstance of our lives *small*, since such as seem most trifling in themselves do often give birth to those which we judge most important. On the other hand, to be able to discover the wisdom and goodness of our heavenly Father, through the darkest cloud of troubles and afflictions ; to see all our trials appointed to us, in number, weight, and measure; nothing befalling us by chance, nothing without need, nothing without a support, nothing without a designed advantage : what a stay must these apprehensions be to the soul? Take away these, and man is the most forlorn, helpless, miserable object in the world ; *pining* for every thing he has not, *trembling* for every thing he has; equally suffering under the pressure of what *does* happen, and the fear of what *may;* liable to thousands of unsuspected dangers, yet unable to guard against those which are most obvious. Were there no future life, it would be our interest to be truly and uniformly religious, in order to make the most of this. How unhappy must they be to whom the thoughts of a God ever present is a burden they strive, in vain, to shake off! But let us learn " to acknowledge him in all our ways," and then " he will direct and bless our paths." Prov. iii.

2d, Since all we have is the gift of God, let this teach us, " in whatever state we are, therewith to be content." Our heavenly Father knoweth what we have need of before we ask him," Matth. vi. " The earth is his, and the fulness thereof;" Ps. xxiv.: and his goodness is equal to his power; a proof of which we have in the text. He has already given us more than ten thousand worlds. Are you poor? Be satisfied with the Lord's appointment. It were as easy to him to give you large estates, as to supply you with the bread you eat, or to continue your breath in your nostrils; but he sees poverty best for you: he sees prosperity might prove your ruin; therefore he has appointed you the honour of being in this respect conformable to your Lord, who, when on earth, " had not where to lay his head," Matth. viii. Have any of you lost a dear friend or relative, in whose life you thought your own lives bound up? " Be still, and know that he is God," Ps. xlvi. It was he gave you that friend; his blessing made your friend a comfort to you; and though the stream is now cut off, the fountain is still full. Be not like a wild bull in a net: the Lord has many ways to turn your mourning into joy.

Are any of you sick? Think how the compassionate Jesus healed diseases with a word, in the days of his flesh. Has he not the same power now as then? Has he not the same love? Has he, in his exalted state, *forgot* his poor languishing members here below? No, verily; he still retains his sympathy: "he is touched with a feeling of our infirmities; he knows our frame; he remembers we are but dust," Ps. ciii. It is because sickness is better for you than health, that he thus visits you. He dealt in the same manner with Lazarus, whom he loved, John xi. Resign yourselves, therefore, to his wisdom, and repose in his love. There is a land where the blessed inhabitant shall no more say, "I am sick," Isa. xxxiii.; and there "all that love the Lord Jesus" shall shortly be. Are any of you tempted? "Blessed is the man that endureth temptation; for when he is tried, he shall receive the crown of life, which the Lord has promised to them that love him," James i. Sure you need no other argument to be content, or, shall I say? to rejoice, and be exceeding glad. "My son, despise not thou the chastening of the Lord, nor faint when thou art rebuked of him." Heb. xii. Be it in poverty or losses, in body or mind, in your own person or another's, it is all appointed by God, and shall issue in your great benefit, if you are of the number of those that love him.

3d, Once more: since it is said that all things are freely given us in and together with Christ, let us "give all diligence to make OUR calling and election sure," 2 Pet. i.; to know that we have an interest in him and his mediation; and then (if I may borrow a common expression) we are made for ever. The Lord Jesus Christ, sent from God on a merciful errand to a lost world, did not come empty : no, he is fraught with all blessings, suitable to all persons, extending to all times, enduring to all eternity. O make it your great care to know him and to please him; study his word, call upon his name, frequent his ordinances, observe his sayings, seek to know him as the only *way* to God, John xiv. : the way to pardon, peace, and Divine communion here, and to complete happiness hereafter. When once you can say, " My beloved is mine," Sol. Song ii., I account all his interest my own, " and I am his," I have given myself up to him without reserve ; you will, you *must* be happy. You will be interested in all his attributes and communicable perfections. His wisdom will be your high tower, his providence your constant shield, his love your continual solace. " He will give his angels charge over you to keep you in all your ways," Ps. lxxxi. In times of difficulty he will direct your counsels; in times of danger he will fill you with comfort, and " keep" you " in perfect peace," Isa. xxvi., when others quake for fear. He will bless your basket and your store, your substance and your families : your days shall happily pass in doing your Father's will, and receiving renewed tokens of his favour; and at night you shall lie down, and your sleep shall be sweet. When afflictions befal you (for these likewise are the fruits of love), you shall see your God near at hand, " a very present help in trouble," Ps. xlvi.; you shall find your strength increased in proportion to your trial ; you shall in due time be restored, as gold from the furnace, purified sevenfold, to praise your great Deliverer. Every thing you meet in life shall yield you profit; and death, which puts a fatal period to the hope of the wicked,—*death*, at whose name thousands turn pale, shall to you be an entrance into a new and endless life.   He who tasted death *for* you, Heb. ii., and sanctified it *to* you, shall lead and support you through that dark valley; you shall shut your eyes upon the things of time, to open them the next moment in the blissful presence of your reconciled God. You, that a minute before was surrounded by weeping, helpless friends, shall in an instant be transported and inspired to join in that glorious song, " To Him who loved us, and washed us from our sins in his own blood, and hath made us kings and priests to God and his Father: to him be glory and strength, for ever and ever.   Worthy is the Lamb that was slain, to receive power, and riches, and wisdom, and strength, and honour, and glory, and blessing," Rev. v. Thus, " blessed shall the man be that fears the Lord," Ps. cxxviii.   " Thus shall it be done (Esth. vi.) to him whom the King delighteth to honour."   Amen.

SERMON V.

ON SEARCHING THE SCRIPTURES.

JOHN v. 39.

Search the Scriptures; for in them ye think ye have eternal life: and they are they which testify of me.

THE phrase in the Greek is ambiguous; and may be either rendered, according to our reading, as a command, *search the Scriptures;* or else as simply affirming, *ye do search the Scriptures.*   And as the words were spoken to the Scribes and Pharisees, who were exceedingly studious in the letter of the Scriptures, this may perhaps have been their first design. The difference is not material; and either sense will afford us instruction. If we receive it as a command, we should consider it as given us by the Lord himself, whose disciples we profess to be; as bound on us by our own acknowledgment, since in them we think, and say, we have eternal life; and as absolutely necessary to be complied with, since it is these, and these only, testify of Christ, in the knowledge of whom our eternal life consists. If we should understand it in the latter sense, as spoken to the Scribes and Pharisees, it may give us a useful caution not to lay too much stress either on what we think or on what we do. For these persons we find had, in some respects, a right sentiment of the holy Scriptures: they believed that in them there was eternal life: and, in a sense likewise, they made this an inducement to read, yea, to search them. But though they thus thought and thus acted; and though the Scriptures, from the first page to the last, do testify of Christ; yet they could not understand or receive this testimony, but rejected the Messiah whom they professed to hope for, and took all their pains in searching the Scriptures to no purpose.

In what I am about to lay before you, I propose the following order: 1st, To mention a few requisites, without which it is impossible rightly to understand the Scriptures: 2d, To shew *how* the Scriptures testify of Christ: 3d, To consider what the import of their testimony is: 4th, To press the practice of searching the Scriptures from the argument used in the text, which is equally applicable to us as to the Jews of old, " that in them we think we have eternal life."

I. The first requisite I shall mention is *Sincerity;* I mean a real desire to be instructed by the Scripture, and to submit both our sentiments and our practices to be controlled and directed by what we read there. Without this, our reading and searching will only issue in our greater condemnation, and bring us under the heavy doom of the servant that knew his master's will and did it not. A remarkable instance of this we have in the 42d and two following chapters of Jeremiah. After the destruction of Jerusalem, and the death of Gedaliah, the people that were left entreated the prophet to inquire of the Lord for them, concerning their intended removal into Egypt. Their request was fair : " That the Lord thy God may shew us the way wherein we may walk, and the thing that we may do." Their engagement was very solemn : " The Lord be a true and faithful witness between us, if we do not even according to all things for the which the Lord thy God shall send to us. Whether it be good, or whether it be evil, we will obey the voice of the Lord our God, to whom we send thee." But their hypocrisy was most detestable. The Lord, who seeth the inmost purposes of the soul, could not be put off with their fair pretences. He sent them in answer an express prohibition to go into Egypt ; assuring them that his curse should follow them, and that there they should certainly perish. Yet they went, and verified what the prophet had told them : " For ye dissembled in your hearts, when ye sent me to the Lord your God, saying, Pray for us unto the Lord our God, and according to all that the Lord our God shall say, so declare unto us, and we will do it." Then they spoke out, and, like themselves, when they told him, " As for the word which thou hast spoken unto us in the name of the Lord, we will not hearken unto thee, but we will certainly do whatever thing goeth forth out of our own mouth." None of us dare speak thus in express terms: but if we bring our preconceived opinions or purposes, not in order to examine them strictly by the test of Scripture, but to find or wrest some passages in the word of God to countenance or justify ourselves; if our desire is not simply to be led in the very way of God's commandments; if we are not really willing to discover every error and evil that may be in us, in order to forsake them; we closely imitate these deceitful, obstinate, insolent Jews, be our pretences ever so fair, and are liable to the like dreadful judgment for our hypocrisy,—the curse of God upon our devices here, and the portion of his enemies hereafter.

Where this sincerity is wanting, every thing is wrong; neither praying, nor hearing, nor reading, can profit. The Scripture abounds with the severest threatenings against those who presume to mock the all-seeing God. I shall only produce one passage from Ezekiel, xiv. 5: "Son of man, these men have set up their idols in their hearts, and put the stumbling-block of iniquity before their faces: should I be inquired of at all by them? Every man of the house of Israel that setteth up his idols in his heart, and putteth the stumbling-block of iniquity before his face, and cometh to the prophet, I, the Lord, will answer him that cometh, according to the multitude of his idols." I say not this that I would have any one throw aside the ordinances of God, especially his public worship. These are the means which God has appointed, in which he has commanded us to wait, and where he is often pleased to be found, even by those who seek him not. But I would entreat such persons seriously to consider the dreadful condition they would be in, if death thould surprise them in such a state of insincerity as renders their very prayers and sacrifices " an abomination to the Lord," and perverts those things which are designed for their advantage, into an occasion of their falling.

A second thing necessary is *Diligence.* This, with the former, is finally described in the Book of Proverbs :—" My son, if thou wilt receive my words, and hide my commandment within thee; so that thou incline thine ear to wisdom, and apply thine heart to understanding: yea, if thou criest after knowledge, and liftest up thy voice for understanding; if thou seekest her as silver, and searchest for her as hid treasures: then shalt thou understand the fear of the Lord, and find the knowledge of God;" Prov. ii. The wisdom of God, in which we are concerned, is contained in his word. The best understanding is to keep his commandments ; Psal. cxi. ; but as we cannot keep them unless we know them, neither can we know them without a diligent inquiry. The word which is rendered *search,* ερευναω, is borrowed from the practice of *miners:* it implies two things, to dig and to examine. First, with much labour they pierce the earth to a considerable depth ; and when they have thus found a vein of precious ore, they break and sift it, and suffer no part to escape their notice. Thus must we join frequent assiduous reading, with close and awakened meditation; comparing spiritual things with spiritual, carefully taking notice of the circumstances, occasion, and application of what we read ; being assured, that there is a treasure of truth and happiness under our hands, if we have but skill to discover and improve it. Only let us be mindful that we have the same views in reading the Scripture, that God has in revealing it to us; which the Apostle thus enumerates : " All Scripture," or the whole Scripture, πασα γραφη, "is given by inspiration of God, and is profitable for doctrine, for reproof, for correction, for instruction in righteousness ; that the man of God may be perfect, thoroughly furnished to every good work;" 2 Tim. iii. And elsewhere it is said to be able to make us " wise unto salvation." How absurd would it be for a man to read a treatise of husbandry with a design of learning navigation, or to seek the principles of trade and commerce in an essay on music ? No less absurd is it to read or study the Scriptures with any other view than to receive its doctrines, submit to its reproofs, and obey its precepts, that we may be made " wise unto salvation." All disquisitions and criticisms that stop short of this, that do not amend the heart as well as furnish the head, are empty and dangerous, at least to ourselves, whatever use they may be of to others. An experience of this caused a learned critic and eminent commentator (Grotius), to confess, towards the close of his life, *Vitam prorsus perdidi, laboriose nihil agendo!* Alas! I have wasted my life in much labour to no purpose! But, on the contrary, when we are diligent and studious, that we may be better acquainted with the Divine precepts and promises, and better inclined to observe and trust them, then we may hope for happy success; for, " blessed is the man whose delight is in the law of the Lord, and who meditates therein day and night: for he shall be like a tree planted by rivers of waters, which bringeth forth its fruit in due season; his leaf also shall not wither, and whatsoever he doth," under this influence, " shall prosper;" Ps. i. Thus God has promised, and thus many have found it, and been enabled to adopt the words of David, " Thou through thy commandments hast made me wiser than my enemies, for they are ever with me :

I have more understanding than all my teachers, for thy testimonies are my meditation." Ps. cxix.

Humility is a third thing very necessary to a profitable perusal of the Scriptures. " God giveth his grace to the humble," James iv. : " He will guide the meek in judgment, he will enlighten the simple in his way," Ps. xxv. The proud he re-sisteth, αντιτασσεται, he draws up against him, he prepares himself, as it were, with his whole force, to oppose his progress. A most formidable ex-pression! If God only leaves us to ourselves, we are all ignorance and darkness; but what must be the dreadful case of those against whom he appears in arms? This has been a principal source of those various and opposite heresies and mistakes, which are the reproach of our holy profession, that vain man, though born a mere " wild ass's colt," Job xi., has undertaken, by his own strength and wisdom, to decide authoritatively on the meaning of Scripture; without being aware of the igno-rance, prejudice, and weakness, which influence his judgment in religious matters; without know-ing the utter inability of the natural man to dis-cern the things of God, and without attending to those means the Scripture itself has appointed for the redress of these evils. But would we not lose our time and pains would we wish not to be misled ourselves, or not to mislead others? Let us aim at a humble spirit : let us reflect much on the ma-jesty and grandeur of the God we serve : let us adore his condescension in favouring us with a re-velation of his will : let us learn to consider the word of God, and the wisdom of God, as terms of the same import : in a word, let us study to know ourselves, our sinfulness and ignorance; then we shall no longer read the Scriptures with indif-ference or prepossession, but with the greatest re-

verence and attention, and with the most enlarged
expectation.

I shall mention but one thing more upon this
head, which is as necessary in itself as any of the
preceding, and likewise necessary in order to obtain them, and that is *Prayer.* Sincerity, diligence,
and humility, are the gifts of God; the blessing
we seek in the exercise of them is in his hands;
and he has promised to bestow all good things,
even " his Holy Spirit, upon those who ask him."
Prayer is indeed the best half of our business while
upon earth, and that which gives spirit and efficacy
to all the rest. Prayer is not only our immediate
duty, but the highest dignity, the richest privilege
we are capable of receiving on this side eternity;
and the neglect of it *implies* the deepest guilt, and
includes the heaviest punishment. A stranger to
prayer, is equally a stranger to God and to happiness, " like a wave of the sea driven with the
wind and tossed," James i. Are any of you, my
friends, unacquainted with prayer ? Then are you
without God in the world, without a guide in
prosperity, without resource in distress, without
true comfort in life, and, while you continue so,
without hope in death. But especially, you are
utterly unqualified to " search the Scripture."
There is a veil upon the mind and heart of every
man (as the Apostle assures us, 2 Cor. iii.), so that
he can neither see nor embrace heavenly truths,
till this impediment is removed : the means of this
is prayer. Therefore David says, " Open thou
mine eyes, that I may behold wondrous things out
of thy law," Ps. cxix. He knew there were wonderful things contained in the law, but confesses
himself incapable of discerning them till the Lord
should interpose. This he has promised to do in
behalf of all who call upon him. But those who

seek not assistance from God can find it no where else: for " every good and perfect gift is from above, and cometh down from the Father of lights," James i., who hath said, " If any man lack wisdom, let him ask of God." A critical knowledge of the original languages, a skill in the customs and manners of the ancients, an acquaintance with the Greek and Roman classics, a perusal of councils, fathers, scholiasts, and commentators, a readiness in the subtilties of logical disputation ; these, in their proper place and subserviency, may be of considerable use to clear, illustrate, or enforce the doctrines of Scripture : but unless they are governed by a temper of humility and prayer ; unless the man that possesses them accounts them altogether as nothing, without that assistance of the Spirit of God which is promised to guide believers into all truth ; unless he seeks and prays for this guidance no less earnestly than those who understand nothing but their mother-tongue; I make no scruple to affirm, that all his *apparatus* of knowledge only tends to lead him so much the farther astray ; and that a plain honest ploughman, who reads no book but his Bible, and has no teacher but the God to whom he prays in secret, stands abundantly fairer for the attainment of true skill in divinity. But happy he, who, by faith and prayer, can realize the Divine presence always with him! who is sincere in his intentions, diligent in the use of means, diffident of himself, yet full of trust and hope, that God, whom he desires to serve, will lead and guide him in the paths of peace and righteousness for his mercy's sake, Psal. xxxi. Those things which are necessary for him to know, shall be made so plain, that he shall not mistake them ; and those things, with which he is not so *immediately* concerned, shall at least teach him humility; teach him to adore the depths of Divine wisdom, and to long for that hour, when " all that is imperfect shall be done away; when we shall no more see in part, but shall know even as we are known," 1 Cor. xiii.

II. I proceed to the *second* thing proposed, To shew *how* the Scriptures testify of Christ. In general, it may be said, that he is the main design and subject, both of the whole Scripture and of each particular book. This will be easily allowed of the New Testament, but is not so obvious with regard to several parts of the Old : I hope therefore it will not be unacceptable to those who love the word of God, if I consider this point something at large, and help them to discover the Lord Jesus Christ in almost every page of the Bible. This will be a new inducement to them to search the Scriptures, when they shall perceive that many passages which they were accustomed to read with indifference, as hardly able to discern any wisdom or meaning in them, do directly testify of Christ.

What is expressed in the Old Testament (for of this I am now to speak) concerning Christ, may be reduced to three heads; prophecies, types, and ceremonies. To open and trace these in their proper extent, would require volumes ; but it is only a hint of each that the bounds of our present meeting will permit me to offer.

The first glimmering of light which dawned upon a lost world was that promise (for I consider the promises as a branch of prophecy) which God (who, in the midst of " judgment, remembers mercy") made to the woman, that " her Seed should bruise the serpent's head," Gen. iii. This was absolute and general, giving hopes of a recovery, but no information of person, time, or place ; but the path of " this Just One was as the light which shineth more and more to the perfect day," Prov. iv. In the time of Noah, the Hope and Desire of all nations was restrained to the line of Shem, Gen. ix., and afterwards more expressly to the family of Abraham : when this divided into two branches, God, to shew that his purpose is of himself, and that he will do as pleaseth him with his own, set aside the elder, and confirmed to Jacob the younger, " that in his Seed all the families of the earth should be blessed," Gen. xxviii. Jacob had twelve sons, which made a still more explicit restriction necessary: accordingly, the patriarch, before his death, declared this high privilege of perpetuating the line of the Messiah was fixed in the tribe of Judah, Gen. xlix.; and the time of his advent was obscurely marked out, by the promise, " that the sceptre should not depart from Judah till the Shiloh come." The last personal limitation was to David, 1 Chron. xvii.; that of *his* family God would raise up the King, who should reign for ever, and over all. Succeeding prophets gradually foretold the time, place, and circumstances of his birth, the actions of his life, the tenor of his doctrine, the success he met with, and the cause, design, and manner of his sufferings and death : in short, to almost every thing that we read in the Gospel, we may annex the observation that the evangelists have made upon a few instances (in order, as it may be presumed, to direct us in searching out the rest), " Then was fulfilled that which was spoken by the prophets." From them we learn, that the Messiah should be born of a virgin, in Bethlehem of Judah, four hundred and ninety years after the commandment given to rebuild Jerusalem ; that he should begin his ministry in Galilee; that he should be despised and rejected of men, betrayed by one of his disciples, sold for thirty pieces of silver, with which money the Potter's field should be afterwards purchased ;

" that he should be cut off, but not for himself;"
and that his death should be followed by the sudden and total ruin of the Jewish government. To
compare these promises and prophecies among
themselves, and with their exact accomplishment
recorded in the New Testament, this alone would
engage us in a close and profitable search into the
Scriptures, and would afford us the most convincing proofs of their Divine original and excellence.

The types of Christ in the Old Testament may
be considered as twofold,—personal and relative :
the former describing, under the veil of history,
his character and offices as considered in himself ;
the latter teaching, under a variety of metaphors,
the advantages those who believe in him should
receive from him.　Thus Adam, Enoch, Melchizedec, Isaac, Joseph, Moses, Aaron, Joshua,
Samson, David, Solomon, and others, were, in
different respects, types or figures of Christ.
Some more immediately represented his person ;
others prefigured his humiliation ; others referred
to his exaltation, dominion, and glory.　So, in the
latter sense, the ark of Noah, the rainbow, the
manna, the brazen serpent, the cities of refuge,
were so many emblems pointing out the nature,
necessity, means, and security of that salvation
which the Messiah was to establish for his people.
Nor are these fanciful allusions of our own making,
but warranted and taught in Scripture, and easily
proved from thence, would time permit ; for indeed there is not one of these persons or things
which I have named, but would furnish matter for
a long discourse, if closely considered in this view,
as typical of the promised Redeemer.

The like may be said of the Levitical ceremonies.
The law of Moses is, in this sense, a happy schoolmaster to lead us unto Christ, Gal. iii. : and it may

be proved beyond contradiction, that in these the Gospel was preached of old to all those *Israelites indeed*, whose hearts were right with God, and whose understandings were enlightened by his Spirit. The ark of the covenant, the mercy-seat, the tabernacle, the incense, the altar, the offerings, the high priest with his ornaments and garments, the laws relating to the leprosy, the Nazarite, and the redemption of lands;—all these, and many more which I have not time to mention, had a deep and important meaning beyond their outward appearance : each, in their place, pointed to " the Lamb of God who was to take away the sins of the world," John i., derived their efficacy *from him*, and received their full accomplishment *in him*.

Thus the Old and New Testament do mutually illustrate each other; nor can either be well understood singly. The Old Testament, in histories, types, prophecies, and ceremonies, strongly delineate Him who, in the fulness of time, was to come into the world to effect a reconciliation between God and man. The New Testament shews, that all these characters and circumstances were actually fulfilled in Jesus of Nazareth; that it was he of whom " Moses in the law and the prophets did write ;" and that we are not to look for another.

We read in Genesis, chap. xxi., that Abraham had two sons: Isaac, the child of the promise, the son of his old age, by his wife Sarah; and Ishmael, born some years before, of Hagar, the handmaid, and servant of Sarah; that the latter, with his mother, were cast out of the family: the occasion some would think trivial, the anger and jealousy of Sarah, because Ishmael had mocked her son. But when it was grievous to Abraham to put them away upon so slight a ground, God himself interposed, and commanded him to comply with her desire. Had we heard no more of this, it is likely we should have considered it as a piece of *family history*, of no very great importance but to those who were immediately concerned in it. We should, perhaps, have wondered to find so much said upon such a subject, in a book which we profess to believe was written by Divine inspiration; we should probably have presumed to arraign the Divine Wisdom, in descending to particulars, in which, according to our views of the fitness of things, we could discern nothing either interesting or instructive. To guard us from these rash mistakes, to explain the true meaning of this particular transaction, and at the same time to furnish us with a key for understanding many passages of the like nature, in which *human wisdom* can discover neither beauty nor benefit; it has pleased God to favour us with an *infallible* exposition of the whole matter. Not for the sake of Abraham, or Isaac, or Ishmael, or Hagar, was this recorded; much less merely to gratify our curiosity. No: " These things," saith the Apostle Paul, " are an allegory; for these are the two covenants; the one from Mount Sinai, which gendereth to bondage, which is Agar. For this Agar is Mount Sinai in Arabia, and answereth to Jerusalem which now is, and is in bondage with her children. But Jerusalem, which is above, is free, which is the mother of us all.——Now we, brethren, as Isaac was, are the children of promise. But as then he that was born after the flesh, persecuted him that was born after the Spirit, even so it is now. Nevertheless, what saith the Scripture? Cast out the bond-woman and her son: for the son of the bond-woman shall not be heir with the son of the free-woman. So then, brethren, we are not children of the bond-woman, but of the free;" Gal. iv. I must not detain you by shewing at large how the Apostle teaches us to discover the spirit and privileges of the Gospel, together with what all who truly receive it must expect to encounter, in a passage which we might otherwise have thought superfluous, if not impertinent. Keep this in your mind when you read the Scripture. Assure yourselves, that there is nothing vain or useless in the *word of God*. Compare one place with another; the Law with the Gospel, the Prophets with the Evangelists: pray unto God that he would open your understandings to understand the Scriptures, as he did for the disciples, Luke xxiv. ; and in a little time you will find, that Christ is not only spoken of in a few verses, here and there, but that, as I said before, he is the main scope and subject of every book, and *almost* of every chapter.

I would add an instance or two of the meaning of the ceremonies, to what I have observed of Hagar in reference to the types. In the law of the passover, it was especially enjoined, Exod. xii., that not a bone of the paschal lamb should be broken. Now, who would have thought that this referred to Christ? yet we see the Evangelist expressly applies it to him, and is filled with wonder at the accomplishment. The legs of those who were crucified at the same time were purposely broken, John xix. ; but our Lord was passed by; and that it should be so, was intimated near fifteen hundred years before, in this charge concerning the lamb. Again, we find that in several places, where a bullock was commanded to be slain for a sin-offering, it is enjoined, that the flesh and the skin should be burnt without the camp; and from the Epistle to the Hebrews, chap. xiii., we learn, that this was not a slight or arbitrary circumstance. We have there this explication: "For the bodies of those beasts whose blood is brought into the sanctuary, by the High Priest, for sin, were burnt without the camp : wherefore Jesus also, that he might sanctify the people with his own blood, suffered without the gate. Let us go forth, therefore, without the camp, bearing his reproach." I must not enlarge any farther, or it were easy, by the clue the Apostles in their writings have given us, to trace the important meaning of many of those institutions, which *scoffers,* who are wise in their own conceits, though neither acquainted with themselves nor the subject, presume to censure as frivolous. The sense of the sacred writings lies too deep for a captious, superficial, volatile survey ; it must be a search, a scrutiny ; a humble, diligent, sincere, and persevering inquiry, or no satisfaction can be expected.

The import of the Scripture testimony concerning Christ, which was the third thing I proposed to speak of, must be deferred to another opportunity. I hope what has been already said, may, through the Divine blessing, engage you to "search the Scriptures." Remember it is the command of our Lord Jesus Christ : it is the only appointed way to the knowledge of Him, whom to know, so as to love, serve, and obey him, is both the foundation and the sum of our happiness here and hereafter. We, as well as the Jews, think we have eternal life in the Scripture, and shall, like them, be inexcusable and self-condemned if we neglect it. Let us not be like fools, with a prize, an inestimable prize, in our hands, but without heart or skill to use it. Better it would have been for us to have lived and died in the

wilds of America, without either means of grace
or hopes of glory, than to slight this record which
God has been pleased to give us of his Son.   But
happy the man whose delight is in the law of his
God!   He has sure direction in every difficulty,
certain comfort in every distress.   The beauty of
the precepts are preferable in his eye to "thousands of gold and silver," Ps. cxix.   The comforts
of the promises are *sweeter* to his taste, "than
honey or the honey-comb," Ps. xix.   He is happy
in life ; for the word of God is to him as a "fountain of living water."   He shall be happy in death ;
the promises of his God shall support him through
that dark valley : and he shall be happy for ever
in the presence and love of Him for whose sake he
now searches the Scripture ; "whom having not
seen," 1 Pet. i., yet, from the testimony there given
of him, "he loves ; in whom, though now he sees
him not, yet, believing, he rejoices with joy unspeakable and full of glory."

Pleraque autem (si detur liberè loquendi venia) quæ etiam in Theologicis scholis tractantur, et magno cum apparatu et strepitu docentur et disputantur, spinosum fortè acumen habent, sed simul certè spinosam sterilitatem : lacerare et pungere possunt, animos pascere non possunt : " Nemo enim ex spinis uvas colligit unquam, aut ex tribulis ficus." " Quorsum alta (inquit quidam) de Trinitate disputare, si careas humilitate, et sic Trinitati displiceas ? " Et aptè St. Augustinus ad illud Esaiæ, " Ego Deus tuus docens te utilia;" " *utilia* (inquit) *docens*, non *subtilia*." Et hoc est quod opto et oro ; ut nobis pro modulo nostro subdocentibus, ille efficaciter vos perdoceat, qui cathedram in cœlo habens, corda docet in terris. —*Archiep. Leighton. Prælect. Theol. pag.* 4. *edit. Lond.* 1693. 4*to*.

SERMON VI.

THE SAME SUBJECT CONTINUED.

JOHN v. 39.

Search the Scriptures ; for in them ye think ye have eternal life: and they are they which testify of me.

IN a former discourse on these words, I mentioned four things as highly requisite, if we would acquire a useful knowledge of the Scripture ; sincerity with respect to the end, diligence in the use of means, a humble sense of our own weakness, and earnest prayer to God for the assistance of his grace and Spirit. To engage us to this practice, and perseverance therein, I next considered *how* the Scriptures, when properly searched into and compared, do clearly and in every part testify of Christ, that he is the end of the Law, the sum of the Prophets, the completion of the promises, the scope of the types and ceremonies, and the great object of the whole Old-Testament dispensation. I am now to say something to the third point I proposed;

III. Concerning the *import* of the testimony the Scriptures bear to Christ.

The principal difficulties on this head are, where to begin on a subject absolutely boundless; and what to select that may be most suitable and useful to this assembly, from the immense variety of topics that offer. For this being the great end and design of the Scripture, to proclaim the excellency of Christ Jesus our Lord, " that we through him may have strong consolation," Heb. xii., it is inculcated in so many places, set in such a diversity of views, and couched under such deep and comprehensive expressions, that not only our present opportunity, but my whole future life, would be too short, if I would collect, state, and explain, all that properly belongs to this single article. For order's sake, I shall reduce the little I must say at this time to three or four distinct particulars, what the Scripture testifies of Christ, as to his person, his offices, his power, and his love.

When we hear of some great undertaking to be performed, we inquire of course about the person who is chiefly concerned in it ; so, when we are told of the mighty works Jesus Christ engaged to perform, to redeem a lost world, to satisfy Divine justice, to make an end of sin, to abolish death, and to bring life and immortality to light ; the first question that occurs is, Who is he ? " Search the Scriptures," and you will have a clear and decisive answer. The Prophet Isaiah, *rapt into future times*, describes him thus : " Unto us a Child is born, unto us a Son is given, and the government shall be upon his shoulder ; and he shall be called, Wonderful, Counsellor, the Mighty God, the Everlasting Father, the Prince of Peace," Isa. ix. 6. The union of the Divine and Human natures in the Messiah is so strongly asserted, the names and attributes of God are so clearly ascribed in this passage, to one who should be *born* into the world, that " he who runs may read ; the wayfaring man, though a fool," must understand it ; and it requires a considerable share of unhappy ingenuity to wrest the words to any other than their obvious meaning. This text, if it stood alone in the Bible (supposing the Scriptures to be a revelation from God), would be a full warrant, and a firm foundation, for that great point of Christian faith and doctrine, That Jesus Christ is very God and very man; or, as the Apostle better expresses it, " God manifest in the flesh." But it is not alone : on the contrary, the Messiah is seldom mentioned, but something is either said of him, or referred to him, which teaches us the same important truth. " Behold the days come," (saith the Lord by Jeremiah, chap. xxiii.) " that I will raise unto David a righteous Branch ; and a King shall reign and prosper, and shall execute judgment and justice in the earth. In his days Judah shall be saved, and Israel shall dwell safely ; and this is his name whereby he shall be called, THE LORD OUR RIGHTEOUSNESS." Isaiah in general styles him, " A Child to be born ;" Jeremiah more particularly, " A Branch of David." Isaiah ascribes to him the name of " The Mighty God ;" Jeremiah says, he shall be called " The Lord our Righteousness." You have the word LORD in capital letters here, as in other places where it is in the original JEHOVAH. Some of the names of God are occasionally applied to inferior subjects ; to angels, to magistrates, and sometimes to idols. But *Jehovah* is allowed by all to signify the essential and incommunicable name of the Most High God. Yet this is not the only place where it is expressly and directly applied to the Messiah. David himself speaks to the same purpose : " The Lord said unto my Lord, Sit thou at my right hand," Psal. cx. That the Messiah was to be David's Son, was known and acknowledged by the Jews in our Saviour's time ; but how he could be the Son of David, and yet his Lord, was a difficulty that utterly posed and silenced the most learned Rabbies and Scribes among them ; because, being destitute of that sincerity and humility we have before spoken of, they could not understand the Scriptures, which were read in their synagogues every day.

Now, although this important doctrine was not to be discovered by the light of nature, or the powers of human reason, yet, since it has pleased God to make it known to us, our reason, humbly tracing the steps of Divine revelation, can easily prove the expedience, and even the necessity, that it should be so. When we are informed from Scripture, that all mankind being sunk into a state of sin and misery, God had in great mercy appointed a person to atone for the one, and deliver them from the other; we may safely, from these principles, infer, by our own reason, 1st, That this person cannot be *mere man:* for as the whole human race, and consequently every individual, is supposed to be previously involved in the same circumstances of guilt and condemnation, it is impossible that any one of these should be able either to answer or satisfy for himself, much less be qualified to interpose in behalf of another. From hence reason may ascend a step higher, and conclude, 2d, That no *mere creature*, however great and excellent, can undertake this part: for the two great points necessary in order to our redemption—to satisfy the justice of God, and to restore the divine image in man—are either of them beyond the sphere of finite power. We read in the Scripture of angels, archangels, thrones, principalities, and powers; and from several texts we may collect, that their number and excellencies are beyond any conceptions we can form. Could we suppose that the virtues and endowments of all these various and exalted beings were united and centred in one of them; however glorious this being would be in other respects, when we consider him as a creature of the Divine power, he will be found to be as *unfit*, and as *unable*, to interfere in the behalf of sinful man as the meanest worm that crawls upon the earth. It is the duty of every being, great and small, to be entirely devoted, according to the extent of its capacity, to the service and glory of its great Creator : therefore an angel is no more capable than a man of performing the smallest work of supererogation. The highest archangel could not magnify the law of God, and make it honourable on the behalf of man, being already bound thereto for himself : much less can we suppose such a being capable of expiating the sins of mankind by suffering. If Divine justice insisted on a propitiation, it must follow, that nothing less than an equivalent could be accepted. But what would be the temporary sufferings of a creature, *or of all creatures,* in this view ? A finite satisfaction, however heightened and exaggerated, would at last be infinitely short of the demand. As to the other branch of redemption, the restoration of the image of God in the soul, I need only mention it ; for it appears, at first glance, that this must be the prerogative of Divine power alone to effect. It remains, therefore, that the deliverance of mankind could be attempted only by Him who, we are assured by the Apostle, agreeable to the passages already cited, is over all, God blessed for ever.

That the Son of God should take upon him the nature and circumstances of our humanity, sin excepted, in order to atone for our transgressions, is indeed such an instance of condescension and love, as must for ever dazzle and astonish the brightest understandings. It is true, some persons in these refined times, affect to speak of this point with admirable coolness and precision. *But in the beginning it was not so.* Either the Apostle Paul was less master of his temper, or more unequal to sublime speculations, than these gentlemen, or else we must allow he had a very different view of the subject; for he cannot mention it without appearing to be transported, and (if I may use the expression) swallowed up by the thought: his ideas seem too great for words; and it is well if his best attempts to explain himself have not exposed him, in the judgment of some of his readers, to the charge of *solecism*. However, though this doctrine, above any other, is a proof that God "is able to do for us exceeding abundantly, beyond all we could ask or think," it is not, upon the premises I before mentioned, in the least repugnant to right reason; rather it is exactly calculated to remove all those surmises which would arise in the mind of a *reasonable sinner*, upon the first intimation of possible forgiveness. In our nature Christ fulfilled the law which we had broken; he sustained the penalty we had incurred; he vanquished the enemies we had to encounter; he trod the path which he has marked out for us; he is entered in our name into that heaven he has promised us; and retains a sympathy with us in all our sufferings and temptations, "in as much as he himself has suffered, being tempted," Heb. ii.

I am next to consider the testimony of Scripture concerning the offices of Christ. These are, in general, included in the character of Mediator. "There is one God, and one Mediator between God and man, the man Christ Jesus," 1 Tim. ii. In this word is summed up all that Christ has done, now does, or will do hereafter, either on the part of God or man. But, for our better apprehension, it is proposed to us under three distinct and principal views, answerable to the three particulars in which the misery of fallen man does principally consist.

And first, Man having departed from God, "became vain in his imaginations, and his foolish heart was darkened," Rom. i.; so that he totally lost the knowledge of his Creator, and how entirely his happiness depended thereon. He forgot God and himself, and sunk so low as to worship the work of his own hands. His life became vain and miserable; in prosperity, without security or satisfaction; in adversity, without support or resource; his death dark and hopeless; no pleasing reflection on the past, no ray of light on the future. Such was the unhappy case when Christ undertook the office of a Prophet; in which character, under various dispensations, first by his servants inspired of old, and afterwards more clearly in his own person, and by his Apostles, he has instructed us in the things pertaining to our peace; not only renewing in us the knowledge of the true God, which, where revelation prevailed not, was universally lost out of the world, but disclosing to us the counsels of Divine love and wisdom in our favour, those great things "which eye hath not seen, nor ear heard," and which never could have entered "into the heart of man to conceive," had not he who dwelt in the bosom of the Father declared them to us. We can now give a sufficient answer to that question, which must have for ever overwhelmed every serious awakened mind, "Wherewithal shall I appear before the Most High God," Mic. vi. We have now learnt how God can declare and illustrate his righteousness and truth, by that very act which, without respect to satisfaction given, would seem the highest impeachment of both; I mean, his justifying the ungodly. We have now a *glass* by which we can discover the presence of the Creator in every part of his creation, and a *clue* to lead us through the mysterious mazes of Divine providence. But who can enumerate the various, the important, the interesting

lessons we receive frcm this Heavenly Teacher,
when, by the influence of his Holy Spirit, he
powerfully applies his written word to the hearts
of his real disciples, who *search the Scriptures* with
a sincere desire to be made wise unto salvation!
Whatever is necessary to make life useful and
comfortable, and to gild the gloom of death with
the bright prospect of a glorious immortality,
is there contained: so that, instructed by these
writings alone, a poor illiterate mechanic has been
often enabled to converse upon a dying bed with
more dignity, certainty, and influence, than any, or
all the philosophers, ancient or modern, could attain.

But, besides the natural ignorance of fallen man,
he was chargeable with aggravated *guilt.* Guilt
and ignorance are reciprocally causes and consequences of each other. Every additional guilt
tends to increase the stupidity of the human soul;
and every increase of this increases, in the same
proportion, the natural indisposition for the practice or the love of virtue; makes the soul more blind
to consequences, more base in its pursuits, and
thus become a more willing and assiduous servant
of iniquity. No wonder, therefore, that when the
understanding was totally darkened as to the
knowledge of God, the will and affections became
wholly disobedient to his *law.* But when a Divine
light has, in some measure, discovered the heart
to itself, and at the same time set an offended God
in view, every such sensible sinner would undoubtedly imitate our first parents, and fly (were
it possible) from the presence of his Maker and
his Judge. " I heard thy voice," says Adam,
" and I hid myself, for I was afraid," Gen. iii.
Vain attempt; and, if it was practicable, a dreadful
alternative, since absence from God imports the
utmost misery to a creature who can be happy

only in his favour. But here the Scriptures bring us unspeakable comfort, testifying of Christ as our great High Priest. To point out and illustrate this part of his character, is the chief end and design of the whole Levitical law; the main points of which are explained, and applied to our blessed Lord throughout the Epistle to the Hebrews. The principal parts of the priest's office were, to sacrifice in behalf of the people, to make atonement, to pray for them, and to bless them in the name of the Lord. No sacrifices could be offered or accepted; no blessings expected, but through the hands of the priests whom God had appointed. Thus Christ, the High Priest of our profession, offered himself a sacrifice without either spot or blemish; he entered with his own blood within the vail, to the immediate presence of our offended God; and through him peace and good-will is proclaimed to sinful men. He continues still to exercise the other part of his appointment; he makes continual intercession for his people; he presents their prayers and imperfect services acceptable before the Throne; he gives them confidence and access to draw nigh to God; and he bestows upon them those gifts and blessings which are the fruits of his sufferings and obedience. The Levitical priests were, like their people, sinners; and were therefore constrained first to make atonement for themselves; they were mortal, therefore their service passed from hand to hand; their sacrifices were imperfect, therefore needed continual repetition, and had at last only a typical and ceremonial efficacy; " for it was not possible that the blood of bulls and goats," Heb. ix. and x., could remove either the guilt or pollution of sin. " The law made nothing perfect." But Jesus, the " Mediator of the New Covenant," is " such a High Priest as became us; holy, harmless, undefiled, separate from sinners; who needeth not (as those of old) to offer sacrifice first for his own sins, and then for the people; for this he did once, when he offered up himself," Heb. viii. The great inference from this doctrine, several times repeated by the Apostle in a variety of phrase, is, That we may now have boldness to appear before God, that our prayers and services are pleasing in his sight, and all the blessings of grace and glory ready to be bestowed on us, if we faithfully apply for them, through the merits of his Son.

Once more: Man is not only ignorant of God and himself, and too full of guilt to plead in his own name, but he is likewise weak and defenceless; unable to make his way through the opposition that withstands his progress to eternal life, or to secure him from the many enemies " that rise up against him," Psal. iii. We read, that when the Gibeonites made a league with Joshua, Jos. ix., which was the only step could save them from utter ruin, the neighbouring states and cities all united to destroy them; so the soul that is desirous to submit to Jesus Christ, immediately finds itself in the midst of war: the world, the flesh, and the devil, unite their forces, either to recal such a one to the practice and service of sin, or to distress him to the uttermost for forsaking it. And none could support this conflict, if not themselves supported by a higher hand. But Jesus, the antitype of Joshua, the true Captain of the Lord's hosts, reveals himself in his word as the King of his Church. He can inspire the fainting soul with unseen supplies: he, " when the enemy comes in like a flood," Isa. lix., can by his Spirit lift up a standard against him; he can take the prey even out of the hand of the mighty. He has said it of

his church in general, and he will make it good to
every individual that trusts in him, that the gates
of hell shall never prevail against them.   What
though a sense of the guilt and remaining power
of sin often fills the humble soul with inexpressible
distress ! He that stills the raging of the sea, and
the violence of the winds, with a word, can, with
equal ease, calm all the unruly motions of the
mind.   What though the world opposes in every
quarter, and presents snares or terrors all around !
what though rage or contempt, threats or allure-
ments, are by turns, or all together, employed to
ruin us ! Behold, " greater is he that is in us, than
he that is in the world," 1 John iv.;   Christ has
" overcome the world for us," John xvi., and has
promised to make us conquerors, yea more than
conquerors, in our turn.   What though " the devil
goes about like a roaring lion, seeking whom he
may devour !" 1 Pet. v̇. It is an argument of the
strongest kind for watchfulness and prayer; but
we need not fear him : the " beloved of the Lord
shall dwell in safety," Deut. xxxiii. ;   " the Lord
shall cover him all the day long; he shall deliver
him from the snare of the fowler," Ps. xci.   " His
truth shall be a shield and buckler," to all who
enlist under his banner;   and at length, yea
shortly, " the God of peace shall bruise Satan
under our feet." Rom. xvi.

It is thus the Scriptures, to help the weakness
of our apprehensions, testify of Christ, under the
threefold view of Prophet, Priest, and King of his
people.   These are his principal and leading characters, which include and imply the rest ; for the
time would fail to speak of him, as he is declared
to be their Head, Husband, Root, Foundation,
Sun, Shield, Shepherd, Lawgiver, Exemplar, and
Fore-runner.   In brief, there is hardly any com-

fortable relation, or useful office, amongst men; hardly any object in the visible creation, which either displays beauty, or produces benefit, but what is applied in the word of God, to illustrate the excellence and sufficiency of the Lord Jesus Christ. The intent of all is, that we may learn to trust him, and delight to serve him; for these must go together. Whoever would be benefited by his mediation as a Priest, must submit to his instructions as a Prophet, and yield him universal obedience as a King. Fatal are the mistakes in this matter now in the world. Some talk highly of the death and sufferings of Christ, who are little solicitous to keep his commandments: others labour in the very fire to observe his law; but " being ignorant of God's righteousness, and going about to establish their own," Rom. x., they labour to no purpose. Dependence on the merits of Christ, and obedience to his commands, are inseparably united; and only the man who aims at *both*, can attain to *either*.

I should now lay before you some Scripture testimonies of the *power* and *love of Christ;* but I have anticipated this part of my subject in what I have already said. His Divine nature proclaims his power, his offices display his love. We have seen, that *he emptied himself* of his eternal glories; that " he bowed the heavens, and came down in the form of a servant;" that he submitted to all imaginable sufferings; all that the malice of men, all that the avenging justice of God, could inflict: and, having by this means opened the kingdom of heaven, and taken possession there, in behalf of all believers, he has caused the glad tidings of salvation to be published through the world, declaring, that " whosoever cometh to him (without one exception), he will in no wise cast out;" John vi.

Are not these proofs of unspeakable, unexampled love? We have seen, that he fully performed the work he undertook; " that he has made an end of sin," Dan. ix. ; " brought in an everlasting righteousness, spoiled principalities and powers," Eph. ii. ; " triumphed over all our enemies, broke down the partition-wall, and brought life and immortality to light by his Gospel," 1 Tim. i. We read, that he is exalted highly; that God has given him a name that is above every name," Phil. ii. : that he is " far above all principality, and might, and dominion :" and what more can be said of his power? Read his own declaration, " All power is given to me in heaven and in earth," Matth. xxviii. Were these two points, the power and the love of Christ, rightly understood, and fully believed, earth would be full of heaven. But, alas! we are *fools, and slow of heart*, to receive all that *Moses and the Prophets*, Luke xxiv., the *Evangelists and Apostles*, have written for our instruction. From hence proceeds our indifference, and that we need so much to be pressed *to search the Scriptures*, though we readily acknowledge that in them *we have the words of eternal life*.

IV. It remains therefore, in the fourth and last place, that I add a few words to recommend and enforce the command in the text, " search the Scriptures," from the argument there subjoined, " for in them ye think ye have eternal life :" and we think right; for it " is eternal life to know the only true God, and Jesus Christ, whom he hath sent," John xvii. : and every article of this knowledge is contained in the Old and New Testament ; nor can any part of it be met with any where else. Yet let conscience judge this day, as in the presence of " the living God, the Searcher of hearts," before whom our private judgments must shortly come under a review : has any book a smaller share of the time, the memory, or the affections of many of us than this book of God ?   Do not the successive returns of business and amusement so far engross our time, and our thoughts, that we have either no leisure or no disposition to attend to the things which pertain to our peace ?   Consider, " in them we think we have eternal life." We know we are posting to eternity as fast as the wings of time can carry us ; we know, that the consequences of our behaviour in this span of life will attend us into an invisible unalterable state ; and we confess, that the necessary directions for our conduct in these most important and precarious circumstances, are to be found only in the Bible : what words then can describe our fatal insensibility, if, all this acknowledged, we have no heart to consult, or to value, this inestimable treasure put into our hands ?

Many inquiries, more curious than useful, have been started concerning the Divine procedure with the heathen nations, and those who never heard of the Gospel of peace.   " The Judge of all the earth will (undoubtedly) do right," Gen. xviii., and will be justified at the great day, when every man shall receive according to his works.   Till then we must *wait* for the knowledge of what he has not seen fit to reveal.   But thus much he has already told us, that, however it may go with those who know not the Gospel, dreadful will be the doom of those who, having it published among them, refuse to obey it.   " The servant who knew not his master's will shall be beaten with few stripes," Luke xii.   But this will not be our case ; at least our ignorance will be rather an aggravation

than an excuse; a wilful, obstinate, infatuated
ignorance.   We have the words of eternal life in
our hands, "line upon line, precept upon precept;" but how do we imitate those (whom perhaps
we have been ready to blame) spoken of in the
parable, who, when they received a kind and gracious invitation to a royal feast, made light of it,
and "all with one consent began to make excuse!" Luke xiv.   It is easy to apply this to the
Jews of old : so David could clearly judge in the
case of the rich man who killed his poor neighbour's lamb, 2 Sam. xii. ; but had not the Prophet
helped him, he would not have collected that he
himself was the person intended.   But to bring
the general truths of Scripture home to the heart
is the work of God; and perhaps, while I am
speaking at random, he may rouse the consciences
of some to say in particular, *Thou art the man.*
Then they will soon see how much it behoves them
to *search the Scriptures*, when they understand the
weighty meaning of the words, *eternal life.*

Some of us, I hope, do already make conscience
of frequent reading the Scriptures; but let us remember the force of the word *search.*   It is not a
careless superficial reading, or dispatching such a
number of chapters in a day, as a task, that will
answer the end.   I have already reminded you,
that it is a business will need your best application; a serious, impartial, humble, persevering
inquiry, accompanied with earnest prayer for the
light and assistance of God's Holy Spirit.   When
we set about it in this method, we shall soon find
happy effects; pleasure and instruction will go
hand in hand, and our knowledge advance as the
growing light.   The precepts shall inspire us with
true wisdom; teach us how to order all our affairs
respecting both worlds, to fill up our several sta-

tions in life with propriety, usefulness, and comfort; and to avoid the numerous evils and distresses which those who live by no rule, or by any other rule than God's word, are perpetually running into. The *promises* shall be a support in every trouble, a medicine in every sickness, a supply in every need. Above all, the Scriptures will repay our trouble, as they testify of Christ. The more we read of his person, offices, power, love, doctrine, life, and death, the more our hearts will cleave to him : we shall, by insensible degrees, be transformed into his spirit. We shall, with the Apostle, say, " I know in whom I have believed," 2 Tim. i. Every thing we see shall be at once a *memorial* to remind us of our Redeemer, and a *motive* to animate us in his service. And at length we shall be removed to see him as he is, without a cloud, and without a vail; to be for ever with him ; to behold, and to share the glories of that heavenly kingdom " which (Matth. xxv.) he has prepared (for his followers) from before the foundation of the world." Amen.

TWENTY SERMONS,

PREACHED AT OLNEY, IN BUCKINGHAMSHIRE.

———————

Blessed is the people that know the joyful sound: they shall walk,
O Lord, in the light of thy countenance. In thy name shall
they rejoice all the day: and in thy righteousness shall they
be exalted.　　　　　　　　　　PSAL. lxxxix. 15, 16.

SERMONS

PREACHED IN THE PARISH CHURCH OF OLNEY,

ON THE FOLLOWING SUBJECTS:

1. The small Success of the Gospel Ministry.
2. The Mysteries of the Gospel hid from many.
3. Of those from whom the Gospel Doctrines are hid.
4. The Nature of Spiritual Revelation, and who are favoured with it.
5. The Sovereignty of Divine Grace asserted and illustrated.
6. Of the Person of Christ.
7. Of the Authority of Christ.
8. The Glory and Grace of God revealed in Jesus Christ.
9. Labouring and heavy-laden Sinners described.
10. Of coming to Christ.
11. Of Believers' Rest in Christ.
12. Of the Yoke of Christ.
13. The Service of Christ easy and pleasant.
14. Believers cautioned against Misconduct in their Profession.
15. The Extent and Sanction of the Third Commandment.
16. The Christian Life compared to a Race.
17. No Access to God but by the Gospel of Christ.
18. Of a Living and a Dead Faith.
19. Guilt removed, and Peace restored.
20. Of the Assurance of Faith.

INHABITANTS OF THE PARISH OF OLNEY.

MY DEAR FRIENDS,

I HAVE principally two motives for publishing these Discourses. The one is, to exhibit a specimen of the doctrine that is taught and most surely believed amongst us, to satisfy those who desire information, and to stop, if possible, the mouth of slander. I cheerfully submit them to examination; in full confidence that they contain nothing of moment which is not agreeable to the general strain of the word of God, and to the principles of the church whereof I am a minister, as specified in the Articles, Liturgy, and Homilies. And that what I now print is to the same purport with the usual course of my preaching, I doubt not but all who statedly hear me will do me the justice to acknowledge.

My other motive is a desire of promoting your edification. It is my comfort that many of you live by the truths of the Gospel, and highly prize them. You will not therefore be unwilling to view the substance of what you once heard with acceptance. But it is to be feared, that the far greater part of the congregation have need to have the things pertaining to their peace pressed upon them again and again, for a different reason; not because they know them, and therefore love to have them brought to their remembrance, but because they have hitherto heard them without effect. For the sake of both, therefore, I am willing to leave an abiding testimony amongst you. I hereby take each of your consciences to witness, that I am clear of your blood; and that, to the best of my knowledge and ability, I have not shunned to declare the whole counsel of God.

In the choice of the subjects I have selected for publication, I have not been solicitous to comprise a succinct scheme of Gospel doctrine, but have given the preference to such topics, which the peculiar circumstances of the times, and of my hearers, make me desirous might be had in continual remembrance.

The Exposition of the Third Commandment, which was first delivered in your hearing, I afterwards preached (nearer the form in which it now appears) at London ; and as it led me to touch on some particulars of a very public and interesting concern, I have given it a place in this volume. And I shall think myself happy indeed, if it may please God to give weight to the testimony of so obscure a person with respect to a grievance under which the nation groans.

As long discourses are in many respects inconvenient, I have chosen to publish no more than a brief summary of what you heard more at large from the pulpit. And as I aim to speak plain truths to a plain people, I have purposely avoided any studied ornaments in point of expression, being desirous to accommodate myself to the apprehensions of the most ignorant.

May it please the God of all grace to accompany my feeble endeavours to promote the knowledge of his truth, with the powerful influence of his Holy Spirit. And I earnestly entreat all who know how to draw near to a Throne of Grace by Jesus Christ, to strive mightily in prayer for me, that I may stand fast in the faith, and increase in the knowledge of Jesus the Saviour ; and that for his sake I may labour, without fear or fainting, in the service to which he has been pleased to call me. May the grace of our Lord Jesus Christ be with you all!

I am your affectionate friend, and servant in the Gospel of Christ,

JOHN NEWTON.

Olney, Jan. 20, 1767.

SERMONS PREACHED AT OLNEY.

SERMON I.

THE SMALL SUCCESS OF THE GOSPEL MINISTRY CONSIDERED.

MATTH. xi. 25.

At that time Jesus answered and said, I thank thee, O Father, Lord of heaven and earth, because thou hast hid these things from the wise and prudent, and hast revealed them unto babes.

OUR blessed Lord perfectly knew before-hand the persons who would profit by his ministry : but his observations, conduct, and discourses, were intended as a pattern and instruction to his followers. He is said to have marvelled at the unbelief of some, and at the fate of others; not as though either was strange to him, who was acquainted with all hearts, and always knew what he himself would do; but it is spoken of him as a man, and to shew how his ministers and people should be affected upon the like occasions. In the preceding verses he had been speaking of Capernaum, and other places, where his mighty works had been performed in vain. He had denounced a sentence against them; and foretold that their punishment would be heavier in proportion to the greatness of the privileges they had abused. But this was not his pleasing work. Mercy and grace were his delight, and he usually expressed sorrow and pain for the obstinacy of sinners. He wept for his avowed enemies, and prayed for the murderers who nailed him to the cross. It was not without grief that he declared the approaching doom of these cities; yet, raising his thoughts from earth to heaven, he acquiesced in the will of his heavenly Father, and expressed the highest satisfaction in his appointment. He knew, that, however some would harden themselves, there was a remnant who would receive the truth, and that the riches and glory of the Divine sovereignty and grace would be magnified. Before I enter upon the particulars, this connexion of the words will afford us ground for some observations.

I. That the small success and efficacy of the preached Gospel upon multitudes who hear it, is a subject of wonder and grief to the ministers and people of God. It was so to our Lord Jesus, considered as a Preacher and Messenger; and they, so far as they have received his Spirit, judge and act as he did.

1. Those who have indeed tasted that the Lord is gracious, have had such a powerful experience in their own souls of the necessity and value of the Gospel, that in their first warmth, and till painful experience has convinced them of the contrary, they can hardly think it possible that sinners should stand out against its evidence. They are ready to say, " Surely it is because they are ignorant : they have not had opportunity of considering the evil of sin, the curse of the law, and the immense goodness of God manifested in his Son ; but when these things shall be plainly and faithfully set before them, surely they will submit, and thankfully receive the glad tidings." With such sanguine hopes Melancthon entered the ministry, at the dawn of the Reformation : he thought he had only to speak, and to be heard, in order to

convince; but he soon found himself mistaken, and that the love of sin, the power of prejudice, and the devices of Satan, were such obstacles in his way, as nothing less than the mighty operations of the Spirit of God could break through. And all who preach upon his principles, and with his views, have known something of his disappointment. Speaking from the feelings of a full heart, they are ready to expect that others should be no less affected than themselves. But when they find that they are heard with indifference, perhaps with contempt; that those whose salvation they long for are enraged against them for their labour of love; that they cannot prevail upon their dearest friends, and nearest relatives; this grieves and wounds them to the heart.

2. They have been convinced themselves, that unbelief was the worst of all their sins: and, therefore, though they pity all who live in the practice of sin, yet they have a double grief to see them reject the only means of salvation; and that this contempt will lie more heavily upon them, than any thing they can be charged with besides. It gladdens the heart of a minister to see a large and attentive assembly; but how is this joy damped by a just fear, lest any, lest many of them should receive this grace of God in vain, and have cause at last to bewail the day when the name of Jesus was first sounded in their ears.

It seems plain, then, that those who are indifferent about the event of the Gospel—who satisfy themselves with this thought, that the elect shall be saved, and feel no concern for unawakened sinners—make a wrong inference from a true doctrine, and know not what spirit they are of. Jesus wept for those who perished in their sins. St. Paul had great grief and sorrow of heart for the

Jews, though he gives them this character; "They please not God, and are contrary to all men." It well becomes us, while we admire distinguishing grace to ourselves, to mourn over others: and, inasmuch as secret things belong to the Lord, and we know not but some of whom we have at present but little hopes may at last be brought to the knowledge of the truth, we should be patient and forbearing, after the pattern of our heavenly Father, and endeavour, by every probable and prudent means, to stir them up to repentance, remembering that they cannot be more distant from God, than by nature we were ourselves.

II. The best relief against those discouragements we meet with from men, is to raise our thoughts to God and heaven. For this the Lord Jesus is our precedent here. He said, " I thank thee, O Father." The word * signifies to confess, to promise or consent, and to praise. As if it had been said, " I glorify thy wisdom in this respect, I acknowledge and declare it is thy will, and I express my own consent and approbation." Our Lord's views of the Divine counsels were perfect, and therefore his satisfaction was complete. It is said, " He rejoiced in spirit †," when he uttered these words. And the more we increase in faith and in the knowledge of God, the more we shall be satisfied in his appointments, and shall see and say, " He hath done all things well." It is needful for our comfort, to be well established in the truth suggested in my text, that the Lord hath provided for the accomplishment of his own purposes, and that his counsels shall surely stand. From this doctrine we may infer,

---

* The original word occurs Matth. iii. 6, Luke xxii. 6, and Rom. xv. 9.
† Luke x. 21.

1. That where the faithful labours and endeavours of ministers, and others, to promote the knowledge of grace and the practice of holiness, fail of success, yet they shall be accepted. The servants of Christ may in their humble measure adopt the words of their Lord and Master, in the Prophet, " Though Israel be not gathered, yet shall I be glorious in the eyes of the Lord, and my God shall be my strength*." When he sent forth his first disciples, he directed them wherever they entered to say, " Peace be to this house! and if a son of peace be there," if there be any who thankfully accept your salutation and message, " your peace shall rest upon it; if not, it shall return to you again †:" that is, your good wishes and endeavours shall not be lost for want of proper objects, but when they seem without effect on others, shall be productive of the happiest consequences to yourselves. You shall receive all you were desirous to communicate. Thus his ministers are to declare his whole will, whether men will hear, or whether they shall forbear. And if they do thus with a single eye to his glory, and in humble dependence upon his blessing, they are not answerable for the event, they shall in nowise lose their reward.

2. Faithful endeavours in the service of the Gospel shall not wholly fail. Though all will not hear, some certainly shall both hear and obey. Though all are by nature equally averse and incapable, yet there shall be " a willing people in the day of God's power ‡." If the wise and prudent turn away from the truth, there are babes to whom it shall be revealed. The Lord renews unto us a pledge of his faithfulness in this concern every time the rain descends. For thus he has promised,

---

* Isa. xlix. 5. † Luke x. 6. ‡ Psal. cx. 3.

" As the rain cometh down, and the snow from heaven, and returneth not thither, but watereth the earth, and maketh it bring forth and bud, that it may give seed to the sower, and bread to the eater : so shall my word be that goeth forth out of my mouth ; it shall not return unto me void, but it shall accomplish that which I please, and it shall prosper in the thing whereto I sent it *."

3. The Divine Sovereignty is the best thought we can retreat to for composing and strengthening our minds under the difficulties, discouragements, and disappointments, which attend the publication of the Gospel. The more we give way to reasonings and curious inquiries, the more we shall be perplexed and baffled. When Jeremiah † had been complaining of some things which were too hard for him, the Lord sent him to the potter's house, and taught him to infer, from the potter's power over the clay, the just right which the Lord of all hath to do what he will with his own. It is only the pride of our own hearts that prevents this consideration from being perfectly conclusive and satisfactory. How many schemes derogatory from the free grace of God, tending to darken the glory of the Gospel, and to depreciate the righteousness of the Redeemer, have taken their rise from vain unnecessary attempts to vindicate the ways of God ; or rather to limit the actings of Infinite Wisdom to the bounds of our narrow understandings, to sound the depths of the Divine counsels with our feeble plummets, and to say to Omnipotence, "Hitherto shalt thou go, and no farther." But upon the ground of the Divine Sovereignty we may rest satisfied and stable : for if God appoints and over-rules all, according to the purpose

---

* Isa. lv. 10.   † Jer. xviii. 6.

of his own will, we have sufficient security, both
for the present and the future.

First, For the present. We may firmly expect,
what Scripture and reason concur to assure us,
that " the Judge of all the earth will do right."
Whatever to us appears otherwise in his proceedings, should be charged to the darkness and
weakness of our minds. We know, that in every
point of science difficulties and objections occur
to young beginners, which at first view may seem
almost unanswerable; but as knowledge increases,
the difficulties gradually subside, and at last we
perceive they were *chiefly* owing to the defects of
our apprehension. In divinity it is wholly so:
" God is light, and in him is no darkness at all :"
his revealed will is, like himself, just, holy, pure
in the whole, and perfectly consistent in every
part. We may safely rest upon this general
maxim, that " the Judge of all the earth shall do
right." Though he does not give us a particular
account of his dealings, and we are not fully able
to comprehend them; yet we ought, against all
appearances and proud reasonings, to settle it
firmly in our minds, that every thing is conducted
worthy the views which God has given us of himself in his holy word, as a being of infinite justice,
wisdom, goodness, and truth.—And farther,

Secondly, For the future. He has appointed
a day when he will make it appear that he *has
done* right. Though clouds and darkness are now
upon his proceedings, they shall ere long be removed. When all his designs in providence and
grace are completed ; when the present imperfect
state of things shall be finished ; when the dead,
small and great, are summoned to stand before
him ; then the great Judge will condescend to unfold the whole train of his dispensations, and will

justify his proceedings before angels and men; then every presumptuous cavil shall be silenced, every difficulty solved. His people shall admire his wisdom, his enemies shall confess his justice. The destruction of those who perish shall be acknowledged deserved, and of themselves; and the redeemed of the Lord shall ascribe all the glory of their salvation to him alone. What we shall then see, it is now our duty and our comfort assuredly to believe.

The great subject of our Saviour's joy, and which, so far as it is apprehended, will bear up his servants above all their difficulties and disappointments; I mean, the consideration of the sovereign hand of God directing the success of his word when and where he pleases; we must defer speaking of till the next opportunity. And we shall close at present with a few inferences from what has been said thus far by way of introduction.

1. Take heed how you hear. The Gospel of salvation, which is sent to you, will be either a " savour of life unto life, or of death unto death," to every soul of you. There is no *medium*. Though, in a common and familiar way of speaking, we sometimes complain, that the Gospel is preached without effect, there is in reality no possibility that it can be without effect. An effect it must and will have upon all who hear it. Happy they who receive and embrace it as a joyful sound, the unspeakable gift of God's love. To these it will be " a savour of life unto life." It will communicate life to the soul at first, and maintain that life, in defiance of all opposition, till it terminates in glory. But woe, woe to those who receive it not! It will be to them " a savour of death unto death." It will leave them under the sentence of death, already denounced against them by the law which

they have transgressed; and it will consign them to eternal death, under the heaviest aggravations of guilt and misery. Remember the doom of Capernaum, and why it was denounced. Jesus preached amongst them the words of eternal life, and they rejected him. This was all. In other things, perhaps, they were no worse than their neighbours, and probably disdained to hear themselves judged worthy of a heavier punishment than Sodom, and those cities which for their abominations were consumed with fire from heaven. But our Lord assures us, it shall be more tolerable for Sodom and Gomorrah in the day of judgment, than for those who slight his word. For this guilt and condemnation is not confined to the Jews who rejected his person, but extended to all who should at any time treat his Gospel with contempt. However inconsiderable his ministers are in other respects, if they faithfully deliver his message, he has declared himself closely interested in the reception they meet with: "He that receiveth you, receiveth me; and he that despiseth you, despiseth both me and him that sent me*." It is therefore at your peril to treat what we say with indifference (if we speak agreeably to the Scripture): the word of God which we preach will judge you at the last day.

2. Be afraid of being wise in your own eyes, lest you should approach to the characters of those from whom the righteous God sees fit to hide the knowledge of those truths, without which they cannot be saved. The Gospel is not proposed to you to ask your opinion of it, that it may stand or fall according to your decision; but it peremptorily demands your submission. If you think

---

* Matth. x. 40.

yourselves qualified to judge and examine it by that imperfect and depraved light which you call your reason, you will probably find reasons enough to refuse your assent. Reason is properly exercised in the ordinary concerns of life, and has so far a place in religious inquiries, that none can or do believe the Gospel, without having sufficient reasons for it. But you need a higher light, the light of God's Spirit, without which the most glorious displays of his wisdom will appear foolishness to you. If you come simple, dependent, and teachable; if you pray from your heart, with David, " Open thou mine eyes, that I may see wondrous things in thy law *," you will be heard and answered; you will grow in the knowledge and grace of our Lord Jesus Christ: but if you neglect this, and trust in yourselves, as supposing this promised assistance of the Holy Spirit unnecessary, the glorious light of the Gospel will shine upon you in vain; for Satan will maintain such hold of you by this pride of your hearts, as still to keep you in bondage and darkness, that you shall neither see it, nor desire to see it.

3. Those of you who have some spiritual apprehensions of these things, have reason to praise God that you see a *little*. You were once quite blind: you neither saw your disease nor your remedy. You could discern nothing of the excellence of Christ, or the beauties of holiness. But now the eyes of your understanding are in some measure enlightened. It is the grace of God has made you thus far to differ from what you once were, and from what multitudes around you still are. Be thankful. Accept it as a token for good. Be not discouraged that the beginnings are small;

* Psalm cxix. 18.

but wait on the Lord, and they shall be increased.
Seek him by prayer. Converse with your Bibles.
Attend upon the public ordinances. In the humble
use of these means (while you endeavour to act
faithfully according to the light you have already
received), you shall gradually advance in wisdom
and comfort. The Christian growth is not instan-
taneous, but by degrees, as the early dawn increases
in brightness till the perfect day*, and as the corn
comes forward surely, though unperceived†. In
this manner your views of Gospel truth shall increase in clearness, evidence, and influence, till
you are removed from this land of shadows to the
regions of perfect light, to behold the truth as it
shines in the person of Jesus, without a veil, and
without a cloud for ever.

SERMON II.

IN WHAT SENSE THE MYSTERIES OF THE GOSPEL ARE HID FROM MANY.

MATTH. xi. 25.

*At that time Jesus answered and said, I thank thee, O
Father, Lord of heaven and earth, because thou hast
hid these things from the wise and prudent, and hast
revealed them unto babes.*

WHEN our Lord appeared upon earth, though he
came on the most gracious and important business,

---

* Prov. iv. 18.   † Matth. xiii. 31, 32.

displayed the perfection of holiness in his conduct, and performed innumerable acts of kindness and love, he met with little regard. He found many enemies, but few hearty friends. Especially those who were most eminent for riches, learning, power, or reputed goodness, disdained him; and most of those who followed him were either people in low circumstances, or whose character had been offensive. Publicans and sinners, fishermen, unlearned and obscure persons, were almost the only friends he had. The Lord Jesus, who was infinitely above the selfish views which are too apt to influence our little minds, was well satisfied with this event. He did not desire honour from men. "The souls of the poor were precious in his sight *." He spoke kindly to those whom men abhorred: and if he mourned over the obstinacy of the chiefs of the people, it was for their own sakes. Yet (as I observed formerly) when he considered the appointment and will of God in this dispensation, he was not only content, but he rejoiced. He expressed his approbation in these words: "I thank thee, O Father," &c. There is something observable in this passage which will be of continual use and application, so long as the Gospel shall be preached. For as it was then, so it is still: the things that are hid from the wise and prudent are revealed unto babes. Five particulars offer from the words for our consideration.

I. What may be intended by *these things?*

II. Where and in what sense they are hid?

III. From whom? *The wise and prudent.*

IV. How the knowledge of them is to be obtained? By revelation: *thou hast revealed.*

* Psalm lxxii. 13, 14.

V. Who are thus favoured? *Babes.*

I. By the things which it pleases God should be hid from the wise, and revealed to babes, we may understand,

1. In general, the things pertaining to salvation. That most men are ignorant of them, and careless about them, is too plain. Out of the abundance of the heart the mouth speaketh, and the tree is known by its fruits. Men speak as though their tongues were their own ; they act as though they were to give no account; they live as though they were to live here for ever. The way of truth is hid from their eyes, and the fear of God has no place in their hearts.

2. More particularly, those doctrines which are in an especial sense peculiar to the Gospel, seem here to be intended. If the principles of what some call Natural Religion, though agreeable to the light of natural conscience, are little regarded ; the more spiritual truths of the Bible are not only neglected, but scorned and opposed. The same spirit, which shewed itself under our Lord's personal ministry, still subsists. The chief doctrines he taught, and for which he met with the fiercest opposition, were precisely the same with those which have awakened the scorn and rage of the world ever since ; and which multitudes who bear the name of Christians in this day oppose with all their strength. Such as,

First, The Divinity of Christ. When he spoke of himself as existing before Abraham, and said that God was his *own* father*, the Jews took up stones to stone him. And this mystery is still

---

* John v. 18. Πατέρα ιδιον ελεγε. He said that God was his *own* father ; in a sense peculiar to himself, and exclusive of all

hid from the natural man. No one can say, acknowledge, and believe, that Jesus Christ is Lord or Jehovah; that He who once hung upon the cross, bleeding to death, is God the Maker of all things, the rightful object of the supreme love, trust, and homage of men and angels; but by the Holy Ghost *.

Secondly, Distinguishing grace. "When Jesus first preached at Nazareth, the eyes of all were fixed upon him †;" but when, making application to themselves, he touched upon this point, from the examples of Naaman the Syrian, and the widow of Sarepta, who were relieved when many lepers and widows in Israel were passed by, they were filled with indignation, and would have thrown him headlong down the rock. And it is to this hour an offensive doctrine to all who do not know the value and the need of it.

Thirdly, The new birth. When this was proposed to a master in Israel, he cried out, " How can these things be ‡?" And by many who are wise and prudent in their own sight, it is at this day accounted nonsense. A small acquaintance with the general strain of what is published either from the pulpit or the press, may prove that modern divinity has, for the most part, found a

others. The Jews well understood the meaning of this assertion, that thereby *he made himself equal with God*; and, therefore, as they did not believe in him, they charged him with blasphemy. It would indeed have been blasphemy in a mere man, or in the highest archangel, to have spoken of himself in these terms. But the force of the expression is lost in our version of the New Testament, through the omission of the word ιδιον, *his own;* which seems one of the most important mistakes to be found in that translation.

* 1 Cor. xii. 3.   † Luke iv. 16—20.

‡ John iii. 9.

smoother path to tread than that by which Nicodemus was conducted to the knowledge of himself and his Saviour. Such a doubtful inquirer
might now be entertained with many ingenious
essays on the beauty of virtue, the efficacy of benevolence, the excellency of the human mind, and
other favourite topics. He would find teachers
enough to encourage and improve the idea he has
of his own importance, but he would hardly meet
with many who would speak to him in our Lord's
language, and refer him to the brazen serpent,
and a new birth, in order to learn the means and
the nature of the Gospel salvation.

Fourthly, The nature of the life of faith. When
our Lord spoke of this, under the metaphor of
eating his flesh and drinking his blood, many,
who till then had professed themselves his disciples, " turned back, and walked no more with
him *." And none can bear it now, who are not
taught of God, to see such an excellency and sufficiency in Jesus, and such emptiness in themselves, as constrains them to cry out, with Peter,
" Lord, to whom shall we go † ? " These things
are hid from the wise and prudent. But,

II. Where, and in what sense are these things
hid ?

1. Where are they hid ?

First, They are hid in Christ. " In him are
hid all the treasures of wisdom and knowledge ‡."
He is the great repository of truth. " It pleased
the Father that in him should all fulness dwell §."
And he is the Messenger by whom the will of God
is made known to man ‖. From hence observe,

---

* John vi. 66.   † John vi. 68.   ‡ Col. ii. 3.
§ Col. i. 19.   ‖ Luke ix. 35, John i. 18.

(1.) You can attain to no saving truth, but in and by the knowledge of Jesus Christ. If they are hid in him, it can be but lost labour to seek them elsewhere.

(2.) Whatever seeming knowledge you have, if it does not endear him to you, it is nothing worth. It is science falsely so called, and can do you no good: for in the knowledge of him, and of him alone, is eternal life *.

Secondly, They are hid in the word of God.

(1.) They are contained there. " The whole Scripture is given by inspiration of God, and is able to make us wise unto salvation † ;" to furnish us with a sufficiency of knowledge and motives for every good work. The word of God is perfect.

(2.) Yet, though contained there, they are not plain to every eye. Though they are *revealed* in the letter, they are still hid from the wise and prudent. Something more is necessary than barely to read, in order to understand them ; otherwise all who can read, and have the Bible, would be equally enlightened with equal application. But experience shews it is far otherwise. This leads me farther to inquire,

2. In what sense they are hid?

First, They are not hid as if it were on purpose that those who sincerely seek them should be disappointed in their search. Far be it from us to think so hardly of the Lord. We have express promises to the contrary, that all who earnestly seek shall find. Fear not, you that sincerely desire an experimental and practical knowledge of the truths of God, and are willing to be taught in his appointed way : though many things appear

* John xvii. 3.　　　　† 2 Tim. iii. 16.

difficult to you at present, the Lord will gradually increase your light, and crown your endeavours with success.

Secondly, But from some persons they are hid, even from the wise and prudent, whom we are to speak of hereafter. Suffer me to offer a familiar illustration of the Lord's wisdom and justice in this procedure. Let me suppose a person to have a curious cabinet which is opened at his pleasure, and not exposed to common view : he invites all to come to see it, and offers to shew it to any one who asks him. It is hid, because he keeps the key ; but none can complain, because he is ready to open it whenever he is desired. Some perhaps disdain the offer and say, Why is it locked at all ? Some think it not worth seeing, or amuse themselves with guessing at the contents. But those who are simply desirous for themselves, leave others disputing, go according to appointment, and are gratified. These have reason to be thankful for the favour ; and the others have no just cause to find fault. Thus the riches of Divine grace may be compared to a richly furnished cabinet, to which Christ is the door. The word of God likewise is a cabinet generally locked up ; but the key of prayer will open it. The Lord invites all : but he keeps the dispensation in his own hand. They cannot see these things, except he shews them ; but then he refuses none that sincerely ask him. The wise men of the world can go no farther than the outside of this cabinet : they may amuse themselves, and surprise others, with their ingenious guesses at what is within ; but a babe that has seen it opened can give us more satisfaction, without studying or guessing at all. If men will presume to aim at the knowledge of God, without the knowledge of Christ, who is the way, and the door; if they have such a high opinion of their own wisdom and penetration, as to suppose they can understand the Scriptures without the assistance of his Spirit; or if their worldly wisdom teaches them, that these things are not worth their inquiry; what wonder is it that they should continue to be hid from their eyes? They will one day be stripped of all their false pleas, and condemned out of their own mouths.

Thirdly, The expression, " Thou hast hid," may perhaps farther imply, that those who seek occasion to cavil shall meet with something to confirm their prejudices. When people examine the doctrines or profession of the Gospel, not with a candid desire to learn, imitate, and practise, but in order to find some plausible ground for misrepresentation, they frequently have their wish. The wisdom of God has appointed, that difficulties, offences, objections, and stumbling-blocks should attend, to exercise and manifest the spirits of these wise ones. How largely do they expatiate on the divisions and difference of sentiments which too much prevail among those who are united in the same leading truths! If they can discover an instance of error, folly, or wickedness, of a single person who professes to adhere to the Gospel doctrine, how do they rejoice as if they had found great spoil, charge the faults of a few indiscriminately upon the whole, and labour to shew, that every mistake and inadvertence is a necessary consequence of the principles which those maintain who commit it! We do not plead for mistakes and errors of any sort, for weakness in judgment or inconsistence in practice. But as these things are more or less inseparable from the present state of human nature, they necessarily increase and strengthen the prepossession of scorners against the truth, and are so far a means of hiding it from their eyes. Yet here again the fault is wholly in themselves; for they seek and desire such occasions of stumbling, and would be disappointed and grieved if they could not meet with them. But those who are babes in their own eyes, humble, sincere, and teachable, are brought safe through, by a simple dependent spirit, and are made wiser every day, by their observation of what passes around them.

Many inferences and advices might be deduced from what has been said. I shall content myself with three.

1. Examine yourselves what understanding and experience you have of the things I mentioned under the first head. So much as you know of these, so far you are Christians, and no farther. " A form of godliness, without the power*," is one of the worst characters of the worst times; yet how common in the present day! How many who choose to be called Christians, reject the testimony which God has given of his Son, deny the efficacy of his grace, speak of the new birth with disdain, as unintelligible and unnecessary, and account all that can be said of the life of faith (though founded upon express Scripture, and attested by many witnesses) no better than enthusiastic jargon! But if you are thus minded, however sober your deportment, or professedly benevolent your disposition, though you may be applauded as a pattern of generosity, a philosopher or a saint, by your acquaintance and neighbours, if the Scriptures are true, you can be but as a sounding brass and tinkling cymbal in the sight

* 2 Tim. iii. 5.

of God. You would have despised Thomas in
your heart, if you had been witness to his joyful
exclamation when he worshipped Jesus, and cried,
" My Lord and my God!*" You would have
despised Paul as a dark enthusiast, had you heard
him say, " The life which I now live in the flesh,
I live by faith in the Son of God, who loved me,
and gave himself for me †." Yea, you must have
despised Jesus himself, if you had been present at
his conference with Nicodemus. Our Lord Jesus
is now in heaven; Thomas and Paul have been
long dead : you cannot reach them; nor do they
stand in your way : therefore perhaps you are
content to speak well of them in general terms.
But those who come nearest to their language and
spirit, are the objects of your scorn and hatred.
How then can you pretend to love him, or presume that he loves you? Jesus is worshipped in
heaven; how then can you expect to come there?
or what pleasure could you find there, in your
present turn of mind? " O kiss the Son, lest he be
angry, and you perish; for in a little time his
wrath will burn like fire."

But to every one who understands, embraces,
and lives under the influence of these truths, I
may safely apply our Lord's words, " Blessed art
thou ‡," however despised by men, or chastened
of the Lord; " for flesh and blood hath not revealed these things to thee;" thou hast assuredly
received them from God by his Spirit. He alone
is able to cause the light to shine into our dark
hearts, " to give us the knowledge of the glory of
God in the face of Jesus Christ §."

---

* John xx. 28.   † Gal. ii. 20.

‡ Matt. xvi. 17.   § 2 Cor. iv. 6.

2. Do not entertain hard and perplexing thoughts about the counsels of God, either respecting others or yourselves.

First, With regard to others. It is a frequent difficulty, either thrown in the way of inquirers after truth by the subtilty of Satan, or perhaps arising from the natural pride of the human heart, that would be thought able to account for every thing. I say, when they begin to apprehend the Gospel way of salvation, this perplexing question arises, If things are so, what will become of multitudes? What! are all the Heathens, Mahometans, Papists, and even all the Protestants except the few who adopt these singular sentiments, to be lost? I shall not attempt to conquer this objection by dint of reasoning, but would rather persuade you to direct your reasonings another way. When the same question for substance was proposed to our Lord, his answer to those who asked him was, " Strive (each one for yourselves) to enter in at the strait gate *." Take care of yourselves, and leave the cases of others to the Lord. Remember he is God, and therefore just and good.

Secondly, With regard to yourselves. Secret things belong to God ; your business is with what is revealed. Some put the word of salvation from them perversely, and think, If the Lord designs me for eternal life, he will call me in his own time ; till then I will go on in my sins. Those who can reason thus, and take encouragement to persist in wickedness, from the consideration of the power and efficacy of God's grace, do thereby avow themselves to be Satan's willing servants. But he terrifies many on whom he cannot thus prevail, with representing to them, that, let them do what

* Luke xiii. 23, 24.

they will, it is all in vain; unless the Lord has chosen them, notwithstanding any good beginnings they may hope he has wrought in them, they will come to nothing at last. It is your business to give all diligence to make your calling sure. If, by a humble waiting upon God, you are enabled to have your conversation according to the Gospel, listen not to vain and perplexing reasonings, but commit yourself to the mercy and guidance of the Lord; and he, in his good time, will enable you to see, and to say, that it is not in vain to trust in him. Your path shall be like the advancing light, that shineth more and more unto the perfect day. The Lord has already provided all that you can reasonably desire.

(1.) The means are pointed out, in the use of which you are to be found, and wherein you may expect his blessing. These are chiefly secret prayer, the study of his written word, an attendance on the preached Gospel, and free converse (as proper opportunities are afforded) with his believing people. If you continue in the observance of these, and act faithfully to the light you have already received, by breaking off from the evil practices of the world, and watching against those things which you yourself know to be evil, you will certainly gain ground in light, strength, and comfort. You will see more and more of the glory of the Lord in the glass of the Gospel; and, in proportion to your views, you shall be "changed into the same image from glory to glory." For,

(2.) The promise is sure. What God has said you may assuredly depend on. And what has he said? What indeed has he not said for the encouragement of those who are sincerely desirous to seek and serve him? "They that seek shall find. They that wait on the Lord shall renew their strength. I will pour water upon him that is thirsty, and floods upon the dry ground. He giveth power to the weak; and to them that have no might, he increaseth strength*."

If, therefore, you feel yourself a lost sinner, see a beauty and sufficiency in Jesus, have a hunger and thirst after his righteousness, and are made willing to expect the blessing in his way; you may look upon this as a token for good. Such views and desires as these never are found in any heart till he communicates them. By nature we are averse and contrary to them. Give him the glory of what he has begun; and oppose your temptations, fears, and doubts, with this argument, drawn from your own experience, as the wife of Manoah formerly reasoned: "If the Lord had been pleased to kill us, he would not have enabled and encouraged us to call upon him; neither would he at this time have shewn us such things as these †."

---

* Matth. vii. 7, 8; Isa. xl. 29—31; Isa. xliv. 3.
† Judges xiii. 23.

SERMON III.

THE CHARACTERS OF THOSE FROM WHOM THE GOSPEL DOCTRINES ARE HID.

MATTH. xi. 25.

At that time Jesus answered and said, I thank thee, O Father, Lord of heaven and earth, because thou hast hid these things from the wise and prudent, and hast revealed them unto babes.

THE judgments of God are a great deep. He does not give us a full account of his matters; much less can *we* by searching find out *him* to perfection; yet if we carefully attend to what he has revealed, and apply his written word with humility and caution to what passes in ourselves, and around us, we may, by his grace, attain to some considerable satisfaction in things which, at first view, seem hard to be understood. The subject of my text is of this nature. That God should hide things of everlasting consequence from any persons, sounds very harsh; but I hope, when the words are explained, we shall see that, though he acts as a Sovereign in his dispensations, his ways are just, and good, and equal.

We have already made an entrance upon this attempt. Besides some general observations in my first discourse, I endeavoured to shew you, in the second, I. What the things are to which our Lord refers; II. When, and in what sense, they are hid. I proceed now to consider,

III. From whom they are hid—*the wise and*

prudent. It will, I think, be readily supposed, that the expression does not mean those who are truly so, and in God's account. He esteems none to be wise and prudent but those who are enlightened with his spiritual wisdom, who now serve and love him in Christ. " The fear of the Lord is the beginning (or, as the word likewise signifies, the head or principal part) of wisdom* ;" and from such as these he hides or keeps back nothing that is profitable for them : on the contrary, that promise is sure, " The secret of the Lord is with them that fear him ; and he will shew them his covenant †." When our Lord said, " The children of this world are wiser in their generation than the children of light ‡," he did not mean they were so absolutely, for their boasted wisdom is the merest folly, but only that they acted consistently with their own principles. The wise and prudent here are either those who are wise in their own eyes, and prudent in their own sight, or those who are generally so reputed by the bulk of mankind. And these two amount to the same : for as the natural wisdom of man springs from the same fountain, *self,* and is confined to the same bounds, *the things of time and sense,* in all alike (though there is a variety of pursuits within these limits, as tempers and situations differ), men are generally prone to approve and applaud those who act upon their own principles.

We may take notice then (as a key to this inquiry), that what is accounted wisdom by the world, is not only different from the wisdom of God, but inconsistent with it, and opposite to it. They differ as fire and water, light and darkness ; the prevalence of the one necessarily includes the

---

* Ps. cxi. 10.   † Ps. xxv. 14.   ‡ Luke xvi. 8.

suppression of the other. See this at large insisted on by St. Paul, in the beginning of his First Epistle to the Corinthians, the first, second, and third chapters.

Who then are the wise and prudent intended in my text? May the Holy Spirit enable every conscience to make faithful application of what shall be offered upon this head!

1. In the judgment of the world, those are wise and prudent persons who are very thoughtful and diligent about acquiring wealth, especially if their endeavours are crowned with remarkable success. If a man thrives (as the phrase is) from small beginnings, and joins house to house, and field to field, so that he has land to call after his own name, and large possessions to leave to his children, how he is applauded (though at the same time envied) by the most who know him! I do not deny, that a proper concern and industry in our secular calling is both lawful and our duty; and I allow, that the providence of God does sometimes remarkably prosper those who depend on him in the management of their business; but I make no scruple to affirm, that, where this is the main concern (as some call it), such wisdom is madness. Such persons are no less idolaters than those who worship stocks and stones. And if the things of God are hid from them, it is surely their own fault; they do not even complain of it as a hardship; they have their choice, their reward, and are satisfied. They are told that these things are in Christ, and there they are content that they should remain; they see no beauty or suitableness in *them*, they have no desire after *him;* he might keep his heaven and truths to himself, if they could always have their fill of the world. They are told that these things are hid in the

Scripture, but they have neither leisure nor inclination to search there for them. Their time is
taken up with buying and selling, building and
planting, &c. O beware of this wisdom! "What
will riches profit you in the day of wrath*," at
death or judgment? If you live and die in this
spirit, you will bemoan your choice when it is
too late.

2. Those are accounted wise and prudent, who
think they have found a way to reconcile God and
the world together. If a man should attempt to
fly, or to walk upon the water, he would be deemed
a fool. How is it that this endeavour, which is
equally impossible (and expressly declared so by
our Lord), should be more favourably thought of?
The deceitfulness of the heart, and subtilty of
Satan, concur in this point. You will have a sort
of religion, but then you take care not to carry
things too far. You are governed by the fear and
regard of men. Something you will do to satisfy
conscience; but not too much, lest you hurt your
interest, disoblige your friends, or draw on yourselves reproach, or a hard name. I must tell you,
from the word of God, your attempt to halve things
is an abomination in his sight. Would it not be
treason by the law, to pay the king an outward
respect, and yet hold secret correspondence with
his enemies? The decisions of the word of God
are to the same effect in this instance. "Love
not the world, neither the things that are in the
world. If any man love the world, the love of the
Father is not in him†." "Know you not, that the
friendship of the world is enmity with God?
Whosoever, therefore, will be a friend of the world,
is the enemy of God‡."

---

* Prov. xi. 4.   † 1 John ii. 15.   ‡ James iv. 4.

3. A man is deemed wise who has considerable knowledge and curiosity about natural things, and all those subjects which usually bear the name of *science;* if he can talk of the magnitudes, distances, and motions of the heavenly bodies, can foretel an eclipse, has skill in mathematics, is well read in the history of ancient times, and can inform you what is found in books concerning the folly and wickedness of mankind who lived some thousands of years ago; or if he understands several languages, and can call a thing by twenty different names. It is true, when these attainments are sanctified by grace, they may in some respects have their use. But, in general, the best use a believer will or can make of them, is to lay them down at the foot of the Cross. When a man, possessed of a large quantity of these pebbles, has his conscience awakened, and his understanding enlightened, he is glad to renounce them all for the Pearl of great price, and to adopt the Apostle's determination, "to know nothing but Jesus Christ, and him crucified*." This was the effect when the word of God mightily grew and prevailed†. We may at least say, that this kind of wisdom is, for the most part, dangerous and blinding to the soul.

1st, It tends to feed and exalt self, to make a person something in his own eyes. This we are prone enough to by nature. An increase of unsanctified knowledge adds fuel to fire.

2dly, It engrosses the time and thoughts. Our minds are narrow, capable of attending to but few things at once: and our span is short, and will hardly admit of many excursions from the main concern. If we were to live to the age of Methuselah, we might pursue some things which at pre-

---

* 1 Cor. ii. 2.   † Acts xix. 19.

sent are highly improper and impertinent from this consideration alone. A man that is upon an urgent affair of life and death has no leisure for amusement. Such is our situation. We are creatures of a day. Time is vanishing, and eternity is at stake.

3dly, The delusion here is specious, and not easily discovered. A person with these accomplishments is not always enslaved to money, or to sensual pleasures : he therefore pities those who are, and, comparing himself with others, supposes he is well employed, because his favourite studies are a check upon his appetites, and prevent his selling himself for gold, or running into riot with the thoughtless. Yet an attachment of this sort equally blinds him with respect to his true interest. Will the knowledge of books, or men, or stars, or flowers, purify the conscience from dead works, to serve the living God ? It is too plain, that the truths of the Gospel are hid from none more effectually than from many of this character. None cast a more daring or public slight upon the revealed will of God, than some who are admired and applauded on account of their knowledge and learning.

4thly, Your nice and curious reasoners and disputers, that will see (as they profess) the bottom of every thing, and trust to their own judgment and inquiries, independent of the Spirit of God, are another sort of wise persons from whom these things are often justly hid. And this character may be found in many, both learned and unlearned : for many have good natural faculties, who have not had the advantages of learning and education. But this spirit is directly contrary to that simplicity, dependence, and obedience of faith, which the Scripture exhorts us to seek after. Its effects are various.

1st, Some (and those not a few) are led to reject the word of God altogether, because it evidently contains many things above and contrary to their vain imaginations. And herein they contradict the most obvious principles of that reason which they lay claim to. A revelation from God can only be thought necessary or probable, but on the supposition that it is to inform us of something which we could not have known without it. Therefore, to pretend to try the Scripture claim to this character, by such criteria or marks as we possess beforehand, is the same thing in effect as to determine to reject it without any trial at all.

2dly, When the Scriptures, as to the letter, are acknowledged to be true, persons of this turn, presuming themselves sufficient judges of the sense, are helped by their ingenuity to explain away all the sublime doctrines of truth, so as to suit the prejudices and apprehensions of their own carnal minds. This, especially when joined with a smattering of learning, has been the chief source of all the errors and heresies which have pestered the church of God in all ages. This is a principal cause why the depravity of man by nature, the Deity and atonement of Christ, the operations of the Holy Spirit, and all the doctrines of grace, have been denied by men wise in their own eyes, and prudent in their own sight, though evidently contained in the book which they profess to receive as of Divine inspiration.

3dly, Even where the doctrines of grace have been notionally received, the same Spirit of wisdom can still find occasion to work. When there is more knowledge in the head than experience in the heart, many and various are the evils that often ensue. Disputes and hard questions are started, contentions and divisions multiplied, and

people are more eager to perplex others, than to
edify themselves.   Thus the name and counsels
of God are profaned by an irreverent curiosity,
and the clear express declarations of his will
darkened by words without knowledge.   When
this natural wisdom puts on a spiritual appearance,
no persons are more fatally deceived, or more
obstinately hardened.   They think they can learn
no more, but are wise enough to teach every one :
they neglect the use of God's appointed means
themselves, and despise them in others : they are
proud, censorious, obstinate, and full of conceit.
Take care of Satan at all times, but especially
when he would transform himself into an angel of
light.   There is reason to think the things of God
are entirely hid, as to their power and excellence,
from some who fondly dream that none are acquainted with them but themselves.

The consideration of this subject may lead to a
variety of improvement.   It may teach you,

1. What to fear.   A worldly spirit.   This in a
prevailing degree is inconsistent with a work of
grace, and, in whatever degree it obtains, or is
indulged, will proportionably retard and abate
the light and comfort of our souls.   The cares and
pleasures of this life are by our Lord compared to
thorns *, unprofitable and painful ; they produce
no fruit, but they wound and tear.   Yea, they are
thorns in the eyes †, which will prevent the great
things of God from being perceived.

A spirit of self-dependence.   " Be not wise in
your own conceits ‡."   " If any man think that he
knoweth any thing, he knoweth nothing yet as he
ought to know §."   God giveth wisdom to the lowly,
but he confounds the devices of the proud.   His

* Matth. xiii. 22.   † Josh. xxiii. 13.   ‡ Rom. xii. 16.
§ 1 Cor. viii. 2.

promises of teaching, leading, and guiding, are made to the meek, the simple, and those who are little in their own eyes.

2. What to pray for. A simple child-like temper; that you may come to the word as to the light, and look beyond yourselves for the assistance of the Holy Spirit, without which your most laboured inquiries will only mislead you farther and farther from the truth.

3. How to examine yourselves. Not by your notions and attainments in knowledge, for these you may have in a considerable degree, and be wholly destitute of true grace. The word of God supposes it possible that persons may have great gifts *, flaming zeal, and much success, and yet, having no true love to God, be in his sight no better than sounding brass, or a tinkling cymbal. But if you would know your state, examine by your prevailing desires. Are your notions of grace effectual to lead you in the path of duty? Do you hunger and thirst for an increase of holiness? Does the knowledge you have of Christ lead you to love and trust him? Are you poor in spirit? You know nothing aright, if you know not yourselves.

4. Ye that are believers may see cause to praise the Lord for his dispensations towards you.

1st, Had you been wise in men's esteem, you might have continued fools to the end of your lives. If the Lord has taught you the secret of them that fear him, if he has shewn you the way of salvation, if he has directed your feet in the paths of his commandments, then you have the true wisdom which shall be your light through life, and in death your glory. Therefore,

* 1 Cor. xiii. 1—3.

2dly, Be not grieved that ye are strangers to human wisdom and glory. These things, which others so highly prize, you may resign contentedly, and say, " Lord, it is enough if thou art mine." Nay, you have good reason to praise his wisdom and goodness for preserving you from those temptations which have ensnared and endangered so many.

3dly, Do you desire more of this true wisdom ? Seek it in the same way in which you have re-received the first beginnings. Be frequent and earnest in secret prayer. Study the word of God, and study it not to reconcile and make it bend to your sentiments, but to draw all your sentiments from it, to copy it in your heart, and express it in your conduct. Be cautious of paying too great a regard to persons and parties. One is your master, even Christ. Stand fast in the liberty with which he has made you free ; and, while you humbly endeavour to profit by all, do not resign your understanding to any, but to him who is the only wise God, the only effectual and infallible Teacher. Compare the experience of what passes within your own breast, with the observations you make of what daily occurs around you ; and bring all your remarks and experiences to the touch-stone of God's holy word. Thus shall you grow in knowledge and in grace; and, amidst the various discouragements which may arise from re-maining ignorance in yourselves or others, take comfort in reflecting, that you are drawing near to the land of light, where there will be no dark-ness at all. Then you shall know as you are known ; your love and your joy shall likewise be perfect, and you shall be satisfied with the rivers of pleasure which are before the throne of God, world without end.

SERMON IV.

THE NATURE OF SPIRITUAL REVELATION, AND WHO ARE FAVOURED WITH IT.

MATTH. xi. 25.

At that time Jesus answered and said, I thank thee, O Father, Lord of heaven and earth, because thou hast hid these things from the wise and prudent, and hast revealed them unto babes.

WE proceed now to the more pleasing part of our subject. The great things of the Gospel, though hid, are not lost: not hid as in the bottom of the sea; but he who hides them from the wise and prudent, is ready and willing to make them known to every sincere inquirer. This discovery, on the Lord's part, is a revelation, and the character of those who obtain it is expressed by the word *babes*. Of the five particulars I proposed to consider from the text, these two yet remain to be spoken to.

IV. The saving knowledge of Divine truth is a revelation. Our Lord uses a parallel expression, when he commends Peter's confession of his faith; " Blessed art thou, Simon Barjona: for flesh and blood hath not revealed this unto thee, but my Father which is in heaven *." Peter had Moses and the Prophets, so had the Scribes and Pharisees; and after their manner they were diligent in reading and searching them. But that he could acknowledge Jesus to be the Messiah, when

* Matth. xvi. 17.

they rejected him, was because the Father had revealed his truth to him, and given him a clearer knowledge of it, than he could have received from the written world alone.   But it may be proper to inquire into the meaning of this term.   What are we here to understand by revelation?

Sometimes revelation is used in an extraordinary sense, as when of old the Lord made known to his servants, the Prophets, those doctrines and events which, till then, were neither heard nor thought of.   Of this we are not now to speak, but of that which is common to all believers, and necessary to salvation.

Now this revelation supposes the things to be revealed were real and certain before, but unknown, and not to be found out in any other way.

Revelation is not the creation or invention of something new, but the manifestation of what was till then unknown.   The great things of eternity, the glorious truths of the Gospel, are real and certain in themselves already, and do not begin to be when we begin to be acquainted with them: yet till God is pleased to reveal them to the heart, we have no more spiritual and effective knowledge of them, than if they were not.   Ignorance of things very near to us, and in which we are nearly concerned, may be from two causes.

1. From a want of light.   Nothing can be perceived in the dark.   If you are in a dark room, though it is richly adorned and furnished, all is lost to you.   If you stand in a dark night upon the top of a hill that commands a fine prospect, still you are able to see no more than if you were in a valley.   Though you were in a dangerous place, with pitfals and precipices, and thieves and murderers all around you, still you might

imagine yourself in safety, if you had no light with you.

2. It may be from some hindrance or obstruction between you and the object. Thus your dearest friend, or greatest enemy, might be within a few yards of you, and you know nothing of it, if there was a wall between you.

These comparisons may in some measure represent our case by nature. God is near; " in him we live, move, and have our being." Eternity is near; we stand upon the brink of it. Death is near, advancing towards us with hasty strides. The truths of God's word are most certain in themselves, and of the utmost consequence to us. But we perceive none of these things; we are not affected by them, because our understandings are dark, and because thick walls of ignorance, prejudice, and unbelief, stand before the eyes of the mind, and keep them from our view, Even those notions of truth which we sometimes pick up by hearing and reading, are but like windows in a dark room; they are suited to afford an entrance to the light when it comes, but can give no light of themselves.

I think, therefore, we may conclude, that God's revealing these things to us only signifies his effecting such a change in us, by his Holy Spirit, as disposes and enables us to behold them. He sends a Divine light into the soul; and things begin to appear so plain, we wonder at our former stupidity that we could not perceive them before. By the power of his Spirit he breaks down the walls which prevented and confined our views; and a new unthought-of prospect suddenly appears before us. Then the soul sees its danger: " I thought myself secure; but I find I am in the midst of enemies. Guilt pursues me behind; fear, and the snare, and the pit, are before me: which way shall I turn?" Then it perceives its mistake: "While my views were confined, I thought there was nothing but this plan of life to take care of; but now I see a boundless eternity beyond it." It obtains a glimpse likewise of the glories of the better world, of the beauties of holiness, of the excellency of Jesus. This light is at first faint and imperfect, but grows stronger by the use of appointed means; and as it is increased, every thing appears with a stronger evidence.

We may more particularly illustrate this work of the Holy Spirit, as it influences those leading faculties of the soul, the understanding, affections, and will. By nature the will is perverse and rebellious, and the affections alienated from God: the primary cause of these disorders lies in the darkness of the understanding. Here then the change begins. The Spirit of God enlightens the understanding, by which the sinner perceives things to be as they are represented in the word of God; that he is a transgressor against the Divine law, and on this account obnoxious to wrath; that he is not only guilty, but depraved and unclean, and utterly unable either to repair past evil or to amend his own heart and life. He sees that the great God might justly refuse him mercy; and that he has no plea to offer in arrest of judgment. This discovery would sink him into despair, if it went no farther; but by the same light which discovers him to himself, he begins to see a suitableness, wisdom, and glory, in the method of salvation revealed in the Gospel. He reads and hears concerning the person, sufferings, and offices of Christ, in a very different manner to what he did before: and as, by attending to the word and ministry, his apprehensions of Jesus, and his understanding, become more clear and distinct, a spiritual hope takes place, and increases, in his soul; and the sure effect of this is, he feels his love drawn forth to Him who so loved him as to die for his sins. Beholding, by faith, the Lord Jesus Christ, as bleeding and dying upon the cross; and knowing for whom, and on what account, he suffered, he learns to hate, with a bitter hatred, those sins which nailed him there. The amazing love of Christ constrains him to account all things which he formerly valued as dross and dung, for the excellency of the knowledge of his Saviour. Nor does his faith stop here; he views Him who once suffered and died, rising triumphant from the tomb, and ascending into heaven in the character of the Representative, Friend, and Forerunner of his people. Having such a High Priest, he is encouraged to draw near to God, to claim an interest in the promises respecting the life that now is, and that which is to come. Thus possessing, in the beginnings of grace, an earnest of the glory that shall be revealed, a real, universal, abiding change necessarily takes place in the affections. Now old things are passed away, and all thing become new : the soul no longer cleaves willingly to the dust, or can be satisfied with earthly things, but thirsts for communion with God, and an increase of holiness. Sin is no longer consented to, or delighted in, but is opposed and watched against ; and every unhallowed deviation from the will of God, excites the sincerest grief and humiliation, and leads to renewed application to the blood and grace of Jesus for pardon and strength. Thus the will likewise is brought into an unreserved subjection and surrender to the power of Christ, and acts as freely in his service as it once did against him. For that what is

termed *the freedom of the human will* should consist
in a suspended indifference between good and
evil, is a refinement, which, however admired and
applauded by many, is equally contrary both to
sound reasoning and to universal experience. The
will, in all persons and cases, is determined by
the present dictates of the understanding, and the
bent of the affections.

By ascribing so much to the Spirit of God, I do
not mean, as you may perceive by what I have
just now said, to seclude his holy word, or
preached Gospel. All these truths and prospects
are already contained in the word of God; but
without the light of the Spirit they are not discerned. They are propounded to you in the public
ministry. We testify, again and again, the things
which we have seen and heard of the word of
life; and when we are in some measure affected
with their evidence, we are ready to wonder how
any of you can possibly avoid perceiving them;
till we remember how it was with ourselves, and
then we know by our own experience, that *we*
must preach, and *you* hear in vain, unless the Lord
is pleased to open your hearts. But observe,

1. The Spirit of God teaches and enlightens by
his word as the instrument. There is no revelation
from him, but what is (as to our perception of it)
derived from the Scripture. There may be supposed illuminations and strong impressions upon
the mind, in which the word of God has no place
or concern; but this alone is sufficient to discountenance them, and to prove that they are not
from the Holy Spirit. For,

2. The Scripture is the appointed rule and test
by which all our searches and discoveries, all our
acquisitions in religious knowledge, must be tried.
If they are indeed from God, they will stand this

trial, and answer to the word, as face answers to
face in a glass, but not otherwise. " To the law
and to the testimony, if they speak not according
to this word, it is because there is no light in
them *." If those who despise all claims to the
influence of the Spirit of God, as enthusiasm, had
not been frequently informed that we expect, we
acknowledge, no internal revelation, but by the
medium of the word of God, and agreeable to it,
they would be less inexcusable in repeating the
charges of folly and infatuation, which they igno-
rantly fix upon the work of the Spirit, and all who
profess a dependence on it. To those who are
indeed candid and sincere inquirers after truth,
what has been said upon this part of our subject
will, I hope, suggest the propriety of two directions.—From hence learn,

1. To set a high value upon the word of God.
All that is necessary to make you wise to salvation
is there, and there only. In this precious book
you may find a direction for every doubt, a solu-
tion of every difficulty, a promise suited to every
circumstance you can be in. There you may be
informed of your disease by sin, and the remedy
provided by grace. You may be instructed to
know yourselves, to know God and Jesus Christ,
in the knowledge of whom standeth eternal life.
The wonders of redeeming love, the glories of the
Redeemer's person, the happiness of the redeemed
people, the power of faith, and the beauty of
holiness, are here represented to the life. Nothing
is wanting to make life useful and comfortable,
death safe and desirable, and to bring down something of heaven upon earth. But this true wisdom
can be found nowhere else. If you wander from

* Isa. viii. 20.

the Scripture, in pursuit either of present peace
or future hope, your search will end in disappointment. This is the fountain of living waters : if
you forsake it, and give the preference to broken
cisterns of your own devising, they will fail you
when you most need them. Rejoice, therefore,
that such a treasure is put into your hand; but
rejoice with trembling. Remember this is not all
you want; unless God likewise gives you a heart
to use it aright, your privilege will only aggravate
your guilt and misery. Therefore remember,

2. The necessity of prayer. For though the
things of nearest consequence to you are in the
Bible, and you should read it over and over, till
you commit the whole book to your memory; yet
you will not understand, or discern the truth as it
is in Jesus, unless the Lord the Spirit shews it to
you. The dispensation of truth is in his hand;
and without him all the fancied advantages of
superior capacity, learning, criticism, and books,
will prove as useless as spectacles to the blind.
The great encouragement is, that this infallible
Spirit, so necessary to guide us into the way of
peace, is promised to all who sincerely ask it.
This Spirit, Jesus is exalted to bestow; and he
has said, " Whosoever cometh to me, I will in
nowise cast out." Therefore water your reading
with frequent prayer.—We proceed to,

V. The characters of those persons who succeed in their inquiries, and have the things of
God savingly revealed to them; they are called
babes.

1. They are, for the most part, babes in the
world's esteem. They are despised by the wise
and prudent for their weak capacities, small attainments, and their seeming insignificance in
common life. But the Lord does not overlook

any on these accounts. He is no respecter of persons. In the blessings of his common providence, those which are more immediately from his own hand, such as air and light, health and strength, the faculties of sight and hearing, &c. he bestows as freely, and in as great perfection, to the poor as to the rich, to the ignorant as to the learned. And thus it is with respect to his grace. Our incapacity is founded in our nature, and is common to all, and not in any particular circumstances. He is as ready to save the mean as the noble. Many of the great and wise are offended at this. As they engross the earth, they would willingly engross heaven also to themselves. But the Lord has appointed otherwise; and it has been one reproach constantly attending the Gospel, that few but the common people have thought it worth their notice*.

2. They are babes in their own esteem. Not that some are more humble than others by nature, and therefore the Lord gives them a preference on that account: by nature we are all alike, equally destitute of the smallest good : but the expression teaches us, that those to whom the Lord is pleased to reveal these things, he first empties and humbles, strips them of all ground .of boasting, and brings them to a dependence on himself. The true believer is frequently compared to a little child ; and it is easy to trace an instructive resemblance.

1st, A child, or babe, has little knowledge, and its capacity and powers are as yet very feeble. All whose understandings have been spiritually enlightened, will acknowledge themselves children in this respect. The little they know convinces

* Mark xli. 37; John vii. 48, 49.

them of their ignorance. They are convinced that
their views of things are faint, partial, confused;
that their judgments are weak; that, if the Lord
prevents it not, they are very liable to be imposed
on by the subtilty of Satan, and the treachery of
their own hearts. They feel that they have not in
themselves sufficiency to think a good thought.

2dly, A child is teachable. Conscious of their
own ignorance, they listen to all about them, and
think every one is qualified to teach them something. Among men none are truly teachable, but
those who know they need to be taught. The
natural man, if possessed of any advantages,
thinks every one needs his help. The humble
Christian gives this proof that the confession he is
ready to make of his ignorance is genuine, and
from his heart, that he is desirous to learn from
all. He is swift to hear, slow to speak, and open
to conviction. Though he will not assent to
every thing he hears without proof or examination, yet he is disposed to receive instruction,
and thankful to those by whom he is profited.
He is fearful of being mistaken, of giving way to
prejudices, and therefore gladly improves every
means of information.

3dly, A child is simple and dependent. He
does not reason, but implicitly receives what he is
told by his parents, or those whom he thinks
wiser than himself. Such a resignation, indeed,
the believer dares not make of his understanding
to any men, however highly he may esteem them
in the main; for he has learned from the word of
God, not to put his trust in man; but this is the
desire of the renewed heart, with respect to the
teaching of God's word and Spirit. He allows
no reasoning or questioning here; nor will he say
with Nicodemus, " How can these things be?"

It is enough for him that God has said it, and is able to make it good. This is a happy temper. In this way innumerable difficulties that arise from appearances and sophisms are avoided; and the mind, by faith, steers in safety across the immense ocean of conjectures and opinions, which disputants and reasoners essaying to do, are sunk and overpowered. It is true, there are various degrees of this simplicity; and in those who possess it in a larger measure, there is a remaining principle of pride and unbelief, which costs them much prayer and many conflicts to subdue. But this, in some degree, is essential to the character of those who are taught of God; they desire and endeavour to submit wholly to his guidance and will in all things.

Here then is a proper topic for self-examination. Let each one ask his heart, Have I this simple childlike disposition?

If you have, if it is the desire of your soul to be taught of God; if his word is your rule, if you depend on his Spirit to teach you all things, and to lead you as it were by the hand, sensible that, unless you are thus led and guided, you shall certainly go astray; be thankful for this, accept it as a token for good. You were not always so: there was a time when you were wise in your own eyes, and prudent in your own sight. You have good warrant to hope, that the Lord, who has already taught you to depend on himself, will shew you all that is necessary for you to know.

But if this is not the case, if you lean to your own understanding, what wonder is it that you are still walking in darkness and uncertainty? Will you say, I have read the Bible diligently; I have taken no small pains to examine things, to see which of the many divisions that obtain

among Christians is possessed of the truth; but I
am still at a loss : surely, if the tenets some plead
for had been in the Scripture, I should have
found them there! I answer, without detracting
from your sagacity or your sincerity, your case is
easily accounted for from the verse we are upon,
if your inquiries are not conducted in a humble
dependence upon the Spirit of God.   Too many
instances we could produce of men, who, having
laboured for years in what seems one of the most
laudable undertakings, the explaining the Scriptures for the use of others, have at last been in a
remarkable degree unsettled themselves; and the
only visible fruits their reading and industry has
afforded, have been error, invective, and dissatis-
faction : so that their labours have been an exem-
plification of the former part of our text, a proof
in point, how entirely the things of God are often
hid from the wise and prudent.

You that are seeking the Lord, and are little
in your own eyes, rejoice that the dispensation of
grace is in his hands.   If men had the disposal of
it, you might perhaps have been overlooked.   We
should have been ready to have accepted the fair-
spoken young man, who accosted our Lord with
so much outward respect, and had so much to say
in his own behalf * : and probably we should have
left the thief upon the cross to perish like a
wretch, as he deserved.   " But the Lord seeth
not as man seeth †."   " His ways are higher than
our ways, and his thoughts than our thoughts ‡."
Therefore there is encouragement for the meanest
and the vilest.   He has excluded none but those
who exclude themselves.   " Behold now is the
accepted time, behold now is the day of salvation.

---

* Mark x. 20.   † 1 Sam. xvi. 7.   ‡ Isa. lv. 7—9.

Let the wicked forsake his ways, and the unrighteous man his thoughts ; and let him return
unto the Lord, for he will have mercy upon him,
and to our God, for he will abundantly pardon."

———

SERMON V.

THE SOVEREIGNTY OF DIVINE GRACE ASSERTED
AND ILLUSTRATED.

MATTH. xi. 26.

Even so, Father, for so it seemed good in thy sight.

THAT the doctrine in the preceding verse is true
in fact, is sufficiently evident from common observation.   The greatest part of those whom the
world esteems wise and prudent, and all to a man
who think themselves so, pay but small regard to
the truths of the Gospel.   They are hid from
their eyes, and revealed to babes, to those whom
they despise on account of their ignorance and
insignificance.   And if a few who are favoured
with considerable advantages in point of genius,
education, or rank, do receive the truth in the love
of it, they have been at least taught that they are
no better than babes, and are glad to count all
outward things but loss, for the excellency of the
knowledge of Christ Jesus the Lord.

If we could give no other reason for this dispensation of grace, than that which is assigned in
our text, it ought to be satisfactory ; and would
be so, if it was not for the pride of our hearts.
Surely that which seems good in the sight of God,

must be holy, and wise, and good in itself. How
vain and presumptuous is blinded man, that
would dare to reply against his Maker, to charge
his holiness with injustice, his wisdom with mistake, his goodness with partiality! All their vain
cavils will be silenced at the great day, when the
secrets of all hearts are opened, and God will be
justified when he condemns. However, though
we dare not venture too far into the depths of the
Divine counsels, yet, from the light he has
afforded us in his word, we may, in our feeble
manner, assert and prove, that his ways are just
and equal: and, besides the argument of his
sovereignty, " that so it has pleased him," he
has been pleased to favour us with some of the
reasons, " why it has so pleased him." And this
is the subject I propose to lead your meditations
to from these words. May his Spirit assist me,
that I may not darken counsel by words without
knowledge.

Let us begin with inquiring, What might be his
principal ends in sending his Son into the world,
that we might have life through him? These, I
apprehend, were chiefly two.

1. The redemption and complete salvation of
all that believe. All mankind are by nature in
the same state of sin and misery. But we are
told, that at the great day there will be an unspeakable difference in the circumstances between
some and others. Many will then stand trembling
at his left hand, to whom the King shall say,
" Depart." But those on the right hand will hear
those joyful words, " Come, ye blessed of my
Father, inherit the kingdom prepared for you
from the foundation of the world." If you ask,
To what is this difference primarily owing? The

answer is provided : " Jesus loved them, and washed them from their sins in his own blood : he redeemed them out of every nation, and people, and language : they came out of great tribulation, and washed their robes, and made them white in the blood of the Lamb ; therefore are they before the Throne." It was then for their sakes, who should be hereafter found at the right hand of God, that " God sent forth his Son, made of a woman, made under the law, to redeem them that were under the law, that we might receive the adoption of sons."

2. But, besides this, God had another and a still higher end in the work of redemption; namely, the manifestation of his own glory. It was unspeakable love to us that he provided the means of salvation at all : and we cannot wonder, much less ought we to complain, that, in justice to himself, he appointed such means, and such a way, as that all the praise and glory of the contrivance should in the end redound to himself alone. In order to this, it was necessary that the following things should be manifested with the fullest evidence.

1st, The greatness of man's depravity, guilt, and misery : that it was not a small thing, but a case worthy the interposition of Almighty power and infinite grace.

2dly, The utter insufficiency of man to relieve himself; that so God might have the whole honour of his recovery, and we might be for ever debtors to his free undeserved mercy.

3dly, That whereas there are, to outward appearance, a great variety of characters among mankind, it was necessary the dispensation of his grace should be so conducted as to shew, that no case was too hard for his power, or too low and miserable for his compassion and condescension.

Upon these grounds we may see something of his wisdom in the methods he has appointed, and in the subjects of his choice; why it has seemed good in his sight, to hide these things from the wise and prudent, and to reveal them unto babes, for such reasons as these:

1. To stain the pride of all human glory.

2. To exclude every pretence of boasting.

3. That there might be a ground of hope provided for the vilest and meanest.

4. That the salvation of believers might be sure, and not subject to miscarry.

1. The Lord of hosts hath proposed it, "to stain the pride of all human glory *." How much men are disposed to admire their own wisdom, learning, and fancied accomplishments, is sufficiently obvious. But now the pride of all this glory is stained, inasmuch as it is proved by experience to be utterly useless in the most important concerns. One man has talents to rule a kingdom, but is himself a slave to the vilest lusts and passions. Another has courage to face death in a field of battle; yet, with regard to religion, is a mere coward: overawed by the feeble breath of the multitude, he is both ashamed and afraid to practise what his conscience convinces him is his duty. Another almost pretends to count the number of the stars, and to call them all by their names; yet has no more thought of the God that made the heavens and the earth, than the beasts that perish. Another delights in books and languages, which few can understand but himself; nothing so false

---

* Isa. xxiii. 9.

or foolish but he accounts it worth his study, if it has but the stamp of antiquity to recommend it; only the book of God (though much more ancient than all his fables), because it may be read in plain English, is thrown by as unworthy his notice. Another who professes to be Scripture-wise, perverts the Scripture, and abuses his own reason, to establish the most absurd errors, or to overturn the plainest truths. Another amuses himself with setting forth the praises of virtue and morality, while his own conduct furnishes a standing proof, either of the weakness of his scheme, or the insincerity of his heart. Time would fail to recount all the achievements of these wise and prudent men. But behold the pride of them all stained. In the midst of all their acquisitions and inventions, they are strangers to God, to themselves, and to peace; they are without Christ, and without hope: those things which alone are of real importance, are hid from their eyes. Here the desperate depravity and deceitfulness of the heart are manifested to the glory of God; and it is clearly seen, that if he does not interpose to save, men are wholly unable to save themselves.

2. To exclude boasting. " Where is boasting then? It is excluded." As the Apostle speaks in another place, " If Abraham was justified by works, he hath whereof to glory*:" so if men were saved, either in whole or in part, by their own wisdom and prudence, they might, in the same degree, ascribe the glory and praise to themselves. They might say, My own power and wisdom gave me this; and thus God would be robbed of the honour due to his name. But now this is pre-

* Rom. iv. 2.

vented. The word of the Lord is, " Let not the wise man glory in his wisdom, neither let the mighty man glory in his might; let not the rich man glory in his riches; but let him that glorieth glory in this, that he understandeth and knoweth me, that I am the Lord*." For whatever outward advantages some may seem to possess, as to the things of God they stand altogether upon a level with the meanest. These things cannot be understood by any sagacity on our parts, but must be revealed by the Father of lights. What could be done in this way, you may collect from St. Paul's representation in the first chapter of his Epistle to the Romans. Many of the heathens were eminent for wisdom and abilities, and made great proficiency in science; but with regard to the knowledge of God, the result of all their researches was error, superstition, and idolatry; professing themselves to be wise, they became fools, and their disquisitions had no other effect than to leave them without excuse. Their practice (as will always be the case) was correspondent to their principles; and, in the midst of a thousand refinements in theory, they were abandoned to the grossest and most detestable vices. If it be said, these had not the light of revelation, we may observe the same or similar effects where the Gospel is known. With this superior light men are still equally vain in their imaginations; and, though they do not pay an outward and formal worship to stocks and stones, they are gross idolaters; for they serve, love, and trust the creature more than the Creator. When there is a difference, it is owing to grace, and grace is acknowledged. Such will readily say, " Not unto us, O Lord,

* Jer. ix. 23, 24.

not unto us, but unto thy name be the praise*."
Thus all pretence to boasting is effectually excluded ; and he that can glory upon good grounds,
must glory only in the Lord.

If it should be supposed that this representation
of things tends to discourage a diligent and serious
inquiry after truth, I answer, when rightly understood, it will have just the contrary effect. What
can be more suited to excite diligence, than to
point out the method in which it will assuredly
be crowned with success? You cannot succeed
without the light and assistance of the Holy Spirit;
but if conscious of this, and aware of your own
insufficiency, you will seek his direction and guidance by humble prayer, it shall be afforded you.
If you know not this, you will certainly be wearied
in the end by repeated disappointments; but if
you depend upon his teaching and co-operation in
the use of the means he has appointed, your knowledge shall advance as the growing light.

3. This method of the Divine procedure opens
a door of hope to the vilest and the meanest. Let
not any be cast down on account of any peculiar
incapacity or difficulty in their case. If none but
the wise and the learned, the rich, and those who
are esteemed well-behaved and virtuous, could be
saved, or if these stood in a fairer way for it than
others, the greatest part of mankind might give
up hope, and sit down in despair at once. But the
case is exactly the reverse. It is true, the persons
I am speaking of are not the worse for these distinctions, whenever they are sensible how vain
and insufficient they are, and betake themselves,
as poor, helpless, miserable, blind, and naked, to
flee for refuge to the mercy of God in Christ.

* Psalm cxv. 1.

But, alas! their supposed qualifications too often harden them to reject the counsel of God against themselves. They think themselves whole, and therefore see not the necessity or value of the Physician. You who are sensible you have nothing of your own to trust to, take encouragement; the Lord has suited his Gospel to your circumstances.

(1.) Are ye poor? The Lord Jesus Christ has sanctified the state of poverty by taking it on himself. He had not where to lay his head. He will not therefore despise you on this account. Only pray that you may likewise be poor in spirit. He looks through all outward distinctions, and often passes by a palace to make his presence and power known in a mud-walled cottage. Perhaps he appointed this state in mercy to your souls, that you might not be distracted with many things, nor take up with a portion in this world. You cannot be in a lower or more afflicted state than Lazarus, who, while he lay neglected at the rich man's gate, oppressed with want, and full of sores, was a child of God, and the charge of angels.

(2.) Are you ignorant? If you cannot read, you miss indeed a considerable advantage which you might derive from the perusal of his good word, and I would wish you to attain it if practicable. If not, give so much more diligent attention to the preaching of the Gospel; entreat others to read the Scripture to you. But especially pray. The Lord can teach you without a book, and make up for every defect. It is very possible for you to attain to know and love God, to love your neighbour, to rejoice in Christ, to keep his precepts, to be content with your station, to live by faith, and to die with comfort, though you cannot distinguish one letter from another. The prophet Isaiah, in the prospect of Gospel times, gives a description of the way of salvation which is peculiarly suited for your comfort : " And a highway shall be there, and it shall be called the way of holiness ; the wayfaring men, though fools, shall not err therein *."

(3.) Have you been notorious open sinners ? Then you are in the less danger of trusting to your own righteousness. And as to the rest, if you are sick of sin, if you sincerely desire to be freed, as well from the power as from the guilt of it, you stand as fair for salvation as the most sober and regular person upon the earth. St. Paul, speaking to those who had been partakers of the saving grace of God, after he had made an enumeration of the blackest sins which man can be guilty of, adds, " And such were some of you : but ye are washed, but ye are sanctified, but ye are justified, in the name of the Lord Jesus, and by the Spirit of our God†."

4. In this way the salvation of believers is sure. If it depended on any thing in man, it might miscarry. Man's boasted wisdom is soon changed. A few hours of a fever, a small blow on the head, may change a wise man into a fool. " But it is of grace, to the end that the promise might be sure to all the seed ‡." Adam had a stock of wisdom ; yet when he was trusted with his own happiness, he could not preserve it. But the Second Adam is all-sufficient. Our dependence is upon him. To those who are babes, he is wisdom, righteousness, sanctification, and all that they want. If this concern had been left to the wisdom of man, it is most probable that Christ would have lived and died in vain, without a single real disciple. But now the dispensation of grace is in his hands,

---

* Isa. xxxv. 8.   † 1 Cor. vi. 11.   ‡ Rom. iv. 16.

we are sure that some will believe in him; and we are likewise sure, that those who truly do so shall never be ashamed of their hope.

Now, from what has been said,

1. Inquire what is the temper of your minds with regard to this appointment. Our Lord rejoiced in it as the wise and holy will, the good pleasure, of his heavenly Father. If you are displeased at it, is it not a proof that you have not the mind which was in Christ Jesus? If God *wills* one thing, and you *will* another, where must the contention end? To what purpose, or with what pretence, can you use that expression in the Lord's Prayer, "Thy will be done," when in effect your hearts rise with enmity against it? This is one topic from whence we may confirm the declaration of Scripture, that man by nature is not only a transgressor of the law, but an enemy, yea enmity itself, against God *. They may pay some profession of regard to the power that made the heavens and the earth, the sea, and the fountains of water, while they worship they know not what, according to their own vain and dark imaginations. But the attributes and characters of God revealed in Scripture, his holiness, justice, truth, and sovereignty, they cannot bear. They are enemies to the declared strictness of his moral government, and enemies to the methods by which he has proposed to communicate his grace. But he is God, and who can control him? Who can say unto him, What hast thou done? You must either submit to his golden sceptre in time, or his rod of iron will fall upon you for ever.

2. Does it not appear from hence, that the doc-

---

* Rom. viii. 7.

trine of free sovereign grace is rather an encouragement to awakened and broken-hearted sinners than otherwise? If you are most unworthy of mercy, and destitute of every plea, should you not be glad to hear, that the Lord does not expect worthiness in those whom he saves; but that he himself has provided the only plea which he will accept, and a plea which cannot be overruled, the righteousness and mediation of his well-beloved Son?

SERMON VI.

OF THE PERSON OF CHRIST.

MATTH. xi. 27.

All things are delivered unto me of my Father: and no man knoweth the Son but the Father; neither knoweth any man the Father, save the Son, and he to whomsoever the Son will reveal him.

THE two preceding verses have led us to consider grace (if I may so speak) in the unfathomable depths of the sovereign will and good pleasure of God. In this verse, our Lord calls us to the contemplation of his own glorious person, authority, and fulness. In him grace is treasured up as in a repository for communication, to be dispensed to needy perishing sinners.

When an ambassador is deputed from an earthly prince, to transact some concern of great importance, he produces his commission and authority, without which all he could propose would be little regarded; and those are most honoured and attended to, who are intrusted with full powers, that is, with a liberty to act and propose as occasions offer, without farther instructions, and with full security that the king will ratify and confirm whatever they agree to, in the same manner as if he had done it in his own person. Thus (if we may presume to compare small things with great) our Lord Jesus Christ, the great Messenger of the Father's love, before he invites every weary heavy-laden sinner to come to him with a gracious assurance that he will receive, and pardon, and save them all, he condescends in this verse (as it were) to open his commission; to instruct us in his own personal dignity, and to communicate to us the ample and unlimited authority which he has received from God to treat with rebels. He knows what hearts of unbelief we have; how greatly an awakened conscience is terrified with guilt; how busy Satan is to urge us to question either his ability or his willingness to save; and therefore he would leave nothing undone that might encourage us to come to him, and find rest for our souls. May his gracious Spirit enable me to speak aright, and so open your hearts to understand what may be said upon this high subject, that we may have joy and peace in believing.

The words contain a threefold declaration.

I. Of his person: " No man knoweth the Son, but the Father; neither knoweth any man the Father, save the Son."

II. Of his authority: " All things are delivered to me of my Father."

III. Of his office; summarily intimated in the expression, " He to whomsoever the Son will reveal him."

To treat these points in their proper extent, would be a subject more than equal to the abilities

and life of man. Much would be left unsaid at
last. We cannot order our speech by reason
of darkness. This is a theme fit for an angel's
tongue; the most exalted angel, or all the angels
in heaven, would be unable to comprehend it, for
it is infinite, as our text declares. None knows
the Son but the Father. Here we are too prone
to think highly of our own knowledge; but when
we arrive in yonder world of light, to see him
as he is, we shall be ashamed of the highest conceptions we had of him, and of our most laboured
attempts to express them, while we were im-
prisoned in this distant land. Then we shall say
with the queen of Sheba, " Behold the half, the
thousandth part, was not told us." In the mean
time, he is pleased to accept our imperfect stam-
merings, to assist our feeble inquiries, and does
not disdain (as he justly might) to hear us take his
name upon our polluted lips.

I. The inconceivable dignity of his person is
pointed out by two expressions.

1. " No man," (or rather, as it might be rendered here and in many other places, " No one *)
knoweth the Son, but the Father." No one.

First, Not the wisest man in a state of nature.
Various degrees of knowledge there are amongst
the sons of men. There is a great difference between man and man; between one who knows
not his letters, or any thing beyond the bounds of
his own village; and another who has a large
acquaintance with arts and sciences, history and
languages, and has surveyed the manners and
boundaries of many nations. But, with regard to
the knowledge of Christ, the philosopher and the
shepherd, the king and the beggar, are just upon

* Ουδεις.

a level. Of two blind men, one may know many things more than the other; but with regard to the knowledge of light and colours, they will be both ignorant alike.

Some of you perhaps think yourselves wiser than many of your neighbours. But I cannot too often remind you, that if you know not Christ, all your wisdom is folly, and you will find it so at last.

Secondly, Neither do his own people know him in the sense of my text. Some knowledge of him indeed they have, which is their differencing character from the world. But how small a portion! That they know him a little, is plain, because they love him and trust him; but how little, is plain likewise, because their love is so faint, and their trust so feeble. Their doubts, fears, complaints, and backslidings, are so many mournful proofs that they are but poorly acquainted with him; and sufficiently evidence, that a great part of what we account our knowledge, is not real and experimental, but notional only. The literal sense of what we read concerning Jesus, is attainable by study and human teaching; but the spiritual import can be received only from Him who teaches the heart, who increases it in us by the various exercises and dispensations we pass through; and the best have much more to learn than they have already attained. There are, indeed, happy moments when he manifests himself to the eye of faith, in his glory, and in his love; as he did to Peter in the mount, and to Thomas, when a sight of his wounds conquered his unbelief, and made him in a transport of joy cry out, " My Lord, and my God." But these visits, though they have a powerful influence to conquer sin and fear, are transient; and when the cause is withdrawn,

there is a proportionable abatement in the effect.
The knowledge of Christ, in the present life, may
be compared to the knowledge which a shepherd
has of the sea, from having viewed it at the top of
a cliff.   In a sense, it may be said he has seen the
sea; but how little has he seen, in comparison of
what lies beyond the reach of his eye!   How inadequate is such a prospect to give him an idea
answerable to the length, and breadth, and depth,
of the immense ocean!   Nay, farther,

Thirdly, The glorified saints, and holy angels,
who behold as much of his glory as creatures can
bear, do not know him as he is.   They are filled
with his power and love.   He comprehends them,
but they cannot him.   A vessel cast into the sea
can but receive according to its capacity.   Thus
are they filled with his fulness till they can hold
no more; but his glory still remains infinite and
boundless.   The glorious seraphim, therefore, are
represented as hiding *their faces* with their
wings, unable to bear the splendour of his
presence.   For,

Fourthly, " None knows the Son but the
Father." This proves his Divinity.   God only
knows himself.   The Son is his eternal Word, his
eternal Wisdom, and therefore beyond the highest
reach of finite understanding.

2. " None knows the Father but the Son."
Here I might repeat the former particulars.   God
has made something known of himself in his works,
much in his word, more still in his grace.   All
men have some faint perceptions of his power
and presence.   He manifests himself to his own
family below, still more to his family above; yet,
after all, he is said to dwell in light which no man
can approach.   None knows him but the Son;
and he knows him perfectly, knows the incompre-

hensible God; therefore he is God himself;—as he said to Philip, " He that hath seen me, hath seen the Father*."

Now, if we had no other proof of this doctrine but the passage before us, since this is the declaration of the true and faithful Witness, it should be accepted as decisive. But as this is the great mystery of godliness, the pillar and ground of truth, the foundation of all our hopes, I shall take this opportunity to confirm it more largely from other concurrent testimonies of Scripture.

By the Son, I mean the person who spoke these words : he who was foretold by the prophets; who in the fulness of time came into the world ; who, with respect to his Divine nature, is called " the Word†," and with respect to his human nature was born of the Virgin Mary : he who was known upon earth by the name of Jesus ; whose history is related by the Evangelists; who suffered a shameful and accursed death upon the cross without the gates of Jerusalem. Of him we affirm, " That he was, and is, the true God, and eternal life ‡." In proof of this, besides what has been already said, let the following particulars be considered.

First, That the proper and peculiar titles of God are attributed to him frequently in the Scriptures ; so frequently, that it would be a very long task to transcribe them all. Let a few, the application of which to Christ is express and indisputable, suffice for a specimen : " The Word was God:" " His name shall be called Emmanuel, God with us :" " Jehovah our Righteousness :" " The Mighty God." In the same style he speaks

---

* John xiv. 9.   † John i. 1.   ‡ 1 John v. 20.

of himself by his servants the Prophets and
Apostles: " Thy Maker is thine husband, the
Lord of Hosts is his name; and thy Redeemer
the Holy One of Israel; the God of the whole
earth shall he be called." " Look unto me, and
be ye saved, all the ends of the earth; for I am
God, and there is none else." " I am Alpha and
Omega, the beginning and the end, the first and
the last, the Almighty*."

Amidst the variety of testimonies which might
be adduced to this purpose, there are two which
are peculiarly observable. The Psalmist expresses the majesty, power, and immutability of
God, in these sublime terms: " Of old thou hast
laid the foundations of the earth, and the heavens
are the work of thine hands. They shall perish,
but thou shalt endure: yea, all of them shall wax
old like a garment; as a vesture thou shalt change
them, and they shall be changed; but thou art
the same, and thy years shall have no end †."
Surely none can deny, but this ascription must be
incommunicably due to the Almighty; yet the
author of the Epistle to the Hebrews ‡ applies
these words directly to the Son of God.—The
other passage I intend is the vision of Isaiah, recorded in his sixth chapter; which not only proves
the point in hand, but irrefragably establishes the
doctrine of the Trinity. For the Lord of hosts,
whom Isaiah saw and heard, is affirmed by St.
John to have been the Son §, by St. Paul to have
been the Holy Ghost ‖. Isaiah, therefore, had a
manifestation of what was afterwards in explicit
words set forth to the faith of the church, that

---

* John i. 1 ; Matth. i. 23; Jer. xxiii. 6 ; Isa. ix. 6 ; Isa. liv. 5 ;
Isa. xlv. 22 ; Rev. i. 8, 11.

　† Psalm cii. 25—27.　　　　　‡ Heb. i. 10—12.
　§ John xii. 41.　　　　　　　 ‖ Acts xxviii. 25.

" there are three that bare record in heaven, the Father, the Word, and the Holy Ghost ; and these three are one *."

Secondly, His works upon earth were such as necessarily suppose a Divine power. Who can control the elements, raise the dead, command the devils, search the heart, and forgive sin, but God alone † ? If it should be said, that many of his servants and followers wrought miracles equal to his, by a delegated power, and therefore this argument is not conclusive; I answer, There is an apparent difference in the manner of their working which proves the disparity between them and him. They could do nothing but in his name, and by his power : they usually addressed themselves to him by prayer, and always ascribed the praise and glory to him ‡. But his power was independent, sovereign, and unlimited : " He spoke, and it was done ; he commanded, and it stood fast." At the breath of his rebuke, the raging tempest and the boisterous seas were instantly hushed into a perfect calm. The deaf heard his voice, and the dead came forth from their graves, at his first call.

Thirdly, His works of office can be performed by none but God. This might be proved concerning each of the offices he exercises in consequence of his high character as Mediator between God and man ; but I shall speak only of two.

(1.) It is his office to keep his believing people in this present evil world, to act § the part of a Shepherd towards them, to supply their wants of every kind, to direct their steps, to control their enemies,

---

* 1 John v. 7.
† Mark iv. 39 ; John xi. 43 ; Luke iv. 36 ; Mark ii. 10.
‡ Acts iii. 12—16.   § Matth. ii. 6. ποιμανει.

to over-rule all things for their good, and to be a very present help in every time of trouble. To execute this important charge, it is necessary that his knowledge, his compassion, his power, and his patience, must be boundless. His eye must be every moment upon all their cases at once; his ear must be incessantly open to receive the prayers of all people, nations, and languages; his arm must be continually stretched out to support so many that stand, to raise up so many that fall, to afford seasonable and suitable supplies, at the same instant, to the distresses and temptations of millions. If this is the office he has undertaken, and if he is acknowledged sufficient and faithful in the discharge of it, what more undeniable evidence can be given, that he has all the attributes we can conceive as essential and peculiar to the Godhead? The provocations, defects, and backslidings of his people, are likewise so numerous, so often repeated, and attended with such black aggravations, that if he was not God, invincible in goodness, unchangeable in purpose, if his mercy was not, as his majesty, infinite, he would be wearied out, and provoked to cast them off for ever. The great reason why he bore with his people of old holds equally strong with respect to us: " I am the Lord, I change not; therefore ye sons of Jacob are not consumed *."

(2.) The like may be said of the high office, character, and appointment he has received, to be the Judge of the world, of angels and of men. For, besides that it is quite incredible that God, who is jealous of his glory, should intrust this most illustrious prerogative to any mere creature, it

---

* Mal. iii. 6.

seems evident at first sight, that no creature can be possibly qualified for the discharge of it. To the great and final Judge all hearts must be open, all desires known, and every secret disclosed. He must be intimately acquainted with the counsels and plans that lay hid in God from eternity; he must have a sovereign, comprehensive, intuitive view of every event, of every design, that took place within the limits of time and creation; he must have unlimited authority to pronounce the decisive sentence which will fix the everlasting state of all intelligent beings, and uncontrolled power for the immediate and irrevocable execution of his supreme decree. And what higher than this can our most laboured conceptions reach of the Almighty God? If it be said, that Christ will act by a delegated authority; we answer, It is a contradiction to say, that God *can* delegate his *omniscience* to a creature: and without this attribute, any assignable measure of wisdom or power would be insufficient. The power and fulness of the Godhead must so reside in the Judge, as justly to denominate him to be " God over all blessed for ever *." And this the Scripture assures us is the case in fact. The man Christ Jesus, who is appointed the Judge of quick and dead, is so intimately and essentially united to and inhabited by the Deity †, that he is the proper object of our faith, as the true God and eternal life.

Fourthly, The honours he claims from us afford a further argument for his proper Divinity. He challenges our supreme love, obedience, trust, and worship: " Ye believe in God, believe also in me." " Except ye eat the flesh of the Son of man, and drink his blood, ye have no life in you." " That all men should honour the Son as they honour the

* Rom. ix. 5.   † Col. ii. 9.

Father." " My sheep know my voice, and I know them, and they follow me ; and I give unto them eternal life." " I am the light of the world." " I am the resurrection and the life*." If we could suppose an apostle or an angel speaking of himself in terms like these, requiring our unlimited dependence, and directing our hope and love to centre wholly on him, we might justly reject him as a blasphemer. How the Apostles understood these expressions, and that they did not mistake our Lord's meaning, is evident from the behaviour of Thomas. He saluted his risen Saviour, " My Lord, and my God†." Had his transport of joy carried him too far in giving this ascription to Jesus, he would doubtless have corrected him, and provided us with a caution against committing the like fault : for who that has tasted his love, and been made partaker of the power of his resurrection, can avoid adoring him with the utmost homage their words can express, or their hearts conceive ?

From hence we may take occasion to observe,

1. His wonderful condescension ; that, for us and our salvation, he stooped so low, drew a veil over his eternal glories, and appeared in the form of a servant, to suffer and to die : " Though he was rich, for our sakes he became poor, that we through his poverty might be made rich ‡." This was love passing knowledge, to pour out his blood, his life, his soul, for those who by nature and practice were enemies and rebels, disobedient to his government, and averse to his grace !

2. What a blessed and glorious hope is set before awakened sinners ! Add to the consideration

---

* John xiv. 1 ; vi. 53 ; v. 23 ; x. 27, 28 ; viii. 12 ; xi. 25.
† John xx. 28.   ‡ 2 Cor. viii. 9.

of his person, what we have yet to offer from the word of God concerning his authority and purpose, and say if these truths do not give sufficient encouragement to believe and be saved!

3. How awful must be the case of those who shall be found in final rebellion against him, and die in a state of impenitence and unbelief! Alas! poor obstinate sinners, that have stood out so long, will you still harden your hearts, and stop your ears, and rush (like the thoughtless horse in the battle) upon your own destruction? Do you consider whom you are opposing? " Did ever any harden himself against the Lord, and prosper * ? " " Have you an arm like God ? or can you thunder with a voice like him † ? " Where will you stand, or what will you say, " when he shall arise to shake terribly the earth ; when he shall be revealed in fire, to take vengeance on all that know not God, and obey not the Gospel ‡ ? " O kiss the Son, throw down your arms, and fall prostrate at his footstool, lest his anger awake, and you perish without hope ; for in a little time the great day of his wrath will be revealed, " which will burn like a furnace, and all the proud, yea, and all that do wickedly, shall be stubble, and the day that cometh shall burn them up, saith the Lord of hosts, that it shall leave them neither root nor branch §." Then will it appear, that those, and those only, are blessed, who put their trust in him : " For those who trust in him shall never be ashamed ; but when Christ who is their life shall appear, they also shall appear with him in glory ∥."

---

* Job ix. 4.   † Job xl. 9.   ‡ 2 Thess. i. 8.
§ Mal. iv. 1.   ∥ Col. iii. 4.

SERMON VII.

OF THE AUTHORITY OF CHRIST.

MATTH. xi. 27.

*All things are delivered unto me of my Father: and no
man knoweth the Son, but the Father; neither knoweth
any man the Father, save the Son, and he to whomsoever
the Son will reveal him.*

WE have spoken something of the dignity and excellence of that Mighty One on whom our help is
laid; and are now to consider,

II. The covenant authority he is intrusted with
to manage the great concern of man's salvation.
He is not only infinitely sufficient, but divinely
appointed for this great work.

Of this covenant there is express mention in
many parts of Scripture, to some of which I have
referred in the note *. It is styled the *covenant* of
peace, the everlasting, ordered, and sure covenant.
The power and efficacy of this covenant respected
the future incarnation of our Saviour. He asserted his right, while in the form of a servant, in
the words of my text; and to the same purpose
are the words of John the Baptist: " The Father
loveth the Son, and hath delivered all things into
his hands†." But the full manifestation of it was
deferred to the time of his resurrection, when, and

---

* Ps. lxxxix. 19; Prov. viii. 23; Isa. xlii. 1—6, compared with
Matth. xii. 18—21; Isa. xlix. 8, 9; Zech. vi. 13.

† John iii. 35.

by which, he was declared to be the Son of God with power *." Hence, before he left his disciples, he assured them, "All power is committed to me in heaven and in earth†."

The sum is, that our Lord Jesus Christ, by virtue of his Divine nature, and his voluntary undertaking in our flesh, to fulfil all righteousness for us, both as to obedience and satisfaction, is exalted in that nature wherein he suffered, to be the sovereign Judge and Lord of all‡. He it is now with whom we have to do. The Holy God, considered without respect to the covenant of grace, is a consuming fire to sinners; and we cannot stand before him. But now he reveals himself: he dwells, as in his temple, in the man Christ Jesus. He has intrusted all his glory and all his grace in his hands; and to him we are to look, on him we are to depend, for all the blessings we need for time and eternity. For " all things are delivered to him of the Father." All things is a most comprehensive expression. We may distribute it as referring to all persons, all blessings, and all dispensations.

1. All persons are in his hands. Hence his sublime title, " King of kings, and Lord of lords§." He doth what he will among the armies of heaven, and the inhabitants of the earth. Thus Isaiah saw his glory, and spake of him.

1st, He is Lord over his enemies, and those that hate him. He rules them with a rod of iron, and so disposes their designs as to make them (though against their wills) the means and instruments of promoting his own purposes and glory‖. They

---

* Rom. i. 4. † Matth. xxviii. 18. ‡ Phil. ii. 6—11.
§ Rev. xix. 16 ; Dan. iv. 35 ; Isa. vi. compared with John xii. 41.
‖ Psalm ii. 9.

are his servants even when they rage most against him. He has a bridle in their mouths to check and turn them at his pleasure. He can and often does control them, when they seem most sure of success, and always sets them bounds, which they cannot pass. So he shewed his power over Pharaoh of old : the haughty king's resistance only gave occasion for a more glorious display of the greatness and goodness of the God of Israel. So he humbled the pride of Herod, and gave him up, in the midst of his guards, a prey to worms *. And thus, sooner or later, all his enemies are brought to lick the dust before him.

2dly, But especially he is Lord of his own people. By nature indeed they likewise are his enemies, but he knows them all by name. They have been in a peculiar manner given to him by the Father†; he accounts them his portion, and he will not lose his own‡. He knows where to find them, and when to call them ; and when his time is come, one word or look from him can disarm them in a moment, and bring them humbly to his feet. How soon did he stop and change the persecuting Saul!§ When they are thus made willing in the day of his power, he takes them under his especial care ; and whoso toucheth them, toucheth the apple of his eye. He guides, and guards, and feeds, and strengthens them ; he keeps them night and day, waters them every moment, and will not suffer any to pluck them out of his hand : nor will he himself leave them or forsake them, till he has done all that he has spoken to them of. He gives them likewise a new heart and gracious dispositions, suited to the honourable

---

* Acts xii. 23.　　　　　　† John xvii. 6.
‡ John x. 15, 16.　　　　　§ Acts ix.

relation he has brought them into; so that they delight in his precepts, and yield him a cheerful, habitual, and universal obedience, from the constraining sense they have received of his inexpressible love.

2. All blessings are at his disposal. Is not this a welcome declaration to awakened souls? What is the blessing you want? Seek to Jesus, and you shall not be disappointed. Hear his gracious invitation, " Ho, every one that thirsteth, come ye to the waters, and ye that have no money; come ye, buy and eat, yea, come, buy wine and milk without money, and without price. Incline your ear, and come unto me: hear, and your soul shall live *." The promised blessings which he holds in his hands, are the very same that the awakened enlightened conscience must have, and can have only from him.

1st, Pardon. How needful, how valuable is the pardon of sin to those who know what sin is, what it deserves, and what a share they have in it! Such are incapable of taking comfort till they know how God may be reconciled, and sin forgiven. These are the persons to whom Jesus says, " Look unto me, and be ye saved. I, even I, am he that blotteth out thy transgressions for mine own sake, and will not remember thy sins †."

2dly, Righteousness. By believing in him sinners are not only pardoned, but justified. They are accepted in the Beloved, and accounted righteous by his righteousness imputed to them, which we are assured is unto all, and upon all that believe, without any difference or exception ‡. Hence his people adore him, and glory in him, by his name, *the Lord our Righteousness.* In him they possess

---

* Isa. lv. 1.   † Isa. xlv. 22.; xliii. 25.   ‡ Rom. iii. 22.

a righteousness answerable to the demands of the holy law, have confidence and liberty of access to God at present, though conscious of innumerable deficiencies in themselves; and they shall stand with boldness before him in this righteousness, and not be ashamed in the great day of his appearance, when he shall come to judge the world.

3dly, Strength. The forgiveness of sin that is past would little avail, unless there was provision made for a continual supply of needful grace. Without this we shall quickly grow weary, yield to the force of surrounding temptations, till at length the latter end would be worse than the beginning. But now every sincere soul may be freed from this fear. The way of prevention is pointed out, and the success infallibly secured by that one promise, though there are many to the same effect, " They that wait on the Lord shall renew their strength*."

4thly, Healing. This is often necessary; for the spiritual warfare is not to be maintained long without wounds. Our great enemy is so subtle, so watchful, so well provided with temptations adapted to every temper and circumstance; and we are so weak, unpractised, and so often remiss and off our guard, that he will at times prevail to bring us into a dark, barren, backsliding state, despoiled of comfort, and oppressed with fears. But see what a good and gracious Shepherd we have: hear his comfortable words: " I will seek that which was lost, and bring again that which was driven away, and will bind up that which was broken, and will strengthen that which was sick †."

5thly, Support under trouble. He has engaged to

---

* Isa. xl. 31.　　　　† Ezek. xxxiv. 16.

lead his people safely *, through fire and through
water. He gives them leave to cast all their care
upon him, with an assurance that he careth for
them.   He has said, " all things shall work together for their good; that his grace shall be
sufficient for them; and that in good time he will
bruise Satan under their feet, make them more
than conquerors," and place them out of the reach
of sin and sorrow for ever.   Besides the habitual
peace which arises from the believing consideration of these truths, he has likewise peculiar
seasons of refreshment, when he manifests himself
to the soul in a way the world knows not of, and
often makes the hour of their sharpest trials the
time of their sweetest and highest consolations :
" As the sufferings of Christ abound in us, so our
consolation aboundeth by Christ†."

3. All dispensations are under his direction. He
is Lord of all, and does according to his pleasure
among the armies of heaven and the inhabitants
of the earth.   He is the Supreme Disposer,

1st, Of those external dispensations which are
distinguished by the name of *providential.*

(1.) Those that are welcome and prosperous, are
both his gift and his purchase To his people they
come free : but he paid dear for them.   And this
gives them their chief value in the judgment of
those who know him, to receive them as the
pledges and fruits of his redeeming love.   When
the blessings of common providence are received
and enjoyed as the gifts of God reconciled in
Christ, they are then, and not otherwise, truly
comfortable.   It is this thought enables the poor

---

* Isa. xliii. 2.; 1 Pet. iii. 17.; Rom. viii. 28.; 2 Cor. xii. 19,
† 2 Cor. i. 5.

believer often to taste a sweeter relish and flavour in bread and water, than the voluptuary ever knew in the wasteful profusion and studied refinements of luxury. To be able to look back and see how the hand of our gracious Lord has led us from our childhood, chose and managed better for us than we could have done, corrected our mistakes, and in many things exceeded our desires; to look round and see all our concerns in his sure keeping, who delights in our prosperity, and will suffer nothing to grieve us, but what he intends to employ as means for our greater advantage; to look forward and see, that he has prepared still better things for us than ever our eyes beheld, or our hearts conceived,—how cheering are these views! Those who are thus stayed upon the Lord Jesus, as over-ruling and managing all their concerns, are not terrified with every shaking leaf; "their hearts are fixed, trusting in the Lord."

(2.) Afflictive dispensations are likewise of his sending. And the consideration of his hand in them, the good he designs us by them, the assurance we have of being supported under them, and brought through them; according to the degrees in which these things are apprehended by faith, and accompanied with a humbling sense of their own demerits, his people submit to his appointment with patience and thankfulness, and say, after the pattern which he has left them, The cup which my Saviour puts into my hand, shall I not drink it?

In brief, it is he who appointed the time and place of our birth, and all the successive connections of our lives. Our civil and our religious liberties are both owing to his favour; and in these he has been peculiarly favourable to *us*. "He has not dealt so with every nation."

2dly, The dispensation of grace. It is he who raises up instruments to preach his Gospel, appoints them their places, furnishes them with that measure of gifts and sufficiency which he sees requisite and best. And it is he only that makes their poor labours successful. He sends his word to some, and brings others to his word: and in both cases he so makes use of ordinary means, that to a common eye he seems to do nothing, when in reality he does *all*. He brought St. Paul to Corinth, and maintained him there a considerable time against all the efforts of his enemies*. He over-ruled the thoughtless rambling of Onesimus †, and led him by a way which he knew not, to the means by which he had appointed to bring him to the knowledge of himself. And these instances are recorded for our instruction, as specimens of what he does in the same kind every day.

3dly, The dispensation of death. Our times are in his hands. He claims it as his own prerogative ‡, that he keeps the key of death and the invisible state. None can remove us sooner, none can detain us a moment longer, than his call. In this likewise he is little observed. We charge death to fevers, frights, and falls: but these are only the messengers which he sends. Sin has brought us all under a sentence of death: but the moment and the manner of the execution befal us according to his good pleasure. Till then, though his providence leads us through fire and water, though we walk upon the brink of a thousand apparent, and a million of unseen, dangers, we are in reality in perfect safety. Having appointed St. Paul to stand before Cæsar, though the tempest greatly assaulted, and seemingly

---

* Acts xviii. 10. † Philem. 11. ‡ Rev. i. 18.

overpowered the ship he was in, St. Paul was as
safe on the stormy sea, when all probable hope of
being saved * was taken away, as Cæsar himself
upon his throne. But when his time is come, in
vain are all the assistance of friends, or the healing
arts of medicines, to procure the smallest respite.

4thly, The dispensation of judgment. "The
Father hath committed all judgment to the Son†;"
and has especially appointed a day wherein he
will judge the world in righteousness by the man
Jesus Christ‡, whom he hath ordained. Then his
glory shall be confessed by all. Every eye shall
see him, and they also that pierced him. Awful
will the day be to those who hate him, when he
shall appear in flaming fire, to convince sinners of
all their ungodly deeds which they have committed, and of all their hard speeches which they
have spoken against him §. They must give an
account of all. Account, did I say? they can give
none; but will be struck dumb before him, and
hear with horror their dreadful doom, "Depart
from me, ye cursed, into everlasting fire, prepared
for the devil and his angels ‖."

But it will be a joyful time to his own people.
The clouds of infirmity, affliction, and reproach,
under which they are now obscured, shall vanish
away, and they shall shine forth like the sun in
the presence of their Father. God, even their
own God, shall wipe away all tears from their
eyes. They shall be glorified, and their enemies
ashamed. What joy will fill their hearts, when
Jesus the Judge shall own his relation to them before assembled worlds, and shall say, "Come, ye
blessed of my Father, inherit the kingdom pre-

* Acts xxvii. 24. † John v. 22. ‡ Acts xvii. 31.
§ Jude 15. ‖ Matth. xxv. 41.

pared for you from the foundation of the world."
Then sorrow and sighing shall be heard no more;
but songs of triumph and shouts of everlasting
joy shall take place, and so shall they be ever
with the Lord.

How are your hearts affected with this subject?
Do you not expect that I should close it with a
suitable word of application?

1. To those who are as yet in their sins. Will
you not tremble before this great Lord God? If
these things are not so, if you can prove that
we have followed cunningly devised fables, go on
secure. But have I not your consciences on my
side? Do you not feel a secret foreboding that
these are the truths of God? And dare you still
persist? Do you not see that you are already in
his hands? In a moment he could break you in
pieces; yet he spares. He affords you one opportunity more. To-day, while it is called to-day,
hear his voice; lest to-morrow should surprise
you into eternity, and the weight of unpardoned
sins should sink you into the lowest hell. As he
has power to punish, so likewise he is mighty to
save. Believe his word and live. His obedience
unto death is a plea with which you may approach
the Mercy-seat. He has power to take away
your heart of stone, to subdue your enmity, to
forgive your sins; and what he does, he does
freely, without money, and without price. You
need not, you cannot, mend yourselves before you
come to him. If you seek him, he will be found
of you; but if you obstinately reject him, you
will perish under the most aggravated guilt, as
sinners against the light and grace of the Gospel.

2. You that see your need of a Saviour, lift up
your heads and rejoice. Is he not, thus qualified,
able to save to the uttermost? Why should you

keep back, when he bids you come unto him, that you may find rest? Could you invent any invitations more free, more full, than those that are recorded in the Gospel? Can you desire any stronger security than the blood of Jesus, and the oath of him that liveth for ever? Do you wish to know how other great sinners have succeeded in their application to him? Search the Scriptures, and read how he saved Mary Magdalene, the dying thief, the cruel jailor, the persecuting Saul, and many of those who were actually concerned in nailing him to the cross. Be patient, continue waiting on him in prayer, and you shall find he has not inclined you to seek his face in vain.

3. To believers I hope this is a comfortable theme. You see all your concerns are in safe hands. He to whom you have committed your souls, is able to keep them. Jesus, who has all authority and power in heaven and in earth, vouchsafes to be your Shepherd. What then can you want who are at his providing? What have you to fear who are under his protection? Why then do you so often distrust, so often complain? It is because your faith is weak. Are you tempted to think you could place yourselves to more advantage than he has placed you, that you could do better without the afflictions he is pleased to send you, that you cannot spare what he takes away, nor do well without something which he withholds? Reject all such thoughts; they are highly dishonourable to your Saviour, and to your profession. Those who know not God *must* reason thus; but you have a covenant promise, that all things are working together for your good. "This is not your rest, it is polluted." But you will soon be at home; and then, when by a clearer light you look back upon the way by which the

Lord led you through the wilderness, you will be ashamed (if shame be compatible with the heavenly state) of your misapprehensions while in this dark world, and will confess, to his praise, that mercy and goodness surrounded you in every step, and that the Lord did all things well. What you will then see, it is now your duty and privilege to believe. If you sincerely desire his guidance in all things, labour to submit to it. The path which he has marked out for you is difficult, but he has trod it before you, and it leads to glory. The time is short. Yet a little while, and you shall receive the end of your faith, even the salvation of your souls.

SERMON VIII.

THE GLORY AND GRACE OF GOD REVEALED IN JESUS CHRIST.

MATTH. xi. 27.

All things are delivered unto me of my Father: and no man knoweth the Son but the Father; neither knoweth any man the Father, save the Son, and he to whomsoever the Son will reveal him.

THE love we bear to the Lord Jesus Christ, and the confidence we place in him, will always be exactly proportioned to the apprehensions we form of him. Therefore, " to grow in grace, and in the knowledge of him *," are spoken of as inseparably connected. On this account the Scriptures are frequent and full in describing him to us, that we may have a large acquaintance with his all-suffi-

* 2 Pet. ii. 18.

ciency, and be delivered from our sins and fears.
An awakened conscience, that sees the need of a
Saviour, well knows, that the person who can deservedly lay claim to its trust must have these
three properties; power, authority, and intention
to save. How these eminently belong to Jesus,
we learn from his own words here. Power be-
longeth to him, for he is a Divine person, the
Creator, Possessor, and Upholder of all things.
Authority is his, for all things are delivered to him.
Thus far we have proceeded, and are now to speak
of his intention or office, the design of his appearance, and for which he is authorised. This is intimated in the close of my text. We are therefore
now to speak,

III. Of his office, summarily included in this
one thing, *To reveal the knowledge of God.* " Neither knoweth any man the Father, save the Son,
and he to whomsoever the Son will reveal him."

The knowledge of God, here spoken of, intends
something more than merely to know that there is
a God. Some faint apprehensions of this, all men
have by nature. This great truth is so clearly
manifested in the works of creation and providence, that any man would be greatly offended,
if he was supposed to be ignorant of it. But as it
is one thing, to know that there is a king over the
nation, and quite another thing *to know the king*
so as to have liberty of access to him and an interest in his favour, so it is in the case before us.
Our Lord did not come to tell us that there is a
God (the devils know this, and tremble), but to
reveal to us such a knowledge of God as may
stand with our comfort; to teach us how poor,
guilty, hell-deserving sinners may draw near to
God with hopes in his mercy, and call him their
Father and their Friend.

Now, besides the revelation of this knowledge in the Old Testament, which may be properly ascribed to Christ, inasmuch as he was the Lord, Guide, and Teacher of his church from the beginning, and instructed Moses and the Prophets in the things concerning himself—I say, besides this (which was made at sundry times, and in divers manners, in a more dark and imperfect way), our Lord Jesus, through his incarnation, has vouchsafed us a twofold revelation of that knowledge of God in which standeth our eternal life.

1. In his person.
2. By his Spirit.

1. In his person.   In this respect he is said to be " the brightness of the Father's glory, and the* express image of his † substance." That God is great, and good, and wise, appears in part from his works; but it is but a small portion of these attributes we can spell out in this way; and there are other perfections in God, of which we can gain no certain knowledge without a farther revelation. But would we see a glorious display of the great God, let us turn our eyes to Jesus, and behold him by faith in two principal views.

(1.) As *hanging upon the cross.*   Could we have seen this awful transaction, and been in a right frame of mind, we should naturally have asked such questions as these, Who is he ?   What has he done ?   Had we been told, This person, thus destitute and tormented, is the beloved Son of God, who knew no sin, neither was guile found in his mouth; we must have farther asked, Why then was he scourged, wounded, and nailed to the tree ?   Why are those barbarous men per-

---

* Heb. i. 3.   † Της Ὑποστασεως.

mitted to mock his sufferings ? Why does he not
deliver himself, and destroy his enemies? The
proper answer to these questions includes a revelation of the Divine perfections.

1st, Wisdom. We had deserved to perish, but
his mercy had designed to save us with an everlasting salvation. Yet this must be in a way worthy of himself. Sin must be punished, and the
honour of his broken law vindicated. How could
this be done, and the righteousness of God made
to harmonize with our peace ? A wisdom astonishing to angels is manifested in devising this
wonderful means. No sacrifices * or offerings, no
acts of obedience or mediation, which creatures
could supply, would have been of the least avail
when the injured Majesty of God demanded a satisfaction. But the eternal Word, united to our
nature, afforded a propitiation worthy of God, and
suitable for us. Jesus, by his obedience unto
death, has made an end of sin†, and brought in an
everlasting righteousness, available for all those
who flee to him as the hope set before them, for
refuge from approaching wrath.

2dly, Love. *God so loved the world.* If you ask,
How ? judge from this instance, words cannot express it. He so loved sinners, enemies, rebels,
that, for their sakes, he abandoned and delivered
up his beloved Son into the hands of wicked men,
permitted him to be assaulted by the powers of
darkness ; yea, it pleased the Father himself to
bruise him, and to make his soul an offering for
sin. This is love without parallel, and beyond
conception. We can only admire and say, " Behold what manner of love the Father hath be-

* Heb. x. 4—7.   † Dan. ix. 24.

stowed on us*." When Jesus Christ as crucified
is clearly apprehended by faith, then we have the
most convincing, the most affecting proof, that
God is love.

3dly, Justice. Wonder not that God's own
Son is thus treated. He stands in the place of
sinners, and therefore he is not, he cannot be
spared. The words his enemies use † to his reproach, will, in the lips of his redeemed people, be
an expression of his highest praise. Having undertaken to save others, and being determined not
to give up their cause, it is in that respect absolutely impossible for him to save himself.

Again; this justice, which was once as a
flaming sword to forbid and exclude every hope
of salvation to fallen man, is now engaged in our
behalf. For since it has pleased the Father to
charge sin upon his own Son, his wrath will turn
away from all who believe. The immense debt
is already paid, and justice will not exact it twice.
From henceforth God is not only gracious and
merciful, but ‡ just and faithful in the forgiveness
of sin, and declares his own righteousness in justifying the believer in Jesus.

(2.) The knowledge of God is made known in the
person of Christ, if we contemplate him as *reigning in glory*. He is no longer a man of sorrows,
oppressed and despised. He is now upon the
throne. In him the fulness of the Godhead dwells;
and from him, as light from the sun, the unsearchable riches of his goodness are communicated to
indigent, unworthy sinners. All the Divine perfections shine gloriously in him, as the God-man,
the Mediator, who is exalted above all conception
and praise, and doth according to his will in the

---

* 1 John iii. 1.   † Matth. xxvii. 42.   ‡ 1 John i. 9.

armies of heaven, and among the inhabitants of
the earth.

1st, Grace.   The great God is pleased to manifest himself in Christ, as the God of grace. This
grace is manifold, pardoning, converting, restoring,
persevering grace, bestowed upon the miserable
and worthless.   Grace finds the sinner in a hopeless, helpless state, sitting in darkness, and in
the shadow of death.   Grace pardons the guilt,
cleanses the pollution, and subdues the power of
sin.   Grace sustains the bruised reed, binds up
the broken heart, and cherishes the smoking flax
into a flame.   Grace restores the soul when wandering, revives it when fainting, heals it when
wounded, upholds it when ready to fall, teaches
it to fight, goes before it in the battle, and at last
makes it more than conqueror over all opposition,
and then bestows a crown of everlasting life. But
all this grace is established and displayed by
covenant in the man Christ Jesus, and without
respect to him as living, dying, rising, reigning,
and interceding in the behalf of sinners, would
never have been known.

2dly, Power.   The whole creation proclaims
that power belongs unto God.   But in nothing
will his power be more illustriously displayed
than in the wonders of redeeming love!   What
power is necessary to raise those who are spiritually dead in sin, to soften the heart of stone, to
bring light out of darkness, and order out of
confusion!   Wherever his Gospel is faithfully
preached, it is always confirmed by this accompanying power.   How quickly, how easily, did
he change Saul from a persecutor to an Apostle!
Again, how is his power illustrated by the care he

* Rom. iii. 26.

takes of all who believe in his name, affording to every one of them seasonable, suitable, and sufficient supplies in every time of need! So that his weak, helpless, and opposed people, are supported, strengthened, and enabled, to hold on, and to hold out, against all the united efforts of the world, sin, and Satan.

3dly, Bounty. How glorious is Jesus in his kingdom! Exalted beyond all conception and praise; wearing upon his vesture, and upon his thigh, the name that is above every name; and having all thrones, principalities, and powers, obedient to his will, and adoring at his feet. But all his riches and honours (so far as their capacities can receive) he condescends to share with his people. He owns their worthless names, he permits them to claim the most tender relation to him, and to call him their Brother, their Friend, and their Husband. Yea, he says concerning them, " To him that overcometh will I grant to sit with me in my throne, even as I also overcame, and am set down with my Father in his throne*." To him therefore we must look for the most astonishing and affecting display of the Divine bounty.

Thus the knowledge of God is revealed in the person of Christ by the word. But great and important as these truths are, we cannot receive and understand them merely by reading. The Lord Jesus therefore has favoured his church with a farther revelation. That is,

2. By his Spirit. This was one principal fruit of his ascension and intercession†. With the promise of this Spirit he cheered his disciples when sorrowing under the apprehension of his de-

---

* Rev. iii. 21.   † Acts ii. 33.

parture. " It is expedient for you that I go
away: for if I go not away, the Comforter will
not come to you ; but if I depart, I will send him
unto you*." The offices of the Holy Spirit are
various as our wants; he teaches, comforts, sanc-
tifies, and seals the children of God; but he effects
all these benefits by revealing the knowledge of
God, as manifested in Christ, reconciling the
world unto himself.

1. In convincing sinners of their lost estate,
which is absolutely necessary to their deliverance.
None will prize the Saviour but those who feel
their need of him.   Two things are necessary to
convince man of his lost condition by nature and
practice as a sinner,—the spirituality of the law,
and the sufferings of Christ : the one shews the
universality of sin, the other its demerit.   But
these can be truly discerned only by the light of
the Spirit of Christ.   While St. Paul (who was
never absolutely without the law) was ignorant of
the law's spirituality, " I was (says he) alive †."
I had so little knowledge, both of the law and of
myself, that I trusted to it for righteousness, and
vainly thought that I yielded it obedience, and
grounded my hopes of salvation thereon.   " But
when the commandment came," when the Spirit
explained and enforced it in its full extent, as
reaching to the very thoughts of the heart, and
requiring an obedience absolutely perfect " then
sin revived, and I died."   All my hopes vanished,
I saw every principle, affection, and action polluted, and the corruptions which I supposed were
tamed, broke forth with redoubled vigour.   Again;
though sin is declared to be displeasing to God
and destructive to man, by all the evils and

---

* John xvi. 7.   † Rom. vii. 9.

miseries with which the world is filled, and all the punishments which the righteous Judge of all the earth has inflicted on the account of it; yet the just demerit of sin is not to be learnt by the destruction of Sodom, or of the old world, but only from the sufferings of Christ, who has borne the curse for sinners. Nor is it sufficient to know historically that he did suffer, and how he suffered. Where these things are not known by the light of the Spirit, they are no more regarded than a worn-out tale. But where the Spirit of Christ reveals by the word, the nature, cause, and end of his sufferings, then sin appears exceedingly sinful. Nothing less than this can make the soul abhor it.

2. The Spirit produces faith in Jesus, as having once suffered, and being now mighty to save. His blood, his righteousness, his intercession, compassion, and power, are presented to the soul in a light which bears down the objections of guilt, unbelief, and Satan. Then the wounds made by sin are healed. Then old things pass away, all things become new, all difficulties are solved, and God is revealed experimentally to the soul, as holy, righteous, and true, in justifying the believer in Jesus.

3. Those whom the Spirit thus comforts, he also seals *. He impresses the image of Christ upon them. Such is the power of the views he gives them of his glory, that they are transformed into the resemblance of their Lord †. Though the first traces of this delineation are faint and indistinct in the sight of men, yet they are perfect *in kind*. The Spirit impresses feature for feature, and grace for grace ‡; and the chief thing he designs and effects by all his subsequent dispensa-

---

* Ephes. i. 13.   † 2 Cor. iii. 18.   ‡ John i. 16.

tions while the soul remains in the body, is to heighten and finish the heavenly signature. Together with this, and in the same degree, he seals and ratifies to their consciences an interest in all the promises of the Gospel; and, by infusing into their hearts the temper of children, he gives them confidence at the Throne of Grace, enables them to cry, Abba, Father, and bears witness with their spirits that they are born of God. Thus God is revealed not only to them, but in them; and they are made conformable to him in whom they believe, in all righteousness, goodness, and truth.

Let me once more address,

1. Poor mourning souls. Are you seeking to Jesus? You have good reason: you see he is a mighty Saviour. He is furnished with full authority, and came expressly on purpose to save such as you. He assures you, that none shall sincerely seek him in vain. Believe his word, and dismiss your fears. He has begun his good work, by revealing to you your misery, danger, and helplessness, by leading your thoughts to himself. He will not stop here; he will in due time accomplish his whole commission, by revealing to you that knowledge of God in which standeth your present peace and eternal life.

2. Careless sinners. How greatly will your guilt be aggravated if you receive this grace of God, the Gospel of salvation, in vain? Do not your hearts tremble when you think of meeting the Lord Jesus in glory? Have you an answer ready, when he shall ask you why you refused his instruction, and cast his words behind you? The light of truth has visited you, how long will you resist it? How long will Satan blind your eyes? To those who accept not his revelation of grace, he will be ere long revealed in flaming fire.

O humble yourselves before him, while the hope
of mercy is yet afforded; and pray for the Spirit
we have been speaking of, that you may be recovered out of the snare of the devil, and made
partakers of the knowledge and image of God.

3. Believers.   This subject is the food of your
souls.   You remember when you had dark, hard,
and uncomfortable thoughts of God; but you
have seen his glory in the person of Christ, you
have received not the spirit of the world, but the
Spirit of God*, that you may know the things
that are freely given you of God.   You were once
darkness, but now you are light in the Lord †.
Walk then as children of the light; remember
your calling, your privileges, your obligations,
your engagements.   Let these all animate you to
press forward, to endure the cross, to despise the
shame.   Let it not grieve you to suffer with Christ
here, for hereafter you shall reign with him.   The
hour is swiftly approaching, when you shall be
out of the reach of changes and sorrow for ever.
Then " thy sun shall no more go down; neither
shall thy moon withdraw itself: for the Lord
shall be thine everlasting light, and the days of
thy mourning shall be ended ‡."

* 1 Cor. ii. 12.   † Ephes. v. 8.   ‡ Isa. lx. 20.

SERMON IX.

LABOURING AND HEAVY LADEN SINNERS DESCRIBED.

MATTH. xi. 28.

Come unto me, all ye that labour, and are heavy laden, and I will give you rest.

WE read that, when David was withdrawn into the wilderness from the rage of Saul, every one that was in distress, or in debt, or discontented, gathered themselves unto him, and he became their captain*. This was a small honour in the judgment of Saul and his court, to be the head of a company of fugitives. Those who judge by outward appearances, and are governed by the maxims of worldly wisdom, cannot have much more honourable thoughts of the present state of Christ's mystical kingdom and subjects upon earth. The case of David was looked upon as desperate by those who, like Nabal†, lived at their ease. They did not know, or would not believe, the promise of God, that he should be king over Israel; and therefore they preferred the favour of Saul, whom God had rejected. In like manner, though our Lord Jesus Christ was a Divine person, invested with all authority, grace, and blessing, and declared the purpose of God concerning himself, and all who

---

* 1 Sam. xxii. 2.   † 1 Sam. xxv. 10.

should obey his voice, that he would be their King, and they should be his happy people; yet the most that heard him saw no excellence in him, or need of him : their portion and hearts were in this world, therefore they rejected him, and treated him as a blasphemer and a madman. A few, however, there were who felt their misery, and desired to venture upon his word. To these he gave the freest invitation. Those who accepted it, found his promise made good, and rejoiced in his light. Thus it is still ; he is no longer upon earth to call us ; but he has left these gracious words for an encouragement to all who need a Saviour. The greatest part of mankind, even in Christian countries, are too happy or too busy to regard him. They think they deserve some commendation, if they do not openly mock his messengers, disdain his message, and offer abuse to all who would press them to-day, while it is called to-day, to hear his voice. Even this treatment his servants must expect from many. But there are a few, like David's men, distressed in conscience, deeply in debt to the law of God, and discontented with the bondage of sin, who see and believe that He, and He only, is able to save them. To these labouring and heavy laden souls, he still says, "Come unto me, and I will give you rest." May his gracious Spirit put life and power into his own words, and into what he shall enable me to speak from them, that they may at this time receive a blessing and peace from his hands.

The text readily points out three inquiries.

I. Who are the persons here invited ?

II. What is it to come to Christ ?

III. What is implied in the promised rest ?

I. The persons are those who labour (the Greek

expresses toil with weariness *) and are heavy laden. This must, however, be limited to spiritual concerns; otherwise it will take in all mankind, even the most hardened and obstinate opposers of Christ and the Gospel. For let your consciences speak; you that account the yoke of Christ a heavy burden, and judge his people to be miserable and melancholy, are not you wearied and burdened in your own way? Surely you are often tired of your drudgery. Though you are so wedded and sold to your hard master, that you cannot break loose; though you are so mad as to be fond of your chains; yet you know, and I know (for I remember the gall and wormwood of that state), that you do not find all that pleasure in your wickedness which you pretend to. So much as you affect to despise hypocrisy, you are great hypocrites yourselves. You often laugh when you are not pleased, you roar out your boisterous mirth sometimes, when you are almost ready to roar with anguish and disquiet of spirit. You court the friendship of those whom in your hearts you despise; and though you would be thought to pay no regard at all to the word of God, there are seasons when (like him you serve) you believe and tremble. And, farther, what visible burdens do you bring upon yourselves? " The way of transgressors is hard *." Your follies multiply your troubles every day. Confusion and uneasiness in your families, waste of substance, loss of health and reputation, discord, strife, sorrow, and shame; these are the bitter fruits of your evil

---

* Compare Luke v. 5, John iv. 6, where the original word is the same.

† Prov. xiii. 15.

ways, which prey on your present hours, and make your future prospects darker every day. Surely you are weary and heavy laden beyond expression.

But this is not the case with others. You avoid gross vices; you have perhaps a form of godliness. The worst, you think, that can be said of you is, that you employ all your thoughts, and every means that will not bring you under the lash of the law, to heap up money, to join house to house, and field to field; or you spend your days in a thoughtless indolence, walk in the way of your own hearts, and look no farther; and here you will say you find pleasure, and insist on it that you are neither weary nor heavy laden. I might enlarge on your many disappointments, the vain fears which are inseparable from those who live without God in the world, and the trouble you find from disorderly, restless, and unsatisfied passions. But, to wave these things, I say briefly, that if you are not labouring and heavy laden, then it is plain that you are not the persons whom Christ here invites to partake of his rest. And though you can rest without him now, think, O think! what rest you will find without him hereafter? If you now say, Depart, he will then say, Depart. And who will smile upon you when he frowns? To whom will you then flee for help? or where will you leave your glory? O that it would please him to touch your hearts, that, as weary and heavy laden sinners, you might fall humbly at his feet, before his wrath burn like fire, and there be none to quench it!

But to proceed: let us,

1. Explain the terms, what it is to *labour* and be *heavy laden.*

2. Shew who are the persons that answer this description.

First, The persons are said to be,

1. Labouring, toiling, weary. This is not hard to be understood. Weariness proceeds either from labour or from weakness; and when these are united, when a person has much to do, or to bear, and but little strength, he will soon be weary. The case of some, however, is, that when they are tired, they can lay down their burden, or leave off their work. But these are not only labouring, fainting, weary, but,

2. Heavy laden likewise. As if a man had a burden, which he was unable to bear a single minute, so fastened upon him, that he could not by any means be freed from it ; but it must always press him down, night and day, abroad or at home, sleeping (if sleep in such a circumstance were possible) and waking. How would the poor creature be wearied ! How could you comfort or give him ease, unless you could rid him of his burden? How desirable would the prospect of liberty be to such a one! and how great his obligations and acknowledgments to his deliverer!

Secondly, This representation is an emblem of the distresses and burdens of those who seek to Jesus, that they may have rest for their souls ; nor can any truly seek him till they feel themselves in such a state. They may be generally comprised under three classes.

1. Awakened sinners. None but those who have felt it can conceive how sinners labour, toil, and faint, under their first convictions. They are burdened,

First, with the guilt of sin. This is a heavy load. When Jesus bore it, it made him sweat great drops of blood. It is true, he bore the weight of all his people's sins ; but the weight of one sin is sufficient to press us down, if God permits it to lie heavy upon us. I suppose the best of us can remember some action or incident or other in

our past lives which we would wish to forget if
we could.   Now, how would you be distressed to
have a person sounding in your ears, from morning
till night, and every day of your lives, that worst
thing that ever you did?   Would it not weary
you?   This is a faint image of the convinced sinner's state.   When conscience is truly awakened,
it acts this officious and troublesome part; but its
remonstrances are not confined to one sin, it renews the remembrance and the aggravations of
multitudes.   Nor is this the voice of a man, but
indeed of God, who speaks in and by the conscience.   The poor sinner hears and trembles;
then the complaint of Job is understood: "Thou
writest bitter things against me, and makest me
to possess the iniquities of my youth *."   Do you
wonder that such a one can no longer take pleasure in worldly things?   It is impossible, unless
you could silence this importunate voice, that
they can bear themselves at all.   Nay, often it is
so strong and urgent, gives them such a lively
sense of what sin is, and what it deserves from a
righteous God, that they are almost afraid or
ashamed to see any person that knows them.
They are ready to think, that people can read in
their faces what passes in their hearts, and almost
expect that the ground should open under their
feet.   O how wearisome is it to be continually
bowed down with such a burden as this!

Secondly, with the power of sin.   Perhaps they
were once in some measure at ease in this respect:
they saw others whom they supposed to be worse;
and therefore trusted in themselves that they were
righteous.   But convictions rouse and inflame our
sinful natures.   St. Paul exemplifies this by his

* Job xiii. 26.

own case before conversion : " I was without the law once; but when the commandment came, sin revived, and I died *." He never was strictly without the law; for he expected salvation by obeying it; but he was without the knowledge of its spirituality, demands, and sanction : and while he remained thus, he was alive, that is, his hope remained good, and he was satisfied with his obedience. But when the commandment came, when its extent, purity, and penalty, were brought home to his conscience, sin revived, and he died. He found all his pretensions to liberty, obedience, and comfort, were experimentally confuted by what he felt in himself. The more an awakened sinner strives against his corruptions, the more they seem to increase. This wearies him; for, besides the greatness of the toil itself, he finds himself weak, weak as water, weaker and weaker. And he is not only weary, but heavy laden; for this likewise is a burden which he cannot shake off. He sees that he cannot succeed; yet he dares not desist.

2. Those who are seeking salvation by the works of the law, are labouring and heavy laden, engaged in what is beyond their strength and baffles all their endeavours. This may appear, from what has been already said. It is a hard task to keep the whole law : and nothing less will either please God, if made the ground of justification, or satisfy the conscience that has any true light. Those declarations of the word, that "cursed is the man who continueth not in all things written in the book of the law to do them†," and, " whoso keepeth the whole law, and yet offendeth in one point, he is guilty of all‡," keep them in conti-

* Rom. vii. 9.   † Gal. iii. 10.   ‡ James ii. 10.

nual anxiety and servitude. The weakness of their flesh makes it impossible for the law to give a ground of hope; yet they cannot lay down their burden, but are compelled to renew the fruitless task. I speak not of mere formalists, who go through a round of external services, without meaning or design; but all who are in a measure sincere, find themselves still followed with a restless inquiry, "What lack I yet *?" Endless are the shifts and contrivances they are put to ; but all in vain : for, what makes it worse, they always add to this burden many inventions of their own, as though the demands of the law were too few.

3. Those who are under temptation. It is a hard and wearisome service to be in close conflict with the powers of darkness. The leading branches of this exercise are,

1st, When the soul is assaulted, and as it were filled with insufferable blasphemies. When Satan is permitted to shoot these fiery darts, none can express (not even those who have felt them) the amazement and confusion that fills the mind. For a person who has received a reverence for the name and attributes of God, to be haunted from morning to night, from day to day, with horrid imprecations, so strongly impressed, that he often starts and trembles with an apprehension, that he has certainly consented, and spoken them aloud with his lips; this is irksome and terrifying beyond description.

2dly, When the foundations of faith and experience are attacked. Many who have thought themselves grounded in the truth, who have hoped

* Matth. xix. 20.

that they had surely tasted that the Lord is gracious, and have in their first comforts been ready to say, " I shall never be moved *, thou, Lord, of thy goodness hast made my mountain so strong," have found themselves afterwards at their wit's end, when the enemy has been permitted to come in upon them like a flood†. One black cloud of temptation has blotted out all their comfortable evidences ; and they have been left to question, not only the justness of their own hopes, but even the first and most important principles on which their hopes were built.

3dly, When the hidden corruptions and abominations of the heart are stirred up. And perhaps there is no other way but this of coming to the knowledge of what our depraved natures are capable. Such things a season of temptation has discovered to some, which I believe no racks nor tortures could constrain them to disclose, though but to their dearest friend. This subject, therefore, will not bear a particular illustration. The Lord's people are not all acquainted with these depths of Satan. As people who live on shore have a variety of trials, dangers, and deliverances, yet know but little of the peculiar exercises of those who go down to the sea in ships ; so, in the present case, there are great waters‡, depths of temptation known comparatively to few. Those who are brought through them, have more to say of the wonders of God in the great deep than others ; and this is his design in permitting it, that they may know more of him, and more of themselves. But while they are under these trials, they are weary and heavy laden ; and this burden they must bear

---

* Psalm xxx. 6.　　† Isa. lix. 19.　　‡ Psalm cvii. 24.

till the Lord removes it. The help of men, books, and ordinances, is sought and tendered in vain, till his appointed hour of deliverance draws near.

These, therefore, convinced, striving, and tempted souls, are the persons to whom Jesus says, " Come to me, and I will give you rest." The purport of this gracious invitation we are to consider hereafter. In the mean time rejoice in this, Jesus has foreseen your cases, and provided accordingly. He says, *Come ;* that is, *believe,* as he himself expounds it : " He that cometh unto me shall never hunger ; and he that believeth on me shall never thirst *." See how his promises suit the state you are in.

1. Are you heavy laden with guilt ? The Gospel message is, " The blood of Jesus Christ his Son cleanseth us from all sin†."

2. Are you groaning under the power of in-dwelling sin ? Hear his gracious words : " I am the resurrection and the life : he that believeth in me, though he were dead, yet shall he live‡." And to the same purpose his Prophet : " He giveth power to the faint, and to them that have no might he increaseth strength §."

3. Are you striving in the fire to keep the law ? " Wherefore will you spend your money for that which is not bread, and your labour for that which satisfieth not ? " Forego the vain attempt. Is it not written, " Christ is the end of the law for righteousness to every one that believeth ‖ ? "

4. Are you in temptation ? He that says, " Come unto me," has been tempted himself **, and knows how to pity you. He has power over

---

* John vi. 35.   † 1 John i. 7.   ‡ John xi. 25.
§ Isa. xl. 29.   ‖ Rom. x. 4.   ** Heb. ii. 18.

your enemy, and can deliver you with a word *.
Did he not thus dispossess Satan in the days of
his humiliation? and if *then*, surely he is no less
able *now;* for since that time he has gloriously
triumphed over the powers of darkness †. And
as his arm is not shortened, neither is his ear
heavy; he has said, without exception, " Whosoever cometh unto me, I will in nowise cast out ‡;"
and thousands who have been in your distress,
have successively found that promise fulfilled,
" The God of peace shall bruise Satan under your
feet shortly §."

SERMON X.

OF COMING TO CHRIST.

MATTH. xi. 28.

*Come unto me, all ye that labour, and are heavy laden,
and I will give you rest.*

THE dispensation of the Gospel may be compared
to the cities of refuge in Israel. It was a privilege, an honour to the nation in general, that they
had such sanctuaries of Divine appointment; but
the real value of them was known to few. Those
only who found themselves in that case for which
they were provided, could rightly prize them.
In like manner, the Gospel of Christ is the highest
privilege and honour of which a professing nation
can boast; but it can be truly esteemed and un-

---

* Mark i. 27.   † Col. ii. 15.
‡ John vi. 37.   § Rom. xvi. 20; Zech. iii. 2.

derstood by none but weary and heavy laden souls, who have felt their misery by nature, are tired of the drudgery of sin, and have seen the curse of the broken law pursuing them, like the avenger of blood of old. This is the only consideration that keeps them from despair, that God has provided a remedy by the Gospel; and Jesus has said, " Come unto me, and I will give you rest." If they could receive the full comfort of these words, and heartily obey the call, their complaints would be at an end; but remaining ignorance, unbelief, and Satan, combine in various ways to keep them back. Some will say, " O that I could come! but, alas! I cannot." Others, " I fear I do not come aright."—Having, therefore, endeavoured to shew you the persons chiefly intended here, under the character of those who labour and are heavy laden, I proceed to consider,

II. What it is to come to Christ. I have observed in general, that it appears to have the same signification with *believing* in him. But, that we may understand it the more clearly, let us inquire,

1. How those to whom he personally spoke these words, in all probability, understood them.

2. How far their apprehensions of them are applicable and suitable to our circumstances.

3. Whether, as we have the same necessity, we have not likewise equal encouragement to come to him with those who were conversant with him upon earth.

1. It does not appear that those to whom our Lord spoke in person were so much perplexed as many are now, to know what *coming* or *believing* should mean: he seems to have been understood* both by friends and enemies. Many questioned

---

* John vi. 30, and xix. 36.

his authority and right to exact a dependence on
himself; but they seemed to be at no difficulty
about his meaning.   It certainly implied more
than a mere bodily coming into his presence.   He
was surrounded, and even followed, by multitudes, who never came to him in the sense of his
invitation.   To such, while standing about him,
he complained, " Ye will not come unto me, that
ye may have life*."   Therefore, if we consult
what is written of those who came to Jesus for
relief, and obtained it, we may conclude, that
coming to him implies,

First, A persuasion of his power, and of their
own need of his help. They knew that they wanted
relief, and conceived of him as an extraordinary
person empowered and able to succour them.
This persuasion of Christ's sufficiency and willingness was then, as it is now, afforded in different
degrees.   The centurion spoke with full assurance :
" Speak the word only, and my servant shall be
healed †."   The leper more dubiously : " Lord,
if thou wilt, thou canst make me clean ‡."   Another, in still fainter language : " If thou canst do
any thing, have compassion on us, and help us §."
The faith of this last was, as the man himself
acknowledged, mixed with much unbelief and
fear; yet Jesus did not despise the day of small
things : he pardoned his suspicions, confirmed
his fluctuating mind, granted him his request;
and his case is recorded as an instance how
graciously he accepts and cherishes the feeblest
efforts of true faith : " He will not break the
bruised reed, nor quench the smoking flax."

Secondly, An actual application. This evidenced their faith to be right.   They did not sit

---

| * John v. 40. | † Matth. viii. 8. |
| ‡ Matth. viii. 2. | § Mark ix. 22. |

content with having heard of him, but improved
it: they went to him, told him their cases, and
implored his compassion. Their faith prevailed
against all discouragements. In vain the multitude charged them to hold their peace*; knowing
that he only was able to relieve them, they cried
so much the more a great deal. Even when he
seemed to discover a great reserve†, they still
waited, and knew not how to depart without an
answer. Nor could a sense of unworthiness, fear,
or shame, keep them back ‡, when once they had
a strong persuasion of his power to save.

Thirdly, When he was sought to as a soul-
physician, as was the case with many whose bodily
diseases he healed, and with others who were not
sick, those who came to him continued with him,
and became his followers. They depended on
him for salvation, received him as their Lord and
Master, professed an obedience to his precepts,
accepted a share in his reproach, and renounced
every thing that was inconsistent with his will §.
Some had a more express and open call to this; as
Matthew, who was sitting at the receipt of custom,
regardless of Jesus, till he passed by him, and
said, " Follow me ∥." That word, accompanied
with the power of his love, won his heart, and
diverted him from worldly pursuits in an instant.
Others were more secretly drawn by his Spirit
and providence, as Nathaniel, and the weeping
penitent ** who silently washed his feet with her
tears; and this was the design and effect of many
of their bodily and family afflictions. The man
who was brought to be healed of the palsy ††,

---

* Mark x. 48.   † Matth. xv. 27.   ‡ Mark v. 37.
§ Luke ix. 23—61.   ∥ Matth. ix. 9.
** John i. 46; Luke vii. 38.   †† Mark ii. 5.

received the forgiveness of his sins; and the ruler, who first came to Jesus with no other view than to obtain the life of his son *, obtained much more than he asked or expected. The Lord afforded such an affecting sense of his power and goodness upon that occasion, that he from thenceforth believed, with all his house.

2. These things are applicable to us. Jesus is no longer visible upon earth; but he has promised his spiritual presence to abide with his word, ordinances, and people, to the end of time. Weary and heavy laden souls have now no need to take a long journey to seek him; for he is always near them, and in a spiritual manner, where his Gospel is preached. Poor and inconsiderable as we are in the judgment of the world, I trust we have a right to claim his promise †, and to believe that he is even now in the midst of us. Therefore come unto him; that is,

First, Raise your hearts, and breathe forth your complaints to him. Do you see your need of him? Be persuaded, and pray to him to assure you more strongly of his power and goodness. He is just such a Saviour as your circumstances require, as you yourself could wish for; and he is able to convince you in a moment that he is so. If he is pleased to cause a ray of his glory to break in upon your mind, your fears, and doubts, and griefs, would instantly give place.

Secondly, Persevere in this application to him. Set a high value upon these his public ordinances, and be constant in attending them. His eye is fixed upon us; his arm is revealed amongst us. I trust it is a time of his grace, and that every day we meet, he does something for one or another in

---

* John iv. 53.   † Matth. xviii. 20.

the assembly. He has a fixed time for every one whom he relieves. He knew how long the poor man had waited at the pool side*; and when his hour came, he spake and relieved him. So do you endeavour to be found in his way; and not here only, but in whatever he has made your duty. Read his word; be frequent in secret prayer. You will find many things arising from within and without to discourage and weary you in this course; but persist in it, and in good time you shall find rest for your souls. These are the means which the Lord has appointed you. Converse likewise at proper opportunities with his people; perhaps he may unexpectedly join you, as he did the two disciples when walking to Emmaus †, and cause your hearts to burn within you. Farther,

Thirdly, You are to follow him, to take up his cross, to make a profession of his name and Gospel, to bear contentedly a share in the reproach and scorn which is the usual lot of those who will live godly in Christ Jesus, in the midst of an unbelieving and perverse generation. You are not only to trust in him as a priest to atone for your sins, but to receive and obey him as your Teacher and your Lord. If you are truly weary and heavy laden, you will be glad to do this, and are crying to him to enable you : and you are likewise willing to forsake every thing that is inconsistent with his will and service. If you are desirous to come to Christ, it is not grievous to you to think of parting with your sinful pleasures and vain companions. Rather these are a part of the burden from which you long to be freed.

Come in this way, and you shall find rest for your souls. Are any of you thinking,—O that I

---

* John v. 6.   † Luke xxiv. 32.

could!—surely if I had seen him and heard him, I should have ventured; but now unbelief and fear keep me back. I observe, therefore,

3. That as we have no less need of Jesus than those of old who saw and conversed with him; so we have at least equal encouragement to come unto him. This I think will appear, if we consider that,

On the one hand, the bodily presence of Christ, considered in itself, had no peculiar or extraordinary influence upon those who saw him, but all was wrought by the power of his Spirit; the same Spirit which is promised to abide with his church for ever.

1st, Multitudes who saw and heard him were unmoved and unconvinced by all the wonders of his love. Though he spoke as never man spoke, and went about doing good, he was slighted, opposed, and hated, even to the death. And those who know the heart of man, and believe that the carnal mind is enmity against God, will allow it highly probable, that upon a supposition he should appear again in the same circumstance of humiliation, and to use the same authoritative freedom in vindicating the commands of God from the vain figments, traditions, and customs of men, he would meet with little better treatment, even in those countries which are called by his name, than he did from the proud, self-righteous, unbelieving Jews. We may warrantably suppose there were many more lepers, blind, &c. in the places where he resorted, than those who came to him to be healed.

2dly, Many of his professed disciples, even after they had followed him for a while, turned back and forsook him*. We have therefore the less

---

* John vi. 66.

reason to wonder when we see any give up the profession of the Gospel, and return to the world again. It was thus from the beginning ; and those who do so now, would have done so if they had lived then. His looks, his voice, his gesture, and even his discourses and miracles, could not engage a single person to cleave to him with full purpose of heart, unless he was likewise spiritually revealed to the eye of their faith, as the image of the invisible God, the brightness of the Father's glory, full of grace and truth.

3dly, Even his true disciples, who were constantly with him, to whom he had personally made the most express and endearing promises, and who sometimes thought themselves assured beyond the power of a doubt, yet could not maintain their confidence longer than his Spirit upheld them. To them expressly, though not to them exclusively, Jesus had said, " I go to prepare a place for you*," and I will come again to receive you to myself, that " where I am, there ye may be also †." When he had concluded that affectionate discourse, their doubts and fears were dissipated, and they could confidently say, " Now we believe ‡ ;" yet it was not long before they found his reply fulfilled : Jesus said unto them, " Do you now believe ! The hour is coming, when you shall be scattered every man to his own, and shall leave me alone §." Will not this instance convince you of your mistake, when you think you could depend more on a voice from heaven, than on the written word ? The Apostles had the strongest of assurance imaginable, the word of the Lord Jesus himself, face to face ; and

---

* John xiv. 2.   † John xiv. 3.
‡ John xvi. 30.   § John xvi. 32.

yet this would not support them, without renewed supplies of strength.

On the other hand, consider if the loss of his bodily presence is not more than made up to us.

1st. By the fuller manifestation of the Holy Spirit than was afforded before his ascension. The Holy Ghost was not then given in that clear and abundant measure as afterwards*, because Jesus was not yet glorified. While he was with them, he was their Comforter and Teacher; but he told them, " When I depart, I will send you another Comforter †," whose office and abode with you will be in many respects so much more advantageous, that on this account it is expedient for you that I go away.

2dly, By the greater number and variety of promises which we enjoy. We have not only the Scriptures of the Old Testament in common with them, but to us the ancient revelations of the will and love of God are enlarged, explained, applied, and confirmed by the super-addition of the new ‡.

3dly, By the experience of multitudes of all ages, people, and languages, who have gone before us, since their time : the cloud of witnesses to the truth and grace of God, the reality of eternal things, and the victorious power of faith, is now increased by the concurrent evidence of thousands and millions, who have overcome all opposition by the blood of the Lamb, and the word of his testimony.

4thly, By the proofs and living witnesses of his power and grace amongst ourselves. Are there not many, with whom you worship and converse from day to day, who can tell you they were even dead in trespasses and sins, but he has

---

* John vii. 39.   † John xiv. 16. and xvi. 7.   ‡ Eph. iii. 5.

quickened them. They were once, as you are, labouring and heavy laden, they waited for him long, had a share in such temptations and conflicts as you now feel, were often at a stand, and upon the point of concluding their case to be desperate, as you may think yours at present; but at length they were enabled to come unto him, and they have found rest. Every such instance should encourage you to gird up the loins of your minds, to be patient and hope to the end. As they have known your troubles, so shall you partake of their consolations in due time. What is it then should hinder you from coming to Jesus that you may find rest? What exceptions can your unbelief devise against the invitations, motives, and examples, which the Lord sets before you by his preached Gospel?

(1.) Is it a sense of your load which makes you say, you are not able? But consider that this is not a *work*, but a *rest*. Would a man plead, I am so heavy laden, that I cannot consent to part with my burden; so weary, that I am not able either to stand still or lie down, but must force myself farther? The greatness of your burden, so far from being an objection, is the very reason why you should instantly come to Christ, for he alone is able to release you.

(2.) But perhaps you think you do not come aright. I ask, how would you come? If you can come as a helpless unworthy sinner, without strength, without righteousness, without any hope but what arises from the worth, work, and word of Christ, this is to come aright. There is no other way of being accepted. Would you refresh and strengthen yourself, wash away your own sins, free yourself from your burden, and then come to him to do these things for you?

May the Lord help you to see the folly and un-
reasonableness of your unbelief.

I have observed already, that coming to Christ
signified more at first than merely to come into
his presence: so likewise it means more now than
to be found among his worshippers. Let none of
you be deceived with a form of godliness. Examine your religious profession by this test. Have
you laboured under a sense of your misery?
Have you known the burden of sin? Has Jesus
given you rest? Or are you earnestly seeking
to him for it? If you understand not the meaning of these questions, you are not yet in that
state to which the promises are made. And why
are you not labouring and heavy laden? Are you
not sinners? Has not the righteous God revealed
a law? Has he not guarded this law with the
sanction of a dreadful curse? Have you not
transgressed this holy law in thought, word, and
deed, times without number? If you have not,
why do you join in the public confession, and
call for mercy when the commandments are repeated? If you have, how will you escape the
penalty? How indeed, if you dare to neglect this
great salvation? The law condemns you already;
if you receive not the Gospel, you must perish
without remedy: for other name or means whereby
men can be saved there is none under heaven.
Once more you are warned of danger; once more
the refuge is set before you. We preach Jesus,
who came to seek and to save those who were
lost; Jesus who was wounded with whips, and
thorns, and nails, that his enemies might be
healed. Does not this thought affect you? Will
you slight his love, despise his blood, and crucify
him afresh? God forbid! Is there not some heart
now relenting, beginning to feel impressions of

fear, shame, and grief? Happy beginning! Obey
the voice of God now opening in your conscience!
Now is the time to pray; before, you knew not
what to pray for: but now you see you want the
blood of Christ, and the teaching of his Spirit.
"Ask, and you shall receive; and seek, and you
shall find." Take your warrant from my text; Jesus
has said, " Come unto me, and I will give you
rest." Let your hearts answer, " Take away our
iniquity, and receive us graciously: Behold, we
come unto thee, for thou art the Lord our God;
and in thee the fatherless, the helpless, the com-
fortless, find mercy."

SERMON XI.

THE PRESENT AND FUTURE REST OF BELIEVERS IN CHRIST.

MATTH. xi. 28.

*Come unto me, all ye that labour, and are heavy laden,
and I will give you rest.*

THE learned have a variety of arguments whereby
to prove the Scripture to be the word of God.
But though that kind of proof, which may be
brought in a way of reasoning and external evidence, is doubtless useful upon proper occasions;
yet, I apprehend, the chief and most satisfactory
argument to those who are capable of receiving
it, arises from the correspondence between the
subject matter of the Scripture, and the state of
an awakened mind. When the eyes of the understanding are opened, we begin to see every thing
around us, to be just so as the Scripture has described them. Then, and not till then, we per-

ceive, that what we read in the Bible concerning
the horrid evil of sin, the vileness of our fallen nature, the darkness and ignorance of those who know
not God, our own emptiness, and the impossibility
of finding relief and comfort from creatures, is exactly true. We cannot but apply the words of
the woman, and say, Come * and see a book that
has told me all that ever I did, the ground of all
my complaints, the true cause and nature of all
the evil I either see, hear, or feel, from day to day.
And as we find our disease precisely described,
so we perceive a suitableness in the proposed remedy. We need a Saviour, and he must be a
mighty one ; but though our wants and sins, our
fears and enemies, are great and numerous, we
are convinced that the character of Christ is sufficient to answer them all. We need a rest, a rest
which the world cannot give. Inquire where we
will among the creatures, experience brings in the
same answer from all, It is not in me. This again
confirms the word of God, which has forewarned
us that we shall meet nothing but disappointment
in such pursuits. But there is a spiritual rest
spoken of which we know to be the very thing we
want, and all our remaining solicitude is how to
attain it. From hence, as I said, we may assuredly
conclude, that the book which gives us such just
views of every thing that passes, must be given by
inspiration from Him who is the searcher of hearts.
This proof is equally plain and conclusive to all
capacities that are spiritually enlightened, and
such only are able to understand it. We are now
to speak,

III. Of this promised rest. And here two
things offer to our consideration.

* John iv. 29.

1. What this rest is ?
2. How it is obtained ?

1. The Greek word αναπαυσω expresses something more than rest, or a mere relaxation from toil; it denotes refreshment likewise. A person weary with long bearing a heavy burden, will need not only to have it removed, but likewise he wants food and refreshment, to restore his spirits, and to repair his wasted strength. Such is the rest of the Gospel. It not only puts a period to our fruitless labour, but it affords a sweet reviving cordial. There is not only peace, but joy in believing. Taken at large, we may consider it as two-fold.

1st, A present rest. So the Apostle speaks, " We who have believed do enter into rest *."

(1.) The common wearisome pursuit of the world is described, as " spending their money for that which is not bread, and their labour for that which satisfieth not†;" wandering from object to object in quest of good‡, but still mortified by incessant and repeated disappointments. We should pity a person whom we should see seeking some necessary thing day after day, which we knew was impossible to be found there. It is, however, the case with all till they come to Christ. Satisfaction is what they profess to aim at ; and they turn every stone (as we say), try every expedient, to meet with it, but in vain. It is only to be found in Him. When they come to him, their wishes are answered. This is exemplified by our Lord in the character of a merchant-man seeking goodly pearls§, who was still upon the inquiry till he had found one pearl of great price.

---

* Heb. iv. 3.
‡ Psalm iv. 6.

† Isa. lv. 2.
§ Matth. xiii. 46.

This answered and exceeded his desires: upon the discovery of this one, he rejoiced to forego all his former acquisitions, and to give up every other possession or purpose that he might obtain it.

(2.) I have spoken something concerning the wearisome exercise of a conscience burdened with guilt: but by coming to Jesus and believing in him, an end is put to this. When we are enabled to view our sins as laid upon Christ, that those who come are accepted in the Beloved, that there is no more condemnation, but pardon, reconciliation, and adoption, are the sure privileges of all who trust in him; O the sweet calm that immediately takes place in the soul! It is something more than deliverance. There is a pleasure more than answerable to the former pain, a comfort greater than all the trouble that went before it. Yea, the remembrance of the former bitterness greatly enhances the present pleasure. And the soul understands and experiences the meaning of those Scriptures, " When the Lord turned the captivity of Zion, then was our mouth filled with laughter, and our tongue with singing*." " In that day thou shalt say, O Lord, I will praise thee: though thou wast angry with me, thine anger is turned away, and thou comfortedst me. Behold, God is my salvation: I will trust, and not be afraid; for the Lord Jehovah is my strength and my song; he also is become my salvation†."

(3.) There is likewise a rest from the power of sin. In vain is this sought from resolutions and endeavours in our own strength. Even after we are spiritually disposed, and begin to understand the Gospel salvation, it is usually for a season rather a *fight* than a *rest*. But when we are brought

---

* Psalm cxxvi. 1, 2.   † Isa. xii. 1, 2.

nearer to Christ, and taught to live upon him as our sanctification, deriving all our strength and motives from him by faith, we obtain a comparative rest in this respect also. We find hard things become easy, and mountains sink into plains, by his power displayed in our behalf. Farther,

(4.) There is a rest from our own works. The believer is quite delivered from the law as a covenant, and owes it no longer service in that view. His obedience is gracious, cheerful, the effect of love; and therefore he is freed from those fears and burdens which once disturbed him in the way of duty. At first there was a secret, though un-allowed dependence on himself. When his frames were lively, he was strong, and thought he had something to trust to, but under a change (and changes will happen), he was at his wit's end. But there is a *promised*, and therefore an *attainable* rest in this respect; a liberty and power to repose on the finished work and unchangeable word of Christ; to follow him steadily through light and darkness; to glory in him *only* when our frames. are brightest; and to trust in him *assuredly* when we are at our lowest ebb.

Such is the *present rest;* in different degrees according to the proportion of faith, and capable of increase even in those who have attained most, so long as we remain in this imperfect state. But there is,

2dly, A future rest besides and beyond all that can be experienced here: " There remaineth yet a rest for the people of God*." Faint and imperfect are our most enlarged ideas of that glory which shall be revealed. " It does not yet appear what we shall be†." Who can describe or

---

* Heb. iv. 9.   † 1 John iii. 2.

conceive the happiness of heaven? The most we can clearly understand of it lies in negatives. It will be as unlike as possible to this wilderness of sin and sorrow where we are now confined. Here we are in a warfare, but then we shall enter into perfect rest.

(1.) A rest from all sin. There no unclean thing shall defile or disturb us for ever. We shall be free from sin in ourselves. This alone would be worth dying for. Indwelling sin is a burden under which even the redeemed of the Lord must groan, whilst they sojourn in the body; and those who are most spiritual are most deeply affected with shame, humiliation, and grief, on this account, because they have the clearest views of the holiness of God, the spirituality of the law, the love of Christ, and the deceitfulness of their own hearts. Therefore the Apostle Paul, though perhaps in grace and talents, in zeal and usefulness, distinguished above all the children of Adam, accounted himself the chief of sinners*, less than the least of all saints †, and cried out under the disparity he felt between what he was, and what he would be, " O wretched man that I am! who shall deliver me from the body of this death ‡?" But we shall not carry this burden beyond the grave. The hour of dissolution shall free us from the inbred enemies (the inseparable concomitants of this frail perishing nature) which now trouble us, and we shall see them no more for ever.

Again; we shall be free from all the displeasing effects of sin in others. Our hearts shall be no more pained, nor our ears wounded, nor our eyes filled with tears, by those evils which fill the earth. Now, like Lot in Sodom, we are grieved every

* 1 Tim. i. 15.   † Eph. iii. 8.   ‡ Rom. vii. 24.

day with the filthy conversation of the wicked*.
Who that has any love to the Lord Jesus, any spark
of true holiness, any sense of the worth of souls in
his heart, can see what passes amongst us without
trembling? How openly, daringly, almost universally, are the commandments of God broken,
his Gospel despised, his patience abused, and his
power defied. To be a silent spectator of these
things is sufficiently grievous; but if (as we are
in duty bound) we dare to stand as witnesses for
God in the midst of a crooked and perverse nation,
we find the spirit of the first-born Cain instantly
takes fire, and denounces war against all who
should presume to say, that we ought to obey and
fear God rather than men. Invectives and ill
treatment are the certain lot of all who openly
and consistently appear on the Lord's side; and
if they escape stripes and bonds, imprisonment
and death, it is to be ascribed to the restraints of
Divine Providence, and (as a means in our happy
land) to the temper of the laws, and to the cle-
mency of the powers under whom we live. These
things often constrain the believer to say, " O
that I had wings like a dove! for then would I
flee away and be at rest †." Let us not be weary
or faint in our minds; ere long this wish shall be
answered. A glorious rest awaits you, where sin
and sinners shall have no place, nor the alarms of
war be any more heard.

(2.) A rest from all outward afflictions, which,
though necessary, and, under the influence of
Divine grace, profitable, are grievous to bear; but
then they will be necessary no more. Where there
is no sin, there shall be no sorrow. Then, believers, God " shall wipe away all tears from your

---

* 2 Pet. ii. 7.   † Psalm lv. 6.

eyes; and there shall be no more death, neither
sorrow, nor crying, neither shall there be any
more pain: for the former things are passed
away*."

(3.) A rest from Satan's temptations. How
busy is this adversary of God and man, what
various arts, what surprising force, what constant
assiduity does he employ to insnare, distress, and
terrify those who by grace have escaped from his
servitude. He says, like Pharaoh of old, " I
will pursue, I will overtake, I will destroy †."
He follows them to the last stage of life, but he
can follow them no farther. The moment of their
departure out of the body shall place them beyond his reach for ever.

(4.) A rest from unsatisfied desires. Here, the
more we drink, the more we thirst: but there
our highest wishes shall be crowned and exceeded; we shall rest in full communion with Him
whom we love; we shall no more complain of interruptions and imperfections, of an absent God,
and a careless heart. Here, when we obtain a
little glimpse of his presence, when he brings us
into his banqueting-house, and spreads his banner
of love over us, how gladly would we remain in
such a desirable frame! How unwilling are we
to come out of the mount! But these pleasing
seasons are quickly ended, and often give place to
some sudden unexpected trial, which robs us of
all that sweetness in which we lately rejoiced.
But when we ascend the holy hill of God above,
we shall come down no more; we shall be for
ever with the Lord, never offend him, never be
separated from him again. We shall likewise rest
in full ‡ conformity to him. Here we find a mix-

---

* Rev. xxi. 4.   † Exod. xv. 9.   ‡ Ps. xvii. 15.

ture of evil in our best moments; when we approach nearest to him, we have the quickest sense
of our defilement, and how much we fall short in
every branch of duty, in every temper of our
hearts : but when we shall see Jesus as he is, we
shall be fully transformed into his image, and be
perfectly like him.

2. But how is this rest to be obtained? Blessed
be God, in that way which alone can render it
attainable by such unworthy indigent creatures.
If it was to be bought, we have nothing to offer
for it; if it was proposed as a reward of merit,
we can do nothing to deserve it. But Jesus has
said, I will *give* you rest. Our title to it cost him
dear; he purchased it for us with his own blood;
but to us it comes freely. Faith in his name puts
us in immediate possession of the first-fruits, the
earnest of this inheritance; and faith will lead us
powerfully and safely, through all hindrances
and enemies, to the full enjoyment of the whole.
Faith unites us to Christ; gives us an immediate
interest in all the benefits of his life, death, and
intercession; opens the way of communication
for all needful supplies of grace here, and insures
to us the accomplishment of all the Lord has
spoken to us of, in a state of glory. " He that
believeth shall be saved*;" saved in defiance of
all the opposition of earth and hell; saved, notwithstanding he is in himself unstable as water,
weak as a bruised reed, and helpless as infancy.
What Jesus will give, none can take away. Only
remember that it is a free gift. Receive it thankfully, and rejoice in the giver. Let him have all
the glory of his own undertaking. Renounce

* Mark xvi. 16.

every hope and every plea, but his promise and
mediation. Commit your souls to him, and then
fear nothing. " The eternal God is your refuge,
and underneath are the everlasting arms*." He
will fight your battles, heal your wounds, refresh
your fainting spirits, guide you by his counsel
while here, and at last receive you to himself.

May we not therefore say, Happy are the people
that are in such a case! Happy they, who have
been enabled to accept this gracious invitation,
who have already entered upon the rest of grace,
and have a well-grounded expectation that they
shall rest in glory! Believers, what should you
fear, or why complain? Look back to where the
Lord found you sleeping in sin, helpless and hopeless, yet insensible of your danger: look forward
to what he has provided for you, an inheritance
incorruptible, undefiled, and that fadeth not away;
a crown of life, a kingdom that cannot be shaken;
think of the love, the sufferings, the glory of him
to whom you owe these blessings; and let these
considerations animate you to run with patience †
and thankfulness the race that is set before you.

Happy likewise are you whose hearts are fixed
upon this rest, and this Saviour, though as yet
you are in heaviness through manifold temptations. The Lord will give you rest. Doubt it not,
he cannot deny himself; wait his hour; though
he seem to tarry long, yet maintain your confidence in his promise. Redouble your prayers,
cry mightily to him, he will not (as perhaps many
around you do) rebuke your importunity, and
charge you to hold your peace. Look at the
generations of old, and see, did ever any trust in

* Deut. xxxiii. 27.   † Heb. xii. 1.

the Lord and was confounded? or did any abide in his fear and was forsaken? or whom did he ever despise that called upon him?

And you who are yet strangers to rest are thus far happy, that you are still spared, and have the Gospel continued to you. The Lord is still waiting to be gracious: he says to all, Come unto me, and ye shall find rest for your souls. Do you not see this rest desirable? What rest, either here or hereafter, can you expect, if you remain in the service of sin? Why may not you obtain your liberty? You are no worse than others, either by nature or practice. Though you have been transgressors from the womb, you are not excluded, if you do not exclude yourselves: though your sinful habits and inclinations are exceedingly strong, he is able to subdue them. There is a power in his blood, and in that Spirit which he is exalted to bestow, sufficient to make the Ethiopian change his skin, and the leopard his spots *, to soften the hardest heart, and to pardon the most aggravated guilt, and to enable those to do good, who have been accustomed to do evil. Arise, he calleth you. O may he accompany the outward call of his word, with the efficacious power of his grace, that you may this instant obey his voice, and flee to him for refuge! Whither can you flee else? Who, but Jesus, can save you from the wrath to come? Be wise, and delay no longer. " But, if you will not hear, mine eye shall weep for you in secret places †." If you will not come to Jesus for life, you must die. If you are out of Christ, God is angry with you every day. The curse of his broken law lies heavy upon you, whether you are asleep or awake, abroad or at home, at the

* Jer. xiii. 23.　　　　　† Jer. xiii. 17.

market or in the church. The wrath of God is revealed against you; if you turn not, he will whet his sword*; he hath bent his bow, and made it ready; he hath prepared the instruments of death to smite you; he hath ordained the arrows of his vengeance against you: and can you, dare you, go on in your sins, and say, I shall have peace? O may you be wise in time! " It is a fearful thing to fall into the hands of the living God†." " Consider this, ye that forget him, lest he tear you in pieces, and there be none to deliver‡."

———

SERMON XII.

OF THE YOKE OF CHRIST.

Matth. xi. 29.

Take my yoke upon you, and learn of me; for I am meek and lowly in heart: and ye shall find rest unto your souls.

Those who are enabled to come unto Christ, not only experience a change of state, but of character, disposition, and practice. They are not only freed from condemnation, but they are made partakers of a divine nature. They are delivered from the slavery and yoke of Satan, and made willing in the day of the Lord's power, to accept and embrace his yoke, which is commended to us in the following verse, as easy and pleasant. Our Lord speaks of his service as a yoke or burden, because it is

* Ps. vii. 12.　　　† Heb. x. 31　　　‡ Ps. l. 22.

so esteemed by all who know him not. They account him a hard master, and think his service wearisome ; but those who have made the experiment, find it otherwise ; though, it must be confessed, it exposes to some difficulties, calls for the daily exercise of self-denial, and will not admit either of competition or composition with the world, nor can be pleasing to the unrenewed part of our nature. But the knowledge of his love, the hope of glory, and those seasonable refreshments with which he is pleased to favour those who come unto him, sweeten every bitter thing, and make them willing to bear his yoke, and to prefer it to all that the world accounts freedom.

Let us inquire,

I. What is meant by the yoke of Christ ?

II. The proper means by which we are enabled to take it upon us; that is, the believing consideration of him as our effectual Teacher and perfect Pattern.

III. The happy effect of bearing his yoke : we shall find rest to our souls.

I. The yoke of Christ, taken at large, includes all that dependence, obedience, and submission, which we owe him as our rightful Lord and gracious Redeemer. He has a double right to us : " He made us *." We are the creatures of his power : He gave us our being, with all our capacities and enjoyments. And farther, " He bought us†:" He pitied us in our low and fallen state, and gave his own life, his precious blood, to ransom us from that ruin and misery which was the just desert of our sins. There is good reason, therefore, that we should be his, and live and cleave to him in love alone ; that we should no longer live

Psalm c. 3.   † Acts xx. 28

to ourselves, but to him who died for us and rose again. In particular, we may consider,

1. The yoke of his profession. This is very pleasing to a gracious soul, so far as faith is in exercise. Far from being ashamed of the Gospel of Christ, he is ready and willing to tell to all who will hear, what God has done for his soul. Many young converts, in the first warmth of their affection, have more need of a bridle than of a spur in this concern. For want of prudence to time things rightly, and perhaps for want of more tenderness mixed with their zeal, they are apt to increase their own troubles, and sometimes, by pushing things too far, to obstruct the success of their well meant endeavours to convince others. But, though this is a fault, it is a fault on the right side, which time, experience, and observation, will correct. And though we are hasty enough to condemn the irregular overflowings of a heart deeply impressed with a sense of eternal things, I doubt not but the Lord, who owns and approves the main principle from whence they spring, beholds them with a far more favourable eye than he does the cold, cautious, temporizing conduct of some others, who value themselves upon their prudence. We should judge thus, if we had servants of our own. If we had one who was heartily and affectionately devoted to our interests, always ready to run by night or by day, refusing no danger or difficulty from a desire to please us, though sometimes through ignorance or inattention he should make a mistake, we should prefer him to another of greater knowledge and abilities, who was always slow and backward, and discovered at least as much care to save himself from inconveniences, as to promote our service. However, this warm zeal usually suffers abatement; we are flesh, as

well as spirit : and there are some circumstances
attending a profession of the Gospel, on the account of which it may be with propriety termed a
yoke to us, who have so many remaining evils
within us, and so many outward temptations to
call them forth. It will certainly stir up opposition from the world, and may probably break * in
upon our dearest connections, and threaten our
most necessary temporal interests.

2. The yoke of his precepts. These the gracious soul approves and delights in ; but still we
are renewed but in part. And when the commands of Christ stand in direct opposition to the
will of man, or call upon us to sacrifice a right
hand or a right eye ; though the Lord will surely
make those who depend upon him victorious at
the last, yet it will cost them a struggle; so that
when they are sensible how much they owe to his
power working in them, and enabling them to
overcome, they will at the same time have a lively
conviction of their own weakness. Abraham believed in God, and delighted to obey ; yet when
he was commanded to sacrifice his only son,
this was no easy trial of his sincerity and obedience : and all who are partakers of his faith are
exposed to meet, sooner or later, with some call
of duty, little less contrary to the dictates of flesh
and blood.

3. The yoke of his dispensations. This none
can bear as they ought, but those who come to
him. It is natural to us to repine, to fret and toss
like a wild bull in a net†, when we are under
afflictions. Believers likewise find their flesh
weak, when their spirits are willing ; yet they see
sufficient reasons for submission, and they know

---

* 2 Tim. iii. 12 ; Matth. x. 36. † Isa. li. 20.

where to apply for grace. Affliction is a touch-stone that discovers what spirit a man is of. The hypocrite may keep up a fair semblance of true piety, while all things go smooth and to his wish; but in sharp troubles the mask will drop off. Satan proceeded upon this maxim in his contest with Job; and the maxim is a truth, though Satan was mistaken in the application.

II. The appointed means by which sinners are enabled to bear this threefold yoke, is suggested in the words, " Learn of me, for I am meek and lowly." However amiable and desirable the dis-position I have described may appear, you will never acquire it by any strength, wisdom, or dili-gence of your own. Our Lord, to prevent you wearying yourselves with unsuccessful efforts and needless disappointments, has assured you before-hand, " Without me you can do nothing *." But here he graciously offers you the assistance you need. As if he had said, I know you are unable of yourselves, but I will help you. Be not afraid of the prospect, but consider what I *can* do. To my power all things are easy: I can make the crooked strait, and the rough smooth: I can sweetly engage your affections, subdue your wills, influence your practice, and deliver you from your sinful fears. Consider likewise what I *have* done: thousands, who, by nature, were as unskilful and impatient as yourselves, have been made willing in the day of my power.

Therefore, *Learn of me*. Be not afraid to come to me, for I am meek and lowly of heart. Great and mighty as I am, you may freely apply to me in every doubt and difficulty. Awakened souls, through a sense of guilt, and the power of unbe-

* John xv.

lief, are backward and unwilling to come to Christ. They think, Surely he will take no notice of such a one as I am. But observe how kind and condescending is his invitation; how graciously suited to engage our confidence. It was said of a Roman emperor, that those who durst speak to him were ignorant of his greatness; but those who durst not, were still more ignorant of his goodness. This was a false and impious compliment when applied to a sinful mortal; but it is justly applicable to Jesus, the King of kings, and Lord of lords. His glorious majesty may well fill our hearts with awe, and humble us into the dust before him; but his immense compassion, tenderness, and love, are revealed to overbalance our fears, to give us confidence to draw nigh to him, and an encouraging hope that he will draw nigh to us.

Again, *Learn of me.* I know the cause why these things appear so hard. It is owing to the pride and impatience of your hearts. To remedy this, take *me* for your example: I require nothing of you but what I have performed before you, and on your account; in the path I mark out for you, you may perceive my own footsteps all the way. This is a powerful argument, a sweet recommendation of the yoke of Christ, to those who love him, that he bore it himself. He is not like the Pharisees, whom he censured * on this very account, who bound heavy burdens, and grievous to be borne, and laid them on men's shoulders, but they themselves would not move them with one of their fingers.

1. Are you terrified with the difficulties attending your profession, disheartened by hard usage,

* Matth. xxiii. 4.

or too ready to shew resentment against those
who oppose you? Learn of Jesus, imitate and
admire his constancy : " consider him who endured
the contradiction of sinners against himself*."
Make a comparison (so the word imports) between
yourself and him, between the contradiction which
he endured, and that which you are called to
struggle with; then surely you will be ashamed to
complain. Admire and imitate his meekness :
when he was reviled, he reviled not again; when
he suffered, he threatened not; he wept for his
enemies, and prayed for his murderers. Let the
same mind be in you which was also in Christ
Jesus.

2. Do you find it hard to walk stedfastly in his
precepts, especially in some particular instances,
when the maxims of worldly prudence, and the
pleadings of flesh and blood are strongly against
you. Learn of Jesus. He pleased not himself †;
he considered not what was safe and easy, but
what was the will of his heavenly Father. Entreat him to strengthen you with strength in your
soul, that, as you bear the name of his disciples,
you may resemble him in every part of your conduct, and shine as lights in a dark and selfish
world, to the glory of his grace.

3. Are you tempted to repine at the dispensations of Divine Providence? Take Jesus for your
pattern. Did *he* say, when the unspeakable sufferings he was to endure for sinners were just
coming upon him, " The cup which my Father
has put into my hands, shall I not drink it‡ ? "
and shall we presume to have a will of our own ;
especially when we further reflect, that as his

---

* Heb. xii. 3. αναλογισασϑε.   † Rom. xv. 3.
‡ John xviii. 11.

sufferings were wholly on our account, so all our sufferings are by his appointment, and all designed by him to promote our best, that is, our spiritual and eternal welfare?

It is thus by looking to Jesus, that the believer is enlightened and strengthened, and grows in grace and sanctification, according to that passage of St. Paul, " We all with open face," or unvailed face, " beholding as in a glass the glory of the Lord, are changed into the same image, from glory to glory, as by the Spirit of the Lord*." The word of God is a glass in which the goodness and beauty of the Lord Jesus are manifested to the eye of faith by the light of the Holy Spirit. In this wonderful glass the whole object is not seen at once, but every view we take strengthens the sight to discover something not perceived before : and the prospect is not only affecting, but transforming ; by beholding we are gradually formed into the resemblance of Him whom we see, admire, and love.

All those whom Jesus thus teaches to bear his yoke, find his promise fulfilled : they obtain,

III. Rest to their souls. Those who are truly awakened want nothing to make them happy, but to be assured they have an interest in the Redeemer's love. Now this satisfaction is peculiar to those who take his yoke upon them, and are daily learning of him, and copying after him.

For, 1. This affords the best and most unshaken evidence that he has begun a good work of grace in our hearts: I say the best, *because* the most unshaken. Many are greatly perplexed to know if they are truly converted ; and are kept the longer in suspense, because they overlook the

* 2 Cor. iii. 18.

ordinary Scriptural method of confirmation.
They expect to know it by some extraordinary
sensation, suddenly impressed upon their minds.
But, besides that there have been many instances
in which this expected evidence has been coun-
terfeited, and a groundless confidence has been
placed in a delusion or vain imagination (to the
hurt of many, if not to their overthrow), even
when they are from the gracious Spirit of God,
they are, for the most part, transient; and when
a different frame takes place, the believer is often
tempted to question the reality of what went before. I think therefore the testimony of an enlightened conscience, judging by the word of
God, and deciding in our favour, that by his
grace we have been enabled to take up the yoke
of Christ, is in some respects a more satisfactory
evidence, that we are his, and that he is ours, than
if an angel was sent from heaven to tell us, that
our names are written in the book of life.

2. The promise of the peculiar manifestation of
his love*, is made and restrained to those who
walk in the path of obedience. If the discoveries
the Lord is pleased sometimes to make of himself to the soul, are not the proper and direct
evidences of a state of grace, they are, however,
exceedingly desirable. Whoever has tasted the
sweets of that water of life cannot but long for
repeated draughts. When he lifts up the light of
his countenance upon the soul, then is love, joy,
and peace within, however dark and distressing
things may be without. But this desirable presence can only be expected while we wear his
yoke, and walk in his steps. If we turn aside
into forbidden ways, if we decline or dishonour

* John xiv. 21.

the profession of his truth, we grieve the Holy Spirit, on whose communications our comforts are suspended; we give the enemies of our souls encouragement to assault us, and are in danger of falling from one wickedness to another, without the power of withstanding either the greatest or the smallest temptation, till the Lord is pleased to turn again to our assistance. In such a situation there can be no rest. " But he that walketh uprightly, walketh surely*," and findeth rest.

And true rest is no otherwise to be obtained. Those of you who refuse the yoke of Christ, well know in yourselves that you are far from rest. Your experience agrees with this declaration in the prophet: " There is no peace, saith my God, to the wicked †." In what respect will you dare to pretend that you have the advantage of those who bear the yoke of Christ ?

We allow the profession of the Gospel is subject to inconveniences; but surely not so many as you meet with who are ashamed, or afraid, or averse, to maintain it. If those who are of your household are not your foes on this account, yet we can see how it fares with those who live without the fear of God. How many, and how sharp, are your trials from disobedient children, unfaithful servants, false friendships, ungoverned passions, and unsatisfied desires! Nor do you save any thing in point of character, not even with those by whom you are most desirous to be esteemed. They cannot indeed reproach you with being a believer; but may they not, do they not, reproach and despise you for being a drunkard, or a liar, or a miser, or an extortioner? And is this more

---

* Prov. x. 9.　　　　† Isa. lvii. 21.

honourable than to suffer shame for the cause of Christ?

Do the precepts of Christ seem hard? Certainly not so hard as that miserable bondage you are under to Satan, the god of this world, who works in you, and rules over you, at his will. He will not allow you to listen to the united remonstrances of conscience, health, interest, and reputation. But you are hurried on in his drudgery, constrained, like a mill-horse, to toil in the same tedious round of folly and sin; though you are aware of the consequenses and wages before-hand. How absurd is it for you to boast of your freedom, while you are compelled to rush into present misery, and to dare your eternal ruin, with your eyes open!

And how greatly are you to be pitied under the many unavoidable afflictions of life, to which you are equally liable with the servants of Christ! When your idols are torn from you, when sickness seizes you, or death stares you in the face, then how do you fret and pine! how many are your fears and alarms! Then you are your own tormentors. The review of the past affords you only shame and regret. If you look forward to the future, you are filled with foreboding fears and distressing apprehensions; you are weary of living, and afraid to die.

Why then will you continue thus, when Jesus says, " Come unto me, that you may have rest?" O may he incline your hearts this day to hear his voice! Have you been hardened in your evil ways, by a suspicion that your case is desperate, that it is now too late, and that he whom you have so often rejected will refuse you mercy? Beware of such a thought: " There is forgiveness with him*." " Behold now is the accepted time; behold now is the day of salvation." He is gracious to pardon, and mighty to save; only acknowledge your offences, and throw down the arms of your rebellion. He is mighty to save, and no less willing than able. As yet there is hope; but who can tell how long his patience may bear with you? Take notice of that awful denunciation, " He that, being often reproved, hardeneth his neck, shall suddenly be destroyed, and that without remedy†." If you seek him to-day, with all your hearts, you shall find him. But who can answer for to-morrow? To-morrow, or to-night your souls may be required of you; or, if your lives are spared, you may be given up to judicial and incurable hardness of heart. If his Spirit should cease from striving with you, you are lost for ever.

SERMON XIII.

THE SERVICE OF CHRIST EASY AND PLEASANT TO HIS PEOPLE.

MATTH. xi. 30.

For my yoke is easy, and my burden is light.

THIS verse alone, if seriously attended to, might convince multitudes, that though they bear the name of Christians, and are found among the Lord's worshipping people, they are as yet entire

---

* Psalm cxxx. 4.   † Prov. xxix. 1.

strangers to the religion of the Gospel. Can it be supposed, that our Lord would give a false character of his yoke? If not, how can any dream that they are his followers, while they account a life of communion with God, and entire devotedness to his service, to be dull and burdensome? Those, however, who have made the happy trial, find it to be such a burden as wings are to a bird. Far from complaining of it, they are convinced that there is no real pleasure attainable in any other way.

What the yoke of Christ is, we have already considered. It includes the profession of his Gospel, obedience to his precepts, and submission to his *will*, under every dispensation. But since it is confessed, that a sinful nature, and a sinful world, will bring many difficulties, trials, and temptations upon all who walk in this way, it may be worth our while to inquire more particularly, what there is in the yoke of Christ that overpowers all these hardships, and makes such amends for every suffering, that, upon the whole, every believer will subscribe to this as a sure and experienced truth, that the " yoke is easy and the burden light."

I. Those who bear the yoke of Christ, act from a principle which makes all things easy. This is love. It is said of Jacob, that when he served a hard master seven years for Rachel, they seemed to him but a few days, for the love which he bare her *. And many of you find it easy to do much for your parents, children, and friends, because you love them. But there is no love like that which a redeemed sinner bears to Him who " has loved him, and washed him from his sins " in his own blood."—Farther, love produces the greatest

* Gen. xxix. 20.

effects, when it is mutual. We are willing to do and suffer much to gain the affection of a person we regard, though we are not sure of success; but when the affection is reciprocal, it adds strength to every motive. Now the believer does not love at uncertainties: he knows that Jesus loved him first, loved him when he was in a state of enmity *; and that nothing but the manifestation and power of this love could have taught his hard unfeeling heart to love *him* whom he never saw †. This love, therefore, affords two sweet and powerful encouragements in service.

1. A cordial desire to please. Love does what it can, and is only sorry that it can do no more. We seldom think much, as I have hinted already, either of time, pains, or expense, when the heart is warmly engaged. The world, who understand not this heart-felt spring of true religion, think it strange that the believer will not run into the same excess of riot with them ‡. They wonder what pleasure he can find in secret prayer, in reading and hearing the word of God; they pity the poor man who has such a melancholy turn, and gravely advise him not to carry things too far. But the believer can give them a short answer in the Apostle's words: "The love of Christ constrains me §." His ruling passion is the same with theirs, which makes his pursuit no less uniform and abiding; but the objects are as different as light from darkness. They love the perishing pleasures of sin, the mammon of unrighteousness, and the praise of men; but he loves Jesus.

2. A pleasing assurance of acceptance. If we

---

* 1 John iv. 19. † 1 Pet. i. 8.

‡ 1 Pet. iv. 4. § 2 Cor. v. 14.

know not whether what we do will be favourably received or not, it makes us remiss and indifferent. But this animates the Lord's people; they are assured that he will not overlook the smallest services or sufferings they are engaged in for his sake. He has told them in his word, " that if they give but a cup of cold water in his name, and on his account, he will accept and acknowledge it, as if it were done immediately to himself*."

II. It makes a service still more easy and pleasant, if, besides acting from a principle of love, the service itself is agreeable to our inclination. Esau would probably have done any thing to please his father, in hopes of obtaining the blessing; but no command could please him more than to be sent for venison, because he was a cunning hunter, and his pleasure lay that way†. Now the believer has received a new nature; so that the Lord's commandments are not grievous to him; but he delights in them with his whole heart. It is true he groans under remaining corruptions; and this is properly his burden, not the service of Christ, which he approves and delights in, but because he can serve him no better. So far as faith is in exercise, he rejoices in every part of the yoke of Christ. He glories in the profession of his name. He has made Moses's choice; he prefers even the reproach of Christ, to all the honours of the world ‡, and has a measure of that spirit by which the Apostles were enabled to rejoice that they were counted worthy to suffer shame for his name §. He heartily consents to the precepts; he esteems them as a light to his

* Mark ix. 41.   † Gen. xxv. 27. and xxvii. 3.
‡ Heb. xi. 26.   § Acts v. 41.

feet; he makes them his meditation all the day. Nothing pleases him more than to find an increasing victory over the hindrances to his obedience; and the time of his greatest grief is, when, through infirmity or the prevalence of temptation, he is seduced to neglect or transgress them, though in the smallest instance, and in what does not pass under human observation. Even afflictions, though not joyous in themselves, but grievous, are cheerfully submitted to, because the Lord has appointed them, and is pleased to account them a filling up of his sufferings *.

III. In other cases, even when there is a principle of love, and the service not disagreeable in itself, yet weakness may render it wearisome or impracticable. Though, perhaps, you would willingly take a long journey to serve a friend; yet if you are sick or lame, what could you do? But the yoke of Christ is light and easy in this respect, that there is a sufficiency of strength provided for the performance. This consideration makes every difficulty vanish; for though these should be increased tenfold, yet if strength be increased in an equal proportion, it amounts to the same thing. What is hard or impossible to a child, is easy to a man; what is hard to flesh and blood, is easy to faith and grace. The believer, though weak in himself, is strong in the Lord: the power on which he depends is not in his own keeping, but it is treasured up in the *covenant* of grace, or in the Lord Jesus, in whom all fulness dwells, and is always to be obtained by prayer. Every child of God is interested in the blessing of Asher: "Thy shoes shall be iron and brass; and as thy day is,

* Col. i. 24.

so shall thy strength be*." By the *day* may be understood,

1. A day of service. Whatever the Lord appoints for us to do, if we depend upon him in the use of appointed means, he will certainly qualify, furnish, and strengthen us, for the accomplishment of it. If David is called out to meet Goliath, though he is but a stripling†, and the other a practised warrior from his youth, he shall not be disheartened or overcome, but be made a conqueror, though all appearances are against him. If we are in the path of duty, and if our help and hope is in the name of the Lord, we may confidently expect that he will uphold us, however faint and enfeebled we may seem to be to ourselves or others.

2. A day of suffering. If, like Daniel and his companions, we should be threatened with lions and flames, we may confidently commit our way to God; he can control the fire, and stop the lions' mouths ‡. While all things are in his hands, whose we are, and whom we serve, why should we fear that they will act beyond the bounds of his permission, or that he will permit them to do any thing which it is not his purpose to over-rule to our advantage? Such considerations in the hour of need, seasonably impressed by his good Spirit, together with a trust in his promises, shall inspire us with new strength to meet the greatest danger undismayed; and, with regard to trials immediately from his own gracious hand, he will so adjust them, in number, season, weight, and measure, to the ability he communicates, that we

---

* Deut. xxxiii. 25. † 1 Sam. xvii. 37.
‡ Dan. iii. 16. and vi. 22; Ps. xci. 13; 2 Tim. iv. 17.

both shall be able to bear, and also find a way made for us to escape. With such assurances, we may boldly say, "The Lord is on my side, I will not fear what man (or Satan) can do unto me."

IV. There is farther a consideration of profit and advantage, which makes the yoke of Christ easy. The believing soul is not mercenary. He loves his Master and his service; yet it is impossible to serve God for nought. In the keeping of his commandments there is a reward, though not of debt, yet of grace *; a great and sure reward, respecting both the life that now is and that which is to come.

Those who sincerely take up the yoke of Christ, and cleave to him in love alone, have ample compensation in the present life for all that their profession can cost them. They enjoy the testimony of a good conscience, which is compared to a continual feast. St. Paul, though a champion for free grace, and determined to glory only in the excellency of the knowledge of Christ Jesus †, expresses a high and just value for this privilege; and that it afforded comfort, yea joy, in a time of trouble. Superadded to this, they are often favoured with the peculiar consolations of the Holy Spirit, which, though slightly esteemed by those who know them not, satisfy the soul as with marrow and fatness, and can change the voice of mourning into songs of praise in an instant ‡. And though these are not their constant food, yet they have real and habitual communion with God, from day to day, in his ordinances and providences. They live in his presence; they converse with him, and he with them; their good things are doubly pleasing, because they receive them

* Ps. xix. 11. † 2 Cor. i. 12. ‡ Ps. lxiii. 3.

from his hand : and this thought likewise sweetens every bitter cup of affliction which he prepares for their good. The mutual intercourse and communion his people have with each other, is likewise a considerable branch of their present reward. How pleasing is it, when, speaking to each other in his name, they take sweet counsel together, they are confirmed in his way, by finding how their experiences answer as face to face in a glass; and he causes their hearts to burn within them, while they are freely declaring what he has done for their souls. Lastly, they are happy in a comfortable expectation of a better world ; and when the appointed time comes, death will put an end to all their troubles ; and then shall they fully know and possess the future reward which the Lord has prepared and reserved for them that love him.

This is briefly summed up by the Apostle: They shall be absent from the body *, and all its inseparable evils; sin and sorrow, want, pain, and every distress that belongs to this mortal state, shall affect them no more; and they shall be present with the Lord, whom they love. Then they shall see his face without a cloud, and share his joy without abatement or interruption; and all this shall be for ever. When they are made pillars of the New Jerusalem †, they shall come out no more. The prospect of this makes them rejoice under all their tribulations; for they know whereto they lead, and how they will end. " These light and momentary afflictions are working for them a far more exceeding and eternal weight of glory ‡."

From these things I hope it will appear, that

---

* 2 Cor. v. 8. † Rev. iii. 12; 1 Thess. iv. 17.
‡ 2 Cor. iv. 17.

the yoke of Christ is easy. His people serve him because they love him; they love his ways: he is their strength; he comforts them now, and will be their portion for ever.

But perhaps some, whom I would willingly comfort, will rather be discouraged by this representation, and say, Alas! if it is thus, I am yet to seek: my love is so faint, my strength so feeble, my consolations so small, my obedience so imperfect, that I am afraid I have not known the easy yoke of Christ. There are therefore some other things to be taken into the account, and which are no just exception to the character our Lord here gives of his yoke.

1. The entrance, or first application of the mind to the yoke or profession of the Gospel, is seldom pleasant. Though the work of grace leads to love, it usually begins in fear. On this point we have already spoken at large. It is no pleasing state to be weary and heavy laden, to see ourselves obnoxious to a curse, and unable to escape; yet by apprehensions of this kind the soul is prepared to embrace the yoke of Christ; and none but those who have experienced the misery of a fallen state will be truly desirous of the Gospel rest.

2. The progress is gradual. The first dawnings of grace in the heart are faint, and hardly perceptible: hence the whole process is compared to things that are very inconsiderable in their first principles. The kingdom of heaven is like a grain of mustard-seed, which is hid and lost in the earth for a season; it is like leaven, which when cast into meal may be concealed and unnoticed for a while, but by degrees diffuses its influence through the whole mass *. It is like the corn which springs

* Matth. xiii. 31—33.

up and comes forward night and day, a man knows
not how *.   The growth in the Christian life being
thus low and indistinct, many, who aim to ascer-
tain their interest rather by the degree than the
reality of grace, are often dejected to find their
attainments proceed no faster.   It is indeed a
humbling consideration, but ought not to rob us
of the comfort arising from a believing view of
what Jesus has completely wrought out for us,
and of what he has promised he will infallibly
perform in us, in his own good time.   A deliverance from this poring into ourselves for the
grounds of our hope, is a part, a considerable
part, of the rest to which he invites us.

3. The difficulties attendant on that course of
faith and obedience, which is included in taking
his yoke upon us, are many and great.   While
we sojourn in a wilderness state, and in a sinful
nature, there will be fightings without, and fears
within.   It is the appointed and necessary rule of
our profession, that " through much tribulation
we must enter into the kingdom of God †."   All
who are against him will be against us for his sake ;
and the evil heart of unbelief will shew itself in a
variety of forms, as it is acted upon by various
impressions, from the things of sense and the
powers of darkness.   But these troubles do not
arise from the spiritual yoke of Christ, but from
our present situation and circumstances, and
shall therefore shortly cease for ever.   His ways
are ways of pleasantness ; though we are sure to
meet with perplexity and uneasiness, so far and
so often as we wander from them into our own
crooked paths.   But,

4. The end is sure.   " He that endureth to the

end shall be saved * ; " and all who are in his way have his promise and power engaged in their behalf, that they shall certainly endure, that he will so lead, guide, support, and strengthen them, that neither life nor death, nor things present, nor things to come, shall separate them from his love †. Your complaints and fears, therefore, are no proof that you are not right. Go on in his name. Trust in him in whom you have believed, and be nothing terrified by your adversaries. The longer you wear the yoke, the easier you will find it.

Let each one examine himself by what has been offered. If you have not a principle of true love to Christ, and a prevailing desire to live in all holy obedience to his will, you are no Christian ; and though you may begin warmly, you will not be able to hold out, but your profession will wither away for want of root and moisture. Nor is it difficult to know whether you love him or no: if you do, you have seen your need of him, and abhor yourself in dust and ashes.

From hence likewise you may discern the difference between the religion of the Gospel, and the formal worship that many are contented with, in which the heart has no place. Remember that " God is a spirit ‡ ; " and unless you love him, you cannot possibly please him. If a man would give all the substance of his house for love, it would be utterly contemned. His commandments likewise are spiritual; they extend beyond the surface of the outward conduct, and take cognisance even of the retired thoughts and intents of the heart. Many sins may be avoided, and many duties performed, from motives and principles which not being derived from his word,

* Matth. x. 22.　　† Rom. viii. 38.　　‡ John iv. 24.

or conformable to it, are therefore sinful in themselves, and make every thing proceeding from
them defective and displeasing in his sight.   If
you are attempting to serve him by your own natural strength and understanding, be assured that
you have not yet taken up the yoke of Christ: if
you had, you would find it answerable to the character he has given of it, for his word is truth.
But your constrained obedience you know in
yourselves, far from being easy and light, is a
heavy burden which you would be glad to cast
off if you durst.   You serve the Lord as a slave
serves a hard master ; not with a willing mind, but
of necessity, and from a dread of punishment.
But in vain do you draw near to him with your
lips while your heart is far from him.   Therefore
spend no longer your labour for that which is not
bread, but come to Jesus that you may find rest
for your souls.   He is able to take away your
heart of stone, and give you a heart of flesh, to
put a new spirit in you that shall delight in his
yoke, to give you strength and ability for every
part of your duty, and to make you a willing
people in the day of his power.

Believers, rejoice in your security.   The Lord
has given you a never-dying principle of love, and
provided for you a never-failing supply of grace.
These will bear you up through all your journey,
and at last bring you safely home to the mansions
provided for you in your Father's house.   Then
shall you praise him world without end.

SERMON XIV.

BELIEVERS CAUTIONED AGAINST MISCONDUCT IN THEIR PROFESSION.

ROM. xiv. 16.

Let not then your good be evil spoken of.

THE immediate occasion of this caution you may learn from the context. It has pleased God from the beginning, to permit his people, who all agree in the great and essential truths of the Gospel, to differ in some things of less importance. This difference of judgment gives room for the mutual exercise of patience, forbearance, tenderness, and charity; but at the same time too often affords opportunity for the remaining corruptions of the heart to discover and exert themselves. The Jewish converts were for some time attached to the observance of that distinction in meats and drinks which had been enjoined by the law of Moses: the Gentiles, on the contrary, claimed a right to be free from this yoke, as a part of the liberty which they had received from Christ. The Apostle does not in this place blame either party with respect to their own judgment and practice; but he reproves them for censuring and despising each other: and he especially reproves those who understood their liberty in the Gospel, for not being prudent in the use of it, but rather forward to provoke and offend their weaker brethren. He confirms their liberty, but admonishes them not to abuse it, either by urging others to act against their consciences, or by treating them with contempt, because they had not entirely laid aside those scruples and prejudices to which they had been long accustomed. " Let not your good be evil spoken of." Be thankful for your liberty, but do not bring it into discredit and reproach, by acting in an unbecoming spirit towards others.

The instruction in my text, understood in this sense, has always been applicable and seasonable in the Christian church, and perhaps never more so than in our land, and in our times. While believers in Jesus, who are led by the same Spirit into the same fundamental truths, and stand in the most endeared relation to each other through their common Head, place such undue stress upon lesser incidental differences, and are professed partisans for the little interests of systems, denominations, and leaders, *love*, the grand characteristic of their profession, is hardly discernible; they censure and grieve each other, retard the success of the cause which they would all be thought to have most at heart, and open the mouths of the adversaries to revile that which they understood not. The prevalence of this wrong disposition calls for the admonition in my text. Be thankful for your privileges; you not only claim the rights of private judgment and liberty of conscience, as men and as Christians, but as Britons you possess them. " Let not then your good be evil spoken of;" allow to others that freedom which you expect yourselves; and if you do not suppose yourselves infallible, suppose it possible that some may be as near to the Lord as yourselves, who cannot agree with you in every sentiment you have adopted.

But this direction may be taken in a much more general sense. It behoves all who honour the Lord Jesus Christ to be careful in every part

of their conduct, that they do not give occasion
for their good to be evil spoken of. To make the
subject as sujtable as I can to the different states
and characters of all present, I shall,

I. Inquire, what is the believer's good.

II. Explain and apply the advice here given,
" Let not your good be evil spoken of."

I. All mankind have something near at heart,
on which their dependence is placed, and wherein
they find their chief pleasure. This (whatever it
is) is their good; and according to the object in
which they delight is their proper character. By
nature the world and worldly things are the
highest good we seek after; and these, in one
view or other, as tempers and situations vary, are
pursued with unwearied earnestness. Riches,
honours, sinful pleasures, are the poor things in
view, when the unrenewed heart cries out, in its
eager pursuits, " Who will shew us any good*?"
If your strongest desires tend this way, your
good will not be evil spoken of by many. Men
will praise you when you do well for yourself:
you are not therefore concerned in the admonition
in my text. Only take notice what the word of
God declares of your good, and of you for ac-
counting it so. Your good is vanity, your fruit is
vexation of spirit, and you who set your hearts on
such a good as the objects of sense can furnish,
are adjudged " enemies to God†." You yourselves will speak evil of this good when you come
to die, if you die in your sins. Then you will see
a propriety in Esau's words to your own case,
" Behold, I am at the point to die, and what
profit shall this birth-right do to me‡?"

As the world is the good of the unconverted, so
a covenant God in Christ is the good and portion

---

* Ps. iv. 6. † James iv. 4. ‡ Gen. xxv. 32.

of all who are called by his grace. They are ever
looking to the obedience and blood of Jesus, applied by the Spirit of grace, as the sole foundation
of their hope and comfort. God is their good in
the highest sense, and every thing else is good so
far as it leads to him, and assists them in maintaining communion with him. In this view we
may mention several particulars, each of which
they account their good, because the means of enjoying and glorifying their God.

1. The Gospel, that gracious revelation by
which they have been taught to know themselves,
and to know Jesus, is their good. All the doctrines, precepts, and promises, contained in the
Scripture, are a very precious treasure, in which
they rejoice more than those who find great spoil.
Each of them can say, in the language of the
Psalmist, "The law of thy mouth is dearer to me
than thousands of gold and silver. How sweet
are thy words unto my taste, yea sweeter than
honey to my mouth! O how I love thy law! It
is my meditation all the day long*." By this
word they are enlightened, quickened, warned,
comforted, and supported : therefore it is the joy
and rejoicing of their hearts, and more than their
necessary food †.

2. The ordinances make a part of their good.
A famine of the word of the Lord would distress
them greatly; and if they may but have frequent
opportunities of this kind, and meet with his gracious presence in them, they can be content to be
without many things which the men' of this world
highly value. When beset with many straits, and
surrounded with troubles, they can find refreshment in the Lord's assurance by the prophet,
" And though the Lord give you the bread of ad-

* Psal. cxix. 72, 97, 103.   † Job xxiii. 12.

versity, and the water of affliction, yet shall not thy teachers be removed into a corner any more; but thine eyes shall see thy teachers*." If this promise is fulfilled to them, they will not greatly complain of the bread of adversity, although that is joined with it. But, on the contrary, they find it a hard trial to be deprived of lively ordinances and faithful ministers, however advantageous and pleasing their situation may be in temporal things, because these are not their good.

3. They account their profession a part of their good. They esteem it a high privilege to bear the name of Christ, though it exposes them to the reproach of the world. They account it a great and important trust to have the honour of the Gospel committed to them, and in some measure dependent on their conduct. When they are in their right minds, they would rather die than be guilty of any thing that might bring it into discredit. Wilfully they cannot, they dare not do it; but through ignorance and infirmity they are prone to mistake, and therefore need, and are desirous to observe, the caution in my text.

4. Their experiences are their good, their choice pearls; I mean the inward dealings of the Lord with their souls,—the proofs they have had of his power and wisdom in bringing them thus far safely on their way to his kingdom, the discoveries he has given them of the deceitfulness of their own hearts, the manifestations of his grace, love, and nearness to them, notwithstanding all their unworthiness and unfaithfulness. Some of these experiences have cost them dear, have cost them many a pang, trouble, and conflict: yet they would not be without them to avoid all that they have suffered; and

* Isa. xxx. 20.

they are content to suffer on, if by any means they may increase this precious stock. They delight to recollect how low they were brought, how wonderfully delivered, what answers they have been favoured with to their poor prayers; and from hence to collect the all-sufficiency and goodness of him to whom they have fled for refuge, and to derive arguments wherewith to combat their unbelieving fears in time to come. Thus far their experiences are their good; not as the foundation of their hope, or the source of their comfort,— for these their whole reliance is on the obedience and blood of Jesus the Saviour,—but as evidences that they have neither " followed cunningly devised fables, nor received the grace of God in vain *."

Thus much in general, that you may all have something whereby to try your spirits, and to know whether you have embraced the good of the Lord's chosen people†. If your good does not lie in such things as I have mentioned, you have no durable riches, nothing but what you must soon leave behind you. Can you be content to be stripped of all, and to enter poor, naked, and friendless, into an eternal world? O that you would take our Lord's advice. He might command, for he has all authority; but he says, " I counsel thee to buy of me gold tried in the fire, that thou mayest be rich; and white raiment, that thou mayest be clothed, and that the shame of thy nakedness do not appear; and anoint thine eyes with eye-salve, that thou mayest see‡."

But some there are whose hearts can go along with me in what I have said. The great God himself is your good. His word and ordinances,

---

* 2 Pet. i. 16; 2 Cor. vi. 1.   † Ps. cvi. 4, 5.   ‡ Rev. iii. 18.

your profession of his name, and your experience
of his goodness, are what you rejoice in. To you
then I address the rest of my discourse. " Let
not your good be evil spoken of."

I am,

II. To explain and apply this advice. The
words plainly imply two things.

1. That there are many ready enough to speak
evil of your good ; many who despise the Gospel,
and you for professing it : they watch for your
halting, and will be glad of the smallest occasion
to expose you. The world, that loves its own,
will make allowances in other cases. Indiscre-
tions, and even vices, will be charged to the account of human infirmity, and the amiable name
of candour shall be employed to conceal or pal-
liate such things as can by no means be justified.
But if you are a professed believer in Jesus, you
must not expect this candour will be extended to
you ; rather all your words and actions will be
sifted, your mistakes exaggerated ; and if any
part of your conduct will bear a double construction, it will generally be viewed in the most unfa-
vourable light. Nay, even when there is no just
occasion afforded, falsehoods and calumnies have
been and will be industriously propagated against
the servants of Christ *. That it must be so, we
are often warned by Scripture, and it is abundantly confirmed by experience.

2. That though it is impossible wholly to stop
the mouths of evil-minded men, yet they would
not be able to talk so fast if the imprudence of believers did not too often afford them advantage.
That such occasions should sometimes be given

* Matth. v. 11.

by those whose hearts and aims are in the main
sincere, will not be thought strange to any person
who is acquainted with the true state of human
nature. Through inadvertence, want of experience, errors of judgment, sudden and unexpected
temptations, and other evils inseparable from our
present situation, persons, whose chief desire is to
adorn the doctrine of their God and Saviour in all
things, may and do in some instances cause their
good to be evil spoken of. It is, however, our
bounden duty, as we regard the honour of God
and his truth, to endeavour as much as possible
to " cut off occasion from them * " that seek occasion in this respect.

In order to this, let us inquire, what are the
most common objections which are made against
the Gospel preaching and profession, not only by
malicious enemies, but sometimes by persons who
discover no very bad intention, but are partly
imposed upon by the misrepresentations of others,
and partly stumbled by the faults of professors?

1st, It is objected, that our doctrine lays no
sufficient stress upon good works. We dare not
indeed recommend them out of their proper place,
or propose them as the ground of our acceptance
with God. But I hope none who attend here will
dare to say, that they are not frequently reminded, that " without holiness no man shall see
the Lord†." However, the world will judge more
by what they *see* in *you*, than by what they *hear*
from *me*. Be upon your guard, therefore, lest by
any instances of a trifling, foolish, unkind, or
unjust conduct, you let your good be evil spoken
of. It will not be a sufficient apology to say,

---

* 2 Cor. xi. 12 ; 1 Pet. ii. 12.   † Heb. xii. 14.

that your principles do not allow of these things, if those who know you can charge them upon your practice.

2dly, It is farther objected, that the evangelical system is a scheme chiefly made up of notions and subtle distinctions, and opens a door to a thousand disputes. This is one unhappy consequence of our many divisions and subdivisions, and the heat with which they are contended for by their respective partisans. Let this engage you to avoid a disputing contentious spirit. " Be swift to hear, slow to speak *;" and when a reason is asked " of the hope that is in you †," give your answers with meekness and fear, lest you cause your good to be evil spoken of.

3dly, It is likewise a very common objection, that a usual effect of this doctrine is to make people idle and careless with regard to the necessary concerns and business of life. Indeed I should not be unwilling to plead with candid and fair reasoners, in behalf of young converts, on this point. At first setting out, the change is so great, their views of eternal things so strong and affecting, that, considering human infirmity, it can hardly be otherwise but that the attention will be almost entirely taken up with them for a season. While a sense of unpardoned sin is fixed upon the conscience, and a person now duly aware of the uncertainty of life is in suspense about the greatest of all concerns, and knows not how or whither he shall be able to flee from the wrath to come, it is no wonder if this solicitude should in a great measure swallow up his thoughts, and leave him but little either leisure or ability to attend to other concerns, which, however proper in their respec-

* James i. 19.   † 1 Pet. iii. 15.

tive places, are confessedly, in comparison of this, of little or no importance. In like manner, the removal of this burden is usually accompanied with such a lively sense of the wisdom, love, power, and grace of God, revealed in Christ Jesus by the Gospel, as may for a little while almost overpower and extinguish the apprehension of inferior things. But if this indifference about common duties continues very long, or is indulged to an extreme, it gives great and just offence. It causes the ways of truth to be evil spoken of; and we hardly know what to say, but this, That the fault is not owing to the Gospel, but to the neglect of what the Gospel teaches and enjoins. This is no new inconvenience; the Apostles observed and reproved it in their day. There were such mistaken persons among the Thessalonians, who supposed or pretended that the Gospel exempted them from labour. Of these he says, " Now them that are such we exhort and command, that with quietness they work, and eat their own bread;" and farther directs, " that if any would not work, neither should he eat *." The Sabbath is the Lord's; and the same command which forbids us to do any work then, requires us to labour on the other six days. " Let not your good be evil spoken of." Be faithful to your trust, diligent in your business, do every thing heartily as unto the Lord, and not unto men. Give no one just cause to say, that since you have become religious, you care not (as the phrase is) which end goes foremost; for this would be to put a stumbling-block in their way, and to increase their prejudices against the truth.

4thly, Once more; The Gospel doctrine is

---

* 2 Thess. iii. 10—12.

charged with weakening the bands of natural and social relation ; that it makes children and servants heady, high-minded, and disobedient, so that they presently think themselves wiser than all about them, and are obstinately bent to have their own wills. This objection will indeed cleave to the Gospel so long as the spirit of the world and the Spirit of God are opposite to each other. For cases will inevitably arise where we must either displease God or man, and then we ought not to hesitate a moment. But professors should take care to be assured that there is such a necessity before they act against lawful authority ; and especially when the point in dispute lies between children and parents. For though we ought to disobey and forsake father and mother when God's commands require it ; yet next, under God, parents are above all to be honoured, consulted, and obeyed : and the excepted cases are not near so numerous as persons in the warmth of their first zeal are apt to suppose. The enemy suits his temptations to our occasions ; and it is no uncommon thing to be drawn to act violently in our own spirits, while we imagine we are striving in the cause of God and truth.

In short, we are directed to examine ourselves, and others are allowed to examine us by our fruits. The people of the world are not proper judges of spiritual experiences, but they can judge tolerably right of tempers and actions. Some will watch you out of ill-will, and some will observe you for information. If they hear you have begun to make a religious profession, they will take notice to see if you are the better for it. They will observe you not only in the church, but in the shop and in the house : and if they perceive you are all of a piece, steady, quiet, humble, diligent, who

knows but this may be a means in the hand of God
to win upon them, and to give them a more favourable regard to the means which have wrought
so effectually on you? But, on the contrary, if
you are imprudent, rash, and careless, if you
either conform to the world, or neglect your acknowledged duty in it, you will cause your good
to be evil spoken of, bring difficulties upon yourselves, and put it out of your own power to be
useful to others. Pray therefore for wisdom and
grace, to make your light so shine before men,
that they, seeing your good works, may glorify
your Father who is in heaven. This is the great
design and proper effect of the Gospel, when
rightly understood. For as it is the grace of God
alone which bringeth salvation, so this grace not
only enlightens the understanding, but purifies the
heart, regulates the conduct, works by love, and
overcomes the world. It effectually teaches and
enforces (what the best schemes of morality and
philosophy have always failed in) the denial of all
ungodliness and worldly lusts *; and by the motives it displays, and the strength it communicates,
enables the true Christian to adorn his character
in every relation, and to fill up the whole circle
of duty as it respects himself, his neighbour, and
the God with whom he has to do. It teaches to
live soberly, righteously, and godly; to avoid
whatsoever is contrary to the purity of the Gospel;
to practice moderation in the use even of lawful
things ; and to do unto others as we would they
should do unto us. It teaches the rich to be
humble and bountiful, the poor to be thankful and
resigned. It teaches superiors to be kind, inferiors
to be faithful. Husbands and wives, parents and

---

* Titus ii. 11—15.

children, masters and servants, magistrates and
people, are all instructed by this grace to a conduct answerable to their high calling, and to the
common relation they stand in to Him who has
loved them and washed them from their sins in his
own blood. For the morality of the Gospel has
a nobler spring, and a more extensive scope,
than the ties of social life. Their sobriety and
righteousness are not substituted in the place of
vital godliness, but are the fruits derived from it.
The grace of God teaches them to live godly, to
delight in him, to obey him, to do every thing for
his sake, as under his eye, and to be continually
governed by a sense of his unspeakable love manifested in his Son, and " an expectation of the
blessed hope set before us, the glorious appearance
of the great God, and our Saviour Jesus Christ,
who gave himself for us, that, by his blood and
Spirit, he might redeem us from all iniquity, and
purify unto himself a peculiar people zealous of
good works." Labour to shew that you are not
only called by his name, but have sat at his feet,
and drank of his spirit; and if, after all, unreasonable and wicked men will speak evil of you,
and your good, be not moved at it, but pity and
pray for them. When He shall return to vindicate
your cause, and wipe away your reproach, then
" every cloud shall be removed, and the righteous
shall shine forth as the sun in the kingdom of
their Father*."

* Matth. xiii. 43

SERMON XV.

THE EXTENT AND SANCTION OF THE THIRD COMMANDMENT.

EXOD. xx. 7.

Thou shalt not take the name of the Lord thy God in vain; for the Lord will not hold him guiltless that taketh his name in vain.

THE foundation of true religion is laid in a right knowledge of God and ourselves. How deficient we are in each of these, how far fallen from original righteousness, is strongly implied in this prohibition; which would be wholly unnecessary, if we were not wholly sunk in stupidity and wickedness. That such worms as we should be liable to trifle with the Divine Majesty, whose presence fills the heaven and the earth, before whom the angels hide their faces; that such frail dependent creatures have need to be cautioned, that we do not profane the name of the God in whom we live, and move, and have our being, is a striking proof of our depravity; and that we can dare to break through this caution, and slight the awful threatening with which it is closed, is a dreadful aggravation of our guilt.

These words when first spoken to the Israelites, were delivered in flames and thunder. The mountain shook; the people trembled; and even Moses, who had been honoured with peculiar freedom of access to God, was constrained to cry, " I exceed-

ingly fear and quake*." Such a scene, or rather
infinitely more dreadful, shall hereafter take place,
" when the Lord himself shall again descend from
heaven with a shout, with the voice of the archangel, and the trump of God; when he shall be
revealed in flaming fire, to take vengeance of all
who know him not, and obey not his Gospel †."
" Then shall sinners be convinced not only of their
ungodly deeds, but of all their hard speeches which
they have spoken against him ‡ ; " and they shall
know the full meaning of that terrible exception
which I have read, " that the Lord will not hold
him guiltless that taketh his name in vain."

The terms of my text require little explanation.
The name of God is in every one's mouth, upon
one occasion or other, in places where his revealed
will is known. In a more eminent and peculiar
sense his name is discovered to his believing people
in Christ Jesus the Lord; those who know the
name § of God in Christ will put their trust in him;
they dare not, they cannot blaspheme that holy
name by which they are called. But I shall take
it more extensively here; for though but few understand the name of God in an evangelical and saving
sense, there is not a person in this assembly but
knows and makes mention of his holy name, so far
as to render them transgressors of this commandment. To take his name in vain, is to use it falsely
or profanely; inconsiderately, without due reverence; or unprofitably, and without a suitable necessity. The sanction, " The Lord will not hold
him guiltless," has indeed a meaning and emphasis
beyond what is expressed. Similar forms of speak-

* Heb. xii. 21.   † 1 Thess. iv. 16 ; 2 Thess. i. 8.
‡ Jude 15.   § Psal. ix. 10.

ing are frequent in Scripture; as, "The Lord will not spare that man *;" that is, he will punish him to the utmost; for it is immediately added, "All the curses of this book shall come upon him." Again, "He spared not the angels;" that is, he shewed them no mercy, as the following words declare : "He spared not the old world ;" he visited them with utter destruction, and swept them all away with a flood. So, "he will not hold him guiltless," implies two things : 1st, That the Lord God has appointed a day to call sinners to an account for their words, as well as their actions. 2dly, That whatever shall become of others, those who have presumed to take his name in vain have their doom already determined. Whoever escapes, they shall surely be punished; whomever he acquits, he will certainly condemn them.

As the import of the expressions is not difficult, so likewise it will be far more easy than agreeable to point out some of the many ways in which this commandment is customarily and carelessly broken. The law in general, and each particular precept, is *spiritual* †, and perhaps this will be found of a more extensive signification than some of you are aware. The delightful theme of a minister of the Gospel is to preach Jesus Christ, and him crucified ; to open the treasures of Divine mercy, and to shew the grace, freeness, and security of the promises; to raise up them that fall, to strengthen those that stand ; " to support the weak, to comfort the feeble-minded ; to preach deliverance to the captives, and the opening of the prison to them that are bound ‡." But these sub-

---

* Deut. xxix. 20 ; 2 Pet. ii. 4, 5.   † Rom. vii. 14.
‡ 1 Thess. v. 14 ; Luke iv. 18.

jects do not comprise *the whole* of our message; and, in general, we find, that the full soul loatheth the honey-comb *; and multitudes, through ignorance of the spirituality and purity of God's holy law, and a partial judgment of their own hearts, can neither see the beauty nor the necessity of the Gospel-salvation. We are therefore constrained frequently to insist on far less pleasing subjects, to lift up our voices like a trumpet †, to demand a general attention while we attempt to shew our hearers their transgressions and their sins, that we may thereby make the doctrine of the cross of Christ welcome and desirable. It is painful to the patient, and, without doubt, unpleasing to the humane artist, to probe a deep and dangerous wound; but necessity commands, and, without it, a complete and lasting cure is not to be expected.

1. The first and most direct way in which the name of God is taken in vain, is by *perjury;* that is, when he is expressly appealed to in confirmation of what is false, or when engagements are made as in his name and presence, which are not *strictly and literally complied with.* I need not take up your time in proving, that this is a *sin of a deep dye* in itself, and attended with peculiar aggravations under the light of the Gospel; and I wish it was more difficult to prove the frequency of it in our land; but this likewise is as obvious as the light. I have sometimes met with a random assertion, that though we are wicked enough, we are not worse than other countries. In other things I am content to wave the parallel; but with respect to the sin of perjury, I fear we are much worse than any nation now under the sun,

---

* Prov. xxvii. 7.   † Isa. lviii. 1.

perhaps worse than any that the sun ever saw. I am afraid, there are *more* and *more daring* instances of this wickedness amongst us than in all the rest of Europe. By an unhappy kind of necessity it is interwoven, as it were, with the very constitution of the body politic, and diffuses itself like a deadly contagion amongst all orders and ranks of people. Oaths are so excessively multiplied, and so generally neglected, that it is equally difficult and rare for a person to engage through a course of years, in any kind of employment, either civil or commercial (O that it stopped even here!) without being insnared. Some are so *expressed*, that it is morally impossible to comply with them ; others so *circumstanced*, that they are usually swallowed without the remotest design of regarding them, either in whole or in part. If here and there a few make conscience of their engagements, and are desirous to perform to the Lord their oaths*, or decline taking such as open a door either to honour or profit, so strong is the torrent the other way, that it is well if they escape the charge of singularity and preciseness. Though wickedness of every kind too much abounds amongst us, *perjury* is perhaps peculiarly and eminently our *national sin:* and I tremble to think it is so ; for it gives too just a ground to fear the approach of national judgments. Surely all who have any regard for the honour of God, any sense of the worth of souls, will pray earnestly that this iniquity may not be our ruin, but that the Lord would be pleased to inspire and succeed the most proper means for the removal, or at least the mitigation, of this evil. This would be an event

* Matth. v. 33.

worthy to stand in the annals of the happy times and auspicious government under which we live.

2. And though the matter of an oath be strictly true, yet if it is not transacted with a serious acknowledgment and homage of that Divine Being to whom appeal is made; such an oath, however lawful and necessary it may be in itself, is, with regard to all such thoughtless triflers, no better than taking the name of God in vain. It cannot but be grievous to every serious mind, to observe the little reverence and solemnity, or rather the total want of common decency, which too frequently prevails among us in this respect; so that sometimes it is not easy to say, whether those who *tender* the oath, or those who *take* it, seem *least in earnest*. Without doubt this indifference may be assigned as one cause of the increase and prevalence of perjury. If those who are authorized to require or receive those solemn appeals, were themselves impressed with a due reverence of the awful majesty of God, and were solicitous to inspire all who came before them with the same sentiments, and would remind them (those especially who appear very positive and unguarded) of the impiety and danger of swearing falsely, it is possible many mischiefs would be prevented. Some persons would probably tremble and start back from the first temptation to this wickedness; and others might be deterred from persisting in it, who, for want of such admonitions and examples, and because they never saw any solemnity observed, precipitately rush upon this enormous evil, and are at length given up to a dreadful habit of wilful and corrupt perjury.

3. If an oath lawful and necessary in itself may thus become criminal through inconsideration,

what shall we say of the throng of profane swearers, who wound our ears, and pollute our language, by a horrid mixture of execrations and blasphemies, in their common conversation? " Their throats are an open sepulchre; their mouths are full of cursing and bitterness, the poison of asps is under their lips*." This I have to say from the word of God, that the Lord will not hold them guiltless. In vain their thoughtless plea, that they mean no harm: in vain their presumptuous comparison of themselves with others, as though these were trivial escapes that did not affect the peace of society. If these were small sins singly, their frequency would swell to a vast amount: but is it indeed a small sin to rush against the thick bosses of God's buckler, and to despise so terrible a threatening as this? Surely " the plague shall never depart from the house of the swearer." " As he clothed himself with cursing like as with his garment; so it shall enter into his bowels like water, and like oil into his bones †." A habit of swearing is a sure sign, not only of an unsanctified heart, but of a conscience hardened, and, as it were, seared with a hot iron, callous, and quite insensible.

4. Some persons who scruple expressly to mention the name of God, accustom themselves to swear by his creatures, by the heavens, by the light, or by their own souls, &c. But that this likewise is a direct violation of the law, and exposes to the same penalties, we are assured by Him who best knew how to explain his own commands. Our Lord determines this point in his sermon on the mount, so as not to leave the possibility of a doubt. " I say unto you, Swear not

---

* Rom. iii. 13, 14.　　　† Psalm cix. 17, 18.

at all; neither by heaven, for it is God's throne:
nor by the earth, for it is his footstool——Neither
shalt thou swear by thy head, because thou canst
not make one hair thereof white or black*."
" And whoso shall swear by the temple, sweareth
by it, and by him that dwelleth therein; and he
that shall swear by heaven, sweareth by the
throne of God, and by him that sitteth thereon†."
" But let your communication be Yea, yea; Nay,
nay; for whatsoever is more than these cometh of
evil." This decision evidently condemns, not only
what is usually deemed swearing, but the whole
multitude of idle expletives, whether fashionable
or vulgar, which have the force of affirmations in
common discourse. Will any who live in a Christian country, and have the Bible at hand, think to
plead ignorance of these things in the great day?

5. If I should stop here, some of you would applaud yourselves, and perhaps not be displeased
with me for what I have hitherto said. Some
who think themselves clear thus far, will join
with me in saying, " Because of swearing, the
land mourns‡." But are there no other ways of
taking the name of God in vain? Yes; many do
it as often as they pray; and it is easily proved
against numbers who join in our established worship. Let each one consider with what dispositions and desires they have engaged in the
service they have already gone through this day.
Our mouths have all spoken the same things; but
have they been the language of our hearts? In
the confession, we acknowledge that " there is no
health in us," and speak as if we were true peni-
tents. In the communion service, we cry for

* Matth. v. 34—36.   † Matth. xxiii. 21, 22.
‡ Jer. xxiii. 10.

mercy as miserable sinners; we pray that the
" thoughts of our hearts may be cleansed by the
inspiration of God's Holy Spirit; that we may
perfectly love him, and worthily magnify his holy
name;" and for this we appeal to God, as " to
whom all hearts are open, all desires known, and
from whom no secrets are hid." More than a few
of you, at certain seasons, publicly declare, that
"the remembrance of your sins is grievous, and the
burden of them is intolerable." Now, what apprehensions can such of you have of God as can
dare to use this solemn language, when your
hearts mean no such thing? Is not this to take
his name in vain in the grossest manner? Is it
not plain that you think him altogether such a
one as yourselves*; nay, more easily imposed
upon, and more safely to be trifled with, than a
fallible mortal? Strange it is to think, that many
can, not only content themselves with this lip-
service, but make it the meritorious ground of
their hope, and conceit themselves religious because they come so often to church to mock the
Power that made them! But hardly can any
wickedness be imagined more daring, and more
dreadfully provoking to the Most High, than such
a religion as this. To all such worshippers I may
address those striking words of St. Peter to
Ananias, " Thou hast not lied unto men but
unto God †."

6. The whole lives of those who live in the allowed practice of known sin, under the profession
of the Christian name, may be considered as
one continual breach of this command. In all
you say and do, you blaspheme that holy name
by which you are called; and still more so, if you

---

* Psalm l. 21. † Acts v. 4.

are declared friends and favourers of evangelical
preaching. By your means, "the ways of truth
are evil spoken of*." You give occasion to those
offences of which it is said, "Wo to that man by
whom the offence cometh." You injure the cause
of Christ, stumble the weak in the faith, grieve
the hearts of all who love the Lord, and make his
enemies rejoice. "Better it would have been for
you never to have known the ways of righteousness †," than thus to abuse your knowledge. You
are now mingled with his faithful servants, as the
chaff is blended with the wheat upon the floor ‡.
But, "behold, the Judge standeth at the door."
His fan is in his hand ; he will thoroughly purge
his floor ; and when he gathers the wheat into his
garner, you will be consumed, like stubble, before
the flame of his indignation. What distress and
remorse will seize your hearts, when you shall
see them with whom you have often joined in the
same ordinances, that have lived with you under
the same roof, dined at the same table, perhaps
slept in the same bed, when you shall see them
received into the kingdom, and you yourselves
excluded, and thrust into that utter darkness §,
where there is weeping and wailing, and gnashing
of teeth, for ever!

From this subject we may observe, by way of
inference and application,

1. The truth and propriety of that Scripture,
"We know that what things soever the law saith,
it saith to them that are under the law; that every
mouth may be stopped, and all the world may
become guilty before God ‖." What person in this
assembly can plead guiltless to every part of this

---

* 2 Pet. ii. 2; Matth. xviii. 7. † 2 Pet. ii. 21.
‡ Matth. iii. 12; James v. 9. § Luke xiii. 28.
‖ Rom. iii.-19.

charge? Must we not all stand silent and self-condemned? And if you are a transgressor, what can you do, either to repair the dishonour you have offered to the Divine Majesty, or to prevent the contagious effects of your own evil example? Nothing can be more false, than a too frequent form of speech amongst us. When a man of some amiable qualifications in social life tramples without fear upon the laws of God, how often is it said, by way of extenuation, he is no one's enemy but his own! when indeed his practice declares him to be an enemy of God, an enemy to his holiness and government; and he is a most mischievous enemy to all who live under his influence, and within the circle of his acquaintance, by tempting and encouraging them to sin, to the hazard of their souls. Things standing thus with all men by nature, with what language can we answer the law's demands? Must we not adopt the pathetic confession of the prophet? " For this our heart is faint; for these things our eyes are dim. The crown is fallen from our heads: wo unto us that we have sinned *!"

2. The necessity and value of the Gospel; otherwise how can you escape the penalty, and stand acquitted before the Supreme Judge? If you refuse this, " there remaineth no other sacrifice for sin †." But if you humble yourself, and apply to Jesus, there is yet hope. He died for sinners, the chief of sinners, and the greatest of sins. For his sake, all manner of sin and blasphemy is pardonable: " He is able to save to the uttermost." But he must do the whole, and have all the glory. Believe in his name. This is the first step; without grace derived from him, you can

---

* Lam. v. 16, 17.   † Heb. x. 26.

do nothing. Remember his agony and bloody sweat, his cross and passion; and that he is now exalted a Prince and a Saviour, on the behalf of those who are ready to perish. Let this be your plea and encouragement to draw near to a Throne of Grace. Pray for his Spirit to reveal his righteousness, power, and love to your soul; and as your knowledge of him increases, your repentance will be more spiritual, evangelical, and effectual. Entreat him to enable you to forsake your former evils, to set a guard upon the door of your lips, and to inspire you with an awful veneration of that holy name which you have hitherto profaned. He can teach your polluted lips to shew forth his praise.

And let the redeemed of the Lord, whom he has delivered from the guilt and power of this iniquity, adore the grace and mercy that has saved them. Look back upon your past lives, and rejoice with trembling. How often have you defied his vengeance and power, and perhaps madly uttered horrid imprecations against yourselves! Why have others been cut off in these sins, and you spared? Yes; " such were some of you; but ye are washed, ye are sanctified, ye are justified in the name of the Lord Jesus, and by the Spirit of our God *." And now your tongues, which once uttered blasphemies almost with every breath, or, under a form of godliness, pronounced a language foreign to your hearts, delight in extolling the name of Jesus, and celebrating the wonders of redeeming love. Now, when you speak of the great God, your hearts are awed with an apprehension of his majesty, yet comforted with the thought, that this God is your God, your almighty Friend, your everlasting Portion. Now

* 1 Cor. vi. 11.

you feel the influence of the Spirit of adoption, whereby you cry, " Abba, Father." Little did you think, in the days of your ignorance, that the God whom you was presumptuously offending, had, in the counsels of his everlasting love, chosen you to salvation by Jesus Christ*. But he was found of you when you sought him not. He passed by you when you was lying in your blood, and bid you live. This was the secret reason why you could not destroy yourselves. And at length his time of love came, the hour which he had appointed to open your eyes, to shew you mercy, to deliver you from the power of darkness, and to translate you into the kingdom of his dear Son. Do not your hearts glow with a sense of your obligations to him who hath loved you, and washed you from your sins in his own blood? Will you not live to him who has saved you from so great a death? Yea, doubtless, you will count all things but loss for the excellency of the knowledge of Christ Jesus the Lord. You will use all your influence to diffuse the savour of his precious name. You will take shame to yourselves, and ascribe glory to him. You will be zealous for his cause, and have a tender compassion for poor sinners, who know not what they do, remembering, from your past experience, the misery and gall of an unconverted state. Let as many of us as have received mercy be thus minded; let it be our great study to shew forth the praises of him who has called us out of darkness into his marvellous light, till the welcome hour shall arrive, when he will say to all who fear and love him, and long for his appearance, "Come, ye blessed of my Father, inherit the kingdom prepared for you from the foundation of the world†."

* Ephes. i. 4; Isa. lxv. 1; Ezek. xvi. 6—8; Col. i. 13.
† Matth. xxv. 34.

SERMON XVI.

THE CHRISTIAN LIFE COMPARED TO A RACE.

1 COR. ix. 24.

—— *So run that ye may obtain.*

THE Scripture teaches us to derive profitable lessons from common occurrences: and since we cannot avoid seeing and hearing the vanities of those who know not God, unless we would go wholly out of the world, we may learn some instruction from them at a distance. The country of Greece, and especially the neighbourhood of Corinth, was famous for trials of skill in a variety of exercises, such as racing, wrestling, fighting, and the like. And because the children of the world are very wise in their generation, and spare no pains to accomplish the point they have in view, the Apostle would stir up believers to diligence from their example; and therefore, in several places, compares the Christian life to one or other of the contests which were managed in the public games, and here particularly to a race. In those ancient races much solemnity was observed. The ground or course was exactly marked out; those who were to run went through a strict regimen and exercise beforehand; a vast concourse of people were assembled as spectators; authorised judges were appointed to award the prize, which was a crown of laurel or oak leaves, to the winner: and before they began, a herald publicly proclaimed the rules to be observed by the competitors; which unless strictly complied with, all their pains and endeavours issued only in disappointment and shame. To each of these particulars the Apostle alludes in different parts of his writings.

Let us then briefly consider wherein the allusion holds, and take notice of some things in which there is a remarkable difference.

I. That the Christian life is compared to a race, may intimate to us,

1. That it is a laborious and strenuous service, and incompatible with an indolent and careless frame of spirit. Not that we can do any thing of ourselves : in this sense, " it is not of him that willeth, or of him that runneth *." But when a believer is animated by a view of Jesus, and the prize of the high calling, to run the race set before him, he finds that it demands his utmost strength, courage, and patience. A spectator may divert himself with the prospect, or the company ; he may make observations upon what passes around him, and ride as softly as he pleases : but then he has no pretensions to the prize. But those who are actually candidates for it, may be easily distinguished without being pointed out : they have no leisure for amusement; their eyes are fixed, and their thoughts wholly engaged, upon what they have in hand ; and they exert all their powers, and strain every nerve, to reach the goal. How inconsistent is the conduct of many professors ? They enter the lists, they inform themselves of the rules, they even presume to expect the prize, though they while away their whole lives, without once attempting to run in good earnest. Not so those who are taught and called of God : a sense of the worth of their souls, of the love of Christ, of the glory that shall be revealed,

* Rom. ix. 16.

of their own weakness, and of the many obstacles
that withstand their progress, stirs them up to
watchfulness, diligence, and prayer, and excites a
holy jealousy, " lest, a promise being made of
entering into his rest, any of them should come
short of it *."

2. That we should still press forward, and not
rest in what we have received. If a man sets out
in a race with the greatest speed, and seems to
outstrip all his antagonists; yet if he does not
persevere to the end, he will be sure to lose. The
Apostle alludes to a race in another place, where
he says, " forgetting the things that are behind,
and reaching forth to those that are before†, I
stretch forward." The Greek word beautifully
expresses the earnestness and energy of those who
run, and are determined to be first : they make no
account of the ground already passed over, but
exert themselves to the utmost, labour with their
hands and feet, and strain every joint to the utmost, as though the whole success depended upon
each single step. We see too many instances of
persons who begin warmly, and seem to run well
for a season; but they are hindered in their progress, slacken their pace first, and then stop short.
Take notice of the exhortation in my text, " So
run that you may obtain :" for it will be a dreadful
disappointment if you should be set aside disapproved, when others receive the prize.

II. The heralds or criers in the Christian race
are the ministers of the Gospel; and their proper
name of office is expressed by the same word.
They have it in charge to invite all to run, and to
declare the prescribed rules : and these must be
carefully attended to; for *if*, or, as it might be

* Heb. iv. 1.   † Phil. iii. 13, 14.

rendered, *although, a man strive**, although he
wrestle, and fight, and run, weary himself, and
excel others; yet, after all, he loses the prize, *he
is not crowned, unless he strive lawfully,* unless he
strictly conforms to the prescribed regulations :
he will be judged unqualified, though in other
respects skilful and diligent, unless he runs in the
limits marked out, fights with the usual weapons,
and observes in all points the discipline of the
place. We are bound in duty, at the same time
that we proclaim the race, and point out the prize
to your view, to tell you, that without faith and
holiness † there can be no acceptance. And we
cannot but be grieved to see how little these
cautions are regarded by multitudes. Some are
labouring, as it were, in the fire, to establish a
righteousness by their own works, and refuse to
believe in Christ for salvation. Others, who profess indeed to believe in him, call themselves his
people, and affect to speak highly of his Gospel,
yet eventually deny him by their works and conversation. But unless you can alter the sure determinations of the word of God, there must be an
alteration in yourselves, or else, when you think
you have attained, and shall confidently demand
the prize, you will hear him say, " I know you
not whence ye are; depart from me, all ye
workers of iniquity ‡."

There is a circumstance in this resemblance
which I would not pass over, because it is
peculiar to the Christian race. The ministers
or heralds are not only to invite others, but
are likewise to run themselves. To this the
Apostle alludes, when he says, "lest, when
I have preached to others, I should be myself a

---

* 2 Tim. ii. 5.   † Mark xvi. 16 ; Heb. xii. 14.   ‡ Luke xiii. 27.

cast-away *;" or be disapproved of the Judge for breaking those regulations himself which he had been authorised to propound to all. We have need to preach to ourselves no less than to you, and to entreat your prayers for us, that we may stand perfect and complete in the whole will of God. And the caution may be proportionally extended to every one that is entrusted with any measure of gifts for the edification of the people of God. Keep close to his word; pray for his Spirit; be diligent and temperate in all things; and maintain a watchful jealousy over your own hearts: these are the means by which the Lord keeps his people from falling. But trust not to any outward talent, calling, or usefulness; for it is possible for a man to be instrumental to the good of others in families and societies, and yet to come short of the kingdom himself at last.

III. I have observed, that a great concourse of spectators attended at the ancient games. The Christian, in his race and warfare, has likewise innumerable eyes upon him, a great cloud of witnesses. We are exhibited a spectacle to the world, to the whole universe, both to angels and to men †. Though he may be placed in an obscure situation, yet his neighbours at least will observe him, to see how his profession and practice agree. Invisible beings attend him in every step; the good angels ‡ rejoice over the returning sinner; and it is probable, by God's appointment, support and refresh him in ways which are beyond our apprehension. The powers of darkness watch him with subtilty and envy, and go to the utmost bounds of their commission, in their endeavours either to divert him from his course, or to make

* 1 Cor. ix. 27.   † 1 Cor. iv. 9.   ‡ Luke xv. 10.

it uncomfortable to him. How should this thought
both animate and humble every sincere soul? Be
not discouraged, because to appearance you are
almost left to serve God alone. If the veil of flesh
and blood could be drawn aside, you would see
you are not alone; all the host of heaven are on
your side; the glorious company that are before
the Throne of God day without night, rejoicing,
are engaged in your cause, and drink of the same
fountain from which you are supplied. The spirits
of just men made perfect, who are now all eye, all
ear, all love, were once as you are, partakers of the
same infirmities, sorrows, and cares; and you ere
long shall be as they are, clothed with light, and
freed from every burden. And Jesus, the Lord
of angels, the King of saints, beholds your toil
and conflict with complacence, and says, "Hold
that fast which thou hast, that no man take thy
crown*." He is always near to succour, strengthen,
and to save. Rejoice, therefore, that you run
not as unnoticed, but rejoice with trembling. Be
ashamed to think how disproportionate your efforts
are to the company that behold you, and to the
prize that awaits you. Remember likewise other
eyes are upon you; Satan envies your privileges,
and scorns your profession; he is every minute
waiting permission to sift you as wheat†; he is
incessantly spreading snares for your feet, and
preparing his arrows against you : therefore be not
high-minded, but fear, and give all diligence so to
run that you may obtain.

IV. The Judge who presides at the end of the
race is Jesus, the *Judge of all.* He holds forth the
prize full in view to the eye of faith, and shall
shortly crown the conqueror with his own hand.

* Rev. iii. 11.   † Luke xxii. 31.

How sweetly does the Apostle spiritualize upon
this circumstance! " I have fought a good fight,
I have finished my course; I have kept the faith.
Henceforth there is laid up for me a crown of life,
which the Lord, the righteous Judge," (who does
not decide by appearances, nor can be influenced
by partiality, as is too frequent amongst men)
" shall give me at that day ; and not to me only,
but to all who love his appearing*." Be of
good cheer, believer: your case may be mis-
represented, or misunderstood by men; but the
Lord, the righteous and unerring Judge, will vindicate, approve, and reward in the great day, when
he shall come to be glorified in his saints, and admired in all them that believe.

Thus much concerning the resemblance of the
Christian life to a race, to which the Apostle alludes. I shall briefly take notice of some particulars in which the resemblance fails; and a
very interesting and important difference may be
observed,

1. In the reward. *The bodily exercise*† employed in the games (for to these the Apostle refers)
profited little: a crown of oak or laurel, or some
such bauble, was their highest aim; and this the
most of the competitors came short of, for though
all ran, *but one received the prize.* Of little more
value, and equal uncertainty, is the prize that has
engaged the time and thoughts of many. *But
godliness* (the whole course and conflict in which
the believer is engaged) *is profitable for all things,*
or in every view, having promises to support the
life that now is, and to crown that which is to
come. " He that overcometh, saith the Lord,
shall inherit all things. I will be his Father, and
he shall be my son. I will give him to eat of the

---

* 2 Tim. iv. 7, 8.   † 1 Tim. iv. 8.

tree of life, which is in the midst of the paradise of God. I will make him a pillar in the temple of my God, and he shall go no more out; yea, I will grant him to sit down with me in my throne*." The Lord will give grace here, and will withhold no good thing from those who walk uprightly; and hereafter he will crown grace with glory, and place his servants out of the reach of every trouble and enemy, in the kingdom which his love has prepared for them from before the foundation of the world. " Having therefore these promises, dearly beloved, let us cleanse ourselves from all filthiness of the flesh and spirit, perfecting holiness in the fear of the Lord †."

2. In races, though many run, one only can receive the prize. But, thanks be to God, it is not so in the Christian race. All who run as the Lord has appointed, shall be sure to win. No opposition can prevail against them, nor will the number of the candidates be any diminution to the happiness of each individual. The inheritance of the saints in light, like the light of the sun, is not diminished by being shared amongst many; each one possesses the whole, in the same perfection as he could do, if there was none to enjoy it but himself.

3. In the races the Apostle alludes to, none were compelled to run. The proclamation was general; but those who did not choose to engage, suffered no disadvantage. But it is not so in the race to which you are invited by the Gospel. The Lord is greatly offended with those who slight the message, and refuse to enter the lists. If you only give his ministers a hearing, and return to your farms and merchandise ‡, forget the worth

---

* Rev. ii. 7; iii. 12—21; xxii. 7; Psal. lxxxiv. 11.
† 2 Cor. vii. 1. ‡ Matth. xxii. 5.

of your precious souls, and suffer your thoughts to be engrossed with the cares and pleasures of this life, to the neglect of this one thing needful, the Lord will account it a contempt offered to himself, and will ere long call you before his tribunal to answer for it.

4. Those who run and did not win the prize, only lost their labour, or at the worst were exposed to shame, but they were liable to no positive punishment. But you who are professors of the Gospel, if you come short at last, will be lost for ever. " So run that you may obtain." Be not content with having set out; the promise is made to perseverance. " He that endureth to the end shall be saved*;" but if any draw back, or stop short, the Lord will have no pleasure in them. They will not only lose the prize, but will receive a heavy and aggravated doom. It would have been better for them not to have known the way of righteousness, than, after they have known it, to turn from the holy commandment delivered to them. If you were forced to run for your lives, you would be very thoughtful about the event. But if you are not found amongst those who come in for the prize of eternal life, you will be cast into outer darkness, and sink under the curse of God for ever.

Fain therefore would I persuade you to address yourselves with earnestness to run the race set before you. Flee from approaching wrath. The wrath of God is already revealed against all unrighteousness, and soon it will be poured forth upon the head of every transgressor. Though God is patient and forbearing, he is angry with the wicked every day. If he turn not, he will whet his

---

* Matth. x. 22; Heb. x. 38.

glittering sword; he hath bent his bow, and made it ready. He hath also prepared for him the instruments of death; he hath ordained his arrows against those who shall finally disobey his great command, to receive the Gospel of his grace. It is impossible to elude his eye, or to withstand his power. You are upon the brink of danger, if you are not already entered in this race : you stand upon a precipice, and hell from beneath has opened its mouth to receive you. But a respite is still afforded; the Lord waits to be gracious; and as yet there is room. The gate of mercy is not yet shut; " turn therefore to the strong-hold, as prisoners of hope: " no longer refuse his gracious invitation, or trifle with your precious souls; seek to Jesus, that you may live; apply to him for faith and repentance; and, in his strength and name, prepare to run this important race. Meditate upon the glorious prize which is provided for all who endure to the end; it is freely proposed to all who run. Pardon, grace, and eternal life, are promised and bestowed, without money, and without price. If, after so many repeated calls, you still harden your hearts, and stop your ears, and determine that you will not come unto Jesus that you may have life, you must assuredly perish, without mercy, and without excuse.

But if you are desirous to run, remember the admonition in my text, " So run that you may obtain." Your steps must be regulated by the word of God, or you will wander wide from the good old way; you must derive your sufficiency and strength from Christ by faith and prayer, or you will faint, and be unable to endure to the end. We read of some*
that ran well for a season, but were afterwards

* Gal. v. 7.

hindered, and turned aside. Be upon your guard; for there are many that will strive to divert you from your course. Satan, the world, and your own evil hearts, will combine, and form various attempts to slacken your pace, and to withdraw your attention from the one thing needful. Dread the thoughts of stopping short, or turning back; and the more you meet with opposition, be so much the more earnest to redouble your diligence, and especially to cry mightily to him who is able to keep you from falling, to preserve you unblameable in love while here, and at last to present you faultless before the presence of his glory with exceeding joy.

Believers, why are not we as wise in our generation as the children of the world? We see how those who are fond of a common horse-race are thinking and talking of it, and preparing for it every day. Does not their diligence shame us, who are so cold, faint, and dilatory, in the most important and honourable concerns? Let us gird up the loins of our mind; some of you have not far to run now; you have taken many a weary step since you were first called; but the end is at hand; the period of your complete salvation is now much nearer than when you first believed *. Think of Jesus the Forerunner and the Judge; he has already entered within the vail for us; his eye is upon us; he is near to assist, and waiting to receive us. May his Spirit and his example animate us to press forward to the prize of our high calling, to tread down every difficulty, and to be faithful unto death, that we may receive the crown of life †.

* Rom. xiii. 11. † Rev. ii. 10.

SERMON XVII.

NO ACCESS TO GOD BUT BY THE GOSPEL OF CHRIST.

MICAH vi. 6—8.

Wherewith shall I come before the Lord, and bow myself before the high God? Shall I come before him with burnt offerings, with calves of a year old? Will the Lord be pleased with thousands of rams, or with ten thousands of rivers of oil? Shall I give my first-born for my transgression, the fruit of my body for the sin of my soul? He hath shewed thee, O man, what is good; and what doth the Lord require of thee, but to do justly, and to love mercy, and to walk humbly with thy God?

THERE is no question that can arise in the mind of man, that is of so high importance as this in my text, and yet, alas! how seldom is it laid to heart! May the Spirit of God impress it upon all your consciences! You are now come before God to worship; ask yourselves, wherewith? On what do you ground your hope, that you offer him acceptable service? You must shortly appear before him in judgment. Are you prepared to meet* him? What plea have you provided? Take heed in time. Be sure that it is such a one as he will admit, lest your hopes should fail, and you perish in his presence as chaff before the devouring flame.

The passage plainly expresses the inquiry of an awakened mind. It is to be feared many of you have often read these words without being suitably

* Amos iv. 12.

affected with their meaning. But if you can indeed make them your own, if you are truly solicitous how you are to come before God both here and hereafter, I hope his good Spirit will enable you to receive satisfaction from the answer given by the prophet.

If you can speak these words from your heart, you will readily acknowledge that they imply the following things.

1. A sense of duty : that you are under an obligation to come and bow before the high God. You are sensible that you ought not, and you find that you cannot live without paying him homage and worship, but that he has a right to your service, and expects it. Too many shew, in this respect, that they are dead while they live; dead to God, insensible and regardless of their many obligations to him, in whom they live, and move, and have their being. They live without prayer; they offer no praises to the God of their lives, but rise up and lie down, go out and come in, without one reflection on his power, goodness, and providence, even like the beasts that perish. But the awakened soul cannot do so. He trembles to think, that he once could neglect that God whom all the hosts of heaven worship; and is convinced, that however fair his character might have been amongst men, he justly deserved to have been struck to hell for so long restraining prayer before God.

2. A sense of the majesty and glory of God. Whoever seriously asks this question, has an awful view of the Lord, as the high God. Many who do not wholly neglect prayer and worship, yet have no spiritual and humbling apprehensions of the God whom they profess to serve. Their prayers, whether in public or private, are only lip-service, as though they thought him altogether

such a one as themselves. Their petitions are not
guided by their desires, but they utter with their
mouths what they find in the book, though their
hearts have no love or relish of the things they ask
for. How often is God mocked by those who join
in our Established worship? Has he not been so
this morning by some of you? How little he is
reverenced by many, is plain from the little regard
they pay to his commands. They will break his
Sabbaths, blaspheme his name, live in drunken-
ness, whoredom, anger, and malice, and yet pretend to worship him. But those who rightly understand the inquiry in my text, cannot do thus. They
consider him as the high God; they know that he
humbles himself to behold even the worship of
heaven, and are therefore struck with this thought,
Wherewith can I, a poor worm, who am but dust
and ashes, come before this high God?

3. A sense of guilt. Alas! says the soul that is
enlightened to see itself, I am not only *mean* but
vile. " I have sinned; what shall I do unto thee,
O thou Preserver of men?* " wherewith shall such
a polluted, obnoxious creature as I am, appear before a holy God? Can my services atone for my
sins? or what service can I perform that is not defiled and rendered unworthy of acceptance by the
evil of my heart? But could I perform ever so
well from this day forward, what would this avail
for what is past? If I had offended a man like
myself, I might think of making some amends;
but my sins are against God. His justice, wisdom,
holiness, and truth, have all demands upon me.
What then can I bring? Will sacrifices appease
him? No: these, though of his own appointment,
are not of themselves sufficient. " It is not pos-

* Job vii. 20.   † Acts xx. 28.

sible for the blood of bulls and goats to take away
sins *." Though all the beasts of the forest, and
the cattle upon a thousand hills were mine, though
I should offer all Lebanon, hills of frankincense,
rivers, yea, ten thousands of rivers of oil, all would
not do. Or should I give my son, my only son,
the fruit of my body, neither would this atone for
the sin of my soul.

Here then you may see, that to an awakened
sinner sin is the heaviest burden imaginable. He
is willing, and would be glad (if it might be), to
purchase the pardon of sin with the loss of every
thing he accounts most valuable. If he had the
whole world, he would freely part with it to be
free from guilt. But at the same time he finds it
a burden that he cannot shake off: he knows that
he never can be delivered for any thing he can do
or propose, and therefore the great subject of inquiry always upon his mind is, Wherewith or how
shall I appear and stand before the high God?

I hope some of you are thus minded: to you I
have a comfortable message from the other part
of my text. But as I cannot hope thus of you all,
I must previously take notice, that there is hardly
any one passage in the Bible more generally misunderstood, and which ignorant and careless men
are more prone to wrest to their own destruction,
than the verses under our present consideration.
Not a few, having their eyes blinded by the god
of this world, and their hearts enslaved to the love
and practice of sin, are content to understand it as
if it was rather a rebuke than an encouragement
to them, who, like † the jailor, are deeply affected
with a concern for the salvation of their souls.
Their comment is to this purpose: "He hath

---

* Heb. x. 4.   † Acts xvi. 30.

shewed thee, O man, what is good;" that is, You need not terrify yourself at this rate; there is nothing so evil in sin, or so awful in God's threatenings, as you suppose. He has said indeed, " The soul that sinneth shall die*;" yet here you see an easy way to escape. " Do justly,"—(which is, being interpreted,) Do not grossly cheat and injure your neighbour; abstain from robbery, extortion, and heavy oppression,—and "love mercy;" that is, be ready to do what are commonly called good-natured offices, and to give a shilling, or a guinea (according to your circumstances), now and then to the poor, and you will be safe enough. How they explain the other clause, "walk humbly," upon this plan, I confess myself unable to conceive, and therefore I believe they are glad to omit it; for I am sure, light cannot be more contrary to darkness, than such language as this is opposite to the idea of walking humbly with God.

According to this opinion, to do justly, and to love mercy, are the whole of religion. They are, indeed, essential parts of it; and miserable will you be who talk in this strain, if God, at the great day, should judge you by this text to which you now presumptuously appeal. How wonderful is the pride and arrogance of fallen man, who will dare to urge a plea before God which must issue in his own confusion! Do you indeed deal justly? It implies something more than not being an arrant knave. Do you at all times, and in all respects, behave to every person as you would they should do unto you? Did you never take the least advantage of the ignorance or necessity of your neighbour? Did you never speak or report any thing to his prejudice, without sufficient

---

* Ezek. xviii. 4.

warrant and sufficient cause? You feel how tender
you are of your own character and interests.
Have you been equally tender of the interests of
others, of all others with whom you have had
connections, without being influenced in any instance or degree by partiality or mercenary views?
If you cannot appeal to the Searcher of hearts
that you have walked in this integrity, your pretence that you have done justly, is vile hypocrisy,
and you may tremble to think how easily you may
be condemned out of your own mouth. Alas! if
God, to whom all your thoughts and actions have
been incessantly exposed, should enter into judgment with you, how unable would you be to answer
him in one of a thousand?

Again; Do you love mercy? Do you *love* it as
a miser loves money? Is it the pleasure of your
hearts to overcome evil with good? If your brother
or neighbour offend you, not seven times, but
seventy times seven *, do you find it delightful to
repeat your forgiveness, to bless them that curse
you, to pray for them that despitefully use you,
and to requite repeated injuries with repeated acts
of kindness? If not, what have you to do with
mercy, either to pretend that you love mercy
yourself, or to indulge a hope of obtaining mercy
from God, if you knew no better way of seeking
it than by your own works. But suppose you was
less culpable in these particulars, can you say that
you walk humbly with God? Alas! how impossible is this, while you trust in your own righteousness, while you slight and despise his threatenings,
while your hearts rise against his Gospel. Are
you not impatient under the afflictions which he
sends, and unthankful for innumerable mercies
which he is daily bestowing upon you? And is

* Matth. xviii. 22.

this to walk humbly with God? Bear with me
for a plain word, which I purposely speak plainly,
that it may not be forgot: I say, that if any man
or woman can be saved in this way, that is, upon
the account of doing justly, loving mercy, and
walking humbly with God, then Satan himself
has no cause to despair.

I return now to those who see and acknowledge
themselves to be sinners, without righteousness
and strength, and are desirous to appear before
God with comfort. To you I bring good tidings;
the Lord help you to believe and rejoice. He
hath shewed you that which is good, which is
the only and sufficient ground whereon to build
your hopes: he has shewed or revealed it, for
otherwise you could never have found it out.
What the law cannot do in that it is weak and
ineffectual through the flesh, God has done by
sending his Son in the likeness of sinful flesh*.
The Lord Jesus Christ is that *good* to which the
prophet refers; Moses and the Prophets, and all
the Scriptures, testify of him, and Micah among
the rest. One of the most illustrious testimonies
to the person and office of our Immanuel in the
Old Testament, is to be found in the chapter preceding my text. " But thou, Bethlehem Ephratah,
though thou be little among the thousands of
Judah, yet out of thee shall he come forth unto
me that is to be ruler in Israel; whose goings
forth have been from of old, from everlasting.
And he shall stand and feed in the strength of the
Lord, in the majesty of the name of the Lord his
God; and they shall abide: for now shall he be
great unto the ends of the earth. And this man
shall be the peace†." All other sacrifices and
saviours are insufficient; but Jesus, by the one

---

* Rom. viii. 3.   † Micah v. 2—5.

offering of himself once offered up, hath made a full, perfect, and everlasting atonement; and now he reigns in our nature, possessed of all the fulness of grace, exercising the power of God in the salvation of men. Would you then come before the High God, come in the name of Jesus, and you shall find acceptance.   In him God is well pleased*; and for his sake he is well pleased with all who honour his beloved Son, and put their trust in him.   He has authority and compassion sufficient to save the most deplorable and the most unworthy. If you read the history of his life and death, you will read of a display of love and grace beyond expression; and he is the same still.   Before he ascended, he left an assurance for your encouragement, that whosoever cometh unto him he will in nowise cast out.   If you say, I want faith, remember it is his gift, and he has promised to do whatever you ask in his name, Therefore, fight against unbelief, resist Satan with the sword of the Spirit.   If it is suggested that you are a great sinner, you cannot deny it, *nor need you;* avow the charge, take shame to yourselves, and give glory to God: but it is equally true, that Jesus is a great Saviour; he is able to save to the uttermost; and though your iniquities are great, yet cast not away your hope, for his mercy is greater than the heavens.

When you come in this way, what does the Lord require of you? Is it to make your own peace? He would as soon require you to make a new heaven and a new earth. Is it to keep your own soul? No more than he requires you to keep the sun in its course. His own arm has wrought salvation, and he will secure it. He

---

* Matth. iii. 17.

requires none of your help here; nay, he disdains the thought: you might as well offer to help him to govern the world. But this he requires of you, " to do justly, to love mercy, and to walk humbly with thy God;" and the methods of his grace will enable you to do so.

1. " To do justly." We are by nature attached to worldly goods, and wholly influenced by selfish principles. But faith in Jesus communicates new motives, views, and aims, to the soul : it teaches us to have our treasure in heaven : to sit loose to the world ; to be satisfied with that station and competence which Divine Providence has allotted us ; and to love our neighbours as ourselves, because they are our fellow-sinners, and are capable of being called to a participation with us in the honourable relation and privilege of the children of God. Upon these principles the practice of justice is attainable, but upon no other; for though there are many characters honourable and blameless in the outward concerns of life, and in the judgment of men, there is no person upon earth who does or can love or practise justice in its full extent, till he has received the Spirit of Christ, and lives upon him by faith, for wisdom and strength from day to day.

2. " To love mercy." None can truly love it but those who have tasted it. When your hearts feel the comforts of God's pardoning love, you will delight to imitate him. When you can truly rejoice that he has freely forgiven you that immense debt, which is expressed by ten thousand talents*, you will have no desire to take your fellow-servant by the throat for a few pence. This sense of God's goodness, and the continual

---

* Matth. xviii. 24.

need you find of his renewed mercy from day to day, will soften your spirit (if you are a believer), disarm and gradually weaken every proud thought that would plead for the exercise of anger and resentment towards those who have offended you. You will be swift to hear, slow to speak, slow to wrath; you will put on (as the beloved of God) **bowels** of meekness *, long-suffering, and compassion, forbearing and forgiving, if you have ought against any; because God for Christ's sake has freely forgiven you. If you find this practice difficult, it is owing partly to the remaining depravity of your nature, and partly because you have had but a faint sense of his mercy. Pray for a more powerful manifestation of it, and you will do better; mercy will be your delight.

3. " To walk humbly." " Can two walk together except they are agreed ? †" When Christ is your peace, you will delight in God; you will set him before you, commune with him, study to please him, and to keep all his commandments. This is to *walk* with God; and you will walk *humbly*, remembering how much you owe to free grace, and how far you fall short in your best endeavours. These considerations, impressed by the Holy Spirit, will humble you, will keep you from being high in your own esteem, wise in your own conceit, and from seeking great things for yourself. You will be habitually thankful when the Lord gives, content when he withholds, patient when he afflicts. You will confess yourself unworthy of the smallest mercies you possess, and acknowledge in your heaviest trials that he has laid far less upon you than your iniquities have deserved.

---

* Col. iii. 12.　　　　† Amos iii. 3.

This is the pattern we are to copy after, and this is the certain tendency and effect of his grace. A measure of this disposition is found in all who are Christians indeed. Yet we may take shame to ourselves, that we are still so far defective in every branch of our duty. Let us stir up ourselves to greater diligence, watchfulness, and prayer, that we may obtain more lively, abiding, and transforming views of that which is our true good, that so we may be enabled to glorify our heavenly Father, and to adorn our profession, by doing justly, loving mercy, and walking humbly with our God.

SERMON XVIII.

OF A LIVING AND A DEAD FAITH.

JAMES ii. 26.

For as the body without the spirit is dead, so faith without works is dead also.

WHOEVER has read the Scriptures with attention, must have observed several passages which, at first view, and till thoroughly examined and compared, appear hard to reconcile to each other. No instance of this sort is more remarkable than the seeming difference of judgment between St. Paul and St. James on the point of justification. St. Paul having said, " That a man is justified by faith without the deeds of the law *," produces the example of Abraham to confirm his

* Rom. iii. 2b.

assertion. St. James (in the chapter before us),
from the example of the same Abraham, draws a
conclusion which seems directly to contradict
this : " Ye see then how that by works a man is
justified, and not by faith only *." Can any two
opinions be more opposite in appearance ? How
then can both be true; or how can we believe both
writers infallible in their doctrine, and influenced
by the unerring Spirit of God ? Must we cleave
to the one, and reject the other ? and if so, how
shall we know which is the real truth ?

We may confidently answer, The Apostles are
both right; their doctrine is equally from God,
and does not clash in any particular. The darkness and difficulty is in the apprehensions of men,
and not in the word of God. Yet a difficulty
there is, and I hope I shall not detain you unprofitably at this time, by endeavouring to clear it,
and afterwards to press upon you the words of my
text as a proper inference from the whole.

When men who are strangers to Christian experience, and who trust more to their own sagacity and learning than to the word and Spirit of
God, attempt to resolve cases of this sort, they
make strange work. And it is no wonder; for
how can any one explain what he does not understand ? It would tire you if I should relate a
tenth part of the conjectures of learned men upon
this very subject. I shall mention one or two as
a specimen. A writer of some eminence in the
world confesses the difficulty I have noticed in
its full strength. He allows and affirms that it is
not only hard, but impossible, to reconcile the
Apostles to each other; and concludes, that since

* James ii. 24.

it is impossible to hold both their sentiments, we must abide by him who wrote the last. This, from many arguments his learning furnished him with, he thinks to have been St. James. Accordingly, he gives up the other, and his doctrine of faith without works, to shift for themselves. He supposes that St. Paul, in the heat of his argument, carried the matter a little too far, and that St. James wrote afterwards to correct him.

But to shew you (excuse a familiar expression) how doctors differ, and at the same time to warn even true believers against hastily judging beyond the line of their experience, I would observe, that the great servant of God, Luther, soon after he began to preach the Gospel, made a mistake no less bold and presuming on the other side of the question. He had felt the power of St. Paul's doctrine in his own soul, and would have defied an angel that should have dared to oppose it : therefore, when his adversaries pressed him with the authority of St. James, not having, at that time, light to give a more solid answer, he ventured to deny the authenticity of the whole Epistle, and rashly insisted, both in his sermons and books, that St. James never wrote it. But Luther, though mistaken in this point, was under the Lord's teaching ; he went on from strength to strength, increasing in knowledge and grace ; and when his judgment was better informed, he publicly retracted his former unguarded assertion.

Leaving, therefore, the authority of men, let us betake ourselves to the word of God, and humbly seek the light of his Spirit, who is promised to guide his people in their sincere inquiries after truth.

Now, if you consider the scope and design of our Apostles, and take in the context, I hope this seeming opposition will be soon removed. St. Paul is evidently treating on the great point of a sinner's justification in the sight of God; he shews that it cannot be of the law, because by the law all men were already condemned, and because then boasting could not be excluded; but that it was freely by grace, through the redemption that is by Christ Jesus. His reasoning will appear to greater advantage by perusing the whole passage, than by producing a few detached sentences. After he had summed up the evidence with respect both to Jews and Gentiles, and pronounced his verdict, that every mouth must be stopped, and that the whole world stood guilty before God, he proceeds thus: " Therefore by the deeds of the law, there shall no flesh be justified in his sight; for by the law is the knowledge of sin. But now the righteousness of God without the law is manifested, being witnessed by the law and the prophets; even the righteousness of God which is by faith of Jesus Christ unto all, and upon all them that believe; for there is no difference : for all have sinned, and come short of the glory of God; being justified freely by his grace, through the redemption that is in Jesus Christ: whom God hath set forth to be a propitiation, through faith in his blood, to declare his righteousness for the remission of sins that are past, through the forbearance of God; to declare, I say, at this time his righteousness: that he might be just, and the justifier of him which believeth in Jesus. Where is boasting then? It is excluded. By what law? Of works? Nay ; but by the law of faith. Therefore we conclude, that a man is justified by faith without the deeds of the law *." And because the Jews had a high opinion of Abraham, he proceeds in the next chapter to shew that Abraham was justified in the same way. " For what saith the Scripture? Abraham believed God, and it was counted unto him for righteousness. Now to him that worketh, is the reward not reckoned of grace, but of debt. But to him that worketh not, but believeth on him that justifieth the ungodly, his faith is counted for righteousness†." The circumstance in Abraham's life referred to is, when he believed the promise of God, that though he was then childless, he should be the father of many nations‡; and that particularly from him should proceed the Messiah, the promised Seed, in whom both he himself and all the families of the earth should be blessed.

St. James expressly treats of those who rested in a notion which they called faith, and accounted sufficient for their salvation, though it had no influence upon their hearts, tempers, and conduct. He shews that their hope is vain, because such a faith as this the devils have. And he proves, by the example of Abraham, that his faith was very different from theirs, because it enabled him to perform the hardest and most painful act of obedience, the offering up his only son. " What doth it profit, my brethren, though a man say he hath faith, and have not works? can (this) § faith save him? If a brother or sister be naked, and destitute of daily food; and one of you say unto them, Depart in peace, be you warmed and filled; notwithstanding ye give them not those things which

---

* Rom. iii. 20—28. † Rom. iv. 3—5.

‡ Gen. xii. 3; xvii. 4. § ἡ πίστις, *this* faith.

are needful to the body; what doth it profit? Even so faith, if it hath not works, is dead, being alone. Yea, a man may say, Thou hast faith, and I have works : shew me thy faith without thy works, and I will shew thee my faith by my works. Thou believest that there is one God; thou dost well : the devils also believe, and tremble. But wilt thou know, O vain man, that faith without works is dead? Was not Abraham our father justified by works, when he had offered Isaac his son upon the altar ? Seest thou how faith wrought with his works, and by works was faith made perfect ? And the Scripture was fulfilled (confirmed), which saith, Abraham believed God, and it was imputed unto him for righteousness : and he was called the friend of God. Ye see then how that by works a man is justified, and not by faith only*." It is exceedingly plain, that he had not the same thing in view which St. Paul had ; for the incident to which he here refers, happened a great many years after Abraham had been declared justified in the sight of God.

The sum is ; The one declares that nothing renders us acceptable to God but faith in the Lord Jesus Christ : the other, that such a faith, when true and genuine, is not solitary, but accompanied with every good work. The one speaks of the justification of our persons,—this is by faith only ; the other of the justification of our profession,— this is by faith not alone, but working by love, and producing obedience.

St. James has the same view in speaking of Rahab † ; and, by producing her as a confirmation, it is still more evident, that he is only considering works as the proofs of our sincerity. We have no sure ground to conclude, that Rahab, in the

---

* James ii. 14—24.   † James ii. 25.

act of receiving the spies, and at that time, had any saving faith, or any view to the Messiah and the covenant of grace: though it is most probable she had, after she was joined to the people of Israel, and became acquainted with Divine revelation. But in Jericho her thoughts seemed to have been confined to a temporal deliverance: and the profession of faith which she made to the spies implies no more. " And she said unto the men, I know that the Lord hath given you the land, and that your terror is fallen upon us, and that all the inhabitants of the land faint because of you. For we have heard how the Lord dried up the water of the Red Sea for you, when you came out of Egypt; and what you did unto the two kings of the Amorites. And as soon as we had heard these things, our hearts did melt; neither did there remain any more courage in any man, because of you: for the Lord your God, he is God in heaven above, and in earth beneath. Now therefore, I pray you, swear unto me by the Lord, since I have shewed you kindness, that ye will also shew kindness unto my father's house; and give me a true token*." Had she said thus, and yet delivered the spies up to the king of Jericho, it would have proved that she did not speak from her heart; but her profession was justified by receiving them into her house, concealing them from the search made after them, and sending them away in peace. Surely this conduct of Rahab will be sufficient to condemn many who would be thought Christians.

We may therefore deduce two propositions, perfectly consistent with each other, from the passage in question.

1. That there is no acceptance for any of the

---

* Joshua ii. 9—12.

sons of Adam, with the just and holy God, but through Jesus Christ as our righteousness received by faith, and that in this concern works of every kind are absolutely excluded.

This is the capital doctrine of the Gospel : it is not only clearly asserted in innumerable passages both of the Old Testament and the New, but is St. Paul's express subject and design in his Epistles to the Romans and the Galatians. Though he was yielding and compliant in many things of less importance, and was willing to become all things to all men, yet he would not give place, no not for an hour, to any who offered to invalidate this foundation-truth. He declares, that to mix any thing, to contend for any qualification or observance, as of necessary influence to concur with the perfect work of Christ in the justification of a sinner, is to darken, alter, and destroy the Gospel which he preached ; and denounces an anathema against every one who should be guilty of this presumption, yea, though he should be (if such* a thing was possible) an angel from heaven. How cordially he rested his own hope upon the truth which he proposed to others, he declares elsewhere, " Yea, doubtless, and I count all things but loss, for the excellency of the knowledge of Christ Jesus my Lord : for whom I have suffered the loss of all things, and do count them but dung, that I may win Christ; and be found in him†, not having mine own righteousness, which is of the ‡ law, but that which is through the faith of Christ, the righteousness of God by faith."

* Gal. i. 8, 9.   † Phil. iii. 8, 9.

‡ Εκ νομυ, of the law : that is, of *any law whatsoever*, not of *the* law, as if he only meant the Jewish law. The article τȣ seems here to be purposely left out.

If this is the Scriptural doctrine, let each one examine on what ground you stand. Has God appointed one way of salvation, and will any of you dare to propose another? This would be both wicked and dangerous : " Other foundation can no man lay than that which is laid, which is Jesus Christ*." You may please yourselves now with what you account your good works; but when God shall " lay judgment to the line, and righteousness to the plummet †," none will be able to abide his appearance, but those who can plead a righteousness perfectly answerable to the law's demands, which can only be found in Jesus Christ, the righteous one.

And as this doctrine is of so great and essential importance, beware how you listen to any other. Take heed how you hear ‡; be not influenced by the names, characters, or stations of men, when the salvation of your souls is at stake. Prize the liberty which, as Protestants and Britons, you enjoy, of bringing every doctrine to the trial of God's word, and freely use it. I account it my honour and happiness that I preach to a free people, who have the Bible in their hands. To your Bibles I appeal. I entreat, I charge you to receive nothing upon my word, any farther than I prove it from the word of God; and bring every preacher, and every sermon that you hear, to the same standard. If this is the truth, you had need to be well established in it; for it is not the current and fashionable doctrine of the times. Let me then farther recommend to you (it is a direction our Lord has given), to examine doctrines by their effects : " By their fruits ye shall know

---

* 1 Cor. iii. 11.   † Isa. xxviii. 17.
‡ Mark iv. 24; Luke viii. 18.

them*." The truths of God, when faithfully preached, in humble dependence upon his blessing, will be attested by his power. At such times, and in such places, a visible change will soon be observable in some or more of the hearers : they cease to do evil, they learn to do well : they acknowledge God in all their ways, and glorify him before men, by living according to his precepts. And if you ask them the reason of this change, they will freely ascribe it to the blessing of God upon that sort of preaching, which by too many is accounted foolishness †.

On the other hand, we are not afraid to challenge those who are most acquainted with men and books, to produce instances of the same effects wrought by any other doctrine than that which commends the Lord Christ in his person, offices, and power, as the only object of a sinner's hope. How much is said and written to tell people what they should be, and what they should do! yet where these principles are not enforced, there is nothing effectually done, nothing indeed attempted, beyond a formal round of dull and heartless service : a little something that looks like religion on the Lord's day, to appear in church at the summons of the bell, to repeat words because other people do the same, to hear what is delivered from the pulpit with little attention or affection, unless something occurs that is suited to exalt self, or to sooth conscience, and then to run with eagerness into the world again.

Or if here and there a person is truly touched by the secret influence and guidance of the Spirit of God, where this evangelical doctrine is not publicly maintained, the consequence always is,

* Matth. vii. 16.   † 1 Cor. i. 21.

that they renounce the things which they before held for truths, are brought into that way of thinking which is agreeable to St. Paul's doctrine, and receive it gladly whenever it comes in their way.

It must be allowed, however, at the same time, that there are counterfeit professors, whose religion lies in notions, and who, while they profess to believe in God, in works deny him ; by reason of whom the ways of truth are evil spoken of*. This the Apostles have taught us to expect ; nay, it was so from the beginning, even while the Apostles were themselves personally with the churches. To such St. James addresses the passage I have been reading to you, of which my text is the conclusion ; and as I dare not hope that there are none such in this great assembly, it is highly proper, that before I conclude I should take notice of a second proposition which naturally offers from the subject we have had in hand ; and more especially from the reasoning of St. James, and from the words of my text.

2. That true faith in the Lord Jesus Christ has a prevailing and habitual influence upon the hearts and lives of those who possess it ; and that they are vain men, and deceivers of themselves, who pretend to faith in him, while their lives and conversations shew them to be enslaved to the love of the world, and the dominion of sin. The Apostle, to inspire us with a just abhorrence of this false profession, makes use of two comparisons which are exceedingly striking. May God open the eyes of those who are concerned in it, to perceive and tremble at the justness and horror of the resemblance.

Ist, He compares it to the faith of devils : "Thou

* 2 Pet. ii. 2.

believest there is one God; thou dost well. The
devils also believe, and tremble*." Are there any
here whom it is needful to address in this harsh
manner? My dear brethren, bear with me; I
wish you well, and would willingly rejoice in
every good appearance; but, alas! how little
does it signify what you believe, or what you
say, unless your acknowledged principles have an
effect upon your conduct!

Do you believe that Jesus is the Christ? so
does Satan? Do you believe the election of God,
the sovereignty of grace, the perseverance of the
saints? It is possible the devil may have a more
extensive [knowledge in these doctrines than the
wisest of men; yet this benefits him not; it is not
want of knowledge, but want of love, that makes
him what he is.

The only effect mentioned of the faith of devils
is, that it increases their terror, and aggravates
their guilt. They believe (there are no sceptics
in hell), and tremble. Is not this too much the
case of some of you? If you knew less, you
would be easier at least, and less inexcusable;
and yet perhaps you mistake your state, and think
yourselves on this account far less blameable than
you really are. Perhaps sometimes, when you
reflect sincerely on your ways, and how strangely
you are hurried to act contrary to the convictions
which the preaching of the Gospel forces upon
you, you are ready to charge the Lord and his
dispensations hardly, and to say, O that he would
give me his grace! but if not, what can I do
without it? Let conscience now speak faithfully,
and it will tell you, that if you are condemned, it
will not be for what you cannot do, but for wil-

* James ii. 19.

fully refusing to improve the power already given
you.   When I tell you, that without holiness no
man shall see the Lord with comfort, and that you
must break off from your vain company and evil
practices, if you expect or desire to be saved, you
know that I speak the truth; and your looks
often testify that you feel the force of it.   Now,
while the word of God is sounding in your ears,
you perhaps are thinking, " It is time, high time
indeed, to break off; though the Lord has forborn
me long, he will surely strike at last, if I go on
thus."   And yet, alas! what I have formerly seen
gives me much cause to fear, that to-morrow, or
the next time they entice you, you will consent
again.   But could I tell you, that by going a different way you might gain a sum of money; or
could I make it appear, that the next time you
went to such a place your house would certainly
be robbed, I make no doubt but you would forbear.   And yet gold is not grace.   It is then plain,
that you have power, but your will is in fault.
God has enlightened your conscience; but you
rebel against it.   O repent, while there is yet
space afforded.   Call upon the name of Jesus;
who knows but he may even yet deliver you?

2dly, He compares it to a dead carcase, which
is not only unprofitable, but loathsome and offensive.   May God shew you to-day, how odious
your profession is in his sight! for by assenting
to the truths of the Gospel, and outwardly favouring the cause, and the instruments whom the Lord
has raised up to promote it, you are so far professors.   May he enable you to be not only almost,
but altogether Christians! for while you thus halt
between two opinions, and stand divided between
God and the world, you are an abomination to
God, a grief to his people, a stumbling-block to

the ignorant, and are (if this was of any weight in comparison of what I have already said) secretly despised by those who pretend to court your acquaintance. Your guilt is in some respects more aggravated, and your example unspeakably more mischievous, than either would be if you openly rejected the truth. You stand in the rank of those wicked servants who know their Master's will, but do it not. The great Judge has determined concerning these, that they shall be beaten with many stripes *." Awake to righteousness, and sin not; look up to Jesus, who is exalted to bestow both faith and repentance, that you may no longer be torn in pieces by those inward contentions, but experience that peace which passes all understanding †.

SERMON XIX.

GUILT REMOVED, AND PEACE RESTORED.

PSALM li. 15.

O Lord, open thou my lips, and my mouth shall shew forth thy praise.

THE history of David is full of instruction. Every thing recorded of him affords us either consolation or caution. In his example, we see much of the sovereign power and providence of God. When a youth, though the least of his father's house, he was singled out, and called from following sheep, to rule a kingdom. We see him supported through a variety of difficulties, and at length established in his throne, to the amazement and confusion of

* Luke xii. 48.　　　　† Phil. iv. 7.

his enemies. In him likewise we have a striking
proof of the evil that is in the heart of man. Who
would have thought it, that David, the man so
highly favoured, so wonderfully preserved, the
man after God's own heart, who in the time of
his distress could say, " My soul thirsteth for God,
even for the living God *;" that he should be
in an unguarded hour seduced, surprised, and led
captive of the devil! From gazing he proceeds
to adultery, from adultery to murder, and at length
sinks into such a stupid frame of mind, that an
express message from God was needful to convince
him of his sin. And in this circumstance we farther see the riches of Divine grace and mercy ; how
tenderly the Lord watches over his sheep, how
carefully he brings them back when wandering
from him, and with what rich goodness he heals
their backslidings, and loves them freely. David
was fallen, but not lost. " The thing which he
had done displeased the Lord †." Yet his loving
kindness and faithfulness were unalterable. He
was interested in that covenant " which is well
ordered in all things and sure ‡;" and therefore,
when he confessed his sin, the Lord assured him,
by his servant Nathan, that " he had put away
his sin, and he should not die for it §."

However, though the Lord is thus gracious in
passing by the iniquity of his children, yet he will
let them know, by sorrowful experience, that " it
is an evil and a bitter thing to sin against him ‖."
Though he will not cast off, he will chasten ; he
will withdraw his presence, and suspend his gracious influences ; and this to a sensible heart is a
heavy punishment. Though David was delivered

---

* Ps. xlii. 2.   † 2 Sam. xi. 27.   ‡ 2 Sam. xxiii. 5.
§ 2 Sam. xii. 13.   ‖ Jer. ii. 19.

from the fear of death and hell, he penned this psalm in the bitterness of his soul. He did not consider the Lord as his enemy, but as a friend and father whom he had greatly offended. He longed to be reconciled, but could not as yet recover his former confidence. He hoped, indeed, that a time of refreshment *would* come from his presence; and therefore he continued waiting; but for the present he made heavy complaints, that his bones were broken, and his mouth stopped. He had lost his strength and life, and found he could not restore himself. He was struck dumb by his late fall; and therefore he breathes out this prayer, " O Lord, open thou my lips, and my mouth shall shew forth thy praise."

From these words I propose to consider that mournful case, which too often happens in the Christian life, when the believer's mouth is stopped, and his lips closed, so that he cannot shew forth the praises of his God. And in this view,

I. I shall point out to you the persons who have reason to make this complaint.

II. Explain what is implied in their lips being thus shut up.

III. Shew you by what means the Lord opens the closed lips. And,

IV. I shall observe, that when a person's lips are thus opened, his mouth, and all that is within him, will certainly shew forth the Lord's praise. May the Holy Spirit apply the word, and command a blessing upon the whole!

I. This petition especially suits two sorts of persons.

1. The *backsliding* believer; one who has formerly known the goodness of God; has rested in his love, and rejoiced in his salvation; has " tasted

that the Lord is gracious *," and walked with
comfort in the way of his commandments; but at
length, by an unguarded conduct, or by building
wood, hay, and stubble upon the Lord's foundation †, has grieved the good Spirit of God, and he
is withdrawn. The comforter ‡ and instructor of
his soul is far from him; and therefore he sits in
darkness and silence. He only retains a sense of
his loss, and can do no more than sigh out this
prayer: "O Lord, open thou my lips."

2. The *doubting* believer. The unbelieving believer, if I may be allowed the expression; I mean
one who has been deeply convinced of sin, and
taught by the Spirit of God, that there is no salvation but in the Lord Jesus Christ;—one who
loves the word, and ways, and people of God,
who is careful to the utmost of his power to abstain from the evil that is in the world, and esteems
" the loving kindness of the Lord to be better than
life §; "—one at whom the enemy has often thrust
sore that he might fall ‖, but the Lord has secretly
upheld him through many a bitter hour, and he
finds he is not cut off yet, though he perhaps expects it every day. Such as these have, indeed,
sufficient ground to say, " If the Lord was not on
my side, I had been swallowed up long ago **."
They have reason to conclude with David, " By
this, if by nothing else, I know that thou favourest
me, seeing my enemies, who have assaulted me so
continually, have not yet prevailed against me ††."
But yet, through a sense of past guilt, a sight of
present corruptions, the prevalence of unbelief,
the workings of a legal spirit, the want of a clear

* 1 Pet. ii. 3.　† 1 Cor. iii. 11—13.　‡ Lam. i. 16
§ Ps. lxiii. 3.　‖ Ps. cxviii. 13.　** Ps. cxxiv. 3.
†† Psalm xli. 11.

apprehension of the Lord's way of justifying the
ungodly, and from the force of Satan's temptations, who is exceeding busy to press all these
things upon the heart, their mouths are stopped
likewise. They cannot believe, and therefore they
cannot speak. However, there are seasons and
intervals when they obtain a little glimpse of hope,
and then the whole desire of their souls is expressed
in the words of my text : " O Lord, open thou my
lips, and my mouth shall shew forth thy praise."

II. I proceed to consider what may be included
in this case, what it is to have the mouth stopped.
The persons I have mentioned have the same
liberty of speech in common affairs as others ; but,
because they cannot converse freely with him who,
notwithstanding all their doubts, and fears, and
follies, still maintains a secret hold of their souls,
they account themselves no better than dumb.
They cannot speak *to* the Lord, nor *of* him, nor
for him, as they wish and ought to do. These
are the three heads of their complaint ; and therefore they sigh, and say, " O Lord, open thou my
lips."

1. 'Alas !' says the believer that has sinned, and
lost his strength, ' " O that it was with me as in
times past ! * " I well remember when I had freedom of access, and found it good to draw near to
my God ; when I could pour out all my complaints
and cares before him, and leave them with him.
I remember the time when my heart was overwhelmed within me, and my spirit was burdened †.
I saw myself a wretched, helpless sinner. Innumerable evils took hold of me. I thought I was
marked out for destruction. I found Satan at my
right hand, waiting for a permission to seize my

* Job xxix. 2.　　　　† Psalm cxlii. 3.

soul, and make me his prey for ever *. I looked
round, but saw no way to escape, and gave up
all for lost.   But, O! I remember, when none in
heaven or earth could help me, how the Lord drew
" near to me in the day of my distress †, and said
unto my soul, Fear not, I am thy salvation." He
revealed himself as an almighty, suitable Saviour.
He said, " Deliver him from going down to the pit,
I have found a ransom ‡." "He brought me out of
the horrible pit and miry clay, and set my feet upon
a rock §." "He brought me into his banqueting-
house, and his banner over me was love. I sat down
under his shadow with great delight, and his fruit
was sweet unto my taste ‖." This was the beginning; but it was not all.   Many a gracious visit he
favoured me with afterwards.   O the sweet hours
of secret prayer! O the happy communion in
which I walked with him all the day long! " Then,
in the multitude of thoughts within me, his comforts refreshed my soul **."   Then I could smile
at Satan's rage, and face a frowning world.   Every
blessing of common providence was doubly welcome, for I could read his name of love written
upon it; and every affliction brought resignation
and peace, because I saw my Father's hand in it,
and found at a Throne of Grace renewed strength
always suited to my need.   Happy were those
times: but, alas! they are gone.   I could hardly
then persuade myself that I should be moved any
more.   I little thought there was such desperate
wickedness in my heart, that, after so much experience of his goodness, I should foolishly wander from him again.   But, O! what a change
have I lived to see!   I have grieved that good

* Zech. iii. 1.   † Lam iii. 57.   ‡ Job xxxiii. 24.
§ Ps. xl. 2.   ‖ Cant. ii. 3, 4.   ** Ps. xciv. 19.

Spirit of God by which I was sealed, and now I
find myself in the hands of my enemies. The
Lord hides himself, and stands afar off; and I
have lost the power of prayer. Those precious
promises which once were the joy of my soul,
which I could boldly plead at the Throne of Grace,
and say, All these are mine, have no longer any
power or sweetness; I read them, but I cannot
feel them; and my trials and sins, which once
I could cast upon my Saviour, and find instant
relief, are now a heavy burden, too great for me
to bear. Mercies have lost their relish, and afflictions have lost their usefulness; since neither the
one nor the other are of force to stir up my soul
to prayer, " O Lord, open thou my lips."

' I remember likewise, when I had this freedom
in speaking *with* God, how pleasing it was to me
to speak *of* him. My heart was full, and running
over with a sense of his goodness, so that it was
my meat and drink to say, " Come unto me, all
ye that fear God, and I will tell you what he hath
done for my soul *." Then the company of his
people was delightful indeed. The meanest of his
children that would sit and hear me speak of his
loving kindness, was precious to me : I esteemed
them the excellent of the earth †, in whom was
all my delight. " We took sweet counsel together
and walked to the house of God in company ‡."
And I thank God I love them still; but I can
neither help them, nor be helped by them, as in
times past. In vain they say unto me, " Come,
sing us one of the songs of Zion. Alas ! how can
I sing the songs of the Lord in a strange land ?
My harp is hung upon the willows, my tongue
cleaveth to the roof of my mouth §." I dwell in

* Ps. lxvi. 16.   † Ps. xvi. 4.
‡ Ps. lv. 14.   § Ps. cxxxvii. 3—5.

darkness and silence, as those who have been long
dead. "O Lord, open thou my lips."

And when I could thus speak *to* God, and *of*
him, I had likewise liberty to speak *for* him. "I
was then very jealous for the Lord of hosts*."
It wounded my soul to hear his name profaned,
to see his commandments broken, and his Gospel
slighted. I had a tender concern for poor sinners.
I could not but wish, that, if possible, every person I met might know what I knew, and feel what
I felt. And especially where I had friendship or
influence, I was ready to improve it to the best
purpose. "The love of Christ constrained me to
lay myself out for his service †." I could not but
oppose sin and self-righteousness, and plead the
cause of my Saviour upon every occasion. "I
was not ‡ ashamed of the Gospel of Christ, for I
felt it the power of God unto salvation in my own
soul, and durst recommend it to every one as the
only balm for sin and sorrow. But now "the
crown is fallen from my head ; woe unto me that
I have sinned §." I am shut out from the fountain,
and all my streams are dried up. My comforts
and my usefulness are declined together. "O
Lord, open thou my lips, and my mouth shall
shew forth thy praise." '

Such is the complaint of the backslider in heart,
when he is filled with his own ways.

And, 2. This, with a little variation, will suit the
doubting, tempted soul too. These will confess,
that the experience I have described is the desire
of their hearts. Such communication with God,
such a freedom in his ways, such a zeal for his
service, is the very thing they mean, when they

---

* 1 Kings xix. 10.   † 2 Cor. v. 14.   ‡ Rom. i. 16.
§ Lam. v. 16.

entreat the Lord to open their lips. And indeed
they cannot, they dare not deny, but they have at
times had some little tastes of them, otherwise
they would not know what I mean. For these
things are to the natural man the merest folly
imaginable: he understands them not, therefore
he despises them; nay, he hates them with a
perfect hatred, and opposes them with all his
heart. But still they complain under a present
burden. One dark hour of temptation blots out
all the traces of comfort they have known, and
they refuse consolation. They will insist on it, I
have neither part nor lot in the matter; I cannot
get near him, and I fear I never shall. When I
attempt to pray, a sense of my sins and sinfulness stops my mouth. I see the Lord not upon
the golden mercy-seat, but upon the fiery throne
of justice, and I am ready to call upon the rocks
and mountains to hide me from his presence.
When I would commune with his people, I am
silenced by that dreadful word, " What hast thou
to do, to declare my statutes, or to take my covenant into thy mouth? * " When I would bear my
feeble testimony for him in the world, conscience
alarms me, and says, " Thou that teachest others,
teachest thou not thyself? † " And then " the
enemy comes in like a flood ‡," with, " God has
forsaken him; persecute and take him, for there
is none to deliver him §." Thus " I spend my
days in groaning, and water my couch with tears ||."
    This is a heavy case indeed; and would be in-
supportable, but that the faithful Shepherd, in a
secret unseen way, affords timely succour, and
sets bounds to the raging enemy, beyond which
he cannot pass. " Hitherto shalt thou come **;"

* Ps. l. 16.　　† Rom. ii. 21.　　‡ Isa. lix. 19.
§ Ps. lxxi. 11.　　|| Ps. vi. 6.　　** Job xxxviii. 11.

thus far thou art permitted to vex, and wound, and
tear, but no farther. The Lord knows our frame,
and has promised with " every temptation to
provide either strength to endure, or a way to
escape *."—Two things are proper to be mentioned for the encouragement of such souls, to
wait on, and expect deliverance.

The first is, The examples of the saints. Think
not your lot strange, as though some new and
unheard-of thing had befallen you. Thousands,
and ten thousands, now in glory, have tasted, yea,
drank deeply of this cup before you. And many
yet upon earth, who are now rejoicing in the light
of God's countenance, have said in times past, as
you say now, " I shall one day perish by the hand
of these enemies ; the Lord hath cast me quite off,
and I shall never live to see his goodness in the
land of the living †." Or, if you choose Scrip-
tnre proofs, you need only read the Book of Job,
the Psalms, and the Lamentations of Jeremiah, to
be convinced, that some whom you number
amongst the Lord's most eminent and highly
favoured servants, have been induced to use such
expressions as suit your case, no less than if they
had been written for you alone. Do not they say,
that " they were broken with breach upon breach;"
that " the arrows of God stuck fast in them ;" that
" the Lord wrote bitter things against them, and
counted them his enemies ;" that he had " shut
them up within stone walls, and covered himself
with a cloud, that their prayers might not pass
through ‡ ? " These are but a small part of their
complaints ; and what can you say more than this ?

Again ; Consider the precious promises of the

---

* 1 Cor. x. 13.   † 1 Sam. xxvii. 1 ; Ps. lxxiv. 1.

‡ Job xvi. 14 ; Ps. xxxviii. 2 ; Job xiii. 26, and xxxiii. 10 ;
Lam. iii. 9—44.

word. Are they not expressly directed to you?
Do you account yourself a backslider? " Return
unto me, ye backsliding children, and I will receive you, saith the Lord *." Do you think yourself a sinner of uncommon size? Yet, saith the
Lord, "Though your sins be as scarlet, they shall
be white as snow; though they be red like crim-
son, they shall be as wool †." Do you say your
neck is as an iron sinew, and your brow brass? Yet
hear the word of the Lord, " Hearken unto me,
ye stout-hearted, that are far from righteousness.
I bring near my righteousness; it shall not be far
off ‡." Is there something peculiarly dreadful in
your case, something that you could hardly be
prevailed on to entrust to your dearest friend?
Yet be not afraid; for Truth has said, " All manner of sin and blasphemy shall be forgiven unto
men. Let the wicked forsake his way, and the
unrighteous man his thoughts; and let him return
unto the Lord, and he will have mercy upon him;
and to our God, for he will abundantly pardon ‖."
But still, when we have said all, we are but miserable comforters. Even with the word of God in
our mouths, we speak too often in vain. It is the
Lord alone that can open the lips. And, O! that
this may be the happy opportunity of his gracious
appearance in favour of all here present, that our
wounds may be healed, and our tongues unloosed
to proclaim his praise! Lift up your hearts to
him, while I endeavour to shew you, by what
means, or in what manner, the Lord is pleased to
open the lips that have been long closed. This is
the third particular I proposed to consider from
my text.

---

* Jer. iii. 14—22.   † Isa. i. 18.
‡ Isa. xlvi. 12, 13.   ‖ Matth. xii. 31 ; Isa. lv. 7.

III. I say then, that when the Lord is about to open the lips, he proceeds by the following steps.

1. He opens the eyes. We are often in a similar case with Hagar in the wilderness. The water was spent in the bottle, and she sat down in despair. There was a well or fountain close to her, sufficient to have supplied her with water to her life's end; but she saw it not till God opened her eyes*." Just so, many a poor soul is distressed, and says, My stock is spent; I had but little grace at the best, and, alas! that little is gone. And now if the Lord should ask some *hard* thing, would you not do it to obtain a supply? You would willingly take a long journey, or part with all your wealth, to have grace abounding in your hearts; but you know you cannot expect help in this way. It is true, all contrivances of our own will have no effect; but, blessed be God, they are as needless as they would be useless. We need not dig in the earth, nor climb the skies, nor cross the seas; our remedy is *near*†. We need no costly offerings of silver or gold; our remedy is *cheap*. Come, pore no longer upon your empty bottle, but look to the fountain, the river, the ocean of all grace. May the Lord open your eyes (as he did the eyes of Elisha's servant‡) and I will undertake to point you to an object that shall answer all your wants. Look unto the Lord Jesus Christ; look unto him as he hung naked, wounded, bleeding, dead, and forsaken upon the cross. Look unto him again as he *now* reigns in glory, possessed of all power in heaven and in earth, with thousands of thousands of saints and angels worshipping before him, and ten thousand times ten thousand ministering unto him; and

---

* Gen. xxi. 15—19.   † Rom. x. 6—8.   ‡ 2 Kings vi. 17.

then compare your sins with his blood, your wants
with his fulness, your unbelief with his faithfulness, your weakness with his strength, your in-
constancy with his everlasting love.   If the Lord
opens the eyes of your understanding, you would
be astonished at the comparison.   Would you
compare a small grain of sand upon the shore,
with the massy mountains which hide their heads
in the clouds, and spread their roots from sea to
sea ? or the spark of a glow-worm with the noon-
day sun? yet there is less disproportion between
these, than between the utmost capacity of your
desires and wants, and the immense resources
provided for you, in the righteousness, compassion, and power of our dear Redeemer.   " He is
able to save to the uttermost * ;" and all our
trouble arises chiefly from this, that our eyes are
holden, so that we do not know him†.   Therefore
the first step towards opening the lips is to open
our eyes, that we may see him, and look upon him
by such a sight as unloosed the tongue of unbelieving Thomas, and constrained him to cry out,
" My Lord and my God !‡ "

2. When the eyes are thus opened, the Lord, in
the next place, and by that as a means, opens the
ear.   When Christ is out of sight, we are deaf to
all the calls, invitations, and promises of the Scripture.   But a believing view of him who died that
we might live, rouses the attention, and makes us
willing and able to hear what the Lord will speak §
to his people.   And what does he say from the
cross ?   " Look unto me, and be ye saved.   If I
be lifted up, I will draw all men to me.   Behold
my hands, my feet, my pierced side ; all this I

---

* Heb. vii. 25.   † Luke xxiv. 16.
‡ John xx. 28.   § Psal. lxxxv. 8.

bore for you. Be not afraid, only believe. O
thou of little faith, wherefore dost thou doubt?
See, sinner, how I have loved thee. I have trod-
den the winepress alone. I have destroyed death,
and him that had the power of death. There is
henceforth no condemnation to them that believe
in me *." And what does he say from his kingdom? " I have prayed for thee that thy faith fail
not. For a season you have sorrow ; but I will
see you again, and your heart shall rejoice. Him
that cometh to me, I will in no wise cast out. I
am the first and the last : that was dead and am
alive. I keep the keys of death and hell, and save
whom I will. Cast thy burden upon me, I will
sustain thee. I will take away thy iniquity. Be
of good cheer, thy sins are forgiven thee. Go in
peace, and sin no more †." *My Saviour, my God,*
what words are these !

3. By opening the eye to see his excellence and
power, and the ear to hear his gracious words, he,
in the next place, opens the heart. He breaks
the prison-doors, forces for himself an entrance,
and sets the prisoner at liberty. He touches the
rock, and the waters flow ‡. Now a true and filial
repentance takes place ; now sin appears exceedingly sinful indeed. There was a sorrow before,
but it was fruitless and ineffectual ; but the sight
of him who was pierced for our sins, and the welcome sound of *pardon* proclaimed in the conscience, produces a sorrow after a godly sort, a
repentance never to be repented of. Thus it was
with the woman who washed our Lord's feet § ;

---

* Isa. xlv. 22 ; John xii. 22 ; John xx. 27 ; Mark v. 36 ;
Matth. xiv. 31 ; Isa. lxiii. 3 ; Heb. ii. 14 ; Rom. viii. 1.

† Luke xxii. 32 ; John xvi. 22 ; John vi. 37 ; Rev. i. 17, 18 ;
Psal. lv. 22 ; Micah vii. 19 : Matth. ix. 2 ; John viii. 11.

‡ Psal. lxxviii. 20.   § Luke vii. 38. 47.

she had been a great sinner; much was forgiven
her, and therefore she loved much. Thus it was
with Peter: he had been a grievous backslider;
he had been with Jesus upon the mount, and saw
the excellent glory; he was stout in his protesta-
tion, " Though all men deny thee, yet will not I :"
but he shrunk at the voice of a girl, and said, " I
know not the man." When the servants spoke to
him, he cursed and swore; but when Jesus looked
upon him, he wept *. Do you think our Lord
looked upon him with disdain and indignation?
rather with a look of love; a look that at once
convinced him of his sin, and gave him to understand that the Lord pitied and forgave him. This
look broke his heart in pieces. He went out, and
wept bitterly. And afterwards, though greatly
humbled as to confidence in himself, yet, when
asked the question, he could boldly appeal to the
Searcher of hearts, " Lord, thou knowest all things,
thou knowest that I love thee †."

And when the eyes, the ears, the heart, are
thus opened; when the understanding is enlightened, the will engaged, and the affections inflamed,
the cure is wrought. Then the lips will open of
course, and the mouth be filled with thanksgiving
and praise. O that it would please the Lord to
give to me, and to each of you, a clearer knowledge
of this blessed change from heart-felt experience,
than is in the power of words (of my poor words
especially) to describe! " Come," my friends,
" let us return unto the Lord; for he hath
wounded, and he will heal us; he hath smitten,
and he will bind us up ‡." Verily we are all
guilty in this matter; we have all provoked him

---

* Luke xxii. 61, 62.   † John xxi. 17.   ‡ Hosea vi. 1.

by unbelief, and wandering from his good way;
and therefore we live so far below our privileges,
and are so often heavy and sorrowful, when we
have in him grounds of continual joy. Now let us
unite in this prayer, " O Lord, open thou our
lips, display thy power in the midst of us, heal all
our breaches, rend the veil of our unbelief, blot
out the thick clouds of our sins, cleanse us from
all our iniquities and idols, and teach our stam-
mering tongues, and barren hearts, to shew forth
the praise of thy abundant goodness."

I proceed to observe, in the last place,

IV. That if the Lord is pleased to answer our
desire, and to open your lips in this manner, then
you will surely praise him. You will praise him
with your mouths, and in your lives; you will
thankfully acknowledge his mercy, his power, and
his wisdom.

1. You will praise his mercy.—Is the cooling
stream welcome to the thirsty soul? is a reprieve
acceptable to a poor condemned malefactor? still
more welcome is a sense of pardoning love to a
soul that has felt the evil and effects of sin. What!
to be taken from the dunghill *, and made a com-
panion with princes! to have all our guilt and
complaints removed at once! to be snatched as it
were from the brink of hell, and placed in the
very suburbs of heaven! to be able to say, " O
Lord thou wast [justly] angry with me, [and I
went mourning under a sense of thy displeasure];
but [now] thine anger is turned away, and thou
comfortedst me!† " Is not this a mercy? especially considering how undeserving we are of the
smallest favour! And, farther, the way in which
it was conveyed! that the pardon, though free to

* 1 Sam. ii. 8.   † Isa. xii. 1.

us, is a pardon " bought with blood : " that it
cost the Lord Jesus his life, his soul, to effect that
blessed reconciliation in which we are beginning
to rejoice! Still more, that all we can now receive
of his love, is but a taste, a small thing, in comparison of what he has reserved for us! O what
mercy is here! O what thanks does it call for!
" O Lord, open thou our lips, and our mouth shall
shew forth thy praise."

2. You will praise his power.—' I thought,' says
the poor soul at such a time, ' I was fallen so low
that there was no help. The more I toiled and
laboured in my own strength, the farther the blessing seemed from me. I know, by experience, that
none but an Almighty arm could relieve me. Creatures, means, and contrivances I had tried, and
tried again, but found them all physicians of no
value. But now " the right hand of the Lord has
done wonderfully, the right hand of the Lord has
brought mighty things to pass*." "What shall
I say? he hath both spoken himself, and also hath
done it†." The work is his; to him be all the
glory. I got not this victory by my own bow‡,
neither did my own arm save me, " but the Lord
himself has been pleased to shew the exceeding
greatness§ of his mighty power in my behalf."
Therefore, " not unto us, but unto thy name, O
Lord, be the glory and the praise‖." '

3. You will praise his wisdom.—" What I do,"
said our Lord to Peter, " thou knowest not now,
but thou shalt know hereafter**." The mourning
soul often asks the question with David, " I will
say unto God my rock, Why hast thou forsaken

---

* Ps. cxviii. 15, 16.   † Is. xxxviii. 15.   ‡ Ps. xliv. 6.
§ Ephes. i. 19.   ‖ Ps. cxv. 1.   ** John xiii. 7.

me? why go I mourning because of the enemy?*"
When the Lord turns your mourning into joy, you
shall know why. You will then see that there was
a need† of all these things. It is to shew you what
is in your hearts, to mortify the spirit of self-
righteousness, "to teach you, that without him
you can do nothing‡;" to make you wise and experienced against Satan's devices; to give you a
tender sympathy and fellow-feeling in the sufferings and infirmities of your brethren, and to enable you to encourage and comfort others§ who
shall be hereafter in your case, by relating what
you have seen and known yourself in your various
conflicts and strivings against sin. These are
some of the reasons why the Lord suffers his dear
children to groan, being burdened, and sometimes
permits their enemies to gain a short advantage
over them, that he may humble and prove them‖,
in order to do them good in their latter end. And,
oh! with what wisdom is all this appointed! A
little of it we may see at present, but we shall not
have a complete view till we get safe home. Then
to look back upon the way by which he led us
through the wilderness, will furnish matter for
eternal praise.

Farther: not only your mouths, but your lives
shall praise him. What is the language of a believing heart, when the Lord pardons his sins, and
binds up his wounds? It is this, "Now, Lord,
I am thine, thy vows are upon me, for thou hast
redeemed me, O Lord God of truth. Shall I continue in sin because grace has abounded? God
forbid! I am crucified with Christ, crucified to

---

* Psal. xlii. 9.   † 1 Pet. i. 6.   ‡ John xv. 5.
   § 2 Cor. i. 4.   ‖ Deut. viii. 2—16.

the world, and the world to me. The love of
Christ constrains me. The time past is sufficient
to have lived in vanity; henceforth I am the
Lord's. He has bound me by his tender mercies
to present myself, body and soul, to his service.
Here, O Lord, I offer my whole self, all that I am,
and all that I have, a living sacrifice, holy and acceptable to thee. O let me never, never wander
from thee again, but walk in the light, as thou art
in the light, and have communion with thee here
below, till thou shalt remove me out of the reach
of sin and sorrow for ever *."

If there are any here who have neither known
the loving kindness of the Lord, nor mourned
under the sense of his displeasure, I am sure your
lips are closed to this hour. And should you die
thus incapable of praising the God who made
you, and the grace which has brought the sound
of the Gospel to your ears, it were better for you
that you had never been born †. You have much
reason to cry out, " O Lord, open thou my lips."
Open my eyes to see my danger, to see the evil
of my nature and life. Open my lips to confess
my wickedness. Open my heart to receive thy
word, that I likewise may bear a part in the
praises thy people pay thee, and not perish (as
without thy mercy I must do) with a lie in my
right hand ‡.—Consider, the time is short §; death
is *near*, and may be *sudden*. May the Lord
enable you to consider the things belonging to
your peace ‖, before they are hid from your eyes!

And you, my friends, who at present enjoy the

---

* Psal. cxvi. 14, 16, and xxxi. 5; Rom. vi. 1; Gal. ii. 20, and
vi. 14; 2 Cor. v. 14; 1 Pet. iv. 3; Rom. xii. 1; 1 John i. 7.
  † Matth. xxvi. 24.　　‡ Isa. xliv. 20.　　§ 1 Cor. vii. 29.
  ‖ Luke xix. 42.

light of God's countenance, who know your sins
are forgiven * for his name's sake, and have a
happy freedom of access at a Throne of Grace,
O be mindful of your privileges; beware of sin,
beware of self, beware of Satan. Your enemy
envies you your liberty: he watches you with
subtilty and malice; he spreads snares for your
feet; he desires to have advantage of you, " that
he may sift you as wheat †." Therefore be upon
your guard, be humble, make much of secret
prayer, keep close to the Scriptures of God—by
the words of his lips you shall be preserved from
the paths of the destroyer ‡—attend diligently
upon the ordinances; and speak often one § to
another, in love and faithfulness, of what the Lord
has done and prepared for you, and of what ‖
manner of persons you ought to be, in all holy
conversation and godliness. Thus you shall be
kept safe from evil. Jesus has prayed for you,
that your faith may not fail **. Fix your eye ††
and your heart upon him, as he that must do all
for you, all *in* you, all *by* you. And he has said,
" yet a little while, and, behold, I come quickly ‡‡.
Hold fast that which thou hast. Be thou faithful
unto death, and I will give thee a crown of life.
Amen. Even so, come Lord Jesus §§."

---

* 1 John ii. 12.　　† Luke xxii. 31.　　‡ Ps. xvii. 4.
§ Mal. iii. 16.　　‖ 2 Pet. iii. 11.　　** Luke xxii. 32.
†† Heb. xii. 2.　　‡‡ Rev. iii. 11.　　§§ Rev. ii. 10 ; xxii. 20.

SERMON XX.

1 JOHN v. 19.

And we know that we are of God.

A WELL-GROUNDED and abiding persuasion, not only that the doctrines of the Gospel are true in themselves, but that we through grace are surely and unchangeably interested in them, is highly desirable. If we may be safe, we cannot be happy and comfortable without it, when once we have received an experimental knowledge of the deceitfulness of our own hearts, and the variety, subtilty, and force of Satan's temptations: and He who knows our frame and situation, has, in his holy word, made a full provision for us in this respect, and declared it to be his intention, that those who flee for refuge to the hope he has set before them, might have strong consolation*; not be left at an uncertainty in a concern of the highest importance, but be rooted, grounded, established, and settled in the knowledge of his love, and be enabled to maintain it as an unshaken principle, through every change of dispensation and frame, " that he who hath begun a good work in them will perform it until the day of Jesus Christ†."

This animating confidence, so well suited, and so necessary, to render the soul superior to all the trials of life, to inspire a noble disdain of the sinful

---

* Heb. vi. 18.   † Phil. i. 6.

pleasures and vain pursuits of the present evil world, and to engage the grateful exertion of every faculty and power in the service of God, is generally expressed by the word *Assurance.* But though the word is in frequent use, the thing itself has been, and still is, a subject of much dispute and controversy amongst professors of the Gospel. Many, not being conscious of such a cheering persuasion in themselves, and too hasty in supposing their attainments must be a standard to others, have ventured to deny the possibility of such an assurance, and treated every claim to it as visionary and enthusiastic. On the other hand, some have maintained the opposite extreme, and held assurance so essential to faith, that without it no person has a Scriptural warrant even to hope that a work of grace is begun in his heart. This sentiment, especially when asserted by persons of undoubted character for gifts, graces, and usefulness, has greatly startled and discouraged weak and feeble-minded souls, and been too often an occasion of adding to the distress of those who rather ought to have been comforted.

Great differences of judgment have likewise obtained concerning the means whereby, the manner in which, and the persons to whom, this assurance is communicated, supposing it attainable. It is not needful to insist on particulars. Perhaps, the best way to prevent or remove mistakes, is to propose the truth simply ; which, so far as it takes place, will necessarily prevent the entertainment of error. I only mention in general, that there is a variety of sentiments on this point, and the most of them supported by respectable names, in order to caution you against paying too great a deference to human authority, and to urge you to praise God for your Bibles, and to be di-

ligent in the perusal of them. If you search the
Scriptures, and pray for the Spirit, you may
arrive to a clear satisfaction for yourselves, no
less than if all the learned were of one mind, and
all of your side.

My text assures us, that this assurance was
possessed in the first ages of the church. There
were some who could say, without hesitation,
" We know that we are of God;" and though
they are an apostle's words, he uses them not exclusively as an apostle, but generally as a believer.

The greatest part of the chapter, and indeed of
the Epistle, shews that he considers those to
whom he was writing as partakers with him in
the common privileges of Christians. So likewise
St. Paul joins the believing Corinthians with
himself, when he says, " We know, that, if our
earthly house of this tabernacle were dissolved,
we have a building of God, an house not made
with hands, eternal in the heavens*." And elsewhere he takes it for granted, that they (some of
them at least) had this assurance, and presses
them to a lively discharge of duty upon that consideration: " Forasmuch as ye know that your
labour is not in vain in the Lord †."

And we need make no scruple of affirming, from
the fullest evidence, that this precious privilege
was not confined, or designed by God to be so,
to the first ages of the Gospel. There have been,
in all periods of the church, where the word and
ordinances of Christ have been faithfully administered, many who could say, " We know that
we are of God;" and we trust there are more
than a few who can say so, and give a solid Scriptural evidence of the hope that is in them, even

* 2 Cor. v. 1.   † 1 Cor. xv. 58.

in this degenerate day. But because arguments from facts, which must depend upon persons' testimony, in their own cases, are not allowed to be fully conclusive; and because the greater part of those who, we hope, sincerely love the Lord Jesus, live far below their just right and privilege, and are perplexed with doubts and fears, which dishonour their profession, weaken their hands, and make their lives uncomfortable; I shall endeavour at this time to state and explain the nature of assurance, to prove that it is attainable, to point out the means by which we are to expect it, and to take notice of the hindrances which keep so many who are interested in the Gospel salvation from enjoying their privilege, and make them unwilling or afraid to say "We know that we are of God." What I have to offer on these particulars, will occur under one or other of the following propositions.

I. Assurance is not essential to the being of faith.—It is a strong faith; but we read likewise of a weak faith, little faith, faith like a grain of mustard seed*. True saving faith in Jesus Christ is only distinguishable by its different degrees; but in every degree, and in every subject, it is universally of the same kind, and produces (according to its degree) the same uniform effects. It purifies the heart from the love and practice of sin; it works by love to the Lord Jesus Christ, his ordinances, ways, and people†; and it enables the professor to overcome the world, to stand fast against its frowns, and to resist the more pleasing but not less dangerous influence of its smiles. Each of these effects is beyond the power, and contrary to the inclination, of the natural man.

---

* Rom. xiv. 1; Matth. xiv. 31, and xvii. 20.

† Acts xv. 9; Gal. v. 6; 1 John v. 4.

"No man can say that Jesus Christ is the Lord*," that is, can give him the honour due to his name, renounce every other hope of salvation, "and count all things but loss and dung that he may win Christ," "but by the Holy Ghost." Yet thus far many have undoubtedly attained, who have not assurance; but while they give sufficient evidence by their conduct that they have received precious faith in their hearts, they go mourning all the day long, and almost pass sentence against themselves as unbelievers. Now, what these mourners want, in order to their establishment and assurance, is not some new principle which they have not yet received, but only a stronger degree of that faith which they already possess. Some good writers speak of faith of reliance, faith of adherence, faith of assurance, direct and reflex acts of faith, &c.; but these are not Scriptural modes of expression, nor do they appear to me to throw light upon the subject, but rather to increase the perplexity of plain people, who are apt to imagine these are so many different kinds of faith. The Scripture mentions only two kinds; "a living and a dead faith†." The true faith is faint and in its beginnings, like the life of a new-born infant; but it is growing up to maturity, and shall increase with the increase of God, "unto a perfect man, unto the measure of the stature of the fulness of Christ‡." From hence it follows,

II. The grounds and principles of faith and assurance are exactly the same.—The first and lowest act of saving faith necessarily includes three things.

1. An apprehension of the sufficiency and authority of Christ to save.—Men that live in their sins will rest upon a slender hope; but a con-

---

* 1 Cor. xii. 3; Phil. iii. 8.   † James ii. 17.   ‡ Ephes. iv. 13.

science truly awakened must have sure grounds to
go upon, and, without the discovery of such a
Saviour as is revealed in the Gospel, would sink
into despair.   It is afraid of being deceived, and
is so far enlightened, that it cannot be easily imposed upon; a sense of the sinfulness of sin, an
impression of the majesty of God, will not suffer
it to rest in any thing short of a perfect atonement and a perfect righteousness.   But when the
eyes of the mind are opened, and Jesus is seen as
revealed by the word and Spirit of God, all scruples of this sort are silenced, and the soul perceives and feels that he is fully equal to the mighty
undertaking.

2. An application to him.—This of course follows a persuasion of his ability to save ; for who
will sit down and perish when there is a possibility
of relief? There is, perhaps, a great questioning
of Christ's willingness ; but still, since there is a
peradventure, a sense of distress on the one hand,
and a view of his power and grace on the other,
will extort a cry, " Lord save me, or I perish*."

3. From hence there arises a hope in his
mercy, which is fainter or stronger, according as
the knowledge of Jesus is more or less distinct,
and the surrender unto him more or less simple
and unreserved; and therefore, in general, it is
very faint at first ; for the knowledge of Christ in
a measure depends upon our knowledge of the
Scriptures, which testify of him, and on the proofs
we have had of his wisdom, grace, and love to ourselves : but the young convert, in whom the seed
of faith is but lately sown, has but little acquaintance with the word ; for he has but just begun to
know the value of it ; and he has but little experi-

* Matth. viii. 25, and xiv. 30.

ence; though his eyes are opened, his sight is not yet confirmed, nor his spiritual senses exercised.

Farther: Though he is sincerely convinced of his need of a Saviour, there is still much of a legal bias, and a principle of self-righteousness in his heart, which, so far from being removed, is not yet discovered to himself; and while he thinks he looks to Christ alone, he is looking in himself for qualifications to recommend him, and afraid to draw near with confidence, because he cannot find them. These things discourage his hopes, and demonstrate his faith to be but weak.

But the strongest and most lively assurance that we can conceive attainable in the present life, is wrought and maintained by the very same principles which have so faint an influence in the infancy of faith. Let us hear the great champion St. Paul, in the close of an exemplary, laborious life, giving an account to a dear and intimate friend of the hope that was in him. He had been honoured and distinguished for grace, gifts, and usefulness, in a peculiar manner; he had laboured more abundantly than all the Apostles; he had fully preached the Gospel, and gathered churches throughout a very large part of the Roman empire*: his first call was extraordinary, by the Lord's appearing to him in glory; and some of his succeeding experiences had been no less singular, for he had been caught up into the third heavens†: finally, his suffering for the Gospel had been as great and remarkable as his services. But when he expresses his assurance of support and salvation, he says not a syllable of these things, but rests the whole upon such points as are common to him with all believers: " I know

* 1 Cor. xv. 10; Rom. xv. 19.　　† 2 Cor. xii. 2.

whom I have believed, and I am persuaded that he is able to keep that which I have committed unto him against that day*." We see there St. Paul's assurance was founded on, first, A knowledge of Jesus Christ, the object of his faith: secondly, A consciousness of transactions which had passed between him and his Saviour; he had committed something to him,—that was, his soul, with all its interests: thirdly, A persuasion of his ability, willingness, and faithfulness, to secure and preserve what he had taken charge of. And these are the very same principles which are necessary to the first act of weak faith; only here they exert themselves with their proper power and efficacy. From hence,

III. Assurance is equally open to all believers. —It is not the exclusive privilege of great services or sufferings; it is not confined to ministers, martyrs, or apostles; but it is a prize set before all who love our Lord Jesus Christ in sincerity, being no other than the growth and establishment of that faith which they have already received. The reasons why all who believe are not happy in this assurance of hope, are to be sought, not in the will of God, who has made abundant provision for our comfort, but in the perverseness, ignorance, and misapprehensions of our own hearts, and from inattention to his revealed word. We are not straitened in him, but in ourselves. It is not easy to enumerate the many ways in which our depravity works to keep this good thing from us. A few of the principal are these.

1. Insincerty. Where grace is really implanted by the Holy Spirit, it will surely prevail at length, and subdue the whole soul to the obedience of

---

* 2 Tim. i. 12.

faith.   But in too many there is for a long time
not only great opposition from indwelling corruption, but a secret cleaving of the will to evil.   A
double-mindedness*, a kind of halting between
two opinions; so that while the desire and prayer
of the soul seems expressed against all sin universally, there is still an allowed reserve of something, inconsistent with light received.   An habitual indulgence of known or suspected evil, or
an habitual neglect of any known duty, will certainly prevent the growth of grace and consolation.   For the Lord claims (what is his just due)
the whole heart, and will not afford the strengthening light of his countenance, while any idol is
deliberately set up in his presence.   " Then,"
says David (and not till then), " shall I not be
ashamed when I have respect unto all thy commandments."   And our Lord Jesus, when asked,
"How will thou manifest thyself unto us?" answered, " If a man love me, he will keep my
words, and my Father will love him, and we will
come unto him, and make our abode with him †."
Till the pride and naughtiness of our spirits are
conquered, and we are made willing to give up
all, to renounce whatever is contrary to his precepts, though pleasing as a right eye, and seemingly necessary as the right hand, it is in vain to
expect a full and abiding assurance of his love.

2. Indolence.—With respect to this valuable
blessing, it may be often said, " Ye receive not,
because ye ask not ‡."   It is too common for those
who were earnest in crying for mercy, while they
thought themselves under the curse and power of
the law, to grow slack and remiss in prayer soon

---

* James i. 8 ; 1 Kings xviii. 21 ; Prov. xxiii. 26 ; Psal. ix. 1.
† Ps. cxix. 6 ; John xiv. 22, 23.   ‡ James iv. 2.

after they obtain some hope of salvation from the
Gospel ; and particularly they do not " give all
diligence to make their calling and election sure*,"
in the careful use of every means appointed for
their establishment in the truth as it is in Jesus.
Therefore that word is fulfilled in them, " The
slothful soul desireth and hath nothing †." They
go on for months or years in a complaining, unsettled state ; and deservedly, because they are
not earnest in seeking, asking, waiting, knocking
at the gate of wisdom, and at the Throne of Grace,
for that blessing which the Lord has promised to
those who persevere in wrestling prayer, and will
take no denial.

3. Misapprehensions.—These arise from a neglect of examining the Scriptures, and an undue
deference to the decisions of men. If assurance
is supposed unattainable, it will consequently not
be sought after. If it is expected as an instan-
taneous impression of the Spirit of God upon the
mind, independent of his word, or to arise from
some sudden powerful application of a particular
text of Scripture, this persuasion will end in disappointment. For though it must be allowed
that the Lord does at times favour his people with
peculiar manifestations of his goodness, and perhaps seal some promise especially suited to their
present circumstances, with a remarkable sweetness and evidence upon their minds ; yet these do
rarely produce the assurance we are speaking
of. These are but visits, seldom vouchsafed, and
quickly suspended; and those who depend chiefly
upon such impressions, instead of endeavouring
to grow in the Scriptural knowledge of Christ,
are generally as changeable in their hopes as in

* 2 Pet. i. 10.   † Prov. xiii. 4.

their frame. While their affections are thus engaged, "their mountain stands strong, and they think they shall never be moved* ; " but when the cause is withdrawn, the effect ceases, and they presently relapse into their former fears and inquietudes. Not to say, that expectations of this sort have a tendency to great inconveniences, and often open a door to the delusions of enthusiasm and dangerous impositions; for Satan, when permitted, knows how to transform himself into an angel of light†. If inherent sanctification, or a considerable increase of it, is considered as the proper ground of assurance, those who are most humble, sincere, and desirous of being conformed to the will of God, will be the most perplexed and discouraged in their search after it. For they of all others will be the least satisfied with themselves, and have the quickest sense of the innumerable defilements and defects, which the Scripture assures us are inseparable from our best tempers and best actions. These mistakes, with others that might be mentioned, prevent many from seeking after assurance at all, and bewilder many more, by putting them upon a wrong pursuit. But what then is assurance? and how is it to be attained? I shall attempt an answer to these questions together in the next proposition.

IV. "Assurance is the result of a competent spiritual knowledge of the person and work of Christ as revealed in the Gospel, and a consciousness of dependence on him and his work alone for salvation." What I apprehend necessary to make my meaning plain, will occur from a brief explanation of the terms I have made use of in this description.

1. By the term " spiritual knowledge," I would

* Ps. xxx. 6, 7.   † 2 Cor. xi. 14.

ascribe it to the influence and teaching of the
Holy Spirit of God, and distinguish it both from
that speculative knowledge of divine things which
natural men may acquire from books and human
instruction, and likewise from that knowledge
which a real believer may attain in the same
way, beyond the limits of his present experience.
Those who are favoured with great outward advantages, particularly the light of a clear Gospel
ministry, may very soon arrive to a notional apprehension of the most important truths; but
with respect to the spiritual and abiding perception of those truths, there is no effectual teacher
but the Spirit of God: and we often find, that what
we think we have learned of men, we have occasion to be taught again by the Lord the Spirit;
for our acquisitions fail us when we have most
need of them, and will not stand the trial of an
hour of temptation. But, so far as we have
received our views of Jesus, his person, offices,
mediation, and promises, from him, we possess
them, and should be able to defy an angel, if he
was to propose to us any other doctrine than that
which we have surely known and believed*.

2. I use the word "competent," because there
is not, that I know of, any determinate standard
where to fix. When our knowledge is so far
increased as to overpower the objections arising
from inward corruptions, defects of obedience,
unbelieving fears, and the temptations of Satan;
when we can cut them short with that question
of the Apostle, "Who is he that condemneth? it
is Christ that died†," assurance follows of course.
For I do not understand assurance in the strictest
sense for the highest degree of certainty imagin-

* Gal. i. 8.   † Rom. viii. 34.

able. Assurance itself is capable of increase ; and
will be so continually, while there is any darkness
in our understandings, or any remaining propen-
sity to a self righteous spirit.   Then only will our
assurance be perfect, when we shall see Jesus as he
is, and be completely freed from all our infirmities.
For these, in whatever degree they prevail, will
so far affect the strength and steadiness of our
confidence in God.

3. This knowledge is wrought in us by the
Spirit, through the medium of the written word.
He teaches no unrevealed truths.   We are not to
expect that he will assure us as by a voice from
heaven, or by a sudden impulse upon our hearts,
that our names in particular are written in the
book of life ; but he opens our understandings to
understand the Scripture*; to assent to, and feel,
that we are such sinners as are there described ; to
see the dignity and sufficiency of Christ Jesus, as
God-man, the Mediator ; the suitableness of his
offices ; the value of his atonement and righteousness ; and the harmony and glory of the Divine
attributes, in the adorable methods of redeeming
love, which renders it just, righteous, and worthy
of God to justify and save the believing sinner †.
He likewise gives us to understand the freedom and
security of the Gospel promises, confirmed by the
oath of God, and sealed with the blood of the Son.
He shews us the establishment and immutability
of the covenant of grace ; convinces us, that there
is a fulness of wisdom, grace, life, and strength,
treasured up in Christ, for the use and support of
those who in themselves are poor, miserable, and
helpless, and to be freely communicated in measure and season as he sees necessary, to support,

---

* Luke xxiv. 45.   † Rom. iii. 26.

nourish, and revive the believing soul, and to lead him in the path of perseverance to everlasting life. Such a discovery of almighty power and unchangeable love engaged for the infallible salvation of every believer, which they cannot lose by their own unworthiness, nor be deprived of by all the opposition which earth or hell can raise against them*, produces a suitable assurance in the soul that receives it. And we can confidently say, " We know we are of God," when we can in this manner know in whom we have believed.

4. Such discoveries of the person and grace of Christ are connected with a heart-felt consciousness that the believer's dependence, for all the great hopes and ends of salvation, are fixed on him and his work alone. They draw forth acts of surrender and trust, and keep the mind from forming any vain scheme of hope or refuge, either in whole or in part, from any other quarter. Indeed, from the very first dawnings of faith, as I have observed, the soul is led to commit itself into the hands of Jesus; but while knowledge was weak, and the heart very imperfectly humbled, there was a secret, though unallowed, dependence upon self, upon resolutions, frames, and duties. But as Jesus rises more glorious in the eye of faith, self is in the same degree depressed and renounced ; and when we certainly see that there is no safety or stability but in his name, we as certainly feel that we expect them from him, and from him only. And the Holy Spirit assists here likewise ; bears a comfortable witness with our spirits†, by drawing us to a Throne of Grace, pleading in us as a Spirit of adoption, and prompting us to renew the renunciation of ourselves, " and to glory in Jesus, as

---

* John x. 28, 29. † Rom. viii. 15, 16.

made unto us, of God, wisdom, righteousness, sanctification, and redemption*," from day to day. And
from hence arises a solid, permanent assurance.
The believer, though weak and unstable as water
in himself, and though continually assaulted by
a powerful combination against his peace, can look
through all to Jesus, and say, " I am persuaded
that neither death, nor life, nor angels, nor principalities, nor powers, nor things present, nor
things to come, nor height, nor depth, nor any other
creature, shall be able to separate me from the
love of God which is in Christ Jesus our Lord†."

What remains, then, but to animate and press
every sincere believer to strive, in God's appointed
way, for a comfortable assurance that they are
accepted in the Beloved, passed from death unto
life, and infallibly freed from all condemnation.
Though this knowledge is not absolutely necessary
to our safety, it is exceedingly needful to make us
unwearied, cheerful, and evangelical, in a course
of holy obedience; to the exertion of all our powers
and faculties in the service of Him who has loved
us, and washed us from our sins in his own blood;
and to give us courage to endure and surmount
the many difficulties and oppositions which we
are sure to meet with in the course of our profession. Unbelief and distrust weaken our hands,
" and make our knees feeble‡." The more steadily we confide in God, the better we shall serve
him; we shall be enabled to cast all our cares
upon him; to rely on his promise to make our
strength equal to our day; and, having a well-
grounded expectation of receiving the end of our
hope, even the salvation of our souls, we shall
stand fast in the evil day, and say, " None of these

---

* 1 Cor. i. 30.   † Rom. viii. 38, 39.   ‡ Heb. xii. 12.

things move me; neither count I my life dear, so that I may finish my course with joy*." I would only subjoin two cautions to those who are thus minded.

1. Remember that the progress of faith to assurance is gradual. Expect it not suddenly; but wait upon the Lord for it in the ways of his appointment. As it depends upon the manifestation of the Holy Spirit, let this engage you to constancy and earnestness in prayer; and as it arises from a knowledge of Jesus, be assiduous in searching the Scriptures, which testify of him. " The blessing of the Lord and the hand of the diligent concur in the attainment of this benefit †." If you persevere in this path, you will be helped forward by the experience of every day; and every dispensation of Providence, as well as every exercise and frame of mind you pass through, will be sanctified, to give you an increasing conviction that you are nothing, and that Jesus is all in all.

2. As you cannot see or maintain a sight of your interest in the covenant, but by the light of the Spirit, beware of grieving him ‡. If you indulge a careless, trifling disposition, or venture upon known sin, you will find dark clouds raised between the Sun of Righteousness and your souls. Assurance is not so invariable, but that it may be affected, weakened, and perhaps for a season quite suspended, by unfaithfulness and backsliding on our part. If you have a persuasion of your interest in the love of God, that remains always the same, though prayer is restrained, the ordinances slighted, and watchfulness intermitted; take heed lest this, instead of assurance, should be vain confidence and presumption. The hope that

---

* Acts xx. 24.   † Prov. x. 4, 22.   ‡ Ephes. iv. 30.

maketh not ashamed, endears every precept and ordinance to the soul, weans the affections from low and trivial pursuits, and strengthens the exercise of every gracious principle.

As it is thus possible and desirable for a believer to " know that he is of God ; " so a concern for many here present will not suffer me to close, without desiring you to consider if you have not cause to conclude, from Scripture testimony, that you are *not* of God.   See the case determined by an Apostle : " Whosoever doth not righteousness, is not of God *."   And again, by another, " If any man have not the Spirit of Christ, he is none of his †."   Are not these decisions plain and absolute?   If your love and dependence are not fixed on the Lord Jesus Christ, if your tempers and practice are not governed by his commands, you are not of God.   Whom, then, do you belong to ? The whole world is divided between two masters, and ranged under opposite banners.   A neutrality is impossible.   If you are not of God, you belong at present to Satan ; you are his captive ‡ ; he leads you blindfold ; and he meditates your destruction when you shall have worn out your lives in his miserable service.   And will you continue fond of your bondage, and follow him like an ox to the slaughter?   There is a redemption-price paid, there is an arm of power revealed, in favour of such helpless, perishing prisoners.   Jesus, whom we preach, " is able to take the prey out of the hand of the mighty, and to deliver the lawful captive §."   The Lord help you to apply to him before iniquity is your ruin.   O may he incline you to believe and be saved! ‖   If you reject him,

---

* 1 John iii. 10.   † Rom. viii. 9.   ‡ 2 Tim. ii 26.
§ Isa. xlix. 24.   ‖ Acts xvi. 31.

you seal yourself to an aggravated condemnation, and must perish without mercy; " But if you hear his voice, and call upon his name, he is able to save to the uttermost, and to bless you, in turning every one of you from your iniquities*."

* Heb. vii. 25 ; Acts iii. 26.

END OF THE SECOND VOLUME.